Living
in
China

Living in China

A Guide to Teaching and Studying in China Including Taiwan

Rebecca Weiner
Margaret Murphy
Albert Li

China Books & Periodicals, Inc. San Francisco, California

Cover design by Linda Revel
Text design in Directories 1, 2 & 3 by Linda Revel

Library of Congress Catalog Card Number: 97-66307

ISBN 0-8351-2582-3

Revised Edition 1997
First Printing

1 3 5 7 9 10 8 6 4 2

Printed in Canada

CHINA
BOOKS
& Periodicals, Inc.

This book is dedicated to our parents:

Midge and Herb
Peg and Joe
Shu-Zhen and Yong-An

Table of Contents

INTRODUCTION

So You Want To Go To China...

You're a student of Chinese, or acupuncture, or calligraphy. You're a teacher of English, or Western culture, or physics. You're a retiree and want to get back in the classroom. You're just starting out and want an interesting first job. You plan a career in Asian business or law or journalism and want to teach or study as an entree to the East. You've just heard how interesting China is, and you want to go live there for a while.

You want to go to China.

This book was written for you.

The *Guide* is for people heading off to China as students, teachers, or researchers. The book will help you choose where to go and how to get there, what to bring and how to make the most of your time once you've arrived. Other books exist for specialized China experts on high-level exchanges (two of our favorites are *Chinabound*, and the *Teaching in China Preparation Series;* see Appendix B for details). Those books teem with suggestions on dealing with officials at the Ministry of Education and the Bureau of Foreign Experts, on how to get books published in China and how to get access to specialized research libraries. This book doesn't re-cross that same ground. Instead, this book is about the nitty-gritty of heading off to China on your own, whether individually or through an exchange organization that provides minimal support. It will tell you which foods you can get in China and how to buy a train ticket, how to combine teaching or studying with travel and how to take advantage of China's freemarkets. It's about real life in China for foreigners without the support provided by high-level exchanges—foreigners who won't be assigned interpreters and guides.

Structurally, the book falls into two parts. Part I runs chronologically through your China experience, from choosing a school to choosing a route home. Part II contains directories of schools and sending organizations. The book is both a reference work for deciding where to go in China and planning how to get there, and a manual on how to make the most of your experiences once you've arrived.

The authors have all been both teachers and students in China. This book contains our views as "insiders" on how life in China really works. We've also bolstered our own experiences by sending out surveys to foreign teachers and students at 552 Chinese institutions, asking about their experiences. Both text and directories have been greatly enhanced by the results of those surveys.

The authors would like to thank the following individuals and institutions without whose help this work would not have been possible. Where the book succeeds, much of the praise is theirs; where it fails, the blame is ours: the National Committee on U.S.-China Relations, and in particular Jan Berris and Elizabeth Kurz; the U.S.-China People's Friendship Association, and in particular Judy Manton and Jo Croom; the Australia-China Chamber of Commerce, and in particular Robert Cousland; the Canadian-Chinese Friendship Association; the Washington, D.C. Embassy of New Zealand, and in particular Lesley Jackman; the British Council's Washington, D.C. liaison, and in particular Margaret Lynch; the National TESOL Organization, and in particular Helen Kornblum; the Council on International Educational Exchange, and in particular Suzanne Fox; AFS Intercultural Programs, and in particular Carol Byrne; Virginia Walden of Sister-Cities International; Jacklyn Levine of the University of Rochester's Study Abroad Office; and the Institute of International Education, and in particular Peggy Blumenthal, Dulcie L. Schackman, and Ed Battle. These people and organizations individually and collectively represent phenomenal wisdom about foreign teaching and study, and about China. They were instrumental in directing us to sources of information. IIE deserves special kudos for their excellent international guides *Teaching Abroad, Vacation Study Abroad,* and *Semester Programs Abroad* (which are updated yearly). IIE provided the format and starting information for the surveys which grew into our Directories of Sending Organizations. Dr. Beatrice Bartlett, Steve Carlin, Dr. Jo Ellen Green, Dr. Bret Hinsch, Lillian Hreljac, Dr. David Kaiser, Dr. Murray Levith, Sr. Anne Phibbs, Barbara Rosenberg, and Paul Williams were extremely generous with their time and helpful with their comments, talking and reading through numerous drafts. Paul Williams was our resident computer wizard. Many Chinese friends (best not named) made possible the gargantuan task of sending out envelopes full of surveys to

552 schools in the P.R.C. Adam Aronson, David Bogart, Jeff Davis, Dan Gaiser, Mary-Ann Hill, Linda G., Carolyn Matthews, and Harlan and Bonnie Seyfer gathered voluminous and invaluable information on Beijing schools on a very tight schedule. Editor Charles Wang and Senior Editor Bob Schildgen at China Books & Periodicals were constantly supportive and inspiring, and the entire China Books staff approached the project with an enthusiasm that reinfected us through the draft #47 blues.

The authors wish to thank all the individuals at sending organizations for teachers and students going to China who took the time to fill out our surveys, allowing us the most up-to-date possible information for our directories. We also thank the following respondents to our survey of teachers and students in the mainland who agreed to be listed in our acknowledgments, as well as the many others who asked not to be listed, but whose thoughtful responses have so enriched our text. These men and women out in the trenches in China's educational system are the real "insiders," and their ideas are as central to this book as our own: Michael Angelasto, Adam L. Aronson, Elmah Baines, Don Barnett, David Bedell, Bernadette Brennan, Ramona and Richard Boyle, Cao Shuang-lin, Molly Deatherage, Keith Dede, Carol DeGrange, Harry and Mo Disney, Laurie Elsen, Sharon Flynn, Patricia Foster, Kevin Gambrel, Erin Gregory, Guo Xian-ting, Ellen Hauser, David Kellogg, Miles Lozinsky, A.S. Maclean-Bristol, Richard Mann, Henri Marcel, Paul Maynard, Heidi Myer, Mik Moses, Jenny Presland, Isabelle Pryor, David Silverglade, Shen Jun-cai, Sun Hong-guang, Judith Valois, Jim Vining, Jon Weston, and Zhang Zhao Xiang.

Finally, we would like to thank our students and teachers in China. In the hopes of sending more and better-prepared foreign teachers and students to China, this book was written also for them.

Note on Transliteration Style and Terminology: Rather than make a political statement by our choice of romanization style, the authors have transliterated all Chinese proper names using the spelling most common in the place discussed. Thus all mainland Chinese names are romanized in Hanyu Pinyin, and all Taiwan names in Wade-Giles. All Chinese phrases are transliterated in Pinyin. See Appendix A for pronunciation guides in both systems.

Throughout the text, the terms "PRC" and "mainland" refer to the People's Republic of China, while Taiwan is called Taiwan. Unless otherwise indicated, the terms "China" and "Chinese" refer to both.

PREFACE TO THE SECOND EDITION

China's economic reform has progressed exponentially in the years since we began the first edition of *Living in China*. Cities which held no fresh fruit in the winter now have imported US cherries and New Zealand kiwis. Schools which had to borrow ditto machines now own photocopiers. International business has replaced English as the nation's most popular major, and recent graduates enjoy competing with their Hong Kong compatriots at picking likely B-share moneymakers on the Shenzhen exchange and swilling XO cognac.

In all this excitement, many Chinese bemoan the death of academia in China today. Our contacts within China's schools, however, say otherwise. Friends now teaching and studying at universities from Beijing to Guangzhou, and many cities in between, continue to share the excitement at learning and growing and exchanging ideas between cultures that made our time as teachers and students so worthwhile.

Economic change has put a squeeze on teacher salaries, foreign no less than Chinese. You'll notice, if you compare editions, that average salaries have doubled or tripled, while many prices have increased by five or six times. This makes teaching in China even more an act of voluntarism than it used to be, while for students, China is no longer an inexpensive study abroad location. Interestingly, with the collapse of Taipei real estate speculation and the recent slower growth in Taiwan's economy, there have been fewer economic changes in the selections on Taiwan.

In the meantime, the broader base of cultural concepts on which this book is founded remains unchanged. The text has been updated to reflect such transformations as the elimination of dual currency and deregulation of Chinese airlines. We were struck, though, by how few changes were, on the whole, required to a text which, after all, deals primarily with culture, learning and education rather than economics. China is richer and more powerful and more economically complex than a few years back, but it is still China. The unbroken 5000 year river of her culture flows still.

Meanwhile, for the authors, though none of us remain teachers in China, China continues to be a central focus in all our lives. Margaret manages the ESL program for international students (many Chinese) at the University of Washington. Albert has gone into international hotel and restaurant management. And Rebecca is Director of Corporate Services for the Shanghai Branch of Bursor-Marsteller Public Relations. As one historian of our acquaintance put it, "Once the Middle Kingdom syndrome bites, it never lets go." May your encounter with China enrich your life as it has ours, and may you, like us, find that the Middle Kingdom fascinates you and expands your imagination through the decades.

PUBLISHER'S NOTE

Although we have tried our best to update and expand all the information in this book, change is constant. By the time we receive the book from the printer, educational programs will come and go, and some information will be out of date. In an attempt to keep the directories located in the back of this book current, we will be posting periodic updates on our web site. Please point your web browser to:

http://www.chinabooks.com/LivChina.html

We would also like to thank Jeremy Brown and Wendy K. Lee for updating the US portion of our directories, and Kitty Su and Liza Liang for updating the listing of schools in China. Michael Rice and Ma Baolin also added valuable insights on conditions in China and Taiwan.

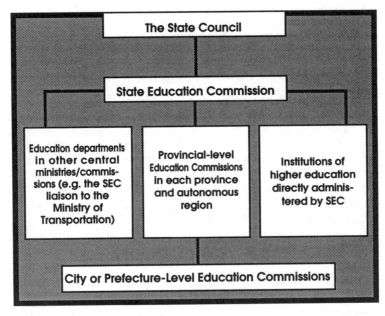

Figure 1:   *Overall Structure of China's Educational Bureaucracy*

1

The Big Picture

CHINA'S EDUCATIONAL SYSTEM

Education, like most things in China, is a top-down affair. The State Education Commission (SEC), primary arbiter of educational policy, fits directly under the State Council in China's governmental hierarchy. This position reflects both the emphasis China places on education and the need felt by China's leadership for strict central control.

The SEC carries out State Council policy through a network of education commissions and officers (see Fig.1). At any one school, teachers (both Chinese and foreign) may be inspected by officials from school-local-provincial and national-level education commissions, and by SEC officials from other ministries related to the school's academic focus (such as railway officials at a School of Transportation Engineering). As might be expected, demands are varied and complex. Chinese schools of significant size hire innumerable vice presidents, and assign at least one to full-time liaison duty with the SEC.

China mandates nine years of public education, from ages 6 through 14, or through middle school (for an international reference chart comparing systems of grade numbering, see Fig. 2). In rural areas, where almost 70% of China's people live, the majority of students make do with those nine years. In cities and more well-to-do rural areas, however, many students begin kindergarten at age 3 or 4 and continue on after middle school. At age 14 students take a municipal or regional exam. Many students then go on to general high schools. Others are tracked into specialized high schools, depending on their exam results (see Fig. 3). Specialized high

1

Approx. Age	Grade Levels	Grade Levels	Grade Levels	Grade Levels	Grade Levels
17	12	Gao 3 (College Exam)	Form 7 (College Exam)	Form 7 (College Exam)	Upper 6 (A Levels)
16	11	Gao 2	Form 6	Form 6	Lower 6
15	10	Gao 1	Form 5 (Nat'l Exam)	Form 5	Form 5 (O Levels)
14	9	Zhong 3 (Nat'l Exam)	Form 4	Form 4 (Nat'l Exam)	Form 4
13	8	Zhong 2	Form 3	Form 3	Form 3
12	7	Zhong 1	Form 2	Form 2	Form 2
11	6	Xiao 6	Form 1	Form 1	Form 1
10	5	Xiao 5	Primary 6	Primus 5	Primus 6
9	4	Xiao 4	Primary 5	Primus 4	Primus 5
8	3	Xiao 3	Primary 4	Primus 3	Primus 4
7	2	Xiao 2	Primary 3	Primus 2	Primus 3
6	1	Xiao 1	Primary 2	Primus 1	Primus 2
5	Kindergarten	Kindergarten	Primary 1	Kindergarten	Primus 1
4	Preschool	Preschool	Kindergarten	Playschool	Kindergarten
3	Preschool	Preschool	Playschool	Playschool	Preschool
Approx. Age	US/Canada	Chinese System	New Zealand	Australia	United Kingdom

Figure 2:   ***Comparative Chart of Elementary/Secondary Grades***

schools include: college preparatory comprehensive school, secondary professional schools (for training to be nurses, technicians, paralegals, and the like), and secondary vocational schools (for training in electronic assembly, auto mechanics, and the like). Students in general or college preparatory high schools compete three years later in the grueling 3-day "College Exam." (*gaokao:* 高考) Based on Gaokao results, students will be accepted into the colleges of their choice, tracked into other colleges, rejected outright, or tracked into tertiary vocational or professional schools. Students in B.A. programs then face a final "Graduation Exam" before receiving their degree, and foreign instructors must teach students what they need to know for this exam. Taiwan's system is structurally identical, except all 12 years are mandatory.

All mainland schools and all departments within schools must have a Communist "Party Secretary" whose full-time job consists of implementing and monitoring "Communist Education and Morality." Until several years ago, Taiwan had "Security Secretaries" from the Kuomingtang party filling comparable roles. Party secretaries form a "dual hierarchy" paralleling the academic hierarchy of department heads and presidents. As might be expected, in some cases the two hierarchies work together well, and in others they bicker constantly. When department heads and departmental party secretaries lock horns, little gets accomplished within the department. Even at its best many Chinese decry the system as wasteful. Deng Xiaoping's 1980s reforms promised a gradual phase out of the dual system. However, in the aftermath of the 1989 Student Demonstrations Movement central control of education once again came to the fore and in the nationalist retrenchment of the succession period, the party has remained strong. For the foreseeable future, foreigners in Chinese schools can expect to keep negotiating between political and academic hierarchies.

Departments appoint a class monitor for each classroom, a student responsible for liaison duty with the department head and party secretary. At larger schools, class monitor functions may be divided among several students, or even a whole class council, with some students responsible for recreation, some for distributing meal tickets, some for attendance records, and so on. At small schools, one student may fill all these roles.

All mainland schools through secondary level, and nearly all colleges and universities, are publicly funded. A few small colleges, such as Xiamen's Overseas Chinese University, are privately funded, but are still administered by SEC policy. In Taiwan many schools at all levels are privately funded and administered, but the Ministry of Education retains veto rights over curricula and teaching. On the mainland, the SEC, like most nations' Ministries of Education (although unlike the US or Canadian Departments of Education), sets detailed national educational policy. At the elementary and secondary levels this control extends to commission and selection of individual textbooks and course curricula. At the tertiary level schools and teachers have more leeway. Nevertheless, all teaching materials and methods are subject to SEC approval. Foreigners working in China need to understand this hierarchy. The teacher who refuses to assign certain materials to foreign students may be following central mandates. Meanwhile, foreign teachers who assign illicit materials to Chinese students mark those students for questioning and suspicion.

The goals of State Council educational policy are best expressed in the inimicable style of the SEC itself: "China lays special emphasis on making students develop morally, intellectually, and physically, on cultivating in them a devoted and hardworking spirit for the welfare of the country and people, on having ideals, morality, culture, discipline, love for the socialist motherland and construction, and on having a scientific attitude and unswerving will of pursuing new knowledge, and bravely creating new things on the basis of seeking truth from facts and independent thinking." (*Study in China: A Guide for Foreign Students, Foreign Student Administration Society* [Beijing Languages Institute Press, 1987], p. 7.)

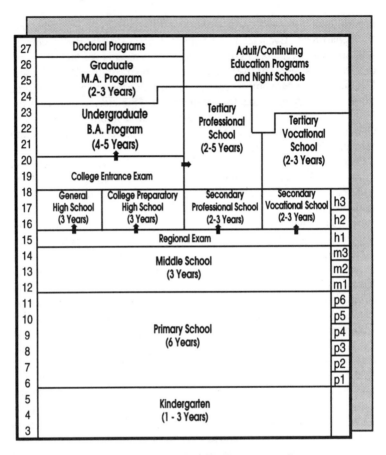

27	Doctoral Programs				
26	Graduate		Adult/Continuing		
25	M.A. Program		Education Programs		
24	(2-3 Years)		and Night Schools		
23	Undergraduate		Tertiary		
22	B.A. Program		Professional	Tertiary	
21	(4-5 Years)		School	Vocational	
20	↑		(2-5 Years)	School	
19	College Entrance Exam		→	(2-3 Years)	
18	General	College Preparatory	Secondary	Secondary	h3
17	High School	High School	Professional School	Vocational School	
16	(3 Years)	(3 Years)	(2-3 Years)	(2-3 Years)	h2
15	↑	Regional Exam ↑	↑	↑	h1
14					m3
13	Middle School				m2
12	(3 Years)				m1
11					p6
10					p5
9	Primary School				p4
8	(6 Years)				p3
7					p2
6					p1
5	Kindergarten				
4	(1 - 3 Years)				
3					

FIGURE 3:   OVERALL STRUCTURE OF CHINA'S EDUCATIONAL SYSTEM

In other words, academic content is only one part of what the SEC hopes to impart to Chinese students (certainly no one stresses the evil of run-on sentences). Many Chinese students have begun to oppose these agendas, and to laugh along with foreigners at SEC "goals." But even these students must take part in non-academic activities. Typical study programs include political study sessions, physical training, military training, inculcation of "moral values," and participation in community projects aimed at "socialist reconstruction" on top of an academic course load. While foreigners are excused from participation in this "other education," both foreign teachers and foreign students should be aware of the demands it makes on their Chinese counterparts.

In this book we lump together all foreigners who teach in China as foreign teachers, small "f," small "t." The Chinese government divides foreigners into Foreign Teachers and Foreign Experts. This distinction means little once your contract is signed (see Chapter 5); Foreign Experts and Foreign Teachers generally live in the same dorms and teach much the same sort of classes. But Foreign Experts receive substantially better salary and benefits than Foreign Teachers. Judging from our surveys, most Foreign Teachers earn between 1000 and 2000Y/month RMB. Foreign Experts generally start at around 2000Y/month.

Try if at all possible to be classed as a Foreign Expert. You'll have substantially better leverage in contract negotiations, and may get first crack at the best dorm rooms and most interesting classes. According to the SEC's brochure "Information on the Recruitment of Foreign Experts," language teachers who wish to be classed as Experts:

1. Should have a relatively high attainment in their own language and literature.

2. Should have been engaged in regular language teaching or the teaching of literature at the college level, or should have been regular language or literature teachers for five years or more in senior high schools, and possess a senior high school teacher's certificate.

3. Should have obtained an MA or higher degree.

As practically applied, these regulations generally mean that anyone with a masters or higher and two or more years' teaching experience can generally expect Expert status. Clever negotiators have also wrangled Expert status with only the degree or the experience.

Following is a breakdown of China's post–high-school educational institutions, the sort most foreigners are likely to become involved with:

1. LIBERAL ARTS COLLEGES/UNIVERSITIES: These are large institutions granting four-year baccalaureate degrees and/or graduate degrees. Most have broad ranging academic departments, from the familiar Chemistry, History, and Music to such uniquely Chinese disciplines as "History of the Chinese Communist Party." Most colleges and universities accept foreign students capable of studying in Chinese into all departments,

and foreign teachers in many departments; many also provide specialized programs taught in English specifically for foreigners. The central government has designated approximately 100 of China's universities as "Key Universities," with special funding and materials. From Peking University to Guangzhou's Sun Yat Sen University, virtually all of China's most famous schools are Key Universities.

2. TERTIARY PROFESSIONAL SCHOOLS: As in many nations (although unlike in the U.S. and Canada), most professional schools in China, from law and medicine to fine arts and normal (teacher preparatory) schools, accept candidates directly from high school. Tertiary professional schools cover a wide range of topics, but are not as broadly focused as the liberal arts colleges and universities. Most tertiary professional schools accept foreigners as both teachers and students. The largest number of students from developing nations on Chinese government scholarships attend professional schools in development-related areas such as Medicine and Engineering. Other students who arrange individual study programs in less conventional disciplines, such as Acupuncture or Peking Opera, often find professional schools more flexible about their needs than the great universities. In China's educational hierarchy the tertiary professional schools sit below the liberal arts schools.

3. TERTIARY TECHNICAL/VOCATIONAL SCHOOLS: China has hundreds of post-high-school vocational schools, teaching everything from textile manufacture to electronics. Many, such as the Postal Workers Institutes, are run by government ministries to prepare workers for their bailiwick; others are run directly by individual factories and workplaces. These institutes accept many foreign teachers, most to train students in English, but some for technical expertise as well. Often these schools offer the best financial packages for foreign teachers. Relatively few technical/vocational schools accept foreigners as students, and those generally only in specially organized programs, such as short-term courses in Chinese banking.

FOREIGNERS IN CHINESE SCHOOLS

The famed Chinese social critic Lu Xun once wrote, "Throughout the ages, we Chinese have had only two ways of looking at foreigners: either up to them as gods or down on them as beasts." Lu Xun may have exaggerated, but some of the attitudes he described still prevail. Foreigners in China live the best and worst of lives. Feted and made into buffoons, welcomed and kept at arm's length, they are both honored individuals and pawns in the struggle of an ancient culture now both embracing and resisting Westernization.

Students and teachers feel these contradictions more keenly than most, for they enter into the deepest social relationship (teacher-student) in Chinese culture other than that of family. Yet they enter as outsiders. The cost is an experience as powerful in its joys as its frustrations. The prize is an understanding closer to the bone of Chinese life than any can claim, be they journalists, businesspeople, or diplomats, who approach China only through official screens.

Whether your time in China is a springboard to a career in Asia, an academic adventure, or just a lark, you are likely to find it an overwhelming experience which changes you, for better or worse, forever. Foreigners who have taught or studied in China tend to love or hate her. Neutrality is rare.

THE UNPLANNED LIFE

The first thing to understand about teaching or studying in China is that however you prepare, including by reading this book, reality will likely turn out quite different from expectation. Conditions in China change rapidly. Then too, few people before they arrive can pin down Chinese institutions on just what they'll study or teach. Those that do often find everything changed on arrival. History lectures become economics seminars, and composition classes conversation classes, often without apparent reason or consideration of your resume.

For many this is the first inkling of the vast unpredictability of life in China, which will soon extend to the availability of such sundries as electricity, water, and transportation. Chinese cooks rarely plan a menu before they shop; rather they see what they can find in the market, and cook accordingly. Likewise, it is the rare teacher, foreign or Chinese, who can plan a semester's syllabus ahead. Who knows if textbooks will arrive or ditto machines work when they are needed?

It may be unclear why you are at the school. The classes promised for you may not have been arranged. Your room may be without heat or electricity. The school may seem very honored to have foreigners around, but may have done very little to prepare.

Foreigners often become uneasy with this lack of predictability. With time, however, most come to see it as part of a larger pattern. How can anyone you depend on be predictable when the people they depend on are not? In time, you may become less predictable yourself. "The nice thing is," points out survey respondent Jon Weston, "whatever you do here—

getting lost, being delayed in travel, etc.—it is interesting and new. Sit back and treat it as a part of a plan."

"Good for the Students" In Whose Eyes?

Everything in China can be seen in more than one way. Once courses get going you'll have to find out what the school expects and what your students or teachers expect, all of which may or may not have anything to do with the course description or with what you want. Teachers will need to learn which exams their students are preparing for, and how to help them both prepare for the graduation exams, and learn useful material beyond. At they same time, teachers need to remember that what they consider useful may not seem so to their students, or the department, or the department's party secretary. Students will need to learn what the school expects them to learn, as opposed to the teacher, as opposed to what they hope to get out of their studies.

If you're at a small institution, you'll likely become a Jack or Jill of all trades, setting up the library and lecturing on topics you never realized you knew anything about. If you're at a large school, you'll become intimate with the Chinese concept of bureaucracy. At either sort of place you'll learn about the complex interplay between politics and expertise in China, between procedure and personality.

Slowly, you'll learn who at your institution has formal power and who has actual power, how they wield it, and how to approach them. You'll learn both official and unwritten rules governing your personal and professional behavior. You'll have freedoms, in travel and in contact with ordinary Chinese people, that no tourist or journalist will ever know. But, at the same time, you'll be held to a higher standard of behavior. You will probably, if you stay in China long enough, become more subtle in human relationships than you are now.

You're Not In Kansas Anymore

Life in China for many foreign teachers and students involves relative physical deprivation, with sporadic water and electricity, and little or no access to cars, stereos, or evening entertainment. You may lose extra pounds you've carried for years, and develop terrific leg muscles. Of course, stores in even small cities now have a wider variety of goods than they did years ago. And, for the independently wealthy, joint-venture hotels in China's large cities stock most any convenience a Western heart could desire. But though the average foreign teacher earns 8 to 10 times the salary of her Chinese counterpart, if she wants to live within that salary, stays at the Great Wall Sheraton are out of the question.

Instead you may rediscover a world of simpler pleasures. Depending on what your city has to offer, and what of it is open to foreigners, you may go dancing, or roller-skating, or to the movies. You will likely go with your students, classmates, and teachers on picnics and for walks. You may relearn the arts of conversation and reading for pleasure. But more, perhaps, than at any other time in your life you will be thrown back on yourself. You may learn as much about yourself as you do about China, by learning what you can do without and what you have within.

You will taste objects you never considered edible, from sea slugs to fried bark to dog. You will come to grips with the sights, sounds, and smells of a people far less inhibited than Westerners about bodily odors and functions. You will learn about overcrowding, and life in an economy of scarcity.

You'll be a racial minority among a very insular people. You'll learn to be stared at and pointed at and endlessly interrogated about your age and income. Even overseas Chinese are subject to this scrutiny because their clothing styles and uncalloused hands set them apart from mainlanders. If you speak Chinese well enough, you'll hear yourself called "outlander" (*laowai:*老外) or even occasionally "barbarian" (*yangguizi:*洋鬼子) and you'll be pushed to the fronts of lines by some people and resented for it by others. You'll most likely be stung badly sometime, just when you think you've understood the culture: the colleague you thought was a friend will turn out to have been assigned to you by the government; your favorite teacher will be fired; your favorite student will report your indiscretions to the authorities. You may decide you can't hack it and go home.

If you stick it out, you'll make your own peace with that mixture of ignorance and vainglory in the Chinese mind, which both is and is not racism. You'll learn to forgive and to understand. You'll appreciate quiet powers of the spirit, and you'll make a few friendships which run very deep.

"I am now 62," writes survey respondent Mik Moses from her teaching post in Shanghai, "and have lived a not uneventful life, but my years in China have been among the most interesting. Teaching in [my home country] had become predictable, the students predictably disinterested and the curriculum predictably unrelated to their needs. After one year here I decided that I would rather work in China. . . . Here, I learn something every day, and absolutely nothing is predictable." If you stay long enough, you'll most likely end up with China under the skin, a part of you and a place you'll want to return to time and again.

MAINLAND CHINA SINCE TIANANMEN: TO GO OR NOT TO GO

This section was written in 1990. Looking back years later, we found it more rather than less true today.

"I can't imagine your motivation," fulminated one survey respondent who preferred anonymity, "to sell China to foreigners now given the present situation. Have you all no shame?" For anyone who cares about China and the Chinese, the tragic events of the spring and summer of 1989, and their aftermath, were horrifying beyond words. The question is, what should a concerned person do? The indignant respondent quoted above wrote us from China, where he continued to teach; and therein, for us, lies the answer.

Teachers and students from the West bring new ideas to China. This inescapable fact lies at the heart of the ambivalence with which the government views foreigners. Western language skills, teaching methods, technological expertise, and currency are valued, but China's government views with alarm the openness foreigners bring to China's academic process, as well as ideas about everything from political democracy to religion to taste in music. Class monitors in Westerners' classrooms are specially instructed to look out for signs of subversive teaching, and teaching materials are carefully screened. Only the foolish foreign teacher would use openly anticommunist teaching materials or language in the classroom. But new ways of thinking get transmitted unavoidably, in informal discussions and ways of talking and living.

It would be foolish to overemphasize the role of Westerners in the "Beijing Spring" democracy movement. The uprising was Chinese in root and leaf, looking back more to the May 4th movement of 1919 than to the Mayflower. Nevertheless, Western influence was present, from the Statue of Liberty–esque "Goddess of Democracy" to the medical students from foreign countries who helped tend wounded after June 4. Westerners provided moral and practical support of many kinds, and, in many instances, were able to protect the Chinese around them from retribution. "Distant water won't put out a near fire," goes the old Chinese saying about the importance of neighbors. Foreign teachers and students enraged at seeing China in flames were in the best position of anyone to do something about it.

For foreigners to boycott China now, we believe, would be to abandon rather than support the people and goals involved in the democracy movement. China's government has demonstrated time and again its tenacity in the face of isolation. As a Chinese friend puts it, "if the West cuts off economic and cultural contacts now, all that will happen is that

China's people will be poorer and more ignorant of the West." If the sad truth be told, the events of 1989 were hardly unique in Chinese history. Westerners in China before Tiananmen always worked in the shadow of "rectification" campaigns from the Hundred Flowers to Spiritual Pollution—and much earlier ones as well. Remember the Boxers? And the crushing of the largest civil war in human history, the Taiping Tianguo Movement in the 1850s and 1860s? Long before communism arrived on the scene China had a highly centralized and totalitarian government, and through the centuries, including our own sad one, that government has perpetrated bloody campaigns that make Tiananmen pale by comparison. The only difference is that in 1850 they didn't have CNN.

Rarely have foreigners ever gone to China to admire her enlightened government. Instead foreigners go today as they have always gone, intrigued by the warm people, astonishing landscapes, and fascinating culture of the Middle Kingdom. Those things haven't changed.

Nor are foreigners in any way unsafe in China today. Even at the height of the 1989 movement foreigners who appeared in the wrong places were spirited away to their hotels or dorms, and perhaps questioned, but not threatened. China's government, ever practical, is too aware of its need for Western businesspeople, teachers, students, and travelers to scare them away permanently. Quite the contrary, a number of survey respondents who had worked in China for several years before 1989 mentioned that their treatment after 1989 was better than ever, as the Chinese government attempted to return to "normalcy" even while trials of 1989 protestors went on.

In terms of numbers, teachers and students continued entering China about as fast as ever. According to a November 1990 Institute of International Education (IIE) report on the "Current Status of Academic and Cultural Exchanges Between US and PRC Institutions a Year After Tiananmen," after some falling off in the 1989–1990 academic year, by late 1990 most programs were back at, or above, their pre-1989 levels. By 1992, levels had returened to 1989 averages.

Data on Westerners heading to China is somewhat more anecdotal. In our survey of sending organizations, we asked the number of students sent in each of the last three years. Most programs showed a sharp drop in 1989 but an increase in 1990 up to, or above, the 1988 level. Among our teacher and student surveys, many respondents mentioned that the number of foreigners at their institutions was as high as ever, and only the one quoted above expressed opposition to new teachers and students arriving. "It is a terrible and wonderful thing that has happened," wrote one teacher who had lived in an interior city for three years before 1989. "People can be killed, but ideas cannot be killed." We believe that for those who care about China, there is no better time to go.

One last concern arises, however, in the special problems of living in China soon after a political campaign. Contact with Westerners and their "Spiritual Pollution" has repeatedly been used against Chinese people during political campaigns. As a result, during times of political stress Chinese people tend to withdraw from foreigners. Some Westerners, concerned that contact with foreigners could make their Chinese friends into political targets, question the morality of ever seeking out intimate friendships with mainland Chinese. We don't support this view, but do note that in politically turbulent times, foreigners do tend to feel cut off.

Many foreigners who lived in China during and immediately after the "Campaign Against Spiritual Pollution" in 1983–1984 reported feeling isolated. "In a year in Nanjing," admits one student of that time with some bitterness, "I was never once invited to a Chinese person's house, or on a picnic. I never even went for a walk with just one Chinese person." In the years just before Tiananmen, almost the opposite was true. Both Margaret and Rebecca found that invitations to dinners, picnics, dances, and parties with Chinese friends came so thick and fast some had to be refused to leave any time for work.

The impact of Tiananmen in these areas is less clear. China's government does seem committed to as swift a return to normalcy as possible, and there has been no repeat of the "Spiritual Pollution" slogans, no organized effort to discourage contact. Still, the spectacle of television trials has cast something of a chill over relationships. As one foreign teacher still in China, who has been teaching since 1987, puts it, "nothing has changed that I could really put my finger on, but everything is a bit more formal." As time goes on, no doubt more relaxed relations will develop again. In the meantime, the best advice is to follow the cues of the Chinese people around you. They know better than anyone what degree of friendliness is safe.

Choosing:
Mainland or Taiwan

In mainland China old men trundle through neighborhoods on tricycle carts shouting *jiu pingzi!* ("drink bottles!"), as they collect the empties for recycling. In Taiwan the same sort of old men perform the same service, only their tricycle carts are motorized and the *jiu pingzi* blares from a tape recorder.

Taiwan and the mainland are amazingly similar in their "Chineseness." Many mainland visitors attribute this to the effects of communism phenomena that appear as well in Taiwan, and which are far more Chinese than communist. Both Taiwan and mainland China claim to be the legitimate heir to Chinese culture. Taiwan is wealthier, more urbane, more international, and more high-tech in daily life than the mainland. Her population includes vast aboriginal and native Taiwanese populations with unique cultural heritages. But Chinese culture as brought to Taiwan by the Nationalists in 1948–1949 still dominates the island's government and much of daily life, particularly in the large cities.

TAIWAN AND THE MAINLAND: AN OVERVIEW

Long lists of similarities link Taiwan and the mainland. Politically, both governments impose order and control. Both have press censorship and political prisoners and essentially one-party rule (opposition parties were illegal in Taiwan until 1987 and remain fragmented). Academically, both Taiwan and the mainland stress centralized educational control, administered by government authorities in the school system. Until recently the Taiwanese had Nationalist Party "security secretaries" in their school system exactly equivalent to the PRC's "Communist party secretaries," and both still have "class spies" in the form of class monitors. (Taiwanese class monitors now have greatly reduced political functions compared with the past, but many Taiwanese students still fear their influence.) Culturally, Taiwanese and mainlanders share language, fine arts, cuisine, and fundamental world view, including the dual idea that foreigners are both gods and beasts which Lu Xun cited. They also share certain other features of Chinese culture. Much political and economic corruption stymies both Taiwanese and mainlanders.

The fact that Taiwan—the richest of Asia's Four Little Dragons and the 13th largest trading power in the world—boasts a thriving capitalistic economy is what most sets it apart from the mainland and makes it an easier place for Westerners to adjust to. You can buy Cadbury Fruit 'n Nut bars at 11:00 p.m. in Taiwan, sample Italian pasta, French haute cuisine, Korean barbecue, and other international fare at all times of day and night. After ten years of economic reform, the same is only beginning to be true in China's largest cities in 1996, and the available choices remain limited.

Taiwan's cities suffer no shortage of entertainment. In Taiwan you can lead a social life much as you do at home, seeing first-run movies and plays and reading what you want. You can choose where you want to live, share apartments with Chinese roommates, and apply for jobs after you arrive. In short, you can have a much more "normal" lifestyle in Western industrialized terms than on the mainland. In the "three big" mainland cities (Beijing, Shanghai and Guangzhou), there are now plenty of discos and bars, and you can rent pirated western movies or laserdisks, just weeks after they've been closed in the West, complete with recorded audience laughs, but even there, choices are very limited (Rocky X or Rambo XII), and in the hinterland they're more limited still.

There is of course a downside to life in Taiwan. Despite Taipei's claim to cultural legitimacy, Taiwanese culture has been heavily influenced by both Japan and the US, as well as by the native Taiwanese heritage. Taiwan does boast some fabulous cultural treasures, from the Palace Museum in Taipei to the temples of Hualien Gorge. In addition, Taiwan's Chinese language schools concentrate on traditional complex written characters, crucial for study of Chinese history, literature, and traditional culture. Mainland schools focus on simplified characters, and offer the traditional characters only in special classes. However, Taiwan's very wealth and cosmopolitanism tend to break up the weight of Chinese tradition so omnipresent on the mainland. Taiwan offers, to some extent, Chinese culture in diluted form. In addition, Taiwanese cities are urban nightmares, with terrible pollution (silver jewelry will tarnish overnight), constant traffic jams, and motorcycle demons who speed through traffic lights, all of which produce a great deal of stress. It's also a bit too easy in Taiwan to move into a foreign enclave, dine on hamburgers and ice cream and socialize with other expatriates.

There are, in fact, many advantages to studying and working in the mainland. Most of the skills, knowledge, and practices of ancient China remain alive there. Even Taiwanese admit the superiority of most mainland artists; "To master Chinese calligraphy," explained a Taiwanese journalist of our acquaintance, "requires constant practice over years. Who has time for that in Taipei? In the mainland that's all they have to do." More programs in ancient traditions exist for foreigners in the mainland as well. Only one medical school in Taiwan, for example, offers courses in traditional Chinese medicine, and it accepts only two foreign students per department. In the mainland, every sizeable city has a College of Traditional Medicine, many with large programs for foreigners. The one thing that it is difficult to explore in the mainland is traditional Chinese religion. While it is possible to make private arrangements for study with local monks in the mainland, no mainland schools offer formal study of Buddhist or Taoist traditions, whereas several Taiwanese schools do.

If you want to study acupuncture, practice martial arts, or paint Chinese landscapes, you'll probably learn more in the mainland. If you desire a steady flow of fascinating (albeit sometimes maddening and depressing) experiences, mainland China won't disappoint you. Also, because at least the smaller cities in the mainland lack the stress which accompanies modern industrialized life, you may find life there very peaceful, allowing you to accomplish more in the way of intellectual or artistic pursuits than you would in Taiwan. Although at times in our mainland years we would have sold our firstborn to see a Western movie or hear live Western music, life there was never dull.

Mainland China is harder to cope with than Taiwan in many ways. Her poverty results in spartan living conditions, little entertainment, and a population made xenophobic by ignorance. Politically, despite similarities, the mainland is also far more repressive than Taiwan. Orchid Island, the Taiwanese *gulag*, holds dozens of political prisoners as compared with probably tens of thousands in the mainland's Qinghai; and independently owned Taiwanese newspapers print stories daily which would mean long sentences to hard labor in Beijing. In fact, the only regularly banned topic for today's Taiwanese papers is Taiwanese independence, and even that, to the horror of mainlanders, is starting to be openly debated.

But many foreigners find the mainland provides a richer experience of Chinese culture in its purest form. In Taiwan's rural areas the ancient Min-An culture preserves many Chinese and Taiwanese cultural traditions. Even Taiwanese urbanites celebrate Spring Festival with plenty of fireworks and the Mid-autumn Festival with mooncakes. In some ways, particularly in religious traditions, Taiwan's festivals can be more traditional than the mainland's. Taiwan also boasts specialists in Chinese culture who, owing to the freer flow of information, can produce better research than anyone on the mainland. But to us, the greatest difference lies in the vitality of Chinese tradition on the mainland, whereas in Taiwan, at least in the cities, many Gucci-booted youth seem to be abandoning Chinese tradition for greater participation in the life of the international jet set. Of course, many of our mainland students had grown up without reading ancient Chinese philosophers and poets, many of whom have been banned in various political campaigns. But they all lived lives steeped in tradition; even our class monitors could tell us ghost tales heard from their grandmothers or give us 32 recipes for dumplings. Our Taiwanese students had memorized Li Bai and Mo Zi for the college exams but often knew more about the television serials "Dallas" or "Dynasty" than about the *I Ching* or acupuncture. Our mainland students took us on hillside picnics in the shadows of temples. Our Taiwanese students were more likely to take us to discos and give us hot stock-market tips.

GENERAL INFORMATION ABOUT TAIWAN

Information on Taiwan appears throughout this book, and we have pointed out in each section which topics refer only to the mainland, which to Taiwan, and which to both. This overview introduces some statistical bases for comparison, as well as broad ways in which foreigners' working lives differ on the "Two Sides of the Ocean Abyss." Taiwan's population hovers around 20 million; the mainland at last official census reported 1.13 billion and climbing. The actual population of the mainland may be considerably higher. Per capita income in Taiwan is first-world level, US$8,000 per year of reported income, and actually considerably higher due to additional incomes in a large underground economy which go unreported. Mainland per capita income is US$300 per year and may be falling due to reclassification of World Bank data. Taiwan is less than 200 miles long, and less than 40 miles wide at her widest point; the mainland has the fourth largest land mass of any nation. Taiwan's climate is subtropical, and heat and humidity can be intense during the summer months. The mainland ranges from the subtropical to the subarctic. Taiwan's countryside is lush and beautiful; the major cities, however, are extremely polluted and crowded, and expensive. The mainland ranges from lush countryside to desert; its cities are as crowded as Taiwan's, but are less polluted due to lower industrialization (though they're still hardly clean). Average families in Taiwan have 1.7 children, and as of 1989 the Taiwanese owned 1 car for every 8 people, and 1 motorcycle for every 2.5

people. Mainlanders may or may not own a bicycle—though there's an increasing number who own a Mercedes as well. Mainland families by official policy have 1 child in cities and 1 or 2 in the countryside, though many in the countryside circumvent these rules. Overpopulation remains the most serious problem on the mainland, a matter of profound concern to people across the political spectrum.

The PRC maintains diplomatic relations with most natons. Taiwan's official diplomatic relations are few, but her trade partners are numerous. In most major countries, Taiwan, though barred from maintaining formal embassies and consulates, posts government representatives in offices marked with cryptic names. In the U.S., Taiwan government offices are called "Taipei Economic and Cultural Office."

In Taiwan, as on the mainland, foreign teachers and students flock to the largest cities; according to one official, over 75% of all foreign students and teachers in mainland China live in Beijing, Nanjing, Shanghai, and Guangzhou. In Taiwan well over half of all foreigners live in Taipei. More daring foreigners (who often report the most lively experiences) scatter to smaller cities throughout both areas—in Taiwan largely to Taichung in the central region, or to Tainan or Kaohsiung in the south.

Standards of living are lower in the mainland, but expenses are also much lower. Housing and insurance is generally free for mainland teachers and students. Teachers instructing Chinese people on the mainland rarely earn enough to save anything (grade-school teachers in the mainland's International Schools generally earn more than Ph.D.'s teaching in mainland universities). But because prices are so low, mainland salaries generally allow significant travel around China, and the purchase of many fine handicrafts and consumer goods.

Taiwanese salaries are competitive internationally, but the cost of living has soared. Years ago Taipei was the destination of choice for Westerners backpacking through Asia in need of a pit stop to reline their wallets. Not today; with Taiwan's booming economy, even after the stock market crash of 1989, housing and food prices have increased vastly since the mid-1980s while foreign teachers' salaries have remained steady. Many foreign teachers report more difficulty living within their means in Taiwan than in the mainland. Because mainland schools assign free housing for teachers and subsidized dorms for students, while the Taiwan-bound fend for themselves in a housing market dizzy with speculation, you may just be able to afford more comfortable quarters in Beijing than in Taipei.

Because Taiwan is more urbane and international than the mainland, it is relatively easy to mingle and develop friendships with the Taiwanese. There is, in fact, quite a bit of dating between Westerners and Taiwanese.

While discouraged by many Taiwanese parents ("you're dating a barbarian?!"), mixing with foreigners in Taiwan carries none of the fear of political retribution so weighty in the mainland. For this reason many young single people prefer Taiwan; the mainland can be a lonely place.

Teaching

The mainland accepts foreign teachers only in formal posts at tertiary schools which must be arranged before arrival. Taiwan offers formal, pre-arranged posts at colleges, universities, and technical institutes as well. These "real school" positions generally require solid teaching credentials, are best applied for in advance, and are fundamentally similar to mainland teaching posts; see Chapters 1, 3, and 6 for details.

Taiwan's more open system, however, allows several other levels of more "entrepreneurial" teaching as well: many small, private, for-profit English Language Institutes; agencies which arrange on-site teaching to employees of foreign subsidiaries; and *buxiban* (补习班) ("study-cramming institutes") dot Taiwan and all will hire foreigners and permit a range of part-time as well as full-time opportunities.

Because of the high turnover in Taiwan's foreign population, you can generally arrive at any time of year and find a job soon. Winter is still the slow season. The easiest time to find a *buxiban* job is right after the schools recess for summer vacation when many students take summer English classes. Tote your resume and transcripts, particularly if you have advanced degrees, and look up "English Teaching" in Taipei's English-language Yellow Pages, or *buxiban* in the Chinese Yellow Pages in other cities. The better English Language Institutes and teaching agencies require a Bachelor's degree and prefer some teaching experience. The *buxibans* vary; many require only that foreigners walk, talk, and speak English, and end up with some astoundingly bad teachers. Be careful, though; some unscrupulous *buxibans* rope in unwary foreigners just off the plane to slave-labor contracts offering dorm rooms, cafeteria board, and some Chinese tutoring in return for unconscionable amounts of teaching. Don't sign anything till you've had a few days to get on your feet and have a look around.

Many foreigners also privately tutor well-to-do Taiwanese in return for cash and/or room and board; look for signs seeking tutors on *buxiban* bulletin boards, or ask other foreigners. As with *buxibans*, be careful. No-shows for classes are common. Try to get payment in advance, and be clear that lessons must be paid for even if not attended. If you get a room-and-board arrangement, make sure that outside a reasonable number of tutoring hours your time is your own. Wealthy Taiwanese may enjoy having foreign live-in maids, but you just may not want to be one.

Studying

Foreign students proficient enough in Chinese to study in it can apply to any degree program in Taiwan. Foreign degree candidates must be high-school graduates. Many schools also have special English-language programs for foreigners. Application for admission should be sent directly to the dean of studies of the host institution.

Taiwan has 5 government-accredited Chinese Language Programs, at National Taiwan Normal University, Fu Jen University, Feng Chia University, Tunghai University, and National Cheng Kung University. There are also major, highly respected Chinese-language training programs at Taiwan University's Interuniversity Program (formerly called the Stanford Center), at the Taipei Language Institute, and the Kuoyu Jipao newspaper. Students wanting to study Chinese at these institutions should submit two copies of their application form, official transcripts, two letters of recommendation from teachers, a health certificate (including proof of no infectious diseases), and a study plan.

There are also numerous other language training programs and programs offered through private colleges and universities. The tuition per semester at private universities ranges from NT$17,740 to NT$24,590 (at an exchange rate of US$1 = NT$27.66 as of April 22, 1997); at public universities tuition runs from approximately NT$4,120 to NT$5,350 (based on 1990 Taiwanese government figures). Evening schools charge approximately NT$580 per credit hour. These schools vary greatly: some are merely visa mills and discourage serious study.

Our Directory #1 lists all major schools in Taiwan after the listing of schools for the mainland. Our Directories #2 and #3 list programs sending teachers and students to Taiwan. For more information and prospects to look for, see Chapter 3.

Accommodations

Mainland schools provide free or cheap housing for foreign teachers and students. This is important since very few buildings in the PRC can legally house forigners, and costs for apartments in those buildings have exploded as multi-nationals compete for expatriate housing in one of the world's most speculative real estate bubbles. A cheap foreign apartment in Beijing these days is anything under US$2,000/month.

In Taiwan, "real school" study programs or posts may include dorm accommodations, but more likely the school will simply assist foreigners in locating housing, and less formal posts involve no housing assistance at all.

When you first arrive in Taiwan you may need to stay in a hostel or hotel until you locate a room or apartment. Relatively cheap places include the YMCA/YWCA dorms and International Youth Hostel dorms which dot the island. Four relatively cheap hostels in Taipei are:

1. The International House, 18 Hsin Yi Rd., Section 3, Taipei, Taiwan (Phone [02] 703-3151).
2. YMCA, 19 Hsu Chang St., Taipei, Taiwan (Phone [02] 311-3201).
3. YWCA, 7 Tsing Tao West Rd., Taipei, Taiwan (Phone [02] 371-4493).
4. The Travel Stop Hostel, 3rd Floor, #35-4, Lane 36, Chungshan N. Rd., Section 2, Taipei, Taiwan (Phone [02] 561-8560).

Get a tourist guidebook for other cities (see Appendix B for suggestions). Just outside Taipei the Academia Sinica runs a longer-term hostel called the "Taipei International Youth Activities Center" which offers single rooms for around US$400 per month, very reasonable by Taipei standards. Be sure to write in advance for reservations, as they dislike unexpected arrivals. Write to Academia Sinica, Nankang District, Taipei 115, Taiwan (Phone [02] 782-2120), or to the Activities Center at 30 Hsin Hai Rd., Section 3, Taipei, Taiwan (Phone [02] 362-1170).

For the longer term, should your school not offer dorms and you do not care to stay in a hostel, you will have to arrange homestay with a Taiwanese family or rent a room or apartment. Some homestays are commercial and arranged through schools; others are free or in return for English tutoring. Check *buxiban* bulletin boards and talk with other foreigners for information. Bulletin boards and word of mouth are among the best sources to find what passes for cheap rents in Taiwan. For those who read Chinese, red rental signs posted on telephone poles are often the only advertising for most apartments. Walking around the rental area of choice can turn up bargains. Also, leases are flexible at *t'ao fang* (studio apartments) in red-light districts. Buildings are filled with prostitutes, but the areas are not dangerous. For those who want short-term leases (by the week), this is a tolerable alternative. Of course your Taiwanese friends might be shocked and/or fascinated when you reveal your address. As in the West, most apartments advertised in the papers tend to be expensive. Although, since Taiwan has an open commercial housing market, the prices are lower than the insane rates on the mainland. As of this writing, a one-room efficiency in downtown Taipei or an upscale suburb such as Shih Lin Tienmu averaged US$700 per month. Many foreigners rent rooms and kitchen privileges from families in such outlying areas as Yung-ho or Pan-ch'iao; these generally start at around US$400 per month.

3

Planning:
Your Institution and How to Get There

Your institution in China will shape your Chinese life; choose it carefully.
Chapter 5 explains in detail the Chinese *danwei,* or "work unit." For now,
suffice it to say that your school in mainland China controls not just the
classes you teach or study, but also everything from your sleeping
quarters to your transport. Beyond that, China's regions, less homog-
enized by television and rapid transit than their Western counterparts,
offer fundamental differences in culture, language, and custom, as well as
geography and climate. City and country in China are different worlds.
Going independently also creates a different experience than going
through an institution. Spend some time thinking carefully about where
you want to be in China and how you want to get there. Read on for
suggestions on the kinds of questions to ask, then flip through our
directories to help you choose where you want to be.

THE INSTITUTION

Before considering specific schools, decide what you want to accomplish
in China. Do you want to work in the capital, making contacts at elite
universities with the children of power? Do you want to live in a region
rich with historical and architectural finds for you to explore? Do you
want to learn Mandarin? Learn Cantonese? Climb mountains? Study
minorities? Keep your overall goals in mind when you make more
specific choices. More than one eager student of Mandarin has chosen a
school in Guangzhou, where only the elite speak standard Mandarin.
Don't let it happen to you!

Aside from your overall goals, three basic considerations should shape your choice of a school: the region of China you want to live in, the choice of big versus small cities and schools, and the services and facilities available at the school itself.

Region

China's regions range from the howling, desolate deserts of Xinjiang, where people speak a language related to Arabic and pray toward Mecca six times daily, to the bustling markets of Guangzhou, where girls in heavy make-up and boys in tight jeans dance to the latest hits from Hong Kong. Space prohibits detailed descriptions of cities here. Our directory gives overviews of each region. But for details, sit down with an atlas and a good tourist guidebook (see Appendix B for suggestions) and make some choices about the kind of region you want to call your Chinese home. Here are some factors to keep in mind:

1. CLIMATE. Chinese live more exposed to the elements than Westerners. Other than in joint-venture hotels, only the northern provinces allow heating, and only the deep south has air-conditioning. Much of daily life, from exercises to cooking to socializing, takes place outdoors due to lack of space. If you suffer in the cold, think south; never assume you can just crank up the thermostat in your Chinese apartment. If you can't stand heat, think north and far west. If you like rain, think south or southeast; for deserts think north central and northwest. Wherever you go, bring adequate clothing for the climate; see suggestions in Chapter 4.

2. GEOGRAPHY. Transportation in China is complicated and slow. You'll relearn the (considerable) joys of walking or bicycling to the places you want to go. However, you'll have to give up the joys of hopping in your car and zipping to the mountains for the weekend or the seaside for the afternoon. Live where you want to be in China. Otherwise you'll have trouble getting there. China offers the world's highest mountains and the world's deepest desert basin, as well as huge lakes, miles of shoreline, rivers, jungles, and high plateaus. Which do you like to live in? And how about travel? Will you feel a need to "escape" to Hong Kong once a month for Western-style entertainment? Want to visit Beijing often? Unless you'll tote heaps of cash for plane fares, live near the places you'll want to see often.

3. HISTORICAL, ARCHITECTURAL, AND CULTURAL RESOURCES. In the jungles of Xishuangbanna, ancient Dai temples shine out among the banyan trees. In the dusty plains of central Henan, centuries of Buddhists have carved images in sandstone. Qingdao, on the coast, combines traditional fishing villages with the Bavarian architecture of the German occupation. Foreign residents with special interests in art, archaeology, architecture, or religion can gain unparalleled access to their region's cultural treasures. Do you want to study Yellow Lamaist scripture on weekends with a local monk? Live in Inner Mongolia, Qinghai, or Tibet. Do you want to learn the needlepoint arts of the Shani, Dai, or Hmong? Live in Yunnan. If you have special interests in any area of Chinese culture, live in the areas richest with those resources.

4. LANGUAGE. Dialect varies tremendously between regions. Many "dialects" of Mandarin, such as Hunanese, are so thick as to be opaque. In the Shandong dialect, for example, *wo* ("I") becomes *an*, and *rou* ("meat") becomes *yo*. Cantonese, Fujianese, and Shanghainese are distinct languages from Mandarin, while Tibetan, Inner Mongolian, and many other minority languages come from wholly different linguistic groups. If you want to speak relatively pure Mandarin on the streets, north central or northeast China is the place to go. For Cantonese, stick to Guangzhou; for Fujianese, to Fujian, for Shanghainese, to Shanghai, and so forth. Mandarin is the official language, and in all areas you'll find fluent speakers with the purest tones. But the average man and woman on the street speak local dialects, and if language study is your chief focus, this should be a concern.

Big City, Small City; Big School, Small School

In general, the larger and more coastal the city, the more Westernized it will be. The larger and more famous the school, the more competition there will be both among Chinese students and among foreigners. The trade-off is a choice between one type of China experience and another—between big ponds and little ponds, of course, but also between making contacts with the known and learning about the new.

BIG CITY, SMALL CITY

Bigger cities offer more formal cultural entertainments—more movies, theater, operas, museums, dance halls, sports events—than their smaller cousins. Guangzhou and Shenzhen are just subdued versions of Hong Kong, where bars and discos stay open till dawn. Beijing is stodgier, but still offers at least one major performance a night. When the Bolshoi Ballet or the Milan Opera tours China their tours include only the largest cities. While cultural offerings in Beijing or Shanghai may seem tame compared with London or New York, they far outweigh those available in the interior towns. Markets are also better in bigger cities, and goods geared towards Western tastes, from cheese and Western liquors to stylish clothing, are generally available only in the largest cities.

Big cities also house large foreign populations, which provide plenty of opportunities to chat about the nature of the universe with unshaven expats in grimy teahouses. Because China's foreign populations are truly international (the Chinese government offers scholarships to needy students from many developing nations), living in Beijing or Wuhan, you'll be as likely to learn about Sri Lanka or Zaire as about China.

Small towns offer none of these things, and if you can't face living where the sidewalks roll up at dusk, stick with the large cities. For the self-reliant, however, small towns offer much greater access to the rhythms of daily Chinese life than the metropolis. Foreigners are special in small towns, and get invited regularly to private homes, even to special events like weddings and birth ceremonies. The Levith family of Saratoga Springs, New York, (Dr. Murray and Tina, and their sons Nathaniel and Willy) spent a year in Qufu, a dusty village in central Shandong famous only as the birthplace of Confucius. But so welcomed were they into village life that they felt they "couldn't have had a richer experience anywhere else." The young boys of the family got interested in stamp and coin collecting, and were showered with the hoarded treasures of local families, including centuries-old coins and rare stamps from the birth of the People's Republic. Their father, a Shakespearian scholar, was able to mobilize the full resources of the college to contact Chinese Shakespeare scholars nationwide.

A note of caution, however: being special also means foreigners in small towns get far more attention than they like. "When I first came to Yan'an," wrote one respondent, "I was the only foreigner, not just at the University, but in the whole city of Yan'an. Thus I came to be a sort of celebrity, or at least an object of great interest." This "zoo" effect appears throughout China, especially in small towns. If you can't stand this sort of scrutiny, best retreat to the relative anonymity of the large city.

BIG SCHOOL, SMALL SCHOOL

As in the West, universities in China fall into an unofficial hierarchy, with schools like Peking University, Fudan University, and Qinghua University being the Chinese Harvard, Yale, and Stanford. If your time in

China is a springboard to a career in Sinology, a time to look good on your resume, a time to make contacts with the political elite, by all means apply to these schools. Be forewarned, however: many foreigners share these goals, and competition for teaching or research posts at the top schools can be fierce. Also, the schools often block foreigners together in foreigners-only compounds, leading to a sense of isolation and what respondent David Silverglade called the "foreigners-in-a-cage syndrome." If he had to do it over, Silverglade avowed, he would "enroll in a Chinese school which was small and liberal."

If you care less about your resume than about the content of what you learn, the elite schools may not necessarily be best for you. To be sure, the top schools get a disproportionate share of funding and resources, and great numbers of excellent faculty and students. However, appointments and acceptances in China are even more political than in Western universities, even depending on such elements as family history, friendship, and the ever-present *guanxi* ("connections"—for more on this topic, see Chapter 6). As a result, a great deal of well-connected driftwood occupy slots at China's top schools. One New York lawyer described his frustrations in teaching a Western law class at Peking University which included the son of an important Communist Party leader. The student did no homework, made noise and fell asleep in class, openly mocked the teacher and disrupted other students' work. When the teacher threatened the boy with a failing grade, he simply yawned. "If you fail me, next semester I'll take a make-up exam administered by a Chinese teacher. Do you think any of them would dare fail me?"

Many of China's finest scholars are scattered throughout the smaller schools, unable or unwilling to make the political connections necessary for appointments at the great universities. If you particularly want to study with an individual scholar, find out where he or she works, and go there. Also, because Chinese are not free to live where they like, China has not seen the general drift of talented people in and out of academia to the great cities typical of the West. Beijing in the '90s is not Paris in the '20s. The greatest of China's poets, painters, and playwrights are scattered throughout the country in places like Chengdu, Kaifeng, and Harbin as much as in Beijing or Shanghai. If you are interested in organizing conferences, editing magazines, and otherwise bringing together talented people and their ideas, you're much more likely to get material and emotional support at a small school where you're one of five foreigners than at a great university where you're one of 500.

The School

China has some 8,000 post-secondary learning institutions, ranging from huge to tiny, from broad-based universities, to technical and vocational schools, to training centers within work units. Some 550 of these institutions accept foreigners as students and/or teachers, and those schools are listed in our Directory #1. Once you've chosen a region and a size of school, spend some time flipping through the directory to decide on individual schools. Notice that the directory is arranged by province or region and city, with Key Universities starred, and schools divided by category in each list, e.g., University, Minorities/Politics/Law, Art/Music, etc. This directory represents the most complete information ever compiled in English about Chinese schools, and we have tried to standardize information in each listing. We sent surveys to each school and consulted all existing directories in both English and Chinese. Nevertheless, complete information for each school was not always available. Where any information you need is missing, we suggest you write to the individual school and ask for it. Here are some factors to keep in mind while you flip through the directory:

1. TYPE OF SCHOOL. If you want to be at a big, academically focused university, with all its advantages and disadvantages (see above under "Big School, Small"), consider one of the "Key Universities" starred throughout the directory. Many of the smaller Key Universities, such as Shandong University in Jinan or Sichuan Academy of Science and Technology in Chengdu, can offer the benefits of the most elite universities without the fierce competition and politicization. Key Universities generally attract the brainiest students in their province or region and have more funding and better facilities than non-Key schools.

If you don't care about being at a Key School, but would like to work with highly motivated students or teachers, consider a Normal School, School of Politics and Law, or Medical College. The teaching, medical, and legal professions are poorly paid in China, but nonetheless are extremely difficult to train for, and, therefore, tend to attract dedicated personnel who believe in what they are doing for its own sake. Some of our happiest comments came from teachers at China's Normal Schools and Medical schools.

Foreigners who wish to study or teach a technical subject may do best at a technical, vocational, or single-subject school. Many schools of Chinese Music, for example, have better performance departments than the Key Universities, with their focus on a general liberal education. Meanwhile, foreigners who would like to contribute to China's technical development will have a freer hand at designing courses at, say, a school of Minerals and Mining than at Qinghua University. Specialized schools in China include schools of Architecture, Art, Chinese Medicine, Chinese Music, Engineering, Industrial Chemistry, Materials Handling and Packaging, Medicine, Minerals and Mining, Music, Police and Army, Post and Telecommunications, Textiles, and Transportation.

2. PROGRAMS AND FACILITIES. Within each type of university, specific programs vary by institution. Our directory lists departments. If you'd like to teach Electrical Engineering, don't choose a school without an Engineering department. If you'd like to study the *erhu,* choose a school with a music department. Best of all, choose a school where the specific program you want has already been set up. Someone else has done the dirty work, and you won't have to run around for weeks getting books and classrooms lined up.

Consider the limits of available facilities. How highly is the library rated in our directory? What about computer facilities? Are there secretaries to help you prepare classroom materials? Of course, you can always bring books and computers and copiers with you, but there's a limit to the patience of the airlines, and if a school's current facilities are totally unsuited to what you hope to do there, best choose another school. Remember, there'll be no photocopy shops on the corner.

3. ACCOMMODATIONS AND TRANSPORT. Most students and teachers headed for China are prepared for some discomfort, but there are matters of degree. Whether you're given two rooms or three shouldn't be the deciding factor in your choice between schools, but if everything else checks out, why not go for comfort? Also, school choices on accommodations can affect your work. Some schools are notorious for refusing Chinese students access to foreign teachers' dorms, which cuts down on your time with your students and lessens your abilities as a teacher. Given the difficulty of transport in China, the willingness of the school to give access to school vehicles can also be important. If you live 90 kilometers from the isolated Buddhist grottoes you hope to study, willingness of the school to let you either get a Chinese driver's license and borrow their car or use a car and driver three times a week can make a big difference in your research.

4. FINANCIAL ARRANGEMENTS AND BENEFITS. Again, no teacher or student goes to China to get rich. But all else being equal, a 2000-yuan monthly salary or $1,000 semester's tuition will allow a more comfortable life than a 1000-yuan monthly salary or $2,500 tuition. But consider the whole package. Will you be charged for your room? For health insurance? What will board cost? What about travel allowances or shipping allowances? Many independent teachers or students will settle these details after arrival (see Chapter 5). But the history in our directory gives a base for comparison.

SENDING ORGANIZATIONS AND INDIVIDUALS

Judging from our survey responses, about 40% of foreign students and teachers in China arrange their stay through some form of sending organization. These range from Sister City programs and university-to-university exchanges to missionary organizations and programs for seniors. The other 60% go as individuals, making arrangements directly with the Chinese institution, the Ministry of Education, or the Ministry of Foreign Affairs.

To Solo or Not to Solo

Sending organizations offer stability, experience, and institutional backing should conflicts arise. Most sending organizations also provide financial compensation, travel bonuses, and training. Individual travel offers greater flexibility in choice of institution and negotiations over program. Going individually also avoids conflicts over organizational philosophy, rules, and regulations. Here are some factors to keep in mind when making your choice:

1. EXPERIENCE. Sending organizations offer experience. Many have been sending teachers and students to China for decades, and are familiar with the politics and culture of China. Often these organizations deal year after year with the same Chinese institutions, and know all the internal politics of their Chinese partners. Virtually all sending organizations arrange some pretravel training for participants; many provide midsemester conferences as well. Most also help in contract negotiations. While a few organizations emphasize voluntarism, and, therefore, arrange minimal compensation for participants, most engage in solid financial negotiations. Unless you're very experienced at business talks, you'll almost certainly get a better financial deal going through an organization than as an individual.

2. ORGANIZATIONAL BACKING. Chinese society functions better at the group than the individual level. Your Chinese institution will feel happier in discussions with a sending organization representing 20 teachers than in 20 discussions with individual teachers. Should conflicts arise, foreigners who represent a sending organization also generally have greater leverage than individuals. Finally, organizations can provide substantial material and professional support, in the form of shipping allowances, teaching materials, and other goodies available to individuals only at their own expense. Also, student sending organizations can generally easily arrange transfer of credit to your home institution, a process which can be agonizing if you go as an independent.

3. AVAILABLE PROGRAMS AND INSTITUTIONS. Most sending organizations deal with a finite set of Chinese institutions and programs. The Chinese institution of your dreams may host no exchange programs, leaving you no choice but to apply as an individual. You may also wish to design a program not offered by any sending organization. Most student sending organizations arrange classes in Chinese language, culture, and, perhaps, business management. For anything else, from Chinese music to minority medicine, you'll likely need to go it alone. Teachers also find more flexibility on their own, particularly when combining teaching and studying. One enterprising man in Kunming arranged to study acupuncture and Chinese music while teaching English and US history. Such an individually tailored program will generally require going it alone.

4. RULES AND REPRESENTATION. Every organization has rules and regulations for participants, and you should consider what sort you want to deal with. You represent your sending organization and they you. If you're uncomfortable with the organization's image, don't get involved; your Chinese institution won't consider You apart from Them. If you hate the organization's rulebook, stay away; you'll only cause confusion trying to bend rules on the sly. Certain religious sending organizations, for example, enforce dress and behavior codes on participants. Some university exchange programs forbid participants to teach or study outside the formal program arranged with the Chinese institution. If you're the rugged individual type, uncomfortable with organizational restraint or eager to be dealt with on your own terms, go on your own.

5. ORGANIZATIONAL PHILOSOPHY. Beyond the rule book, be aware of the sending organization's underlying philosophy. Many sending organizations have specific religious or political agendas. Be sure these goals agree with or complement your own. You'll be very far from Kansas in China, and you won't want people whose basic ideals you detest to have power over your life.

MAKING CONTACT

Once you've made your choice, it's time to make initial contact.

1. CONTACTING SENDING ORGANIZATIONS. Our Directories #2 and #3 offer the most complete list ever compiled in English of student and teacher sending organizations dealing with China. We have tried to collect the most up-to-date information possible on sites in China, subjects taught, eligibility, credits granted, available positions, and other information needed for an educated choice. We've also included any ratings of each sending organization given by respondents to our survey, as well as any information we had on each program's special focus or affiliations. Write or call the organizations directly for more detailed information and for application materials.

2. MAKING CONTACT AS AN INDEPENDENT—USE PERSONAL CONTACTS. Our Directory #1 lists addresses and phone numbers of all schools in mainland China that accept foreigners as teachers and/or students, and all major schools in Taiwan. Once you've chosen a school, write to it directly. However, your first challenge will be getting the Chinese institution to write back to you. Chinese people dislike dealing with strangers and prefer introductions. Chinese institutions are no different. Institutions that receive blind letters and resumes often have no idea what to do with them or how to evaluate them, and more than one such letter is gathering dust on a shelf while a fine position goes begging.

If possible, get yourself an introduction to the institution from someone whose name will be familiar. If you know anyone who has worked with a Chinese institution, ask for a recommendation. Try asking at your local community college if anyone has been to China on a speaking tour. Write your local Chamber of Commerce or your local chapter of one of the China-related resource organizations listed in Appendix C.

If you or anyone you know will be going to China, stop in at a school there. Meeting in person can break the ice in ways a resume and cover letter can't.

Try meeting representatives of Chinese institutions in the US. Check with your local college or community college to ask about visiting scholars, speakers, or exchange students you might hook up with. One Chinese exchange student in Maine has arranged several placements for American teachers and students simply by writing letters of recommendation to his, his wife's, and his friends' alma maters.

Try also attending a conference of the Teachers of English to Speakers of Other Languages (TESOL) Association (write: National TESOL Association, 1600 Cameron Street, Suite 300, Alexandria, VA 22314, Phone (703) 836-0774, for a schedule). Many Chinese institutions send representatives to regional TESOL conferences, and every national conference boasts 15 or 20 different institutional representatives. Visit the Educational and Cultural Section of the mainland Chinese Embassy or Consulate, or of Taiwan's government representative nearest you. Helpfulness of staff varies, but they can probably direct you to a number of institutions in China, and may even help with applications. Appendix C lists Chinese Embassies and Consulates, and Coordinating Councils for Taiwan.

If you can't get any sort of introduction, try applying through the Foreign Expert's Bureau (get an application from a Chinese Embassy or Consulate, or write P.O. Box 300, Friendship Hotel, Room 71633, Beijing 100088 PRC. Phone 86-10-6-849-8888).

As a last resort, write blind letters to the institutions listed in our directory. But leave plenty of time and send as much information as possible. A detailed, descriptive Curriculum Vitae, for example, works better with Chinese institutions than a resume, whose terseness reads to them as opaque. Send photographs, copies of diplomas, and awards of merit, anything that will help establish a personal relationship. Be patient, and if necessary write several times. Just remember, if you start to get frustrated, it'll make great tales for the grandkids.

Choosing a Route; Saving on Tickets; Exotic Routes

If you're going through a sending organization, or if your Chinese institution buys your ticket, you'll likely have little choice of route. If you go on your own, however, you'll probably be looking for bargain airfares. As of this writing, the cheapest (APEX) regular round-trip airline fares to China are approximately US$1,400 from the East Coast of the US or US$1,100 from the West Coast. You can get much cheaper rates by flying through Hong Kong. If your school is very far north or west, however, the savings might not be worth the trouble. Much cheaper fares are available through "overbooking agencies," which specialize in buying up blocks of tickets and reselling them at a discount. These fares run as low as US$1,000 from the East Coast or US$800 from the West Coast to the mainland, and even cheaper for Taiwan. Chinese-language newspapers and magazines are the best places to find ads for overbooking agencies that deal with China. Be careful, though, as many of these tickets have stringent limitations. In general, avoid "fixed tickets" (tickets which must be used for the flight indicated, so that if you miss the flight you forfeit the fare), or "open tickets" good for less than one year. Try to purchase round trip tickets, or have someone at home make return arrangements. In most PRC cities, buying international tickets is nightmarish, and because of exchange rates, buying tickes in Taiwan is far more expensive than buying them at home.

Note that Taiwan visas are good for a maximum of six months (minimum of two months). Travelers to Taiwan must leave the island at least one week out of every six months, and might, therefore, find it cheaper to buy their ticket through to another destination (Boston-Taipei-Bangkok round trip, for example). This makes the six-month visa trip abroad far cheaper. For example, you could fly Boston to Taipei in August; then fly Taipei to Bangkok round trip in February for a visa trip and vacation; and then return to the US from Taipei in July.

If you have some time, you might also want to consider a more exotic route. Foreigners have entered China via the Trans-Siberian Railroad from Moscow; the Karakoram Highway from Pakistan; the Friendship Road through Tibet from Nepal; and the Mekong River. Get a good tourist guidebook geared toward independent travel (see suggestions, Appendix B) for ideas.

Packing:
Psychological, Personal, and Professional Baggage

You've decided on an institution and chosen a route there. Now's your time to prepare your baggage, both the kind you'll lug with your arms and the kind you'll tote in your head. Remember as you do that China is another world, in both material standards of living and cultural norms. You should consider both mental preparation and physical needs, as well as your professional requirements as teacher, student, or researcher. The following are tips on what to bring— and what not to bring—to help make your adjustment to China as painless and joyful as possible.

PSYCHOLOGICAL BAGGAGE

One of our survey questions asked teachers and students how they'd prepare differently if they went to China again. Over 90% answered they'd *"learn more about China before going."* This goes for Taiwan as well as for the mainland, for while Taiwan's material standards of living are closer to the West's, her culture is not. You can *never* overprepare yourself for China, read too many books, see too many movies, nor talk with too many people who've been there. Forewarned, as the saying goes, is forearmed.

Cultural pride compels prearrival study. Considering China's rank as the world's most populous nation with the world's longest uninterrupted cultural heritage, most Westerners remain woefully ignorant of her history, economy, geography, and traditions. Chinese people feel this ignorance keenly. Some resent it, some are depressed by it, and some use it for intellectual one-upsmanship ("My favorite American authors are

Faulkner, Wilder, and Twain. Which Chinese authors do you prefer?").

Immerse yourself in Chinese culture before you go. Knowing China will earn you respect from students, teachers, and colleagues and help break the ice with Chinese friends. After all, imagine a "Visiting Scholar" from China lecturing as an expert at a university in the UK, and suddenly asking the name of the current prime minister, or whether Dublin was next to Dorset. Wouldn't such basic ignorance raise questions in your mind about the scholar's competence and level of concern about Britain and British students? Foreigners who can't separate Zhou Enlai from Zhao Ziyang, or who wonder which province Shanghai is in, open themselves to the same suspicions.

Every language student knows the raptures Chinese people pour forth on hearing Westerners attempt their tongue, even a word as simple as *ni hao* ("hello"). Deeper interest reaps even greater rewards. One student in Kunming wrote of asking a Bai minority classmate about Bai wedding customs, and getting an invitation to the classmate's sister's tribal wedding, a three-day affair which was the height of the student's China stay. Quote a passage from the poet Li Bai, and Chinese friends will fête you with the ultimate compliment for a Westerner in China, calling you a *zhongguo tong* (中国通 : "China Hand").

1. LANGUAGE. Despite great stress in recent years on English education, very few Chinese have gone beyond "hello." Speaking even a few words of pidgin Chinese will open new worlds of communication and possible friendships for you. Attaining fluency in Chinese presents many hurdles. A chasm divides Chinese from all Western linguistic groups; remembering characters is fiendishly difficult (native speakers often forget the more obscure ones); thousands of regional dialects confuse even the locals; and the infamous "tones," by which words take on different meanings depending on their musical pitch, terrorize many a learner.

Survival Chinese, on the other hand, can be learned remarkably quickly. Several factors simplify learning basic Chinese. First, Chinese grammar ranks among the world's simplest. No verbs conjugate, nor do nouns decline. Adding particles like *le* and *yao* magically transports sentences to past or future tense. Compared with English (ever try to list all possible forms of *to be?*) this simplicity is sublime. While few cognates (words with related pronunciation) link Chinese to Western languages, Chinese uses phonemes (building blocks of pronunciation) virtually identical to English; see the pronunciation guide in Appendix A for details. A few cognates exist as well to cheer the learner's way; even the most dispirited students recognize *ka-fei* as "coffee" and *han-bao-bao* as "hamburger." Consider a semester or two of language before you go. For the time-pressed, many schools offer intensive summer courses packing a year's worth of Chinese into eight or ten weeks. Even if you're heading to China to study language, consider studying some beforehand. Any language learning proceeds faster from a base; you can build that base more comfortably with the teaching methods of your homeland than with the Chinese equivalents; and you'll sidestep dealing with regional dialects at the same time as you struggle with your first words of the language. In addition, many PRC programs are very poor, with presence in China being the main draw. Taiwanese language programs are generally (though not always) better, but require learning *bo po mo fo*. Most Chinese-language semester and summer programs in your home country offer college credit and financial aid. See Appendix A for a list of programs, and write individual schools for detailed information and applications.

Non-students might try self-study courses, using one of the fine book/tape series available (see our list of suggestions in Appendix B). Even without formal study you can pick up a little Chinese. Try calling your local college or university International Students Association and offering to help Chinese exchange students with their homework in exchange for tutoring in Chinese. Failing that, tote your Berlitz guide. Even a few words of Chinese can make the difference between dependency and independence in Asia.

2. READING, LOOKING, AND LISTENING. Hundreds of books, movies, and tapes published in English explore every aspect of China's culture, history, and peoples. Appendix B contains an annotated bibliography of our favorite suggestions, divided by category. Don't neglect the videos; images give a visceral reality to your understanding missing from even the best books.

Also, talk to people who have been to China, as tourists, teachers, students, or businesspeople. Learn what they thought and felt, regretted bringing or leaving behind, or found difficult to adjust to. Ask how they suggest you prepare. Find the best advice you can, and take it. You'll need it. "This place," swore one respondent, "can be heaven or hell." Learn everything you can to improve your odds.

3. CROSS-CULTURAL AWARENESS. A cultural gulf separates China from the West. Some thought on cross-cultural communication and conflict can save much pain. Any number of books have come out full of advice on coping with culture shock and understanding cultural differences. You may find some of these books useful; Appendix B contains a suggested list.

But the most important preparation for cross-cultural sensitivity occurs in the mind. Take some time to consider life in a wholly different culture, and how you'll react to it. In many ways, Chinese etiquette and cultural values are opposite the Western. How will you adjust to Chinese values, or not adjust to them? For example, when meeting for the first time, many Chinese people ask about age, income, and marital status. These questions, considered frightfully personal in the West, are in China a common way of expressing friendly interest in another person, regardless of nationality. Will you answer these questions (literally hundreds of times, as you'll meet many strangers during your stay)? Will you explain the Western reserve regarding these topics, and ask that Chinese people respect your privacy—also hundreds of times? Will you follow the example of one teacher in Yunnan, who had a T-shirt printed with his name and all relevant details, and wore it incessantly to avoid being asked?

Planning a strategy for coping with cultural conflict saves much hair-pulling and allows a happier, more productive stay. Only you know which approach will work for you. Just remember, Chinese culture will not change, nor should it change, simply because it makes you uncomfortable. The Chinese themselves say *ruxiang suisu,* (when you enter a village, follow its customs), a rough equivalent of "When in Rome. . . " Whether you should imitate Chinese custom in China or politely explain your preference for your own ways depends on your character and tolerance for adjustment. But preparing yourself mentally to recognize cultural differences and develop a conscious strategy for coping with them works better than yelling at people whose manners make you uncomfortable, or sniggering at them behind their backs.

Recognize also that mental preparation has its limits. No doubt, whatever resolve you make to politely answer the questions listed above each time asked, one day on an unvented train, steaming through the jungles of Guizhou, the poor soul who happens to be the 40th person to ask your income that afternoon will trigger an explosion. Prepare yourself mentally for that day as well. Recognize that you are human. Screaming at the poor soul in Guizhou is hardly noble, and will do little to improve the image some Chinese hold of foreigners as not quite civilized. But it's understandable, probably inevitable, and may even have some therapeutic value. If you can recognize your limits of cultural tolerance, and forgive yourself for outbursts when those limits are crossed (while recognizing that little good comes of such outbursts), you can minimize their frequency.

For more on this topic, see Chapter 6: "Adjusting: The Big Seven Hate List of Cross-Cultural Conflicts."

4. SUNDRIES: TOOLS TO PREVENT WESTERN WITHDRAWAL SYNDROME. Despite all best preparations and plans, you'll sometimes feel so frustrated with Chinese culture you could gleefully murder, and other times feel so homesick you could weep. For both of those times, prepare a few treats to help you relax and forget about China.

Think about what you do on days when you really want to relax and get away from it all at home. If your answer is "go for a spin in my Porsche," you're probably out of luck in China. But most people can think of a few favorite activities that revive them after a hard day, and which are portable: listening to music, reading a trash novel, drinking a big mug of hot chocolate, playing the guitar, going for a hike. Whatever it is, and whatever you need for it, bring it along. When you need it, it'll be there; lock yourself away and enjoy.

PERSONAL BAGGAGE: THE NECESSITIES

Material living standards in China can't compare with the West though they are improving rapidly, especially in the big cities. Taiwan is coming very close (who knows— if current economic trends continue, Taiwan may soon race past the West).   But in the mainland, and particularly in smaller cities, life is spartan, as we have already noted. You can't do much about the plumbing, but you can make choices about material goods. Many products we take for granted are rare or unknown. Other products exist, but not in familiar brands. While international trade with China is developing rapidly, the government limits importation of consumer goods to preserve hard currency. In Taiwan you can buy virtually any import goods, for a price. But in the mainland American shampoo and

Canadian beer and Swiss skin cream available at your local US supermarket may be sold only in large cities, or not at all.

Obviously, more than a billion people thrive on Chinese products. Very flexible foreigners fascinated with Chinese culture may decide to wear the clothes, eat the foods, and use the toiletries of the natives. But most mortals find a total break from all familiar material goods downright unpleasant. Adjusting to real cultural differences causes enough trouble; making more anxiety by weaning yourself from your favorite shampoo at the same time is pointless.

The following sections suggest which Western products are sold in China, which are unavailable but have reasonable local equivalents, and which you should bring from home. Obviously, bringing a year's supply of every product you use is impractical, and given the many joys of modern travel, you will want to keep your luggage to a minimum. But if you must have Grape Nuts for breakfast, by all means ship 20 boxes of Grape Nuts. Better pay excess baggage charges than go stir-crazy over lack of a breakfast cereal.

Necessity #1: Clothing

Before you stuff your duffle bag to head for Asia, try a quick experiment. Check the tags on each piece of clothing you've bought in the last five years. Chances are much of what you planned to haul to Asia came from there in the first place.

The moral is that China makes very high-quality clothing and sells it at very reasonable prices. Many Chinese-made clothes sold in the West are export only, not officially sold inside China because of their hard-currency earning potential abroad. But many other fine brands are sold in China, particularly in the freemarkets. Even supposedly "export only" brands, with the designer labels sewn in, often find their way to the freemarket stalls. The larger the city, the more variety the local freemarkets yield. We've bought Jordache jeans in China for $4.00, polo shirts for $3.00, and a Pierre Cardin 3-piece wool suit for $50.00, including tailoring. Taiwan sells equally high-quality clothing at only somewhat less modest prices.

Most foreign teachers and students buy clothing in China, so starting out with an overstuffed bag makes little sense. Heavy or very tall people will have trouble finding sizes that fit (though they can have apparel tailored). But most others should pack with the assumption they'll go home with more clothes than they brought. Many foreigners, in fact, bring a favorite outfit which fits well from home and have it copied by Chinese tailors in a variety of fabrics and colors. For more on this topic, see shopping suggestions in Chapter 8.

Obviously, however, you'll want a few changes of clothes to start out with. The Taiwan-bound can bring clothes they'd bring to any Western country, remembering weather conditions and slightly more modest necklines. But the mainland demands special consideration. The following guidelines should help you pack.

"DRESS CODES"

Most mainlanders care less about fashion than Westerners. In the Hong Kong–ized cities, such as Guangzhou (Canton) and Shenzhen, fashion reigns supreme. Many foreigners unfamiliar with the scope of reforms have been shocked to see low-cut dresses and punk hairdos. Yet dress codes even in Guangzhou remain informal. No one looks askance if shoes don't match handbags or socks are the wrong shade of gray.

Chinese in interior cities dress more casually still. The days when foreign journalists mocked China's "blue ants" are long gone and unlamented. Blue cotton "Mao Coats" and "Mao Hats" (the Chinese call them "Sun Yat Sen Coats" *(zhongshanfu)* and "People's Hats" *(renminmao)* remain cheap, durable, and common; during (increasingly rare) political campaigns everyone dusts them off. But only the rare Chinese now gets through life wearing nothing but monotone cottons. Nevertheless, dress codes are hardly exacting. Plaid skirt, striped shirt, and polka-dotted jacket may match just fine in Chinese eyes, so long as they display similar colors.

Bring one nice dress, or sports jacket, and tie for the banquets you'll inevitably attend. But for everyday wear, so long as your clothing is neat and clean, Chinese won't mind if it's less than fashionable, or notice if it's more. Indeed, foreigners living in depressed areas, such as the mining towns of Northern Shanxi now hit by heavy unemployment, should avoid expensive clothing and accessories, which could easily raise resentment or scorn.

Three points to bear in mind, however: First, Chinese appreciate neatness. The preppy "unfashions" of the West—the untied Docksiders worn without socks, the holes in the knees of the designer jeans—to most Chinese appear merely slovenly. Second, most Chinese find very bright colors inappropriate for wearers over 40. If you live to wear lime green sweaters and scarlet suits, by all means wear them. You may even strengthen cross-cultural understanding by explaining Western "young at heart" views. But be prepared for puzzled stares from folks on the street who may wonder why you don't "act your age." Third, while the Hong Kong–ized belt is quite permissive, in most of China wearing revealing clothes is still not done. Most Chinese find tight pants, short shorts, micro-bikinis, and low necklines vulgar, and wearers risk reducing their professionalism in the eyes of students, teachers, and colleagues.

PRACTICAL CONSIDERATIONS FOR CLOTHING

Wise packers remember that China is dry and dusty; that many gooey goods get carried throughout her streets without packaging; and that travel by crowded bus is far messier than travel by private car. At the same time, China lacks the abundance of both water and electricity that makes the Western push-button laundry possible. In other words, it's a lot easier to dirty your clothes in China than in the West, and a lot harder to clean them; this is largely true in Taiwan as well as the mainland. Your very best clothes should stay at home, lest they get stained forever with chicken blood from the freemarket butcher or axle grease from your bike. Clothes you bring should be sturdy and easily washable; cotton-synthetic blends, for example, clean easier than pure cotton. Depending on accommodations, you may have to wash your clothes with a scrub board and lye soap. Even if you've access to a washing machine, it'll be Chinese style: fill it from the tap, let it swish, haul out the clothes wet, and put them through the wringer. Take it from us: you may enjoy your burgeoning biceps, but you'll want no clothing one iota harder to clean than necessary.

Leave the dry-clean–onlies at home. Outside of joint-venture hotels, mainlanders dry-clean with kerosene, which leaves a stench that lasts for days and may stain fine fabrics.

Bring a good variety of warm and cool clothes. China's chronic energy shortages leave her people far more exposed to the elements than in the West. Warm clothes for winter and breezy for summer are essential. Even in Taiwan, you should have sweaters and jackets for winters, which can be surprisingly cold and damp. The Chinese make lovely and warm, if rather shapeless, padded trousers and jackets, and also make very nice silk thermal undies, though high-tech fabrics are fairly rare. Recently, The North Face and other outdoor clothing manufacturers have also started producing Gore-Tex jackets and other accessories in China at very reasonable rates.

Shoes, particularly women's shoes, can be a problem; most Chinese versions qualify as arch-crushing torture instruments. Bring all the dress shoes you'll need, and also any hiking shoes or boots you want. Nike, Adidas, and Reebok now manufacture in China, so you can buy trainers cheaper in China than at home.

Necessity #2: Food

China's cuisine is as varied as it is ancient. From the spicy stews of Sichuan to the tangy garlic sauces of Shandong to the sweet gooey treats of Guangzhou, Chinese food offers an endless, mouthwatering array. You'll likely fall in love with many a delicacy, and probably even lose weight and lower your cholesterol in the process, for the Chinese diet emphasizes plenty of grains, fish, and fresh vegetables. Many foreigners never miss their native cooking and feel no need to carry any foods from home.

Most foreigners, though, need some familiar foods to eat happily. You may or may not have a kitchen, but much can be done on a hotplate, or even with just thermoses of hot water. Shops in Taiwan's cities (and to some extent even rural areas) hawk any Western food you could want, and though you may not be able to afford it on a teacher's salary, splurging there is still probably cheaper than shipping from home. But the mainland is another story.

The following chart suggests foods available and unavailable in the PRC. Pack any unavailables you'd feel happier tasting now and again. Strictly speaking, food imports are controlled, but most officials won't bother about small amounts. A familiar meal can help you relax after a tough day, and few of the agonies of cultural withdrawal are as poignant as craving a hot chocolate and knowing the nearest cocoa powder is 8,000 miles away.

Few Whole Grains

Chinese people prefer highly refined flour and rice. Western preferences for brown rice and whole wheat flour seem inexplicable; the Chinese eat them only when they can't afford finely milled versions. If you insist, your schoolmates will search out a place to buy whole-grain staples, but it may gain you a strange reputation.

Herbs and Spices Hints

Many Western herbs and spices aren't sold as food, but as medicine. Bring the list of herbs and spices, with translations in Appendix A, to any Chinese herbal medicine store. Upscale markets in large cities now also hawk common Western seasonings (oregano, thyme, rosemary, onion and garlic salts). But many out of the way seasonings aren't sold in China, and neither are non-Chinese spice mixes such as curry powder or garam marsala; bring your own.

Dairy Hard to Find

Chinese people detest most dairy products. Many Chinese lack lactase, the enzyme necessary to digest the lactose in milk, so dairy foods give them stomachaches. Additionally, much as many Chinese delicacies seem repulsive to foreigners (would you believe sea slug and fish maw soup?), Chinese find Western love of cheese faintly horrifying. Look at cheese as an outsider: moldy milk so curdled it's gone solid.

As a result, few Chinese stores sell many dairy products. Upscale stores in large cities stock a full range; many a foreigner has lugged a wheel of cheese on the train from Beijing or Shanghai back to their school.

Mongolians and Tibetans like dairy products, so in Inner Mongolia and Tibet you can eat hearty—though yak butter and powdered goat cheese may take some getting used to. But elsewhere in China your dairy choices are limited to three: yoghurt, powdered milk (fresh in large cities), and ice cream. Chinese yoghurt (*suannai:* 酸奶) is runnier than Western, but delicious and widely sold in plain and fruit flavors. Powdered milk is also easily available; our polls indicate Anchor Steam Brand from Australia tops most foreigner's lists. Chinese love ice cream, but be warned that most Chinese like far less milkfat than Westerners; you'll taste more ice than cream. Foreign tastes are being incredibly catered to, though. Bud's Ice Cream is now available in all major cities, and Haagen-Dasz premiered in Shanghai in 1996.

BRING COFFEE IF YOU NEED IT

Real perk coffee exists only in joint venture hotels, which sell it only by the cup. In the largest cities dried beans and filters are available, but elseware fresh-roast addicts should bring a drip pot with a year's supply of filters and beans (a re-usable Melitta-style filter is best). They will guarantee popularity with the expatriate crowd, but don't be surprised if your Chinese friends can't tell the difference between your best Columbian roast and Maxwell House. Just imagine how they feel when you prefer Orange Pekoe to a prizewinning Oolong or Longjing tea.

LIQUORS AND WINES

Friendship Stores and upscale private stores sell many Western wines and liquors at steep but not outrageous prices, though for fine brandies or cognacs you'll have to try Hong Kong. China also sells a few indigenous "brandies," which are quite tasty but very unbrandy-like; more like a cross between Southern Comfort and Old Thunderbird. Most Chinese wines taste like Manischewitz with added sugar, but a few palatable varieties exist; China's first varietal vintage winery, Huadong Winery in Shandong province, produces a lovely Riesling and a Chardonnay whose 1986 vintage took a Silver Medal at bordeaux. Traditional Chinese liquors, such as Shao Xing, Mao Tai, and Lao Jiao, take some getting used to. Most pack a punch, as much as 180 proof. Experiment, however. You may develop a taste for them. Beer is widely available, with Carlsberg, Heineken, San Miguel and Pabst producing in local joint ventures.

Necessity #3: Personal and Health-Care Products

Chinese use most toiletries Westerners use, though often less liberally. In Taiwan virtually any product is available, though, again, often at inflated prices (at last check, a 5-ounce tub of Nivea Brand skin cream sold for US$15 in Taipei). Since Procter & Gamble and Johnson & Johnson have

Product	Readily Available	Large Cities Only	Easy to Find Good Substitutes	Unavailable
Staples				
MEATS, FISH	X			
GRAINS	X: *also see Note 1*			
FRUITS, VEGETABLES	X: *in North, in cold months, choices can be very limited*			
FLATBREAD, BUNS	X			
YEAST, YEAST BREADS		X		
SOFT NOODLES	X			
HARD DURUM PASTA		X		
CHINESE SPICES	X			
OTHER SPICES: SEE NOTE 2				
DAIRY: SEE NOTE 3				
Beverages				
CHINESE TEAS	X			
WESTERN TEAS		X	X	
INSTANT COFFEE	X			
FRESH-BREWED COFFEE: SEE NOTE 4				
NON-DAIRY CREAMER	X			
DRINKABLE TAP WATER				X
BOILED WATER	X: *thermoses in every room*			
COKE, PEPSI, FANTA	X: *but not in diet varieties*			
OTHER SOFT DRINKS	X: *but many Chinese sodas are very sweet*			
PURE FRUIT JUICE		X: *except the kind in the fruit*		
GOOD COCOA POWDER	(*Chinese brands would insult dishwater*)			X
BEER	X: *Tsing Tao is the best local brand, but experiment*			
LIQUOR AND WINE: SEE NOTE 5				
Other				
CONVENIENCE FOODS	X: *Chinese*			X: *Western*
CANDY	X			
WAXY CHOCOLATE	X			
GOOD CHOCOLATE		X		

Chart 1:   **AVAILABLE FOODS**

made huge inroads into the China market, products of those two companies are available throughout China. See Chart 2 for suggestions of what
else is available in the mainland.

TAMPONS

Amusingly, because Chinese remain conservative about premarital sex
and the preservation of the hymen, until recently, some tampons in China
were sold with a warning on the box against use by unmarried women!

PRESCRIPTION DRUGS: BRING FULL YEAR'S SUPPLY

Be sure to bring a full supply of all prescription drugs. Most foreigners get
the best care that China's medical system offers, but nevertheless,
especially in rural areas, quality varies. Then too, quite aside from
practitioners' qualifications, many Chinese generic medicines have chemical compositions slightly different from their Western equivalents, enough
to cause problems. If you are prone to respiratory or digestive troubles, be
sure to ask your doctor for preventatives and remedies, as China's dry air
and lax hygiene attack those two systems with particular vigor. See
"Medical Preparations" below for required shots.

RECREATIONAL DRUGS?

The answer is: *DON'T*. The Chinese have a deep-rooted racial horror of the
influence of foreign drug users dating back to the Opium War. Nothing,
with the possible exception of rape, raises such fury as a foreigner
providing illegal drugs to a Chinese. Nor will any other activity, including
underground political activism, be as likely to land you in jail. If you have
a drug problem, keep it out of China. Period.

Necessity #4: Professional Supplies

Mainland teachers and students rely much less than Westerners on
professional presentations. Everything you might need, from art supplies
to computers, is available, but not always in the quality you might be used
to. See Chart 3 for details (unless otherwise noted, all items are available
in Taiwan).

PHOTOCOPYING DIFFICULT

Most Chinese schools have photocopiers, but restrict their use because of
expense (China needs to import toner). Instead, materials are dittoed. If
you want to assign large sections from books be sure your school has a
thermal transfer machine to create ditto masters from photocopies.
Otherwise, everything will have to be retyped. A sad comment on Chinese
wage structures appeared from this fact. When Rebecca's school's
thermal transfer machine broke down, the school hired a typist to retype
book sections Rebecca wanted to assign onto ditto masters: the typist's
wage cost the school less than the price difference between dittos and

PRODUCT	READILY AVAILABLE	LARGE CITIES ONLY	EASY TO FIND GOOD SUBSTITUTES	UNAVAILABLE
Toiletries				
SHAMPOO, CONDITIONER	✗ *(P&G, J&J)*	✗ *Western Brands (other)*		
MOUSSES, GELS, SPRAY	✗ *(P&G, J&J)*	✗ *(other)*		
HAIR COLORING	✗ *(black only)*	✗ *(P&G, J&J)*		
SOAPS	✗ *Zest, Lux, other imports—also many good Chinese brands*			
PERFUMES, COLOGNES			✗ *(Chinese brands very sweet)*	
MAKE-UP			✗ *(some easy-to-find Chinese brands OK)*	
MOISTURIZERS	✗ *(P&G, J&J)*		✗ *(you'll need them in the North or West)*	
LIP BALM	✗ *we recommend Double Horses Brand*			
Feminine Care				
TAMPONS	✗ *See note 1*			
PADS	✗			
PMS/CRAMPING MEDICATION				✗
Contraceptives				
CONDOMS/FOAM	✗ *(though selling to foreigners may cause giggles)*			
DIAPHRAGMS/JELLY				✗
IUDs				✗
PILLS	✗ *(but Chinese doctors often prescribe very high doses)*			
Eye Care				
EYEGLASSES	✗ *simple correctional lenses, nice frames (complex lenses can be difficult, best bring extras)*			
CONTACT LENSES		✗		
CLEANING SOLUTIONS	✗			
Skin Care				
FIRST-AID NEEDS	✗			
INSECT REPELLENTS				✗
SUN-TAN LOTIONS		✗		
Medicines				
VITAMINS	✗ *synthetic*	✗ *naturally derived*		
ASPIRIN	✗			
IBUPROFEN-BASED PAINKILLERS				✗
COLD MEDICINES	✗ *Chinese*	✗ *Western*	✗ *herbal*	
PRESCRIPTION DRUGS: SEE NOTE 2				
RECREATIONAL DRUGS: SEE NOTE 3				
Cleaning and Maintenace Supplies				
DISH SOAP	✗			
LAUNDRY SOAP	✗			
BLEACH, FABRIC SOFTENERS		✗		
SPECIAL SOAP FOR FINE WASHABLES	✗ *(Woolite)*			
CLEANING TOOLS	✗			

CHART 2:   PERSONAL AND HEALTH-CARE PRODUCTS

photocopies. If you intend to produce your own materials, remember only wide-carriage typewriters hold Chinese ditto masters.

ABOUT COMPUTERS

China makes several personal computers; best is the Langchao, an IBM PC clone (rumored, in fact, to be pirated from IBM technology, but that's another story). It's hellish to buy in China (export only), but many schools have them available for foreign teachers. Should you bring your own computer, your students, teachers, and friends will crowd into your quarters at any opportunity to fiddle with it. Most larger cities have stores selling moderately good computer paper in standard sizes, a few sizes of ribbon cartridges, 5.25" (very occasionally also 3.5") floppy disks, and software. Software pirating is _rampant_. Pirated copies of Windows '95 were for sale in China before the real thing was released in the US. But given China's spotty record with intellectual property rights, any software you buy in China may be subject to confiscation back home (equally true in Taiwan, and computer viruses are rampant in pirated Taiwanese software).

Computer users _must_ use a current stabilizer and a surge protector in addition to the step-down converter (see below). In the case of 3, 6, or 9 volt laptops, an AC/DC adaptor is also required. Many computer stores sell international current adaptor/surge protector/stabilizer kits in one box, with hefty price tags; or just buy components. Bring the surge protector and adaptor from home; Chinese stores sell bulky but excellent current stabilizers for about $15. The order of plug-in, from the wall out, should be: stabilizer, surge protector (and any grounding wires necessary for the surge protector), step-down converter, AC/DC adaptor (if necessary), computer. The experts say China's erratic electricity will still wear down your computer faster than use in the West, but we used ours for 2 ¹/₂ years with no noticeable ill effects.

OTHER ELECTRONIC GADGETS

Both mainland and Taiwan electrical systems feed 220 or 240 volts AC into wall sockets. US/Canadian travelers bringing their own appliances will need a simple step-down converter changing 220/240 into 110/120. Buy a converter with a variety of plug adaptors, as Chinese wall sockets vary widely. Radio Shack sells a converter/plug adaptor set in a carrying case for $10.95. Walkman-style tape recorders also require conversion from 110 volts AC to 3, 6, or 9 volts DC. Bring both the step-down converter and an AC/DC current adaptor from home; in China, from the wall out, plug in the step-down converter, the adaptor, and the recorder. Chinese stores sell AC/DC adaptors which convert 220 volts AC directly

Art/Display Supplies

PRODUCT	READILY AVAILABLE	LARGE CITIES ONLY	EASY TO FIND GOOD SUBSTITUTES	UNAVAILABLE
CHINESE ART GOODS	X (inkstones, silk, rice paper, ink, Chinese brushes, etc.)			
WESTERN ART GOODS	X (standard goods—premixed pigments, pre-made canvases, etc.)			
HIGH-QUALITY/NON-STANDARD WESTERN ART SUPPLIES			X	
EASELS	X			
FLIPCHARTS/DISPLAY PAPER		X (and can be hard to find there)		
LIGHTWEIGHT PAPER	X	all colors/styles, but all flimsy		
HEAVY DUTY PAPER/CONSTRUCTION PAPER	X			
HIGH-QUALITY CRAYONS/MARKERS		X		

Writing Materials/Desk Supplies

PRODUCT	READILY AVAILABLE	LARGE CITIES ONLY	EASY TO FIND GOOD SUBSTITUTES	UNAVAILABLE
PENCILS, PENS	X			
SCISSORS, GLUE	X			
STAPLERS, RULERS	X			
PAPER CLIPS	X			
EASY-TO-USE CLEAR STICK TAPE	(the Chinese kind sticks to itself) X			
CARDS, POSTCARDS	X			
HIGH-QUALITY STATIONERY		X		
MANUAL TYPEWRITERS	X			
STANDARD RIBBONS	X			
GOOD ELECTRIC TYPEWRITERS, NON-STANDARD RIBBONS				X
DITTO MACHINES	X			
DITTO MASTERS	X			
PHOTOCOPIERS: SEE NOTE 1				
COMPUTERS: SEE NOTE 2				
ELECTRICITY: SEE NOTE 3				

Audio-visual Supplies

PRODUCT	READILY AVAILABLE	LARGE CITIES ONLY	EASY TO FIND GOOD SUBSTITUTES	UNAVAILABLE
TAPE RECORDERS	X (but pocket-sized portable recorders are rare)			
CASSETTE TAPES	X (blank and prerecorded)			
VCRs: MOST SCHOOLS HAVE, BUT MAY BE NTSC FORMAT—ask ahead				
VIDEOTAPES		X (or through school supply office)		
SLIDE PROJECTORS: ask ahead if your school has one				
SLIDE FILM/SLIDE FILM PROCESSING				X
OVERHEAD PROJECTORS: ask ahead if your school has one				
TRANSPARENCIES		X	X (acetate sheets)	
RECORD PLAYERS		X		
LPs		X		

CHART 3:   PROFESSIONAL SUPPLIES

to 3, 6, or 9 volts DC, but the plugs often don't fit tape recorders made for sale in the West.

Very few foreigners bring televisions, as most schools provide televisions in foreigners' quarters. Should you insist, however, ask an expert at your local electronics store for advice. Hz cycles in China's electrical current may disrupt TVs made for sale in the West, and TV conversion requirements differ. PRC video uses PAL-D. If you bring a VCR or LDP, make sure they're multi-use stystems. Otherwise, inexpensive local-use systems are sold in China.

PROFESSIONAL BAGGAGE

The Taiwan-bound may not even know where they'll teach or study, let alone what. The mainland-bound will know school, but should take any prearrival advice regarding courseload with a grain of salt, regardless of how definite and specific it sounds. Many people hold sway over foreigners in China, responsible ministries are frightfully slow giving or forbidding consent to curriculum planners, and bureaucrats nurture jealous rivalries, so that whatever A approves B forbids. Chinese officials are often far too enthusiastic about their students' or teachers' abilities. People who give you course lists are probably acting in good faith. But they assume foreigners understand the unpredictability of Chinese life, and this results in much rancor.

Think of any prearrival course lists as guidelines, rather than specific courses. If the list reads, "Seminar in Grammar Development, 2nd level; Seminar in Fiction Writing, 4th level; Lecture in British Literature, 1st Year Graduate," assume you'll be teaching a grammar course, a writing course, and a literature course, but assume nothing else. Don't bother preparing a syllabus or planning classes; your work is too likely for naught.

What this means for teachers is that you must bring a library of materials on each of the subjects you'll teach, materials designed for different levels, class sizes, interests, and goals. What this means for students is that you must bring supplementary materials and study aids for topics, rather than classes. In Taiwan, foreign-language bookstores have selections of language study and reference books, and photocopying for students is readily available. As a result, Taiwan-bound teachers needn't bother bringing books, unless they have particular favorites. But, even there, students will want some materials of their own.

As much as possible, continue to politely press your Chinese contacts for specifics on your course load. Recognize that too much pressure may encourage false advice of the sort detailed above. But quiet, courteous, continuous prodding may encourage openness regarding the behind-the-scenes negotiations. You may learn, for example, that you'll definitely teach a conversation course, though the level hasn't been settled.

At the same time, ask for a list of last year's courses. The courses taught or studied by foreigners at each institution differ little from year to year. Narrowing your possibilities reduces the professional materials you must pay excess baggage charges for.

Keep contacting your institute's representatives about your expectations. Teachers can sketch a draft syllabus or sample readings to send over. Students can send lists of topics they hope to cover, or ask for suggested prearrival reading lists. Chinese are often puzzled over what foreigners want, and find waiting until arrival the easiest course. By getting as much information as you can before you leave, you can prepare in your homeland, where familiar facilities are at hand, and avoid wasting your first weeks in China while the institution scrambles to make arrangements.

Students: Becoming Your Own Reference Library

Western students assume that they can both choose their courses and that materials they need for research will be at hand. Chinese students can assume neither of these, partly because government ministries and political policy hold sway over curriculum developers in China, and partly because Chinese universities have severely limited budgets and their libraries are understocked. Many books in Chinese libraries may also be off-limits, depending on your status and relations with the librarian. Foreign students have many advantages over Chinese students, but these basic facts of Chinese student life restrict foreigners as much as Chinese.

Courses offered can vary based on available staff, space, and political directives. Largely apolitical topics such as language and Chinese medicine are least affected; students of such volatile topics as history and sociology should be prepared for surprises.

Chinese libraries simply haven't the resources, especially in Western languages, taken for granted in Western community colleges, let alone in major research institutions. This is still largely true in Taiwan as well as in the mainland. Taiwan's new National Central Library has a good collection of recent Western books and subscribes to a huge number of English academic and popular periodicals, and the government has recently upgraded several key local schools, such as Chiayi University, providing substantial library endowments. But at many schools, resources are much more sparse. Assume there'll be an encyclopedia, a few dictionaries, and a small collection of books on a variety of topics. Specialized books and books on politically controversial topics may simply not exist.

Bring or ship a box full of books related to your topic. If you're interested in acupuncture, bring acupuncture treatises. In China you'll find charts, medical school/acupuncture texts in Chinese, and probably a very sketchy textbook in English written for foreign students. You may also find ancient and wonderful manuscripts stored in the university library, or in a temple nearby, wholly unknown in the West. But basic reference information on background, philosophy, varying methodologies, and interpretations may just not exist. For more on this see Chapter 7.

Teachers: Syllabus ex Nihilo

Because pinpointing course load before arrival verges on the impossible, you'll likely spend your first days in China frantically determining courses and creating syllabi. The following tips should help smooth the process.

First, if you'll be teaching English and have no experience teaching (a common state for many foreign teachers), try to learn some methods before you go. Chapter 7 contains a crash course in EFL teaching; see also the list of suggested EFL texts in Appendix B. If possible, take a course at your local community college in TEFL. If you're thinking about a career in ESL/EFL, consider enrolling in a program. Many schools offer one-year intensive MA-Teaching degrees, which will earn you higher salaries both in China and after. At the very least, attend a conference of the TESOL (Teachers of English to Speakers of Other Languages) Association, either a huge international convention or a regional meeting in your area. For information in the US, write National TESOL Association, 1600 Cameron St., Suite 300, Alexandria, VA 22314. Phone (703) 836-0774.

Next, try to determine at least the subject you'll be teaching before arrival. At home, stock up on texts and supplementary materials on the topic, and have them there when you arrive (for tips on shipping, see below). Chinese university libraries may have a variety of EFL/ESL texts, but resources can be imbalanced, with 40 preparation manuals for the TOEFL (Test of English as a Foreign Language, the dreaded exam used as entrance criterion for foreign exchange students by many US universities), and only one grammar guide. The Taiwan-bound should assume a wide variety of texts will be available in stores, but bring your particular favorites anyway.

Try also to tote bundles of supplementary "authentic" materials. Recent ESL/EFL methodology stresses "real world" materials and "communicative competence" over grammatical perfection. Bring menus, magazines (*Sports Illustrated, National Geographic,* and columns from Ann Landers and Miss Manners remain perennial favorites with Chinese students), newspapers, maps, advertisements, packages, music tapes, sheet music, want ads, board games, monopoly money, recorded lectures, videotapes (remember to ask if your school has a VCR), video games—anything in English. Think as you go through your daily life of every type of English material you encounter, and bring samples of all of them. Your students will learn more and have more fun "shopping" in a "supermarket" of empty packages brought from home than reading any textbook lesson about shopping.

Many foreign teachers establish and maintain a "Student Library" of English-language books, tapes, and periodicals. Most official libraries are closed-stack to Chinese students, and can be quite discouraging for unsure learners. Maintaining an easily accessible collection of materials for students to read or listen to on their own encourages self-study and mental expansion. We started a student library at Qingdao University in Shandong which, four years later, is being managed and augmented by each year's foreign teachers, and averages dozens of borrowers each day. Good sources of inexpensive materials for such libraries include garage sales, library sales, and neighbors' basements. Try also writing your local paper, college or university library, or Rotary or Elk's Club; or to a publishing conglomerate such as National Geographic or Time-Life, explaining your endeavor. They all responded to us generously, adding to our new library by hundreds of volumes.

By your arrival in China, or shortly before, your course load should be set. Ask if a standard text exists for the course; the answer will generally be yes. In most cases you should use the text even though it may be poorly written, for two reasons. First, the text will contain everything the student will be tested on in the national exams. China's national exams stress grammar and vocabulary, and many who pass with high scores can't communicate in real-world situations. Most teachers hope to teach communicative ability far beyond textbook content. However, your students must pass the national exams to graduate, and if you ignore exam content you do them no service.

Second, the standard texts are available. Chinese text, whether written locally or pirated from a foreign text are printed cheaply and are available to your students at affordable rates. You may find a wonderful text with great illustrations, but your students can't afford it at full price, and even if you choose to aid and abet its pirating, you can't get it printed up in time to start class. Using the standard text gives your students something in hand. You can reorder the lessons or add topics as you like. Just make sure to cover all textbook content; then you can copy à la carte from texts you have brought or write your own supplementary materials, remembering that everything must be transferred or typed onto ditto masters.

China has been working hard to improve its record on intellectual property protection, particulary as part of the drive to attain WTO status. In many cases the standard Chinese texts will now have a license agreement attached. In some cases copyright licenses will still not have been purchased from the foreign publisher, but this is not an issue foreign teachers need to be concerned with at present.

MISCELLANEOUS PREPARATIONS

Shipping

Shipping to China, mainland or Taiwan, is expensive, inconvenient, and slow. All packages are opened and inspected by Chinese customs, which runs a constant backlog and, therefore, takes weeks. In addition, many classes of items, from the "pornographic" to the "politically offensive," any of which can be defined at the customs officer's whim, are subject to confiscation. Taiwan is less stringent than the mainland, but still can be difficult to deal with.

When possible, carry everything with you. Your first month's clothing, all prescription medicines, valuables, and texts you will use immediately on arrival must be in your luggage, the last three in your carry-ons.

If you ship, plan ahead. Assume that *any* package shipped surface could take up to *six months* (occasionally even more), so send materials you'll need in November by May. The cheapest surface rate from the US is through printed-matter "M" bags—ask at your post office for details. Air mail runs faster, but is exceedingly expensive, and still never guarantees delivery under a month. Express mail generally arrives within a week, but occasionally takes several.

Some packing tips: use stout boxes and plenty of filler, and wrap messy items in plastic; Chinese postal workers can be brutal. Make and copy a list of all contents before shipping; keep one copy and paste another in the box. This discourages pilferage and, if theft occurs, can help with reimbursement. Also, the more potentially problematic the material in any box, the slower it will get through. Large amounts of religious material (mainland only); politically controversial texts; anything to do with Tibet, Taiwan independence, or the Democracy movement; anything pornographic or perceivable as pornographic by prudish customs officials (such as drawings of scantily clad women on the covers of pulp novels) will slow down your package by months while everything is read to determine possible offensiveness. When in doubt, customs will confiscate.

Pack necessary and obviously inoffensive materials, such as EFL texts, classic novels, and your backup supply of vitamins separately from anything that could slow up the works. If possible, carry video and audio tapes. If not, pack them separately and securely, label them "Video and Audio Materials for Use in Teaching English Language," and label each tape with both name and a brief description (" 'The Music Man,' " "US musical drama," etc.).

We do not recommend shipping or carrying materials which are likely to have been banned (such as the Dalai Lama's memoirs, or a collection of speeches by dissident Fang Li-zhi). If discovered, they'll draw attention to you, and to any Chinese people who associate with you. Then too, little purpose is served by bringing them. You and other foreigners can read them at home. Chinese can't read them, for being found with banned texts remains cause for imprisonment. Distributing banned materials in China involves risky and delicate timing best judged by those who make it their life's work. Inexperienced foreigners blundering in generally do more harm than good.

Medical Preparations

Both mainland China and Taiwan have eradicated yellow fever and other epidemic diseases. But hygienic conditions remain below First World par. All foreigners entering should have a series of vaccinations against hepatitis B, and should consider a supply of gamma globulin to combat hepatitis A. Foreigners heading toward southern provinces or Taiwan should bring antimalaria pills. Try to avoid getting shots on the mainland, where doctors often reuse needles. Many foreigners bring disposable needles from home; ask your doctor for some along with his or her note explaining your medical need for them so they don't get impounded at customs.

Other recommended shots fluctuate, but may include Japanese encephalitis vaccine, antiparasitics, and others. Ask your doctor or a physician specializing in immunology for further advice.

Money Matters

Taiwan has a complex, modern economy. You can use most major credit cards and all major-bank traveler's checks throughout the island. Taiwan's currency, the National Taiwan Dollar or NT, is fully convertible and can be purchased with hard currency at banks throughout the island at fairly rational rates. You can also set up savings and/or checking accounts at any bank, at current exchange of US$1 to NT$27.66 (as of 4/22/97). Foreign teachers in Taiwan are also subject to income tax, at approximately 20% of income, though they are exempt for their first six months of residence. US citizens on the mainland are not required to pay Chinese income tax, due to a bilateral treaty, but they must file a US income-tax form. Due to a foreign-earned–income exclusion of up to $70,000, you'll owe no tax on your Chinese salary but you may have to pay Social Security self-employment tax. Other foreigners owe tax to the PRC government at 30% of any earnings over 800 yuan per month, though your *waiban* (see Chapter 5) may or may not enforce this.

Mainland China still has a cash-based economy. Joint-venture hotels accept major credit cards, but most other places don't. Foreign students will be expected to pay their school in cash or traveler's checks, and foreign teachers' wages come in cash. Bring enough cash with you to last a month including set-up costs (no less than US$500), since some schools won't pay the first month's salary up front. Travelers checks are safer than cash, and American Express are the most widely accepted.

The mainland "People's Currency" (*Ren Min Bi* 人民币), or RMB is semi-convertible since January of 1994. Before then, foreign currency was converted at Bank of China offices to "Foreign Exchange Certificates" (*Wai Hui Quan:* 外汇券), or FEC, which were not technically a currency, but functioned as one. FEC were eliminated in 1994 and the RMB is now only semi-controlled. As a result, the formerly flourishing black market for money in China has largely disappeared and unless you're trading really large amounts and are a very savvy black market trader, you're far better off sticking with the banks.

You can withdraw cash from most foreign banks through large Bank of China offices using any major international credit card. American Express Card members are entitled to home-country currency withdrawals, though Bank of China officials may be peevish about it. MasterCard, Visa, and Diner's Club allow withdrawal in RMB "equivalents," at exchange rates determined by the Bank of China. In the largest cities, American Express also has cash machines.

You can set up a savings account at Bank of China; checking accounts are very rare. But read the fine print; interest is generally negligible, and BOC sometimes requires deposits of six months before withdrawal. Many foreigners just imitate their Chinese neighbors and "stuff it into the mattress." BOC now issues the Great Wall "credit card" (it actually functions as a debit card), which is widely-enough accepted at places which won't take Western cards to be worth having; your *waiban* can help you apply.

Visas and Arrival Procedures

Your mainland Chinese school will probably arrange your resident visa and contact the nearest embassy or consulate in your home country. You can then just go in or mail in your passport (certified or registered mail only!) for the visa stamp. In rare or rushed cases you may have to enter on a tourist visa. The easiest way is to fly to Hong Kong and get a one-month tourist visa there, either in the PRC travel office or at a commercial travel agency. If you enter with a tourist visa, be sure your *waiban* begins the paperwork to convert to a work visa as soon as possible. You must have a valid work visa to get a resident card, which gives you permission to live long term in a Chinese city.

The Taiwan-bound can enter on a six-month visitor's visa; simply apply at your nearest Taiwanese government representative (see list in Appendix C). Students never need any other documents (though remember to leave Taiwan for one week every six months to get your renewal!). Students can also get a student resident visa, which requires proof of full-time study (16 credit hours undergrad or six grad/semester in degree programs, or tex hours/week of language classes). Foreign teachers technically require a commercial visa, which is expensive and cumbersome, but few ever get one. Most simply get a six-month visitor's visa, then register with their local foreign affairs bureau in Taiwan to get a temporary work permit.

Both Taiwan and the mainland have strict health codes, and may require a clean-health inspection, including a negative test for HIV antibodies. Check with your *waiban* or the local Taiwanese government representative for details. If the Chinese government insists on retesting you for HIV after entry, insist they do so with an unused disposable needle.

The mainland also technically requires that you fill out a detailed summary of all valuables you carry in, especially electronic goods and jewelry. Keep this list; it may be rechecked on exit. Customs has become increasingly lax recently but still better safe than sorry. Chinese import duties on electronics and jewelry are steep, and on paper the government strongly discourages foreigners from presenting them as gifts, though overseas Chinese can import goods to the PRC more easily. Practically speaking, as long as it's in accompanied luggage, foreigners can too now. Shipped bags are another matter, so be sure to carry as much as you can of any valuable items you require.

Arriving:
Your Danwei,
Your Waiban, *and You*

China hits new arrivals full force. Bleary-eyed and jet-lagged, you'll stumble off your plane to a cacophony of families greeting their returnees. Customs officials will poke through your underwear. Cabbies will shout to cram you and ten others into a swaybacked cab which belches monoxides as it careens through crowded streets at high speeds. A representative of your institution may or may not greet you, perhaps bearing a contract you'll be urged to sign immediately.

Many foreigners react first to China with an overwhelming urge to flee. Chinese people stand closer to one another than Westerners, talk louder, knock less before opening doors, and use less deodorant. The Chinese construct buildings, streets, hallways, and rooms narrower, shorter, and more crowded than in the West. Claustrophobia can set in.

Your first and best defense remains mental preparation. Before arrival, gear yourself up by packing the mental baggage described in Chapter 4. After arrival, strive to adjust to Chinese culture by finding your own combination of imitation, adaptation, and acceptance. The following sections should help you develop a sense of how things work in China and what will be expected of you, and suggest a few strategies for adjustment.

BOSS/LANDLORD: YOU AND YOUR *DANWEI*

The Danwei *for Chinese People*

Chinese people grow up in an interwoven web of mutual responsibility networks. The family, the street association, the neighborhood or village brigade all bond the individual to society through complex ties. Misbehaving children reflect badly on parents, siblings, and even neighbors. A thief shames and potentially brings punishment to co-workers and superiors.

In Taiwan mutual responsibility networks have become attenuated, but in the mainland they flourish. In mainland cities the strongest mutual responsibility group is the work unit, or *danwei* (单位). Village brigades function as rural *danwei*. Urban *danwei* range from individual factories, schools, or hospitals to massive national *danwei,* such as the Ministry of Transportation. Each *danwei* both cares for and controls its workers, managers, and dependents. Omnipotent by comparison with Western employers, the *danwei* not only assigns work duties, salaries, and benefits, but also arranges housing, health care, transportation, travel benefits, rationing coupons, and internal sales of reduced-priced goods. *Danwei* can give or deny permission to marry, move, travel, and bear children, and are the front line of the Chinese justice system.

Westerners would find such omnipotence intolerable, but most Chinese find it comforting. If bad feelings develop, *danwei* leaders can consign workers to hell on earth. But most Chinese get along with their *danwei*, and enjoy job, housing, and neighborhood stability unknown in the West. Westerners accept social instability and professional insecurity as part of the price of freedom. Chinese accept autarchic control over their lives in return for stability and certainty.

The Danwei for Foreigners

Taiwan has no *danwei*, and Taiwanese schools function much as do Western equivalents. But mainland-bound foreigners, like it or not, join China's mutual responsibility network from their first day in China till their last. Lacking families in China or membership in neighborhood brigades, foreigners tie in solely through their *danwei*. This relationship is frequently explained as one between "guests" and "hosts," reflecting the traditional Chinese emphasis on hospitality. The foreign guest is received by a Chinese host *danwei* responsible for the foreigner's needs and actions.

Guest-host relationships for tourists can be tenuous. Individual tourists issued transit or tourist visas at the border may never see their *danwei* at all unless they run into trouble, yet all remain guests of the Ministry of Travel and Tourism.

The longer foreigners stay in China, however, and the more they participate in Chinese life, the more aware they become of their host *danwei* and their mutual obligations as guests. Businesspeople negotiate through their host *danwei* for materials, transport, import/export licenses, currency exchange, and inter-*danwei* contractual agreements. Much has been written on the importance to traders of selecting a suitably influential host *danwei*.

As a foreign teacher or student you must choose your *danwei* very carefully indeed, for it controls you very directly. Your *danwei* has nowhere near the power over you as over your Chinese counterparts. Your *danwei* is, however, your employer, landlord, health insurer, transport company, food supplier, and many other things, including scapegoat for your indiscretions. Should you break laws during your stay, your *danwei* will take the rap. In extreme cases, while you may be deported, the *danwei* member responsible for you could go to jail.

THE WAIBAN

The *danwei* section directly responsible for foreigners at a school is the Foreign/External Affairs Office (FAO)—*waishi bangongshi* in Chinese, or *waiban* (外办) for short. The *waiban* has many duties unrelated to foreigners, such as inter-university contracts and liaison with city government. But for your purposes, the *waiban* is your link to the *danwei*. Depending on *danwei* size, your *waiban* may be a single person assigned liaison duties, or a large office responsible for everything from preparing visa extensions to hiring maids to swab the foreign toilets.

Your *waiban* bears direct responsibility for you, suffers more than anyone else for your indiscretions, and wields great power over your daily life. Not surprisingly, many Westerners, unused to such control, come into conflict with their *waiban*, most frequently about money. The central government gives *waibans* a yearly or monthly allowance per foreign teacher set by geographic region, and determines the amount of student tuition remitted to the school. This money the *waiban* controls, using part for your salary or stipend; part for room, any board subsidies, medical insurance, travel and shipping allowances, and other benefits; part for banquets and other organized activities, and part for *waiban* coffers. As might be expected, *waibans* vary, some using every penny for the foreigners, others reducing foreigners to penurious wages while buying official *waiban* stereos and official *waiban* cars. Foreigners too vary, some working long hours and volunteering to coach basketball, others shirking class and whining year-round.

But most *waibans*, like most foreigners, are reasonably professional, moderately materialistic, and hope to cooperate happily. Work from that base. Strive for cordiality with your *waiban*, if not warmth, and much happiness can be yours. Your friend, the *waiban*, can get you theater tickets, be your guide and cultural interpreter, help you buy artwork, and gain you access to research facilities. Most *waibans* love to be asked for advice by "their" foreigners. By playing up to the Chinese system's paternalistic tendencies you stand to gain.

At all costs avoid becoming mortal enemies with your *waiban*. Your enemy, the *waiban* can move screaming babies to the room next to yours, start construction projects by your window and order workers to start at 5:00 AM, arrange for a transfer of your favorite teacher, or refuse to extend your visa or arrange travel permits to restricted areas. Quite aside from these horrors, troubles with your *waiban* can taint your whole stay. Years down the line you'll have forgotten about the time the *waiban* didn't keep his promise, but you will remember the time you argued with the *waiban* and got excluded from every field trip from then on. Better to keep on an even keel.

THE CONTRACT FOR TEACHERS AND STUDENTS

Your contract governs your legal and financial relations with both *waiban* and *danwei*. It merits serious attention. This is true in Taiwan as well as in the mainland, though Taiwan contracts deal only with the categories familiar in Western versions. Contracts can be negotiated before or after arrival, depending on whether you and your *waiban* feel more comfortable negotiating in person or by FAX. Prearrival contracts allow more time for reflection and consultation with friends, but tend to be abstract, as you sign them without knowing details of local conditions. Post-arrival contracts allow inclusion of nitty-gritty details like which building you'll sleep in and whom you'll teach, but can be subject to time pressure; much paperwork can't be completed till you sign, and your *waiban* may push for speedy negotiations.

Student contracts tend to be straightforward. At long-established programs, like the Beijing Language Institute's Chinese program, schools present fixed packages. Newer programs may still be plagued with bugs. One student promised a master's program in Chinese literature arrived to find no curriculum, merely a tutor assigned to meet with her twice per week. Particularly, if you're among the first foreign students to attend an institution, be sure the courses to be offered you are clarified on paper; you won't be able either to transfer or to obtain a refund after payment. For this reason, you may prefer postarrival contracts and payment, with specifics in writing about classes, teachers, books and materials, access to facilities, and hours of instruction per week.

Be sure also to clarify in writing any arrangements for transcripts and credit, as China has no standardized academic credit system, and you may otherwise have trouble arranging transfer of credit to your home school. See also the suggestions below on housing and benefits under teacher contracts. Otherwise, student contracts rarely pose problems.

Teacher contracts, on the other hand, vary across the map, both between and within institutions. Negotiate vigorously. Too many foreigners, starry-eyed about Asia, inexperienced at negotiation, and perhaps succumbing to unscrupulous *waiban* pressure to sign a contract while still gripped by jet lag, neglect the contract's importance, or sign without careful scrutiny. When later discovering their colleagues teach half the courses for twice the wage they howl and scream, but to no avail.

Such foreigners feel cheated, but they shouldn't. Your contract is a business arrangement in which emotions have no place. Chinese understand this and will give absolutely nothing away in negotiations. Neither should you. You may feel idealistic about contributing to Chinese society; attend to your idealism later. No one will stop you from doing more than required in your contract. If you sign up for 12 class hours per week, then teach four more without pay, your commitment and sacrifice will be recognized and appreciated. If you sign up for 16 hours, those 16 are taken for granted, and refusal to do any more appears intransigent. Getting a reasonable set of conditions down on paper protects both you and your *waiban*.

Space prohibits detailed suggestions here on negotiating with the Chinese, but, in any case, several fine books cover the subject in detail (see Appendix B). Suffice it to say that patient, reasonable discourse, and a clear focus on objectives are key. The following, while by no means cut in stone, show our suggested guidelines for discussion.

TEACHING HOURS

Most Chinese teachers run five to ten class hours per week. Foreign teachers are expected to hold down 12 to 16 hours per week (more variable on Taiwan). This alone should help dispel any guilt you may feel about earning a higher wage than Chinese teachers. We suggest agreeing to no more than ten hours per week of academic classes (history, literature, culture, etc.) or of composition classes (all those essays!), or no more than 12 to 14 hours per week of straight language classes.

"WHITE CARDS"

White Cards (which are now, in fact, yellow) identify foreigners who work for the mainland government. They allow access to some restricted areas and greater ease in applying for re-entry visas, but their chief benefit is financial. For hotels, trains, and many other expenses foreigners are expected to pay at approximately twice the Chinese rate. The White Card allows payment at or near Chinese rate. Students can get student cards, which allow still greater discounts. Even Taiwan student cards are sometimes accepted for discounts on the mainland. We suggest insisting on a White Card unless you're being paid at least 50% in a hard currency, and at least 3,000 yuan per month.

SALARY RANGE

Mainland salaries range from 600 yuan RMB per month to upwards of 3,000 yuan RMB per month (even more for technical experts), depending on age, experience, academic background, and subject; 900 to 1,500 yuan is average. Salary may be paid wholly in RMB, or partly in hard currency. Part hard-currency payment is desirable even if you have a White Card, as some places won't accept White Cards. Mentally convert all hard-currency payments to RMB to figure your wage; as of late 1996, approximate value was US$: RMB at 1:8:3 (note: these exchanges change rapidly; talk with someone who's visited recently or check the weekly rates published in the Far Eastern Economic Review.). We suggest teachers with master's degrees or higher and two or more years' full-time teaching experience accept no lower than 2,000 yuan RMB per month, while inexperienced teachers with bachelor's degrees only accept no less than 800 yuan RMB per month (students without a B.A. will get less). Taiwan salaries range from NT$400 to NT$600 per hour at *buxibans*, and up to NT$900 per hour at "real school" posts. We suggest not less than NT$550 per hour for experienced teachers, or NT$400 for new. Salary is generally paid monthly on the mainland. In Taiwan, insist on weekly payment, especially from *buxibans*: many are literally run by crooks. *Note:* some schools will insist on   a one-month "trial period" at a lower wage. This is acceptable *only* if: a) the contract may be cancelled by either party at the end of theone-month trial, and b) should both parties choose to continue the relationship, an acceptable wage hike is mandated in writing as of the end of the one-month period. Also, insist on salary for your entire time teaching, including Spring Festival Break and (if you'll teach two consecutive years) Summer Break.

ACCOMMODATIONS

Most mainland teachers get a private bedroom, and one or more other rooms which may be shared with other foreigners. Foreign students generally sleep one or two to a dorm room. Taiwan schools may offer dorms, but most foreigners are on their own; see Chapter 2. Given China's premium on space (Chinese students generally sleep six or eight to a room), we advise against griping about room size. Mainland rent, however, should be negligible or free unless wages are very high. Also, be sure you have heat, hot water, electricity, and other facilities comparable with others on campus. We advise against accepting a room whose electricity or running water "will be hooked up soon." Construction projects drag on forever in China, and "soon" may not arrive till you've left.

Other possible accommodations include a kitchen (much to be desired), furnishings, Western flush (as opposed to Chinese squat) toilets, TV, washing machine, refrigerator, bicycle, tape recorder, space heater, fan, and VCR. No foreigner gets all of these, though the school might buy one of each for all foreigners to share. Again, relative equity matters more than absolutes. Foreigners who agree to substantially poorer facilities than other foreigners become pushovers in Chinese eyes, even if they mean well.

Determine the school's policy on guests. If friends visit, can they stay in your room for free? For a small charge? One school in Sichuan drove away foreign teachers by insisting their visiting boyfriends, mothers, and friends stay in separate rooms at hotel rates. Avoid problems by getting fair policy in print.

Food

Most mainland schools provide foreign teachers with kitchen facilities, and/or the choice of the dining hall or a chef; Taiwan schools rarely arrange board. We suggest the mainland-bound press for a kitchen with cafeteria privileges. You won't always want to cook, but Chinese cafeteria fare is no better than Western institutional food as a steady diet, and chef service is expensive and can be inflexible about timing. Also, freemarkets and cooking are focal points of Chinese life, and you'll miss much insight into the culture if you don't go shopping and invite Chinese friends to dinner.

Should you choose chef service, we suggest agreeing to no more than 45 yuan per day or half your salary, whichever is less, for 3-meal 7-day service. Many foreigners enjoy getting chef service a few nights a week, and cooking other times thesmselves.

International Travel

Most foreign teachers teaching at least two full semesters at regular posts in China, mainland or Taiwan, get at least one-way international airfare. We suggest this as a minimum. Because of the cost of airfare to China, you might also consider flexibility on salary in return for a round-trip ticket. Some mainland schools will suggest cash payments in lieu of tickets. If so, get an adequate cash payment mandated in the contract. If cash payment is to be made in RMB, figure at 8.3:1 for US dollars, and remember that you'll have to pay airfare out of your hard currency savings, using RMB payments for expenses in China.

DOMESTIC TRAVEL

Taiwan schools rarely provide domestic travel benefits. Mainland *waiban* usually greet foreign teachers on arrival, providing two to five days of paid sightseeing at the port of entry. Most *waibans* happily agree to this, as they get to accompany you. Some schools also offer travel bonuses for the Spring Festival Break and/or the Summer Break, ranging from 400 yuan to 2,000 yuan per break. We make no suggestions here, but note that those with low salaries may wish to push for a travel bonus.

SHIPPING ALLOWANCE

Some mainland schools give foreigners shipping allowances, either for shipping books to China or for sending belongings home. Cash allowances range from 500 to 3,000 yuan RMB, and kind allowances are generally half or one cubic meter of door-to-door ocean shipping. Shipping allowances can also be used to boost low-range salaries.

MEDICAL BENEFITS

Most mainland schools enroll teachers in China's national health system; the Taiwan-bound may receive benefits, but, otherwise, must arrange private health insurance. The mainland system's caregivers vary widely. As in the West, some of the worst care comes from school clinics, often staffed by inexperienced interns. We suggest pressing for rights, in the event of serious illness, to hospitalization in the nearest main city hospital, rather than at the school clinic.

VISA EXTENSIONS, MULTIPLE ENTRIES

These cost your *waiban* little or no money, though admittedly much paperwork, and would be considerable trouble and expense for you. We suggest asking, but not pressing, for these services.

CONTRACT REVISIONS

We suggest a clause in the contract stating that it may be revised by either party, providing that all revisions are mutually acceptable to both parties.

To recap, remember the following Golden Rules of contract negotiation:

1. Negotiate patiently and politely, remembering that the contract is a business arrangement in which emotion has no place.
2. Be sure all agreed-upon terms appear on paper. Rely on no oral promises.

3. Should contract revision become necessary, renegotiate with patience and respect, remembering that anger is counterproductive.

4. Once you sign a contract, honor it.

TROUBLES WITH WAIBANS

Despite the best of contracts, some troubles will inevitably arise. Following are the three most common "hot spots," and some suggestions on how to keep things cool:

Hot Spot #1: The Ogre

Most mainland schools put foreign teachers and students in special dorms with doorkeepers. These doorkeepers, unfondly known as "ogres," officially protect the foreigners' security and privacy. Practically, ogres also watch who comes in and out, at what times, and how often. Visitors may or may not have to sign in; whether or no, you can be sure their arrival is noted. Ogres also bear responsibility for locking doors after hours and deciding who to let in after lockup.

Try having a frank talk with your *waiban* and chief ogre soon after arrival regarding your hours and visiting habits. If you want Chinese students to have free access, say so; try to get a *waiban* promise, in the ogre's presence, that they'll not be interfered with. As to your own hours, be reasonable but firm. Chinese schools impose curfews on their students but have no right to impose them on you. Try to negotiate a key to your building (unlikely), or a promise that you can come home whenever you like and be let in.

To maintain good relations, don't abuse any privileges you gain. Most ogres moonlight at day shifts, and need their beauty sleep after the doors lock at night. If you study Beijing opera with the local diva eight to 11 each Friday night, by all means let the ogre know you'll be in each Friday after 10:00 PM lockup. But waking the ogre three times a week so you can spend an extra hour at the local bar is unwise.

Foreign guests should try to be in before lockup, and Chinese visitors should be careful. Never let Chinese friends stay past curfew, especially friends of the opposite sex. Also, very frequent visitors should meet you elsewhere sometimes. Records of constant visits to foreigners go in files and can cause damage should anti-Western campaigns start.

You can also help defuse your ogre by a courteous, responsible manner and the periodic distribution of small gifts.

Hot Spot #2: Friendly and Intimate Relations

How friendly mainland Chinese can be with foreigners changes from year to year. Your *waiban* must monitor your relations with Chinese people and report anything untoward. Be sensitive to the political climate. Never press Chinese people for more closeness than they solicit. Even when friendships have developed, never initiate politically sensitive discussions. If Chinese initiate these discussions, best hold them outdoors, away from crowds, with people you trust. (Foreigners' rooms have often been bugged.) And never use a Chinese person's real name in a politically sensitive conversational context, even with someone you think of as a friend; it can take years to recognize a snitch.

If you arrive in China at a time of openness, enjoy. Dinner at a Chinese home is an all-evening affair, marked by plenty of good food, drink, and conversation. Bring food, candy, or something from your country or some faraway part of China. Chinese bring cut flowers to funerals, however, so they traditionally make inappropriate dinner gifts (though they are becoming more common in Westernized areas). Also, never give an older Chinese person a clock; the phrase *song zhong* ("to give a clock") is homophonous with a phrase meaning "to wish death."

Chinese are aware of political conditions, and you can safely follow their lead in matters of friendship. Physical intimacy, however, is a different story. Taiwan is as Westernized in ideas about sex as it is in its banking structure. Mainland Chinese, however, remain conservative about courtship, dating, and sex. Recent surveys indicate changing attitudes among Chinese about premarital sex especially in the big cities. But most Chinese still harbor romantic ideals about one true and eternal love. Premarital sex is still more often than not assumed to be between partners who will soon marry. This cultural background predisposes Chinese to take any physical intimacy as a sign of very strong commitment. Never take romance with a Chinese person lightly. Your abandoned amour may feel deeply wounded and be subject to ridicule and censure, potentially even to punishment. This is especially true of matches between foreign women and Chinese men, a combination still far less accepted than the reverse. Both men and women with Western passports should remember just how much draw that passport has, and not allow their heads to be turned. No, that cute waitress asking which city you grew up in isn't necessarily swooning over your witty conversation.

In general, unless you strongly believe you might marry, best not get involved romantically with Chinese people. Should your needs be purely carnal, we suggest you consider other foreigners. Prostitution has returned to some Chinese cities, but liaisons with foreigners open the prostitute to grave political and juridical consequences. In the meantime, as Chinese prostitutes still rarely use condoms, the foreigner exposes himself to many a nameless disease. Gay people face particularly complex restrictions and prejudices; see section under cross-cultural conflicts in the next chapter.

Should you decide to marry a Chinese person, you'll both need permission from your *danwei*. Proceed cautiously, particularly if your partner is still a student. Greedy *waibans* have forced foreigners to cough up huge "release fees" to free Chinese from their *danwei*. Make sure your plans are set when you approach the *waiban*, come bearing gifts, and be careful.

Hot Spot #3: Travel and Other Restrictions

Travel to many areas on the mainland requires permits and possibly pre-travel registration of any Chinese people you'll be traveling with and what their relationships are. Many dance clubs, bars, and other social gathering points are closed to foreigners. Drug laws are draconian. Lack of cars limits mobility. Many foreigners fret over these restrictions.

Your *waiban* bears responsibility for you and will be punished if you break the law. Therefore, the job of enforcer falls to the *waiban*. No doubt you'll resent having to get travel passes from your *waiban* like a grade-schooler getting permission to go potty, and resent not being able to choose where you want to eat, or drink, or dance. You may even be tempted to flout the rules a bit, sneak onto a train into a restricted area, or into a Chinese discotheque. Our advice is, don't. Just remember, the *waiban* doesn't make the laws, but does take your punishment when you break them.

Consult with your *waiban* before traveling, especially together with Chinese people, and take any advice you're given. Don't bother trying to sneak into closed clubs. More and more open clubs rock through the night anyway, especially in big cities. Closed clubs generally tend to attract the financially poor and fashionably retro anyway. Long-term good relations are more important than a glimpse at Chinese guys dressed up like John Travolta. If you feel too claustrophobic, try the withdrawal techniques described in Chapter 6, or a weekend in Hong Kong.

Adjusting:
How Not to Be a Foreign Barbarian

Adjusting to China, rhapsodized respondent Miles Lozinsky, is "like a roller coaster, sometimes up slowly, slowly and then down fast, fast, sometimes it makes you sick to your stomach, sometimes the thrill cannot be beat, and there are always twists and turns where you least expect them."

For most foreigners, adjusting to life in China involves many uncomfortable unfamiliarities along with the excitement. Some are cultural, some political, and some economic. Most in the first two categories apply as much to Taiwan as to the mainland. The following sections describe some of the most common annoyances, and some suggestions for coping.

THE BIG NINE HATE LIST OF CROSS-CULTURAL CONFLICTS

Cultural conflicts can be harrowing, since we all have the inbred certainty that the customs of our youth are the right ones. Still, understanding goes a long way toward coping, so the following attempts to describe some of the more common conflicts in terms of Chinese culture.

Conflict #1: The Litany of Tedious Questions

What is your name? Where are you from? How old are you? Is this your first trip to China? Are you married? How much do you earn? Do you have any children? What do you think of Chinese people? Where did you buy your clothes/bag/tape recorder? How much did it cost?

As mentioned earlier, Chinese people on first meeting ask each other these and many similar questions. You too will face several thousand such queries. However much you try to appreciate each questioner as a unique individual, eventually, the sheer mass of China's people will make it seem as if you're confronting an unending conveyor belt of interrogators from the ninth circle of Dante's Hell: the dreaded Chinese question torture.

Try to remember that Chinese people mean well by this scrutiny. Such questions reveal their interest in you, and are meant to serve as icebreakers—standard openers for people who want to get acquainted and aren't sure how to start a conversation otherwise. Remembering these things will not always prevent annoyance, but it may help you skirt the edge of outrage, at least till you're alone in a room of your own.

Think about which of such questions to answer. If talking about your age or income would seriously bother you, then don't. Explain instead the Western reticence on those subjects. Or just be Chinese and stonewall, saying "It's not clear"; "It varies"; or "We calculate it differently." Whatever your response, develop a strategy for responding.

When you feel like you've had too much, and your best intentions will not prevent you from snapping at the next person who asks your income, withdraw. Go home, and shut the door. Read a book. Listen to some music. Go for a walk in an isolated section of a park (most Chinese parks have isolated sections, as Chinese people prefer togetherness, and tend to crowd into the popular sections). If you're on a bus or train and can't escape, try pretending you're asleep, or curling onto an upper bunk of the sleeping car, or burying your nose in a book or some writing. If all else fails, simply tell your interrogator you don't feel well and wish to be left alone.

Conflict #2: Lack of Privacy

Chinese lacks a word for the Western concept of privacy. Related words such as *sishi* or *sichu* all carry overtones of secrecy, loneliness, or misanthropy. Chinese people live, birth to death, in crowded rooms and have developed a culture based on sharing everything; not even bathroom stalls are fully enclosed except in hotels that cater to foreigners. To the Chinese, the Western need for privacy seems inexplicable. As a result, Chinese tend to assume foreigners want company more than may in fact be true, to show up unannounced and stay long, enter without knocking, peek in windows, and, otherwise, express friendly curiosity which to the foreigner seems monstrously invasive.

Remember the Chinese world view and remember that such actions, whatever their effect, generally stem from friendly intent. Try explaining these differences to your students, teachers, and friends. You may not fully convince them, but you'll be left alone. If not, by all means lay down rules about anything that makes you uncomfortable. Announce that visitors to your room must knock before entering; if your visitors keep forgetting, install a latch inside and a sign on the door. Hang curtains that fall below the sill to discourage peeking. Prepare a bilingual sign to hang on your door to announce when you don't want company, something along the lines of "Dear Friends: Please excuse me for not entertaining you now. I feel rather tired and wish to be alone. I hope, however, that you will come back another time."

Conflict #3: Staring and Pointing—the Monkey in the Zoo

"The sights of the city are free for the beggars. . . . The temple fairs with their merrymaking crowds, the candy sticks with fluttering pennants. . . . There is drama on the open-air stage." These lines come from an oral autobiography of a Chinese woman transcribed by a foreign missionary half a century ago (*A Daughter of Han: The Autobiography of a Chinese Working Woman.* Ida Pruitt, Stanford: Stanford University Press, 1945, 1967). Yet any Chinese person could say the same today. Lacking both the funds to attend formal entertainments and the tradition of enclosed theaters so popular in the West, many Chinese are accustomed to viewing life as one great pageant. Street jugglers and musicians segue into colorful crowds, vendors, families on outings, men sleeping on the sidewalks on hot nights, to form an ever flowing river of life, all of which is joyful to look at and legitimate entertainment. Chinese mothers rarely teach their children not to stare or point at what is interesting or strange.

Westerners, alas, are unaccustomed to being part of the "drama on the open-air stage." White or black skin, blond or brown hair, blue or green eyes, hairy limbs, and foreign clothes, all make foreigners different, interesting, worth pointing at, staring at, commenting on, and even holding babies up to look at. Foreigners never quite get used to this, and often wonder how Chinese people, famed for their politeness, can be so rude.

Just remember: staring and pointing at the new and different is not rude for Chinese people. It reveals Chinese lack of exposure to the western world, which is the cumulative effect of centuries of closed-door policies. In wealthier Taiwan, for example, only in remote areas do foreigners feel the zoo effect. On the mainland, staring reveals poverty and lack of opportunities for education or travel. But for Chinese, staring is not rude, nor is it truly racist, however much it feels like racism. You can waste your lungs yelling, and Chinese will only stare more.

Rather, try to understand being stared at in terms of China's sense of pageantry. Notice that Chinese stare just as much at other Chinese who dress, act, or talk differently, are handicapped, or are otherwise extraordinary. Most white Westerners never experience life as a racial minority, and can take their China time as a lesson in racial sensitization. Try cutting back on the staring by dressing and acting as inconspicuously as possible. In the meantime, if the staring gets to be too much, withdraw.

Conflict #4: Our Great Culture: No Foreigners Allowed

Chinese call China *Zhongguo,* literally "the Middle Kingdom," the center of China's ancient world. Ever since Confucius codified the rules of human behavior over 2,500 years ago, Chinese have had a sense of knowing the correct way to live. "I have noticed," writes long-time China teacher Nancy E. Dollahite, "that every Chinese I have encountered hangs a towel on a rack the same way, wrings a wet cloth the same way, folds paper to form a parcel the same way, and chops vegetables the same way... this is within China's very bones. There is a Chinese way to do things."

Few Chinese hold foreigners to these standards of behavior, partly because some Chinese recognize legitimate differences in cultural values, but more often because they assume Westerners can't quite master all the rules of propriety. Chinese admire, feel abashed by, and envy the West's technical superiority, and argue endlessly among themselves as to which dynasty lost China's technological edge. But only the rare Chinese doubts China's cultural and moral superiority.

In practical terms, at least on the mainland, foreigners may also be excluded from much of Chinese life by segregation laws controlling housing and social centers. These rules are particularly galling for overseas Chinese, who may be welcomed to some areas off-limits to "foreigners," but excluded from others.

Segregation laws can even depend on precise racial mixes. Overseas Chinese who marry Chinese nationals can enter mainland China with a special "Visiting Your Relatives" visa, which allows limited duty-free importation and other privileges. Non-Chinese people are officially eligible for Visiting-Your-Relatives visas, but in practice may be denied, regardless of how long they've been married to a Chinese national. This is what Mark Salzman calls the Chinese bureaucratic game of "Let's make a regulation." The position of mixed-race children of such marriages is unclear. One white foreigner we know applied for a Visiting-Your-Relatives visa based on her marriage to a Chinese national, but was denied. She asked if her children would be eligible. "Is your husband pure-blooded Chinese?" the immigrations official wanted to know. Our friend assured the official he was. Then, she was told, the children would be eligible. And what about the grandchildren, if the children also married white people? After some consultation the answer came back. No, if the grandchildren were 3/4 white, they would not be eligible for a Visiting-Your-Relatives visa.

You may be angered by such rules till your face mottles purple, but rage changes nothing but your blood pressure. Someday greater education and openness will drive China's racist tendencies to the shadows. In the meantime, keep explaining, encouraging your students, teachers, and colleagues to think in more open ways. Many teachers find some of their greatest satisfaction in China came from convincing a few of their students to think more logically about race, and thus, in a small way, to have left the world a better place.

Conflict #5: Black Devils

Dark-skinned people suffer out-and-out racism in China, as in much of the world. Blacks, Sri Lankans, and others are unabashedly seen as inferior to Chinese and whites. Although many regulations have been passed to improve the treatment of "African guests," the overall tenor of Chinese attitudes toward dark-skinned foreigners remains quite negative. China's intellectual community, cut off in many ways from world discourse, continues to harbor racist theories of separate evolution now debunked in the West but once credited as "scientific." The terrifying race riots of Spring 1989 in Nanjing illustrate the effects of such thinking. Fights broke out between Chinese and African students which culminated in the arrest and incommunicado incarceration of hundreds of black students, destruction of black dorms, and three days of marches with Chinese townspeople chanting "kill the Black Devils." Hollywood deserves a share of blame for this sad situation, for while few Chinese have ever met a black person, many have seen blacks stereotyped as hoods or maniacs in celluloid extravaganzas. Having no strong black constituency to contest these images, and few blacks around to act as contrary role models, most Chinese have swallowed these stereotypes whole. This is as true in Taiwan as in the mainland.

Conflicts with African and subcontinental exchange students have unfortunately, in some cases, further inflated racism and xenophobia on the mainland. China invites thousands of students each year from developing nations in quid pro quo exchanges for oil and other resource rights, and in political tit-for-tats. These students, most in "developmental" disciplines, such as medicine, nutrition, engineering, and sanitation, study in China for two to ten years, earn a degree, and return home to contribute to national construction. While in China, their studies and housing are subsidized by China's government, which also distributes monthly per-student stipends of around 300 yuan—nearly twice the average Chinese worker's monthly wage. Most are among the elite of their own countries, and consequently have more money than their Chinese counterparts, even without stipends from the Chinese schools. Many Chinese resent special treatment for exchange students, pointing out that stipends for Chinese students hover near 15 yuan per month. Yet few Chinese understand what China gets in return for hosting these students, and the government does little to enlighten them. Further, when Chinese students or scholars go to African or subcontinental nations, they are invariably given far more special treatment than exchange students from these nations receive in China.

Economic tensions have formed the base for a vicious circle of conflicts between African/subcontinental students and Chinese students, which in turn reinforces stereotypes of dark-skinned people as violent and irrational. As a result, hundreds of small and large clashes have marred relations through the years; the 1989 Nanjing riots are just a particularly vicious example.

Foreigners can ease this tragic situation by quiet insistence on more equitable discussion of race relations. If you're teaching, you could assign your students readings from Stephen Jay Gould and other debunkers of racist theories of evolution. For students, open discussions with your teachers regarding historical and economic causes of racial inequity in the US are helpful. Changing people's minds doesn't happen in a week or a year or even a century, as Western racism itself demonstrates. But by making your small mark you help push the whole project forward.

At the same time, dark-skinned foreigners need to do some serious soul searching before heading off to China. Chinese racism toward dark-skinned people is at least as virulent as Western. If you can't steel yourself to maintain good humor and optimism in a land where you'll be called "Black Devil," then it's probably best not to go. On the other hand, if you are resourceful, self-reliant, and resilient in your humor, you can probably make the greatest sort of contribution of anyone to increased understanding. One of our favorite moments came watching a mixed-race band from New Orleans perform at the Cyclone Disco in Beijing. The lead singer, a black woman, had memorized the highly nationalistic, almost crypto-fascist Chinese lyrics to the popular song "Eastern Pearl" (*Dong fang zhi zhu*). She belted out the song with the biggest, most innocent smile, and the audience cheered and clapped and sang along until she came to the line about "my beautiful yellow face." At that point the audience faltered, but the New Orleans gal kept right on singing, white teeth flashing against dark chocolate skin. When she finished, there was a terribly awkward half-second, while a bar full of suddenly embarrassed Chinese people shuffled their feet. One started applauding, though, and then the whole bar gave her a standing ovation. China needs more moments like that, and more people with the guts and good cheer to create them.

Conflict #6: Cut Sleeves and Certain Parks

China has ancient traditions accepting homosexuality that probably date back farther than those of Greece. One classic expression for same-gender affection is "love of the cut sleeve", referring to Emperor Han Wudi, who reportedly ordered the brocaded sleeve of his imperial robe cut off, rather than make the young courtier who had fallen asleep cross it . For more on China's traditional attitudes, see Dr. Bret Hinsch's *Passions of the Cut Sleeve*.

In modern times, however, China's traditional acceptance of homosexuality has disappeared, and, in both the mainland and Taiwan, homosexuality and gay culture are seen as signs of corruption coming from the West.

In both places, gay people are less likely to be actively persecuted than to be used as scapegoats. A few years back, gay life across China was very much like in the US or England in the 1950s; the love that dare not speak its name. Sex was largely anonymous and casual, taking place in certain bars and parks (especially Dongdan in Beijing and Xingongyuan Park in Taipei) with much fear of police raids and exposure.

In Taiwan these pressures have largely ceased. While Xingongyuan Park (recently renamed 2-2-8 Peace Park" in one of the more stunning examples of the DPP's new leadership in Taipei) remains an old standby, and active gay culture has created a degree of social acceptance, at least in Taipei. Gay bars like Funky's flourish, while AIDS activism has become almost chic. In fact, one couple of our acquaintance, who had a rock thrown through their apartment window in the US, now believes Taiwan is more accepting than the West.

On the mainland, a few signs have also appeared indicating a more accepting official attitude. In Beijing, Shanghai, and Guangzhou, a few health department HIV information centers have been set up. Word on the street is that parks such as Dongdan are rarely raided anymore, except when the police wish to clean up "undesirable elements" prior, to, say, the Olympics bid or the Women's conference. In fact, a few quiet gay clubs have started to open in the mainland, and certain discos have de facto "gay corners". Ask gay foreign residents and friends for current information.

Though all signs indicate a gradually more open attitude, foreigners in both places, and especially on the mainland, need to be aware just how stigma is still attached to homosexuality. Police on the mainland can still arrest gay people and hold them for long periods without trial, simply on a whim. Reports of beatings and torture are far fewer than in the past, but not unheard of. Be extremely sensitive, in any same sex encounter with a Chinese person. While most safe sex practices should be followed in China as elsewhere, exchanging names may not be practical. Take cues from your partner as to where and when. Don't assume that radical activism would be a good thing in China (indeed, there's a case to be made that extremist activism has negative effects in the West, too, but that's another story). Above all, should you take any sort of strong public pro-gay stance, be sure no flak could harm any Chinese gay people around you.

That said, quiet, thoughtful discussion on this topic, as on racism, can help overcome prejudice, a person at a time.

Conflict #7: My enemy, My Brother—Overseas Chinese

Taiwanese by and large have a relaxed attitude towards people of Chinese ethnicity visiting Taiwan (except for Chinese from the mainland, who are carefully controlled, and tend to make the Taiwanese nervous). It wasn't always so. In the early 1980s when most Taiwanese scholars who went abroad didn't return, relations could be brittle between those "sticking it out" in Taipei and those who had gone to "get rich" in Tokyo or Paris or New York. Now that Taipei itself has become a more wealthy, cosmopolitan city, and returnees outnumber new student abroad, everything has relaxed. There is little reason for mutual fingerpointing.

It's to be hoped that eventually the mainland will go the same way, for the same good reasons. At present however, there's still a love-hate relationship between mainlanders and their overseas cousins, whether first generation immigrants or many steps removed. As with Taiwan in the past, most of the tension is a combination of economic difference and complex feelings of jealousy and anger towards those who "abandoned the struggle for the homeland in favor of the good life abroad."

In essence, because overseas Chinese are still viewed primarily as Chinese, mainlanders resent economically successful overseas compatriots in ways they don't resent white Westerners. Many companies have reported morale troubles with local employees after hiring returning PRC émigrés on non-local packages. Similarly, overseas Chinese are far more often the targets of theft and violent crime (including kidnapping) than are whites. This is especially so with Hong Kong and Taiwanese visitors, since, for political reasons, residents of those areas aren't granted as much special attention or protection from the PRC police as are US citizens and other Westerners.

In some cases, this is a two-way street. Certain overseas Chinese are given to statements about how poor and backwards the mainland is, perhaps without realizing how inflammatory such statements can be, especially coming from a "compatriot." Nothing can justify police turning a blind eye to kidnapping and murder. Unfortunately, a few particularly notorious cases seem to have come to symbolize mainland handling of criminal cases involving overseas Chinese, especially from the perspective of the Taiwan press. This then becomes a viscous cycle, as Taiwanese visitors become more likely to make inflammatory statements, and tempers continue to rise. On a macro scale the same thing is happening between the PRC and Taiwan governments as a whole. The authors devoutly hope the current (1996) round of name calling does not deteriorate into armed conflict. The authors also believe that thoughtful discussion by overseas Chinese teachers and students could help defuse current tensions as, perhaps, nothing else could.

On a scale less terrifying and more annoying, overseas Chinese should be aware they may be subject to various pressures not normally applied to "pure Westerners." These may range from requests for money from long-lost 42nd cousins; to pressure on those working for Western firms to "try to represent the Chinese side"; to pressure on teachers to accept longer class hours for less pay than the white teachers as a "sacrifice to the homeland."

Our advice is that overseas Chinese should react to emotional appeals the same way other foreigners do, only more so. A business negotiation is a business negotiation. Don't let yourself be pushed into a corner through emotional blackmail. After the contract is signed, attend to your idealism in whatever way seems appropriate. And as for that 42nd cousin, don't allow yourself to be guilt-tripped into something you'll regret. China's poverty isn't your fault, nor will all your disposable income cure it. Set reasonable limits to your generosity and stick to them.

Conflict #8: Polite Refusals

"Would you like some tea?" "Oh, no." "Please, really, would you like some tea?" "No, no, of course not. I'd hate to be any trouble." "Oh, it's no trouble, really, I'd love to get you tea."Well, if it's really no trouble . . ." "No trouble at all." "Well, maybe just one cup." This exchange, almost pathological by Western standards, seems quite normal to Chinese. Proper Chinese manners require self-effacing pro forma refusals of compliments, refreshments, and gifts as part of politely accepting. Chinese would never accept refreshments from each other without three or four polite refusals first. Accepting straightaway seems proud or greedy.

All this politeness confuses foreigners, and many amusing errors have resulted when Westerners took polite refusals at face value. Many a hapless Chinese has spent a visit with a foreigner suffering from thirst after refusing a cup of tea, and never getting follow-up offers.

More Westernized Chinese understand Western directness, and may adopt Western manners when visiting foreigners. With your more sophisticated Chinese friends you'll be able to ask directly, "is that a Chinese 'no' or a Western 'no'?" But most Chinese still operate under old rules. Westerners who omit polite refusals seem uncouth.

Compliments should also be turned aside. Polite Chinese reply to compliments with *nali, nali,* literally "where, where?" meaning "where is the trait you are complimenting, which I surely do not possess?" Chinese also never open gifts in front of the giver, and are reticent in discussing sexual matters.

If you feel comfortable, try adopting Chinese manners. Adding in a few polite refusals costs nothing and will help Chinese feel more comfortable with you. Westernized Chinese may find Sinicized foreigners quaint, but never rude. Meanwhile, meeting a foreigner who "knows a bit about manners" may just help dispel those myths about us barbarians.

Conflict #9: Truth and Consequences

Westerners value truthfulness in and of itself. We may tell "little white lies," and we may tell big lies, but we aren't proud of telling them. We put a premium on being honest with ourselves and others.

Chinese look at truth quite differently. From a philosophical standpoint, China created the Daoist and Yellow Buddhist traditions which hold that all the world is falsehood and trickery of the senses, a mirage which, if we believe in it too much, keeps us from nirvana (Buddhist) or immortality (Daoist). Imagine trying to reconcile that view with the Judeo-Christian tradition! From a practical standpoint, Chinese simply feel that telling the truth for its own sake merits less emphasis than other values, such as preserving face.

Direct refusals of requests, for example, are impolite in Chinese etiquette. Chinese prefer to create reasons why doing so-and-so is impossible, rather than refuse to help. Some bus companies lack government permission to carry foreigners. Many a foreigner, asking for a seat on a bus run by such a company, has been told the seats were all full, and then fumed and fretted as the bus drove away half empty. In fact, to the Chinese, lying about the seats is far more polite than saying, "no, we cannot carry you." When Chinese lie to you, look around and see what the reasons might be. Very few Chinese lie for the sake of lying. Have you made a request which the Chinese might be unable or unwilling to carry out? If so, take the lie as a polite refusal or, at worst, as laziness. Has something perhaps gone wrong, which the Chinese might hesitate to admit to you? If so, take the lie as a polite way of avoiding discussion. You may prefer to hear all the gory details, but you can't change Chinese etiquette. Look at it this way: you never have to admit to anyone in China when you goof up, either.

"POLITICAL INDECENCY" AND OTHER INVASIONS

The Chinese customs service, both in the mainland and in Taiwan, has the legal right to open all packages sent into or out of the country to ensure that they contain no illegal material. Illegal imports for the mainland include pornography, anticommunist literature, large quantities of evangelistic religious materials, and all banned books. Illegal imports for Taiwan include pornography, communist literature, anything that advocates Taiwan independence or the overthrow of the KMT ruling party (*Kuomintang*), and all banned books. Illegal exports from both include, among other things, national treasures (for the mainland, read: antiques that haven't been approved for export and/or on which you haven't yet paid tax).

Both post offices claim not to open letters, but many foreigners have found missing pages, steamed-open letters, and even parts of pages cut off. Phones may also be tapped, rooms may be bugged, and cameras on the street may monitor meetings. Foreigners should be very sensitive to this government scrutiny in order to avoid causing political fallout for Chinese people around them. One foreigner we know chatted with a Reuters reporter from her hotel room in Lhasa. The call was bugged and traced, and the family of the Chinese person she was traveling with were interrogated, first by the Public Security Bureau and later the National Security Bureau (China's CIA).

Political control measures are far more relaxed in Taiwan than in the mainland, and are likely to relax still further. Back in 1984, on Rebecca's first trip to Taiwan, her Chinese-English dictionary was even confiscated at customs because characters were romanized in Pinyin, the official romanization system of the mainland, and usage examples included pro-communist phrases. Letters can now be sent back and forth between the "Two Sides of the Ocean Abyss," and Taiwan residents can visit the mainland fairly freely (although Taiwan continues to sharply restrict the number of mainland visitors it will accept). On the mainland, however, watchfulness against political indiscretions will have to become part of your daily routine. After the 1989 democracy movements, many among the hundreds arrested were apprehended simply because they had been videotaped chatting with foreigners known to be stringers for Western news agencies.

Even though Westerners often find these political controls intolerable and may be tempted to protest, the importance of caution can never be overemphasized. Remember, before you get too caught up in a self-righteous reaction to Chinese politics, that this is not your country, and that any of your objections must be voiced with extreme tact and caution if they are to have any effect at all. Most Chinese do not view human rights as a priority, relative to economic growth. If you doubt this, try asking ordinary Chinese you meet what they think of even other Chinese who become "professional protestors," such as Wei Jingheng or Wu'er Kaixi; let alone what they think of western groups like Human Rights in China.

Meanwhile, if you learn to view problems as Chinese do, they can become a challenge. The secret is not to say anything politically controversial unless it is in person, away from ears and eyes, with someone you have good reason to trust. Some foreigners have actually made a game of thwarting their censors, writing cleverly designed letters that appear to be coded but in fact hide nothing, while others convey sensitive meanings through bland but misleading language.

ECONOMICS MAKE A BIG DIFFERENCE

Some difficulties in adjusting to China stem neither from culture nor from politics, but merely from poverty. Due to the differences in wealth, such problems appear more rarely in Taiwan. Still, even on the island these problems appear in rural areas, and to some extent in cities, where old habits die hard. The Taiwan government has instituted a six-year, US$300 billion plan to rebuild Taiwan's infrastructure at a level commensurate with the island's newfound wealth. But for now, even in Taiwan, cities remain dirty and crowded, and the tap water undrinkable outside Taipei. On the mainland it's the same, only more so.

1. SANITATION AND HYGIENE. China's streets are often littered with filth. Open-air markets sell freshly slaughtered animals whose blood run in the gutters. In small towns, the gutters may also act as sewers. In other words, China is a land of many smells, which can be even more overpowering than the sights.

As is common in Third World countries, standards of hygiene also remain below First World par. Hundreds of Anti-Rat Campaigns, Anti-Spitting Campaigns, Cleanliness Campaigns, ad nauseum (one wag of our acquaintance claims what China really needs is an Anti-Campaign Campaign), have improved the situation somewhat. But many people still have no running hot water, and so must boil water for dishes, clothes washing, or baths, and, therefore, simply wash less often than Westerners.

Most foreigners will contract some illness during their time in China, for the crowdedness and the still unstamped-

out habit of spitting in the streets makes every common cold
a city-wide event. In addition, northern and western China's
dry, dusty air irritates the throat and lungs and encourages
bronchitis. Finally, eating off plates washed in cold water, or
maybe only dunked in a pail of suds between uses spreads
many stomach ailments.

Try to minimize your illnesses, as being sick anywhere
is no fun, and being sick in unheated rooms floored with
concrete is horrid. Take your vitamins and get plenty of rest
and exercise. Drink, as the Chinese do, many cups of hot
liquid a day. Don't drink unboiled water. Wear surgical
masks in the winter; they protect you from the dust, the cold,
and many a floating germ. Be careful where you eat. Street
stands often have the best food but the worst sanitation; one
delicious type of mutton skewer commonly sold in the North
has so often borne illness that foreigners call it "hepatitis-on-
a-stick." Many Chinese restaurants sell inexpensive disposable balsawood chopsticks. For those that don't, carry a pair
of your own. Peek into the kitchen to see how spanking clean
it is—or isn't. As a general rule, shun any restaurant that
lacks running water.

Some differences in cleanliness between China and the
West are also cultural. Chinese tend to judge cleanliness of
garments by sight, for example, while Westerners judge by
smell. We pick up a worn shirt and sniff at the armpits to test
whether or not to wear it again. Chinese peer closely for
stains. Thus the Chinese might disdain the Westerner whose
clean-smelling shirt has been smudged, while the Westerner
looks down on the Chinese whose clean-looking shirt smells
worn.

Historian Joseph Needham has also pointed out what he
calls the Chinese people's "courtyard vision of the world."
Traditional Chinese houses surround courtyards, which become the center of daily Chinese life. In traditional China,
housewives cleaned their courtyard and threw the trash just
outside it; the city bore responsibility for cleaning the streets.
Needham argues this attitude continues today, and explains
the contrast between cleanliness in private homes and filth in
the streets surrounding them. Chinese homes may be spot-
less, but the yards just outside may be littered with old cans,
fallen leaves, disintegrating paper, and construction debris.
To the Chinese, no shame is attached to dirt outside the

courtyard of personal responsibility. The Chinese themselves say, "only shovel the snow in front of your own door." Western selfishness centers on individuals; Chinese selfishness centers on the family.

Remembering the cultural and economic bases of differences in cleanliness may not prevent your dismay at walking down a street with open sewers. But it should help you avoid regarding the locals with what old Chinese women call "bitterness in your heart."

2. HEAT, ELECTRICITY, AND WATER. Westerners, and especially North Americans, take for granted hot showers, cheap and reliable electricity, and heating. In China, these facilities vary by the city and by the day. Expat business people live in compounds with back-up generators and emergency cisterns, protecting foreigners from dealing with unpredictable utilities. On campus, however, you'll live more like the Chinese. China abounds with leaky pipes, archaic power plants, and poorly installed wiring. In addition, drought conditions and energy emergencies occur often, during which city governments control water use not by Western-style anti-waste campaigns, but by simply shutting off supplies.

Learn to conserve. Chinese pay much more for electricity as a percentage of income than Westerners, and so are far more conscious of care with resources, and so should you be. Turn off lights when you leave rooms, turn off TVs or radios you're not listening to, avoid using electric heaters, and use electric ovens sparingly, without excessive preheating times. Most schools absorb the cost of foreigners' electric bills, but you alone using more electricity than a family of six down the hall will not foster good feelings. Also, stock candles, a flashlight, and/or a kerosene lamp against sudden blackouts and brownouts.

Don't waste water either, particularly in the North and West. Many Chinese recycle water, using it first to wash food, then dishes, then to scrub the floor, then finally to flush the toilets. You needn't go that far, but neither should you, in a drought-stricken country, leave the shower running while you brush your teeth. Actually, even if you have a hot shower, it'll likely use a tiny self-contained water heater, giving you very little warm-shower time, so you'd be foolish to let it run anyway. And those without water heaters must shower the Chinese way: heat water on the stove, mix it with cool in a bucket, and pour it over yourself with a scoop. Always keep extra thermoses of boiled water and buckets or other containers of unboiled water available in case the water is suddenly shut off by accident or plan; shut-offs can sometimes last for days.

South of the Yangtze River no heating is permitted in schools or other public areas. This blanket (no pun intended) energy conservation measure ignores local and seasonal variation, and in cold years with snow on the ground, the southern Chinese suffer. You'll suffer with them, and we advise carrying lots of thermal underwear. Even Northerners receive ungenerous heat. You may have radiators or a pot-bellied stove with a moderate supply of coal. In neither case will you swelter. Bring sweaters and long underwear.

3. TELEPHONES. Many mainland Chinese cities, and rural areas in Taiwan, still rely on ancient switching systems which make phone calls a nightmare. International calls to China may meet only with "this call cannot be completed in the country you have dialed." Within China even local calls can be blocked by a seemingly endless variety of whistles and beeps. Long distance calls can be made direct from expat hotels in compounds, and more and more Chinese have IDD lines. But if your school doesn't have IDD or DDD service, making a long distance call still means putting a call through the operator and waiting several hours, or even overnight. Once you've gotten through, indifferent operators may take eons to connect you. If possible, have someone who speaks Chinese well help you place your call. If not, speak slowly and clearly, and stress that the call is long distance and important. It may help to identify yourself by unit rather than name; "I'm with Xi'an University" is better than "I'm Joe Smith," and "I'm calling from America" is best of all. Patience and good humor are also key.

4. *GUANXI* AND *HOUMEN:* CONNECTIONS AND BACKDOOR DEALING. The first two Chinese words many foreigners learn, by virtue of their constant repetition, are *meiyou* and *buxing:* "we have none," and "we can't." From ancient times Chinese have suffered an economy of scarcity. Population always out-stripped resources; consumers always outnumbered available goods and services. Desire and ability to pay have never guaranteed possession.

Because of this sense of struggling against limits, Chinese have set up distribution networks for scarce goods and services unrelated to money. Most Chinese rely instead on personal relationships, which they call *guanxi:* literally "connections." Chinese call using *guanxi, zou houmen:* "entering through the back door." Westerners use *guanxi* and *houmen* as well; the English terms "connections" and "back door" have the same connotations as their Chinese equivalents. We might use connections to get jobs or coveted theater tickets. We go in the back door to buy exclusive apartments. But China's imbalance between supply and demand forces Chinese to use *guanxi* for many mundane items taken for granted in the US. Train tickets, TVs, good liquor, cigarettes, and many other items are now routinely available in the pricy upscale stores in the big cities. But in smaller cities they may be unavailable at ordinary prices if the buyer lacks *guanxi*. Notably, Taiwanese use *guanxi* as well. TVs and train tickets are readily available on the island, but decent housing and good jobs are not. *Guanxi* is a Chinese tradition, not a communist invention. Its rampant use on the mainland is aggravated by an economy still struggling with overpopulation and profound problems of underdevelopment, to name just two of China's major difficulties.

Foreigners have certain advantages outside the *guanxi* network. Many cities offer special train-ticket windows for foreigners and high officials, which sell tickets long after regular windows sell out. Friendship Stores sell many hard-to-get items, sometimes for hard currency only, and sometimes to foreigners only, regardless of currency.

But most foreigners get drawn into regular *guanxi* networks as well. Foreigners have much to offer in barter trade through the *guanxi* system; tutoring in English, foreign liquor and tobacco, tickets from the foreigner window, goods from the Friendship Store, goods from your home country, and counseling on job, or school hunting in the West are all legal tender in the world of *guanxi*.

Beware of the manipulators most Chinese scorn as *guanxi dawang:* "*guanxi* masters." People who seem bent on showering you with gifts without at some point asking for something, and without any feeling of real friendship, may be setting you up for a kill ("now that we're such good friends, how about letting me use your passport to transfer some currency?"). Most Chinese prefer an even *guanxi*) balance sheet; owing too much is bad face. *Guanxi* masters arrange *guanxi* deals professionally, taking percentages or piling up *guanxi* credit. *Guanxi* masters are China's loan sharks.

However, ordinary *guanxi* with ordinary people can improve your life in China and hone your understanding of the Chinese experience. Albert, for example, used *guanxi* with a restaurant manager to arrange lovely banquets for all our friends at restaurant cost plus a tiny margin. He created wonderful evenings and happy memories we could other-wise not have afforded.

You may tire of having your Chinese friends always asking for favors; "it's difficult," wrote one survey respon-dent, "to sort out who's a sincere friend and who just wants something from me." But try not to see requests as a betrayal of friendship, but rather as people sticking together in hard times. As you get a better feel for China, your instinct will tell you who's a real friend using *guanxi* out of need, and who's a *guanxi* loan shark.

Do be careful, however; *guanxi* can be complex. For-eigners often have trouble gauging the barter worth of goods and services. It is easy for inexperienced foreigners either to get used ("I've taken you to dinner. Now will you give me English lessons once a week for a year?") or to cause Chinese to lose face by presenting gifts so valuable that the Chinese person has no way of repaying them. Also, only rarely is *guanxi* a direct tit-for-tat trade, such as one train ticket in return for one painting. More often a series of gifts or favors establishes a relationship, which can then be tapped.

To illustrate some of the subtleties, Rebecca was once approached by a Chinese friend's cousin, who asked her to help his wife apply to US graduate schools. The friend brought several gifts—coffee, seafood, and candy. Rebecca agreed to help the wife. She at first declined the gifts, but later took them when told that accepting nothing would lose face for the husband by putting him too deeply in *guanxi* debt. The gifts, she was told by Chinese friends, were valuable enough to establish limited commitment on Rebecca's part.

Rebecca wrote several graduate schools for applications and helped the wife fill them out. A superior candidate, the wife was accepted with full scholarship, and began preparations to leave. The husband then appeared with more gifts: a beautiful jade necklace, and a large sum of cash. Rebecca refused these gifts. Chinese friends confirmed that accepting such large gifts would commit Rebecca to responsibility for the wife's welfare after her arrival in the States. In the end, the husband sent a lovely, but far less valuable, ink seal carved by a well-known seal artist. Helping the wife find a school was worth more than the coffee and food; the seal "paid off" the extra *guanxi* debt, and left everyone's "balance sheet" even.

Because *guanxi* can be confusing, we suggest that you avoid being drawn into *guanxi* trading until you have been in China long enough to develop a sense of the territory, and to make a few friendships with people whose judgment and advice you can trust.

7

Working:
In Spite of the School

A teacher who responded to our surveys was told one day not to work so hard preparing lessons for her conversation class. The students, explained the teacher's school official over her protests about rising test scores, were vocational pupils from the countryside. As such, they were basically stupid, and not worth the waste of time. Better to spend extra effort on the liberal arts students.

This official typifies China's rigid expectations for her teachers and students, whether Chinese or foreign. Though few officials would discourage performance as openly as this one, such attitudes remain common. The college entrance exam taken in the third year of upper middle school determines much of the rest of Chinese students' lives. Based on exam results, students are not only assigned to colleges, but in many cases assigned to majors. Under economic reform, this system has loosened somewhat, but remains essentially intact.

Once assigned to a major, Chinese students have few or no electives. Chinese view education as a process not of learning how to think and creating an individual philosophy, but of memorizing the standard knowledge of a field. Chinese teachers and department administrators determine classes for students. Within classes, memorization and recitation are far more common pedagogical techniques than conversation or independent research. Exposure to Western teaching methods, through both foreign teachers in China and Chinese teachers returned from abroad, has created demand for more open education in recent years; some of these demands influenced the 1989 democracy movement. But change comes slowly and old influences remain strong.

All this affects foreign teachers and students in myriad ways. You'll have fewer choices than you're used to in classes, course content, and pedagogical techniques. Chinese students may be puzzled by Western-style teaching methods, while Chinese teachers may be offended by Western-style students. Because Chinese teachers rely largely on standardized textbooks and curriculum, even where school officials welcome new teaching methods from foreigners, few facilities exist to accommodate them. Every step in the creation of a new syllabus, from library research to photocopying to using classroom displays, becomes cumbersome.

To some extent, persistent foreigners can overcome these difficulties. Your keys are patience, humor, and an understanding of the Chinese system. As our contribution to the latter, we hereby offer the following roadmap to getting things done within a Chinese educational institution.

FACILITIES, OR, "THE MAN WITH THE KEY IS ON VACATION"

From long habit, Chinese institutions prefer hierarchical, clearly defined worker responsibilities. Westerners understand divisions in managerial duties, but not with material resources and facilities. In Western schools, for example, a central Audio-Visual Department controls the overhead projectors, VCRs, and other display equipment. In China, each piece of equipment will likely "belong" to a "Responsible Person" (*fuze renyuan:* 负责人员); Miss Jia controls the English Department's overhead projector, and Mr. Yi controls the History Department's mimeo machine. These Responsible People bear personal responsibility for loss of or damage to equipment, and guard their "trusts" jealously. Using even the simplest facilities may require much placation of Miss Jia and Mr. Yi.

As soon as you've arrived in China and recovered from jet lag, start scouting around to find who controls all the facilities you need access to: copiers, ditto machines, thermal transfers, AV display equipment, supply rooms, library stacks, computers and printers, telephones, FAX machines (yes, many schools have them), language labs, science labs, school cars, exercise equipment, anything you might need during your stay.

Once armed with a list of names, begin your campaign of conquest. Visit each Responsible Person, introduce yourself (through an interpreter, if necessary), and express your sincere wishes for happy cooperation. Offer a token gift from home—a school pin, or postcards from your hometown, for example. Invite your "new friend" the RP to your apartment for tea (be sure to lay in a good stock of tea, soda, and snacks in case they take you up on it). Then begin feeling out how much access you'll be allowed to the facilities each RP controls. How often can you use it? Regularly, frequently, never? Under what circumstances can you use it—can you borrow it? Use it in the RP's presence? Ask the RP to use it for you? What can you do to make life easier for the RP?

A little extra effort at the outset can reap great rewards down the road. Many resources don't exist school-wide, and departments guard their assets jealously. No amount of pleading with the Foreign Language Department Head on the benefits of students seeing *Singing in the Rain* will help if the school's only VCR lives in the Biology Department. On the other hand, a cup of tea with Clerk Bing of the Biology Department may let you not only organize an English-language videofest, but also take the machine home for a Saturday night party with expat chums.

Depending on how crucial the equipment is to your happiness in China, continued free access may merit periodic visits to the RP bearing gifts of homebaked cookies, fresh fruit, or the jet-fuel Chinese liquors known as *baijiu*. Also, keep in touch with the RP about when you'll need access. You don't want to plan your videofest for the week the RP is on vacation without arranging to borrow in advance.

Always remember that the RP bears full responsibility for all charges; no one wants to land in hot water for your misdeeds. Your visits and conduct should build up trust, and reinforce the RP's image of you as an upstanding citizen who would never cause trouble or return a busted VCR. Bear up your end of that trust. Use equipment responsibly, returning it clean and in good condition in a timely fashion. If something breaks, offer the funds to fix it. If the library RP gives you open-stack privileges, don't mess up the shelves or drop crumbs on the floor. Above all, never cause political trouble for the RP. Just because you get FAX privileges, don't use the school's FAX to submit your controversial stringer articles to UPI. You never know who is listening in on transmissions, and that's what rental FAXes in joint-venture hotels are made for.

SQUEAKY WHEELS: KEEPING YOUR NEEDS TO THE FORE

Foreign students get only slightly broader class choices than their Chinese counterparts. Large foreign-language schools use fixed curricula. Smaller schools may offer more choice, but classes will still be bound by available teachers, materials, and ideology. China has no interlibrary loan system; don't ask for course reading materials from the Beijing National Archives at a school in Nanjing. Teachers tend to be specialized within institutes; don't expect classes on Suzhou embroidery at the Xi'an Railway Institute. Prevailing politics also controls class offerings. The autumn after the Tiananmen Incident and the "Beijing Spring" would be a bad time to ask for a course on the "Hundred Flowers Movement." Remember to let the school know your needs early and often; see suggestions in Chapters 4 and 5. Before arriving in China, let the Chinese school know in detail the topics, books, skills, and areas you hope to study. You'll still probably have no choice between courses, but at least the courses the school arranges should be moderately relevant.

Once classes begin, continue to communicate your needs politely but firmly to your teachers. Use specifics: "Can you please show us finger methods one-on-one for the Pipa?" works much better than "I'm learning nothing in music class." Save approaching the teacher's superiors as a last resort, as it causes the teacher to lose face and may breed hard feelings.

Foreign teachers generally have even less freedom of class choice than students, as they must teach within the Chinese curriculum and only certain courses may be taught by foreigners (no, they won't assign you the Marxist Philosophy class). As with students, best provide as much information as you can as early as possible as to your background, strengths, weaknesses, and interests. If you're allergic to teaching class X, say so.

Remember, though, a limited number of courses must be shared among all the foreign teachers, and everyone likes advanced conversation, composition, and content-based classes such as History, Literature, and the ever-popular "Survey of England and America." Don't grieve if you get a class or two you're not thrilled with. But neither need you teach six intro grammar classes and one intensive remedial reading. If class distribution seems inequitable, by all means sit down with other foreign teachers and negotiate. Most *waibans* will agree when the foreign teachers present a united front on teaching requests.

If, on the other hand, you find yourself the new foreign teacher on the block amid crafty old pros who have conspired to give you all the intro grammar classes, consider switching schools. Early in the semester it should be easy enough to find another position, and generally just the threat will be enough to help the Bozos reconsider.

CLOSED-STACK LIBRARIES AND OTHER HURDLES

Both teachers and students should make early visits to the school library. Determine whether or not the books you need, in the languages you require, are available early enough that your friends can still ship extras from home. Don't neglect the importance of good relations with the library RPs. Most Chinese libraries are closed-stack, with card catalogs that range from the confusing to the useless. Most librarians, however, are perfectly willing to allow open-stack privileges for foreigners who appear responsible; you can even use your open-stack privileges to get books for Chinese students, colleagues, and friends, though be sure to keep a list of what you lent to whom. Teachers need to check library facilities with special care, as you can't assign your students research papers on any topic for which the library is inadequately equipped.

Academic honesty tends to blur in China, for along with the emphasis on memorization comes an assumption that the best sort of research consists of looking up the authorities on a topic and quoting them. By long tradition Chinese teachers are lax about requiring quotation marks, so be very careful about accusing Chinese students of plagiarism, even when they've copied an article word-for-word. Foreign teachers can teach about the Western emphasis on creative analysis and insist on proper documentation in their classes, but should be sensitive when students slip. Foreign students should also remember that many Chinese teachers will give higher marks to an unoriginal paper filled with quotes from known authorities than to even the best-documented and most creative paper which deviates from accepted interpretations.

Finally, many educational officials seem to care more about officialdom than education. "There are really," explains respondent David Kellogg, "two kinds of bureaucrats here: lazy, and actively obstructive." Kellogg continues with the tale of one Party secretary at his school: "This man, who has far more power than any of the actual school presidents, is a high-school drop-out himself and bears a terrible grudge against intellectuals, which pits him against the entire school." Strive for appeasement with school officials, even if good working relations appear impossible. Always praise them at banquets, and present them with gifts from your home country. They haven't nearly as much power over your life as they have over your Chinese counterparts, but they have enough to foul up your work and make your life unpleasant; a little sycophancy never hurt anyone.

Also, advises survey respondent Jon Weston, "set reasonable goals (for China) and be happy when you reach the goals. If you expect results found in Western countries, you'll go mad."

THE CHINESE TEACHER-STUDENT RELATIONSHIP: MASTER AND ACOLYTE

One winter, claims an ancient parable of Chinese propriety, the master was cold. His student, having nothing else to warm the master with, burned his shirt for firewood and subsequently perished with cold.

Now outmoded at its most exteme, this traditional respect of students for teachers continues in a host of ways. Most Chinese teachers stand erect at the front of class, reading from formal scripts. A variety of customs and events, from National Teachers Day to the detailing of students, even in university classrooms, to take turns washing the blackboard, underscore the continued respect given to teachers. In recent years, teachers' fixed salaries have fallen far behind inflation, and the profession is out of favor for young graduates. But the tradition of respect remains strong.

Students, for their part, look to teachers for advice and as role models as well as for instruction, far more explicitly than in the West. Chinese teachers routinely advise their students on dress, eating, dating, and other matters which would seem strange or improper coming from a Western teacher to Western students. The Chinese government is keenly aware of the degree to which Chinese students consciously model themselves after their teachers; after various student demonstrations, the first to be arrested have been teachers and administrators fingered as ringleaders.

Chinese expect foreigners to be different, and you shouldn't feel constrained to imitate the Chinese way. Still, enough traditional values are attached to the student-teacher relationship, even with foreigners, that you should be aware of these traditions and not trample them.

At least at first, both students and teachers should err on the side of formality in dress and action. Chinese may interpret your torn blue jeans and shabby tweeds as unprofessional or disrespectful. Carry yourself a little more formally than you might at home; don't stick your feet up on the table. Remember, not only will the Chinese expect somewhat more formal behavior, but you will also represent, in their eyes, Western people. Don't let the rest of us down by acting like a boor.

Your Chinese teachers will likely offer you all manner of advice. You may not have to take it, but do try to accept it graciously. Your Chinese students may turn to you with as many questions about fashion and dating as about grammar. Should you choose to answer such questions, remember that you are taking on the traditional role of Master, at least in some degree, and don't answer lightly.

CRASH COURSE IN TEFL FOR THE NOVICE TEACHER

Many foreign English teachers in China are first-time teachers. As suggested in Chapter four, if you have no teaching and/or Teaching of English as a Foreign Language (TEFL) experience or training, try to get some before leaving home. Think about your own process of learning Chinese in order to gain insight into effective language learning. Set clear goals for your classes in terms of communicative ability, and use your imagination in laying out road maps to achieve your goals. The following is a very brief overview of the 4 language areas and some ways of teaching them.

Listening

Language students learn to listen before they learn anything else. Some teaching theory so emphasizes this fact that teachers are urged not to press students to speak in the target language till they begin to voluntarily. Whether or not you agree with this, you'll need to work to fill your students' minds with English. Remember, you are probably one of very few models of native English your students will ever have.

Try to have your students listen to English in a variety of contexts: in dialogues with each other and with you; in monologues presented to the class; in pronunciation practice with minimal pairs (ship/shop); from tapes; in songs; in word games; in lectures; in conversations between several native speakers. Use your imagination and have fun!

Remember that students can usually either learn new information with old vocabulary, or new vocabulary about old information, but not both at once. Try giving listening selections on familiar topics ("How to Make Chinese Dumplings"), while introducing new vocabulary, then reinforcing the old vocabulary while listening to a new topic ("How to Make Vichyssoise").

Whenever using a lengthy listening selection, use several exercises to reinforce the students' grasp of material and vocabulary. Use pre- and post-listening comprehension questions; pre- and post-listening topic discussion; vocabulary drills; comparison with written transcripts; creative use of new vocabulary. Linguistic research suggests language learners need to hear a new word in at least 50 different contexts before the word becomes completely familiar; try to provide at least a good number in class.

And remember that students need several different types of listening skills. Listening in a general way to a casual conversation is different from listening for details from a newscast, and different again from listening for note-taking purposes in a lecture. Try to teach different skills by asking for details ("how many . . . ?" "what type . . . ?"), sometimes for general comprehension ("why?" "how?"), and sometimes for main ideas ("what were the main points?").

Speaking

Chinese teachers of English tend to emphasize speaking only in rote recitation and repetition. This sort of teaching stems from traditional grammar-based curricula now generally debunked in Western teaching theory (though often, alas, still in practice in Western classrooms). Most new teaching theory emphasizes "communicative competence," the ability to effectively communicate ideas in the target language. Rather than teaching students by grammatical structure, try organizing the material in chunks of real-world communicative needs, either by topic ("at the bank," "at the doctor's office") or by "notional-functional" order ("making requests," "having an argument").

For each class, make a lesson plan. If you're an absolutely new teacher, physically write out the lesson plan; it will help you organize your thoughts. Decide which topic or notion/function you'll teach, what vocabulary and/or grammatical structures naturally attach to it, and how to get them across.

Have your students speak about the topic or notion/function in a variety of ways: repeating after you, in pair drills with each other, in small groups, in prepared skits, in unscripted situations. The more realistic you can make your students' language production, the better they'll be able to communicate. Having your students make dumplings on a hotplate in class while discussing what they're doing in English will imprint forever on their minds the words and notions/functions for foods and cooking and eating in ways no repetitious drills can touch.

And try to make your classroom a fun place, a place where students don't have to feel afraid. Never correct harshly; instead if a student uses a word or structure incorrectly, try using it in the correct context yourself, or pointing out the proper usage to the entire group without assigning blame. Have your students stand up and move around and use the entire classroom. They'll have more fun and learn more, and so will you.

Reading

We read in countless ways, from the bored skim of the cereal box to the consuming intensity with which you are doubtlessly devouring this book. Teach different types of reading in different ways. Teach students to scan charts, maps, menus, and phone books for specific information; to skim articles for main ideas; to read books for analytic understanding.

Chinese teachers tend to teach only intense analytic reading, from sentence patterning and breakdown of complex sentences to memorization of articles. You can help students learn analytic reading in more creative ways; teach them:

- to guess word meanings from context;
- and from common roots (anthropology, misanthropy);
- to summarize author meaning and intent rather than to memorize;
- to analyze writing critically ("we know Faulkner is supposed to be a great writer, but do you like this story, and why or why not?").

But your greatest challenge will be getting Chinese students to read English unintensively. Native readers of alphabetic languages like English relate to words on the page wholly differently from native readers of ideographic languages like Chinese. Bridging that gap is awfully difficult. Teach your students to recognize writing they don't need to read analytically and to read it quickly without looking up every new word in their dictionaries. For skimming and scanning try:

- timed reading exercises;
- bingo games and other competitions;
- reading "realia" like packages, application forms, menus, and maps.

Writing

Have students write copiously, both to reinforce vocabulary and grammar and to sharpen creative and analytic skills. For straight language skills, try sentence writing:

- have students write five or ten sentences with each new vocabulary word or grammatical structure;
- or make complex sentences using connecting words (in addition, although, despite, as if);
- and use peer correcting, which reinforces reading as well as collective learning.

Teach paragraph structure as the base for longer writing:

- give students topic sentences and have them write the body of the paragraph, or vice versa;
- give lists of information to be organized into paragraphs;
- teach about language flow by giving models from great writers with straightforward language (Hemingway, et al.).

Finally, teach students to write essays and short works of fiction:

- assign writing journals, with either assigned or free topics;
- teach outlining and research;
- discuss and assign examples of different expository styles (description, comparison/contrast, classification, etc.);
- produce student-written newsletters and "books."

Straight language sentences you can mark up, or have students mark up in peer exercises, with plenty of red ink. But longer, more creative pieces you should correct in terms of structure and analysis rather than language use, as the latter discourages communication. Correct language errors by giving examples of correct use. For student newsletters and "books" assign at least two drafts. Finally, work together with other teachers at your school. Try coordinating assignments to reinforce vocabulary and ideas ("you have them read Poe while I teach storytelling"), or even having schoolwide projects such as a Broadway-style musical production or a weekly English paper or radio program.

All this may sound like a lot of work—and it is. Most survey respondents rated materials provided by their schools as "terrible"; you'll spend hours producing supplementary materials and arranging for dittoing. As the old saying goes, "Teaching is the easiest job in the world to do poorly and the hardest job in the world to do well." Your Chinese students, by and large, will be serious and hardworking, and deserve your best shot too.

Thriving:
Making the Most of Your Chinese Life

Your work is going smoothly and you've stopped quaking at the filthy streets; it's time to enter more deeply into Chinese life. You'll want to accomplish many things in China, from shopping to traveling to just piling up good memories. Following are some of our suggestions on how.

CULTURAL INTEGRATION

Learning to cope with cultural differences creates the foundation for a good life in China. Building on that foundation requires reaching out, joining Chinese life, and introducing Chinese people to Western life. The following suggest some activities other foreigners have used in their own process of integration.

1. ENGLISH CORNER. In most Chinese cities, groups of dedicated learners meet regularly to practice English. In parks, teahouses, and school campuses, these learners enjoy talking in English, or reading English articles and discussing them. Participants range from rank beginners to the flawlessly fluent.

    Appear at English Corner and you'll learn the meaning of stardom. Ask around to find the English Corner nearest you, and try joining. There you'll find many potential friends, guides, and instructors. You may not want to commit yourself to regular English Corner attendance—too much like another class! Also, be a little wary. Some English Corners attract English-speaking *guanxi* masters, who prey on easy foreigners, and they may appear at your door more often than you'd like. But occasional appearances just may remain a favorite way to meet people and relax.

2. THE ARTS OF CHINA. Many foreigners study one or more of China's traditional arts. Chinese cooking, painting, calligraphy, seal carving, embroidery, martial arts, acupuncture, and other arts continue as vibrant social traditions today. Students learn as much about Chinese life and culture as about their topic.

Mention to your students or teachers any special interests you have in anything Chinese. Rest assured they'll find someone for you to study with, either as part of a group or under private tutelage.

Traditional teachers accepted no pay. Students brought gifts of food, fuel, and other necessaries to sustain the teacher. Beyond subsistence, the joy of seeing traditions passed on was supposed to be its own reward. Today some teachers accept wages. Others still work under the old system. If you're not paying your teacher cash, be sure to bring gifts. You might tutor your teacher, or a relative, in English; bring food or liquor or cigarettes; invite your teacher to dinner regularly; or offer gifts from your home country.

3. LEARNING TO BE CHINESE. Many foreigners find their happiest days in China came when they felt themselves to be most Chinese. Every foreigner needs to escape now and then to a kvetch session with other foreigners or even to Hong Kong for the weekend. But constant separation from day-to-day Chinese life is a recipe for loneliness and disappointment. You'll have few opportunities to appreciate your Chinese friends if you spend your days saving for trips to the disco at the Beijing Great Wall Sheraton or the Taipei Lai Lai Hilton.

Instead, try joining in with daily activities at your school. Go for walks with your students or teachers. Join morning exercises. Invite Chinese friends over for dumpling-making parties. Join a sports team or a choir. Write articles for the school English newsletter. Go to school dances and parties. Even joining in the performances that schools organize for the foreigners ("I feel like a dancing bear!" wrote one student) can be fun. In Taiwan and Beijing these performances are occasionally televised, and there's nothing more charming than playing the buffoon for an audience of 1,200,000,000.

Lacking funds to hire professional entertainers, most Chinese live quite simple lives by Western standards. Yet China's social life provides closeness and a sense of purpose, which you can share by joining in.

4. TEACHING THE CHINESE ABOUT US. Chinese love to learn about the West. Set up Western activities for your students or classmates. Teach Western cooking (we found fruit salads and deviled eggs to be perennial favorites), teach Western songs, or start a choir. Teach dances to Western rock music. Play chess, or poker, or bridge. Start a baseball team. Organize parties for Western holidays. Your students or classmates will love baking Christmas cookies, learning how to make a Seder, or coloring Easter eggs.

Your Chinese friends will love their "Western activities," and you can relieve homesickness by bringing a bit of the West near you. Besides, togetherness promotes international understanding, and isn't that what it's all about?

5. BRINGING CHINA HOME WITH YOU. China changes foreigners. Your time in China will transform your ideas about family, society, and individualism. When you return home, you'll want to share the power of your China experience with your family and friends. Buying souvenirs just isn't enough.

Try keeping a journal, or writing articles for publication at home. Write regular letters, either to individuals or the gang. Many foreigners leave postage and copying money with a friend or family member, and send that person regular thick, newsy letters to be photocopied and distributed. The act of writing not only keeps your loved ones current on the many transformative experiences you'll have in China, but also helps you sort out feelings while there. We found happiness in China came easier when we had a running commentary on paper about how China was making us tick.

You might keep a scrapbook and/or a photo album as well. Many wonderful artifacts of Chinese life will come your way, from old Maoist posters to bus tickets from the Qinghai/Tibet line. Keeping a collection, even while still in China, can help you make sense of your China experience.

TRAVEL IN CHINA

You can't spend a year in China and not go see the Great Wall and the Terra Cotta warriors, or the Palace Museum in Taipei, and at least a few other treasures of the world's oldest continuous culture. For students and teachers in Taiwan, travel presents little problem. The island is small and transport is good. The longest bus ride in Taiwan, from Peit'ou at the north tip to Kenting at the south, is less than 12 hours. A newly proposed train will cut the trip from Taipei, the northernmost large city, to Kaohsiung, the southernmost, to 93 minutes. Mainland-bound foreigners, however, face many problems, and need to plan their time wisely.

Your *waiban* should organize outings to temples, museums, and natural wonders in your area; this is one reason to live near sites you don't want to miss. More ambitious *waiban* also organize weekend regional trips. Larger-scale tours you'll need to organize yourself, but your *waiban* can help with travel arrangements; see suggestions below.

Weekend travel presents problems because China is vast and her transport slow and crowded. Some enterprising foreigners have crammed all their classes into three or four days a week in order to maximize travel time. Never press your *waiban* on this, however; many Chinese get only one day off a week, and your balking at two will seem babyish. Barring long weekends, weekend travel of any distance means flying; see below.

Most foreigners get six or seven short vacations of two to five days each for holidays as varied as National Teacher's Day (September 10) and the Grave Sweeping Festival. Most schools allow a four-to-six week break between semesters at Spring Festival, and six to eight weeks in the summer (summer vacation is paid only for instructors teaching consecutive years). But remember, spring break is very crowded because everyone in China travels at that time.

When traveling you'll see, if you haven't before, how the other half of foreigners in China live, the tourists ignorant of *waibans* and bucket-and-scoop showers who are ferried about by the China International Travel Service (CITS). You may envy them; one teacher from Jinan scrawled in despair "if I had it all to do over again, I'd see China in three weeks on one of those air-conditioned cruises." Just remember: those folks may not have to deal with cold-water showers, but neither will they drink *mao tai* in the moonlight with their students on a hillside. We all have our own goals in life.

While traveling, you can mix and match lifestyles as well. Most foreign teachers and students, especially those living within their China earnings, travel the way middle-class Chinese do, which means trains, dorms, and the public bus. Using your White Card, it's possible to see China on US$6 or $7 a day. But remember you're on vacation, not an endurance contest. When you tire of Chinese-style travel you can always pay for planes, nice hotels, or air-conditioned tour vans. Bring extra cash so you can treat yourself to a private room now and again.

Some foreigners even invite along a Chinese companion when they travel, from among their students, teachers, *waiban* personnel, or class-mates. A Chinese travel companion can negotiate for hotels and tickets; you may end up saving money even after paying the companion's travel expenses. Be careful, however; register any Chinese travel companions with your *waiban*, and get an official *waiban* letter introducing the Chinese person as your tour guide. It's also best not to share hotel rooms with a Chinese person you're not married to. In the case of opposite-sex travel companions, you can't; Chinese hotels check Chinese peoples' marriage licenses.

Tickets

Travel tickets, whether train, plane, bus, or boat, are a hassle to get in China. No computers link nationwide systems for ground transport. The only way to buy round-trip or connecting tickets is to get a package tour. CITS no longer has a monopoly, though, and many good local agencies provide quite reasonable packages. These can be well worth the hassle saved. Ask local friends for recommendations. Plan trips early. Many more Chinese want to travel than Chinese transportation has seats for, especially at Spring Festival time. Consider seeing fewer cities in more depth, especially if you're not on a package; city-hopping without a package tour can be very stressful.

If you travel without a package tour, you'll need to buy tickets in each city to the next stop on your tour. Depending on relations and his or her prestige, your *waiban* may be able to arrange connecting tickets using *guanxi*, getting people in the cities you'll visit to wait in line for you. That way you can make detailed plans ahead. Otherwise, as soon as you arrive in each city, get in line for your ongoing ticket and plan your sight-seeing only when you know how many days till you leave.

Chinese ticket classes are as follows:

Air

Domestic Chinese air travel, except between a few coastal cities, is monopolized by the Civil Aviation Association of China (CAAC). Baby-CAAC airlines generally have original names like "China Eastern Air-lines" and "China Southern Airlines." The baby-CAACs offer First Class and Coach seats and, aside from indifferent service, compare with any international airline. Given China's distances, if you want to cover much ground quickly, you'll have to fly. Note that in addition to the baby CAACs, since deregulation, China has added many airlines, run at city or provincial level. It is, by and large, these airlines that have given China the world's worst air safety record. One, Air Urumqi, was shut down after its fourth crash in five months. Proceed with caution. Unfortunately, though a few foreign airlines (United, Cathay, etc.) run flights between major coastal cities, tickets on those flights can <u>only</u> be sold as part of an international journey. Airfares have shot up in recent years; at last check, a one-way flight from Beijing to Urumqi was 3,750 yuan RMB, even with a White Card, and climbing. The same trip via train costs 175 yuan, but took five days. CAAC hawks tickets at airports and at downtown ticket offices.

Trains

Slow as they are, trains are the travel mode of choice for most students and teachers, allowing countryside viewing at a stately pace. Chinese trains offer the following five classes of service. Because train trips can last several days, choosing a class merits serious thought.

1. SOFT SLEEPER cars hold 10 to 12 rooms, each containing four berths with mattresses, sheets, blankets, quilts, a small table, thermoses of hot water, and a private luggage rack. Only in Soft Sleepers can doors lock and the train announcements be shut off. Also, Soft Sleeper companions will either be other foreigners or Party cadres, frequently with incomprehensible accents. At last check, a Soft Sleeper berth from Qingdao to Beijing costs 350 yuan RMB with White Card.

2. HARD SLEEPER cars hold 18 to 20 rows of padded bunks in three tiers, arranged perpendicularly to one wall with tables between rows, while a narrow aisle with fold-down chairs runs along the other wall. Hard Sleeper berths include sheets, blankets, and no privacy, but unless your neighbors chain smoke or yell all night, Hard Sleeper is quite pleasant. Most teachers and students try for Hard Sleeper tickets. At last check, a Hard Sleeper berth from Qingdao to Beijing costs 240 yuan RMB with White Card.

3. HARD SEAT cars contain thinly padded benches surrounding large plywood tables, chickens hanging from the luggage racks, squatters stuffed in the aisles, and much misery. During the day Hard Seat is merely loud and filthy. At night it can be unbearable. Hard Seat, Qingdao-Beijing, costs 80 yuan RMB with White Card.

4. HARD STAND—see under Boats.

Buying train tickets involves advanced *guanxi* maneuvering. Some train stations offer foreigners-only windows; you may or may not get

White Card rates there. CITS also often has ticket offices, which sell tickets only days in advance with service fees. Otherwise, it's the huge lines at the general windows, the scalpers outside, or boarding without a ticket. Should you brave the general windows, find out which to wait at before you step in line; some cities sell Soft and Hard classes, or same-day and advance tickets, at different addresses. Also be careful: theft at train stations has shot up. Should you board without a ticket, bustle past the ticket collector muttering *shang che bu piao* ("I'll buy it on the train"), and then run—don't walk—to the on-train ticket stand (usually in car #8), proffer cigarettes, and start haggling for a sleeper berth. We recommend this last method for over night trips only for the daring with solid Chinese-language abilities, or for the desperate. For day trips, bring a tiny folding bamboo stool. Sitting on one in the space between cars can be quite bearable.

Buses

Long-distance Chinese buses are rattly, smoke-choked affairs best avoided except for trips to places accessible only by bus. Most buses leave from train stations on an irregular schedule (as soon as they have enough passengers); buy tickets at a ticket window near the bus stop or from the driver.

Boats

Passenger boats ply China's rivers and seacoast offering stately travel for those not in a rush. Riverboats sell six classes of tickets. First Class is rarely sold, consisting of one or two luxury staterooms reserved for VIPs. 2nd Class staterooms contain two curtained beds with mattresses, linens and quilts, maid service, and thermoses of hot water. First and Second classes contain foreigners and cadres only, for the most part. Third Class staterooms offer five bunks, heat, and a private sink; Fourth Class, eight bunks, no heat, and no sink; and Fifth Class, tiers of bunks massed in the boiler room and no linens. Most teachers and students try for third or fourth Class. Sixth Class, or *sanxipiao* (散票) ("loose seating"), like Hard Stand on the trains, is a class created for people who need to travel but have no money. For token fares poor Chinese travelers can squat in unheated freight cars on the trains and in the stairwells and aisles of the boats. Chinese will not sell Hard Stand or *sanxi* tickets to foreigners, and believe us, you wouldn't want them anyway.

Ocean boat classes are the same as riverboats, except that fifth Class gets linens and there is no sixth Class.

Room and Board

Use your vacation travel to sample China's culinary varieties. As in most countries, hotel restaurants offer the blandest fare. Get out into the neighborhoods and eat like the locals. But remember the safety cautions in Chapter 6 under "Hygiene." Hotels in China range from five-star joint ventures with five-star prices to hostels. Generally, only the better hotels accept foreigners. Most joint-venture hotels don't accept White Cards, but Chinese hotels do; you're entitled to pay RMB at Chinese rate. Some hotel managers will deny this; how much you care to argue depends on your personal balance between blood pressure and finance.

Most cities have at least one budget-rate hotel that accepts foreigners and offers spartan rooms and/or dorms; get a good tourist guidebook for advice (see Appendix B for suggestions). Your *waiban* may also be able to arrange stays in school dorms. Even without specific arrangements, try to get a general letter of introduction from your *waiban* when you travel; other *waibans* will often allow you in based on such a letter. School dorms usually offer cheap, clean rooms and access to other facilities, such as bicycles. In some relaxed cities you can also stay in any inn. The best way to find out is just to march up and ask for a room. If the innkeeper accepts you, it's fine.

SHOPPING

China offers unparalleled shopping opportunities for purchasers of knick-knacks, handicrafts, and cheap consumer goods. Shopping in Taiwan is much like shopping in the West. The basic types of mainland shopping are as follows:

Department Stores

Department stores are large, government-run stores selling consumer goods and occasionally handicrafts. They're usually the best place to start looking for things, as prices are fixed and low. Note that the "departments" are hardly as clearly separated as in the West; tea kettles may be next to tape recorders. Also, in all but the most expensive stores, most goods are kept on shelves or behind glass counters; you have to ask service people to see things, and most speak no English. In many stores you'll buy tickets for items at one counter and pay at another; in some cases you may need to wait some time to pick up the goods. For large-ticket items, ask a Chinese friend for help.

Government Food Stores

State food stores are the culinary equivalent of department stores. Once again, because prices are cheap and fixed, they are the best places to start looking for things. We found staples, spices, canned goods, and, when available, fresh produce tended to be great buys at state food stores, but their meat was moldy a bit too often for our tastes.

Small Stores

Many small stores crowd China's streets, hawking everything from eggs to auto parts. Some are public, some are run by *danwei* cooperatives, and some are private. You can usually tell the first two because the workers will be wearing those little white caps. Prices at public stores are fixed. Private stores invite haggling. Prices at small stores tend to be higher than at the large state stores, but selections are often better, and hours more convenient.

Freemarkets

Since economic reform, private peddlers have been able to set up stalls at neighborhood markets throughout China. Most cities also have at least one large central freemarket and, by now, usually one in every neighborhood of any size as well. Freemarket size is arguably the best measure of current government tolerance for liberalization. For the foreseeable future, freemarkets will continue to thrive, as even during the 1989 crackdown the leadership stressed the sanctity of economic reform.

Freemarkets are wheeling, dealing, open air markets full of pig farmers selling porkers from baskets slung on the backs of their bikes, old women hawking embroidery, and young men touting electronic gewgaws. Freemarkets have the best variety of goods in China, the freshest foods (farmers come daily to the freemarkets, and, in the better ones give discounts on day-old eggs!), and the widest price range. Always check prices in state stores first to get some idea of what you should pay. Expect to pay 30–50% more in the freemarket than you would in a state store, though in some cases, freemarket prices may be at or below state levels. But don't get suckered in by what we call the "foreigner tax." Many freemarket sellers see foreigners as marks, and that 18-yuan sweater will suddenly cost 128 yuan when you ask the price. Learn to haggle, or bring a Chinese friend who is adept at bargaining.

Also, beware of freemarket antique stands. Fakes are increasingly common. Then too, by law all antiques must be inspected by the government, and only those not classed as "national treasures" may be exported. In practice, this means that virtually all goods over 120 years old, and many newer high quality goods, are illegal exports. The only legal place to buy exportable antiques is at state antique stores, where you'll pay a hefty surcharge for that red wax seal on the bottom which satisfies customs. You can try your luck smuggling out freemarket purchases, but customs has the right to confiscate anything they find which even looks old but has no seal. Some unscrupulous peddlers, in fact, work hand-in-glove with customs, bribing corrupt officials for confiscated items, which they then resell to other foreigners.

Friendship Stores

Friendship Stores are large state stores selling items of particular interest to foreigners, from handicrafts to export-only goods. They are generally pricier than regular state department stores, and if you can find comparable items, better buy them at department stores. Some Friendship Stores are open to Chinese, others to foreigners only; some may or may not accept White Cards. Larger cities may also offer state "Arts and Crafts" stores and "Antique" stores.

MOONLIGHTING

Living in China offers many chances to further your professional goals. Don't neglect these opportunities.

Writers can publish articles in both Chinese and foreign periodicals; work as stringers for Western news agencies; update tourist guidebooks and business directories, or plug China experiences into first novels. Writing requires no special permission from your *waiban*; be sensitive, however. Never transmit politically sensitive material using school equipment or use the real names of any Chinese people you know in your writing, particularly in sensitive contexts.

Many Chinese companies need foreigners to check English-language technical documents or promotional literature; to help with videotapes; or to do part-time translation. Check with your *waiban* before doing any paid work for an outside *danwei*, as some schools and programs have restrictions.

Foreign companies also often need extra help with translation, writing, sales, research, and many other areas. Resident foreigners in China who appear with resume in hand can often pick up lucrative and interesting part-time jobs that the company couldn't justify relocating a full-time employee for. Some foreigners have found this sort of part-time work led later to full-time careers.

So long as your outside activities don't interfere with your schoolwork, most *waibans* will be very supportive. A happy foreigner means a good working relationship, for them as well as you.

Leaving:
Fruitful Farewells

"I wish my mother lived in a trailer park," survey respondent John Weston bemoaned. "Everything I could buy as a gift or receive as a gift would find a fitting home." As your time to leave China draws near, friends will load you down with pink plastic poodle tumblers, mass-produced ceramic horses, and machine-embroidered rayon wall-hangings featuring scenes from Suzhou.

Take it all as a tribute to international friendship and to the relationships you've developed. And remember: it's not that they have no taste, it's just that they have no money. Your students probably spent a lot of time selecting that puce-and-mauve ashtray, so accept it graciously. Years from now you may still be displaying it proudly as a war trophy.

Aside from how to thank the donor of your third machine-made tricolor horse, many factors will occupy your time and mind in your last days in China, from shipping and routes home to saying your goodbyes. Pay these last-minute activities the attention they deserve. To paraphrase the old saw, "you never get a second chance on a last impression." It's easy in the rush of things to get argumentative about promises not met or to "forget" to say goodbye to a troublesome *waiban* official. In the end, though, the taint on your memories won't be worth it. Take the time to do it right; you'll feel better in the long run.

And remember to leave room in your bags for the pink poodle tumblers.

1. SHIPPING. Depending on the wealth of your material goods, your best bet is probably sea shipment. China's post office is

expensive, slow, and notorious about loss and breakage. Air shipment is both pricey and restrictive. And given the difficulty of transfers in China, you'll not want to carry much with you. Instead, your *waiban* and/or Chinese friends can help you arrange for sea shipment. A one–cubic-meter crate (which your *waiban* can probably get made for free, though you may be charged for it) costs approximately US$150 to ship to North America regardless of weight (less to New Zealand or Australia and more to Europe); many *waibans* will ship for free as part of the foreigner's benefits. You can pack a good-sized apartmentful of goods into a cubic meter, and it'll arrive at your home seaport about two months later.

Remember to pack tightly with plenty of padding; most breakage in sea shipment occur from jostling within the crates. Close and ship off your crate as late as possible so as to have room for those last-minute gifts (surely you have a cousin living in a trailer park somewhere who'll appreciate the rayon wall-hangings). Add liberal amounts of mothballs and desiccants to the crate to protect against shipboard rats and salt spray. And if you've room left in your crate, see it as an opportunity to spend those extra unconvertible RMB. Many items you may have come to take for granted in your Chinese life would make fine additions to your home or excellent gifts, such as woks and other Chinese cookware, those surprisingly effective Chinese thermoses, bicycles, and handicrafts from the Friendship Store.

Customs in your home country will unlikely charge duty on gifts or items for personal use. One exception is any new luxury items, such as hand-loomed carpets or expensive jewelry. For this reason, buy any luxury items early, use them in China, and import them as used goods.

Actually, even commercial importation on a small scale is remarkably easy. In the U.S. any commercial goods bought for less than $1,800 in total can be imported "informally," with a standard 10% duty rate and minimal inspection. One enterprising college student filled the space left in her crate with silk scarves and resold them in her college's dining hall for enough to pay for her next China trip.

2. TRAVEL HOME. Be as specific as you can as to your travel plans, especially if the Chinese institution will buy your ticket home. If you request early, for example, they may be able to route you

with a stopover in, say, Tokyo or Singapore. But once tickets have been bought, adding stopovers ranges from the expensive to the impossible. If you plan extensive travel in Asia before going home, best fly out of Hong Kong. Arrange for a lengthy Hong Kong stopover, then buy bargain Asian airfares there, and return to Hong Kong for your flight home. If you plan to leave via one of the more exotic routes, overland through Pakistan, Nepal, or Russia, best travel very light and consult early and often with your *waiban* and a good travel guidebook (see Appendix B). Trans-Siberian railroad fares can be bought from other foreigners at cheap hotels in Beijing, or from CITS.

3. BUSINESS CONTACTS. Make the rounds of anyone you've done any moonlighting for, especially if you hope for more work from them in the future. Leave them with your business card, memories perhaps of a farewell banquet, and some idea of how you can continue to serve them from your home country. One foreign teacher we know set up contacts before leaving China with several export trade companies, and started a thriving import business at home.

4. GOODBYES. If you can, try to leave a week or so between your final exams or when grades are due and your flight out. Your school will likely give at least one farewell banquet for all foreign teachers and/or students, and many other friends will want to invite you out. At farewell banquets you'll probably be asked for your overall impressions of your time in China. Remember this is a pro-forma question, and not the time for you to remind the *waiban* that the heat was never hooked up in your room. Chinese put great store on face and smooth impressions. Whatever has gone before, try to leave on good terms.

You should also do something for your Chinese friends. Take time to go round with gifts for all your friends and for those who have done things for you (yes, even the ones you didn't get along with); by now you should understand what we mean by "leave your *guanxi* balance sheets even." Go and talk with anyone you may have crossed swords with and be sure all is, at least on the surface, forgiven. You might also consider putting on farewell banquets of your own, either in a restaurant (expensive), or at your home (you can always hire in a chef if your own culinary skills rank low: about 30 yuan RMB/hour or 15 yuan RMB/hour for an assistant would be a generous amount for the service).

Even if you think you'll never go to China again, your Chinese contacts can be useful, sending you handicrafts or meeting your Aunt Jane at the airport when she goes to Beijing. Then too, however you feel now, you may just start hankering for China again someday. You'll want to have folks there feel able to welcome you home.

List of Schools by Province

This directory lists all schools in the PRC, followed by schools in Taiwan, that accept foreigners as teachers and/or students. The information in this directory was gathered from a variety of sources. Our starting points were 2 directories/atlases of education in China published in Chinese by the PRC government, and a directory, Higher Education in the ROC, published in English by Taiwan's government. We translated the PRC directories and reorganized information from the Taiwan directory, then cross-checked our data with U.S. Department of Education information. We then sent out surveys to each of the schools listed asking for updates and new information. Responses varied, and so accordingly does the amount of information in each listing. Wherever information in a directory listing appears in quotation marks, it is a direct quote from a survey respondent; we include these tidbits for flavor, with the proviso that they represent the views of individual respondents and not necessarily those of the authors.

The PRC portion of the directory is arranged in alphabetical order of province, and schools within each province are grouped by type of school: University, Minorities/Politics and Law, Arts/Music, Finance/Commerce/Economics, Foreign Languages, Normal, Medical, and Technical. Please note that schools are also cross-referenced in Appendix D by lists of Key Universities. Key Universities are noted throughout the directory by an asterisk (*).

ANHUI — Most famous as home of Huang Shan, China's most often-painted mountain, Anhui is also a newly developed industrial region, with production at the capital Hefei having increased by a factor of more than 10,000 since 1949. The provincial museum at Hefei also features archeological and artistic treasures from throughout the region. Foreign residents in Anqing and Wuhu, along with unparalleled opportunities for climbing Huang Shan, have been able to study with local monks. Language is fairly heavily accented Mandarin, weather temperate, and food bland but rich in produce.

UNIVERSITIES

Anhui University*
Responsible Bureau: Provincial Education Administration
Departments: Radio Technology, Chinese, History, Philosophy, Foreign Languages, Library Science, Mathematics, Computer Science, Physics, Biology, Economics, Law
Teachers: can teach English, Western Culture

Anhui University, cont'd
Students: growing program in Chinese Language/Culture
Contact: Foreign Affairs Office, Anhui University, Hezuohua Rd., Hefei, Anhui PRC
URL: (in Chinese only) http://www.seu.edu.cn/EC/ah614.htm

Bengbu Unified University
Responsible Bureau: City Government
Departments: Textile Dye Arts, Inorganic Industrial Chemistry, Agricultural Construction, Secretarial Science, Management, Statistics, Packaging
Contact: Foreign Affairs Office, Bengbu Unified University, Dongfengsi St., Bengbu, Anhui PRC

China University of Science and Technology*
Responsible Bureau: State Department of Science
Departments: High Temperature Physics Engineering, RadioTechnology, Systems Science, Computer Science, Precision Mechanics, Mathematics, Physics, Chemistry, Power Studies, Earth and Atmospheric Sciences, Biology
Teachers: Key University w/ good science facilities; can teach English, technical subjects
Contact: Foreign Affairs Office, China University of Science and Technology, Jinzhai Rd., Hefei, Anhui 230026 PRC

Hefei Unified University
Responsible Bureau: Provincial Education Administration
Departments: Management, Finance and Accounting, Taxation, Mechanical Electronics, Environmental Studies and Industrial Chemistry, Information Science, Architecture, Chinese, Foreign Languages, Economics, Experimental Technology, Applied Microbiology
Contact: Foreign Affairs Office, Hefei Unified University, Huangshan Rd., Hefei, Anhui PRC

Huainan Unified University
Responsible Bureau: City Government
Departments: Radiation, Industrial Chemistry, Agricultural Construction, Secretarial Science, Management, Statistics, Packaging
Contact: Foreign Affairs Office, Huainan Unified University, Tianjiaxiang, Huainan, Anhui PRC

Ma'anshan Unified University
Responsible Bureau: City Government
Departments: Mechanics, Computer Science, Agricultural Construction, Chinese, Industrial Management, Accounting
Contact: Foreign Affairs Office, Ma'anshan Unified University, Ma'anshan, Anhui PRC

Wuhu Unity University
Responsible Bureau: City Government
Departments: Mechanics, Management, Agricultural Construction, Farming Technology, Geology, English, Secretarial Sciences, History, Finance, Accounting
Contact: Foreign Affairs Office, Wuhu Unity University, Zhuangyuanfang, Wuhu, Anhui PRC

FINANCE/ECONOMICS

Anhui Institute of Finance and Trade
Responsible Bureau: Ministry of Commerce
Departments: Commercial Economics, Statistics, Finance, Commercial Goods, Cotton Processing
Contact: Foreign Affairs Office, Anhui Institute of Finance and Trade, Hongye Village, Bengbu, Anhui PRC

FOREIGN LANGUAGES

Hefei Foreign Language Technical Institute
Responsible Bureau: Provincial "93 Studies" Society
Departments: English, Japanese
Contact: Foreign Affairs Office, Hefei Foreign Language Technical Institute, Dongchengang, Hefei, Anhui PRC

NORMAL SCHOOLS

Anhui Normal University
Responsible Bureau: State Education Commission/Provincial Government
Departments: Education, Politics, Chinese, History, Geology, Biology, Mathematics, Physics, Chemistry, Physical Education, Art, Music, Foreign Languages, Experimental Physics, Environmental Protection
Sister School: Germany—Univ of Osnabrück
Contact: Foreign Affairs Office, Anhui Normal University, Wuhu, Anhui PRC

Anqing Normal School
Responsible Bureau: Provincial Education Administration
Departments: Political Education, Chinese, History, Mathematics, Physics, Chemistry, English, Biological Pharmacological Production
Contact: Foreign Affairs Office, Anqing Normal School, Linghu S. Rd., Anqing, Anhui PRC

Fuyang Normal School
Responsible Bureau: Provincial Education Administration
Departments: Political Education, Chinese, Mathematics, Physics, Chemistry, Industrial Arts, Foreign Languages
Contact: Foreign Affairs Office, Fuyang Normal School, Xiqinghe, Fuyang, Anhui PRC

Huaibei Mining Normal School
Responsible Bureau: Ministry of Coal Mining
Departments: Political Education, Chinese, Mathematics, Physics, Chemistry, Physical Education, Arts, English
Contact: Foreign Affairs Office, Huaibei Mining Normal School, Huaibei, Anhui PRC

MEDICAL SCHOOLS

Anhui College of Chinese Medicine
Responsible Bureau: Provincial Administration of Sanitation and Hygiene
Departments: Chinese Medicine, Acupuncture, Chinese Pharmacology
Contact: Foreign Affairs Office, Anhui College of Chinese Medicine, Meishan Rd., Hefei, Anhui PRC

Anhui College of Medicine
Responsible Bureau: Provincial Administration of Sanitation and Hygiene
Departments: Medicine, Oral Medicine, Sanitation and Hygiene, Management
Contact: Foreign Affairs Office, Anhui College of Medicine, Meishan Rd., Hefei, Anhui PRC

TECHNICAL SCHOOLS

Anhui Institute of Agriculture
Responsible Bureau: Provincial Education Administration
Departments: Veterinary Medicine, Gardening, Forestry, Agricultural Science, Crop Protection, Silkworm and Mulberry Cultivation, Agricultural Mechanics, Agricultural Economics
Contact: Foreign Affairs Office, Anhui Institute of Agriculture, Shushan Rd., Hefei, Anhui PRC

Anhui Institute of Mechanical Electronics
Responsible Bureau: Provincial Education Administration
Departments: Mechanics, Electrical Equipment, Nutrition, Textiles, Industrial Arts
Contact: Foreign Affairs Office, Anhui Institute of Mechanical Electronics, Jihe Rd., Wuhu, Anhui PRC

Anhui Polytechnical University*
Responsible Bureau: Ministry of Mechanics
Departments: Mechanical Production, Power Production Mechanics, Electrical Equipment, Management
Contact: Foreign Affairs Office, Anhui Polytechnical University, Liu'an Rd., Hefei, Anhui PRC

Bengbu Medical College
Responsible Bureau: Provincial Administration of Sanitation and Hygiene
Departments: Medicine, Medical Examination
Contact: Foreign Affairs Office, Bengbu Medical College, 108 Zhihuai Rd., Bengbu, Anhui PRC

Hefei Institute of Technology
Responsible Bureau: Ministry of Mechanics
Departments: Geology, Electrical Equipment, Industrial Chemical Material, Mechanics, Precision Timing Equipment, Management, Computer Science, Architecture, Civil Engineering, Physics
Contact: Foreign Affairs Office, Hefei Institute of Technology, Tunxi Rd., Hefei, Anhui PRC

Huainan Institute of Mining
Responsible Bureau: Ministry of Coal Mining
Departments: Geology, Materials and Mining, Mechanical Electronics, Industrial Chemistry
Contact: Foreign Affairs Office, Huainan Institute of Mining, Dongshan, Huainan, Zhejiang PRC

Ma'anshan Institute of Steel
Responsible Bureau: Ministry of Industrial Metals
Departments: Industrial Metals, Industrial Chemistry, Mechanics, Industrial Automation, Economic Management
Contact: Foreign Affairs Office, Ma'anshan Institute of Steel, Hudong Rd., Ma'anshan, Anhui, PRC

University of Science and Technology of China
Responsible Bureau: Chinese Academy of Sciences
Departments: Mathematics, Physics, Chemical Physics, Modern Physics, Modern Machines, Biology, Precision Machinery & Instrumentation, Automation, Computer Science and Technology, Applied Chemistry, Thermal Science & Energy Engineering, Materials Science and Engineering, School of Business
Chinese Students: 7,000   **Foreign Students:** 80
Foreign Teachers: 8   **Sister Schools:** 28
Teacher Salary/Benefits: USD$200-300/month   **Teaching Conditions:** 12-16 hrs/wk
Contact: Shi Wenfang, Foreign Affairs Office, University of Science and Technology of China, Hefei, Anhui 230026 PRC
∎ **Phone:** (86-551) 360-2847   **Fax:** (86-551) 363-2579
e-mail: lao@USTC.ac.cn

BEIJING — Capital of the PRC, second largest city, political and cultural hub of the Chinese universe, Beijing is a world unto itself. No other city in China comes close to the capital's cultural and historical treasures, or to the access the city provides to the halls of power. The Imperial Palace, the Great Wall, Tiananmen Square, the Summer Palace, the Temple of Heaven, the nation's greatest museums—the list of attractions goes on. Beijing also offers nightly cultural performances, and the opportunity to visit the Great Hall of the People (home of China's legislative branch) and other government organs. All the cuisines of China are featured in the capital restaurants, as are all traveling cultural troupes.

By one government official's estimate, nearly 50% of all resident foreigners in China live in Beijing. This means several things, of course: competition is fierce, and foreigners are nothing special in Beijing, will get precious little support for any independent projects they may conceive, and will be herded and watched precisely because they are so close to the government's power. Very discreet, clever, and motivated foreign residents have gained unparelleled access to research and governmental facilities in Beijing; one longtime British resident reportedly tutors central leaders inside the fortresslike compound at Zhongnanhai. For many, however, living in the capital means more of a headache than it's worth. "I feel like in a year here I've learned nothing of China," complained one student. "It's like trying to learn about the American Southwest from D.C., or the Scottish Highlands from London. China is somewhere else."

But Beijing remains one of the world's great cities, capital for 7 centuries of the world's most enduring nation. Weather is abominable, furnace-like and polluted in summer, harshly dry and windy in winter. Language, while standard Mandarin, bears the acrid nasal "r's" of the Beijing accent. But Beijing remains the capital, and the fact that foreigners still pour in to view her treasures is ample proof for Chinese of her continuing status as center of the central kingdom of the world.

UNIVERSITIES

Beifang Transportation University*
Responsible Bureau: Ministry of Railroads
Departments: Mechanics, Computer Science, Agricultural Construction, Shipping, Economics, Communications Control, Materials
Sister Schools: 5 in US and Germany
Contact: Foreign Affairs Office, Beifang Transportation University, Xizhimenwai, Beijing PRC

Beijing Unified University
Responsible Bureau: Beijing City Higher Education Bureau
Departments: Mechanical Engineering, Light Industry, Finance, Foreign Languages, Humanities, Medicine, Radio Electronics
Contact: Foreign Affairs Office, Beijing Unified University, Haidian District, Beijing PRC

Beijing University* (Peking University)
Responsible Bureau: State Education Committee
Departments: Mathematics, Physics, Engineering, Applied Physics, Geophysics, Radiology, Computer Science, Chemistry, Geology, Sociology, Japanese, Russian, Western Languages, Psychology, Library Science, Geography, Economics, Law, International Politics, Chinese, History, Archaeology, Philosophy
Sister Schools: over 50 in over 20 countries
Accommodations: small, but pretty; 2-3 rms in old bldg, w/ cooking facilities, TV, tape recorder, bike (students 2/rm, no cooking facilities); strict curfew, and visitors strongly discouraged; in walled compound, isolated from Chinese students, at edge of lovely but huge campus
Teaching Conditions: 10-16 hrs/wk; excellent language lab and library, but student access limited; Beijing Univ is China's most prestigious university
Student Tuition/Expenses: variable; many students are enrolled through home-country universities
Contact: Office of International Scholars & Students, Peking University, Beijing, 100871, PRC
■ **Phone:** (86-10) 62751243, 627512422, 62751246, or 62751247
URL: http://www.pku.edu.cn

Beijing Polytechnic University*
Responsible Bureau: City Higher Education Bureau
Departments: Mechanics, Radio Engineering, Agricultural Construction, Environmental Chemistry, Computer Science, Automation, High Temperature Engineering, Metallurgy
Contact: Foreign Affairs Office, Beijing University of Technology, PO Box 327, Eastern Suburbs, Beijing PRC

Chinese People's University (Renda)*
Responsible Bureau: State Education Committee
Departments: Languages and Literatures, Journalism, History, Philosophy, File Management, International Politics, Party History, Population Studies, Scientific Socialism, Finance, Political Law, Trade, Economic Information, Planning, Statistics
Accommodations: not bad, but free agent can't use shared kitchen facilities
Teaching Conditions: "classes tend to be gargantuan," sometimes 90 students to a

class, "which makes conversation class a logistical impossibility"; students "great
. . . very motivated"; most classes language, some liberal arts, teacher training;
this year's batch of freshmen "are like nothing anyone at this university has ever
seen before: very outgoing and energetic . . . everyone is amazed"
Contact: Foreign Affairs Office, Chinese People's University (Renda), Haidian
District, Beijing PRC

Qinghua University* (Tsinghua University)
Responsible Bureau: State Education Committee
Departments: Agricultural Construction, Mechanical Engineering, Power
Production, Radio Electronics, Computer Science, Automation, Hydrology, High
Temperature Engineering, Precision Equipment Engineering, Electronics, Chemical
Engineering, Physical Engineering, Power Engineering, Economic Management,
Applied Mathematics, Physics, Foreign Languages, Foreign Literatures
Foreign Experts: over 231 foreign experts in 1996 - 22 long term, 209 short term,
coming from 18 countries and regions
Accommodations: 2-3 rms in foreigner compound, w/ shared kitchen and fridge
but no stove; cafeteria food poor—also have separate dining hall for foreign teach-
ers; reasonably lax visitor registration
Teaching Conditions: approx 12 hrs/wk, but "school then tries to lure you, later,
into teaching more classes which are so interesting they're 'hard to refuse'";
school also arranges, for minimal fees, tutoring in Chinese Language, Painting,
Martial Arts, etc.
Student Tuition/Expenses: varied; many students are from developing nations on
Chinese gov't scholarships
Learning Conditions: good variety of classes
Sister Schools: 72 universities of 22 countries and regions of the world
Contact: Foreign Affairs Office, Center for Overseas Academic & Cultural Ex-
changes, Qinghua University, Haidian District, Beijing PRC
∎ **Phone:** (Foreign Student Office) (86-10) 62784621
URL: http://www.tsinghua.edu.cn/

MINORITIES/POLITICS & LAW

Central Minorities Institute
Responsible Bureau: National Committee of Minorities
Departments: Chinese, Minority Languages, History, Minority Studies, Politics,
Music, Dance, Art, Mathematical Physics
Contact: Foreign Affairs Office, Central Minorities Institute, Haidian District,
Beijing PRC

Chinese People's University of Police and Security
Responsible Bureau: Ministry of Public Security
Departments: Chinese, Journalism, English, Asian and European Languages,
Science and Technology, Police Protection and Safety
Foreign Teachers: 3
Accommodations: excellent; 5-1/2 rms, w/ washer, TV, tape recorder, fridge, cook-
ing facilities, use of car and driver once weekly to Beijing (campus 45 min by car
from Beijing, 1-1/2 hrs by public bus); no curfew, relaxed about visitors and guests
Teaching Conditions: 16 hrs/wk; great language lab; good videos; secretarial assistance, but photocopies discouraged; library: good recent foreign newspapers and
magazines, but back copies sold and only limited access for students; plenty of
books in stacks but due to uncooperative librarians students are usually not able

to check them out—"basically the books are being held prisoner"
Contact: Foreign Affairs Office, Chinese People's University of Police and Security, Daxing County, Beijing PRC

Chinese People's University of Public Security
Responsible Bureau: Ministry of Public Security
Departments: Public Security Management, Law, Intelligence, Security, Protection, Political Work
Contact: Foreign Affairs Office, Chinese People's University of Public Security, Fuxingmenwai, Beijing PRC

Chinese University of Politics and Law
Responsible Bureau: Ministry of Justice
Departments: Law, Economic Law, Politics
Contact: Foreign Affairs Office, Chinese University of Politics and Law, Haidian District, Beijing PRC

College of Foreign Affairs and Diplomacy
Responsible Bureau: Ministry of Diplomacy
Departments: Diplomacy, Foreign Affairs
Accommodations: "great"; 2 rms for teachers, 1 for students, w/ washer, TV, kitchen; central location and very relaxed about visitor registration
Teaching Conditions: not bad; 12-14 hrs/wk, great language lab and "fair" library; classes in English, Japanese, and French; school trains diplomats, so experienced teachers are a must; school has excellent library and film-showing facilities
Contact: Foreign Affairs Office, Institute of Diplomacy, Xicheng District, Beijing PRC

Institute of International Relations
Responsible Bureau: State Education Committee
Departments: Chinese, Journalism, English, Japanese, French, International Economics
Teaching Conditions: institute trains many of China's diplomats; students are all children of high-ranking officials. Institute screens foreign teachers very carefully and is extremely strict, especially about contact w/ students. Foreign teachers are barred from living on campus; live instead in Friendship Hotel and are picked up each day for class; "no fraternizing with students is allowed"
Contact: Foreign Affairs Office, Institute of International Relations, Haidian District, Beijing PRC

ARTS/MUSIC

Beijing Film Academy
Responsible Bureau: Ministry of Culture
Departments: Literature, Directing, Acting, Photography, Art, Recording
Foreign Students: 100
Sister Schools: Australia—Australian Film and Television School, Ryerson Polytechnical Inst
Learning Conditions: High-quality independent film study possible, including with some of China's masters. Some students have done joint programs with NYU or USC film schools.
Student Tuition/Expenses: (1996) USD$1,800 for film classes, USD$900 for Chinese classes

Contact: Foreign Affairs Office, Beijing Film Academy, Xi Tu Cheng Lu 4, Han Dian District, Beijing PRC

Beijing Institute of Dance
Responsible Bureau: Ministry of Culture
Departments: Dance Composition, Dance History, Performance, Ballet
Contact: Foreign Affairs Office, Beijing Institute of Dance, Xuanwu District, Beijing PRC

Central Academy of Fine Arts*
Responsible Bureau: Ministry of Culture
Departments: Chinese Traditional Painting, Oil Painting, Wood Block Painting, Comic Book Painting, Calendar Painting, Sculpture, History of Art
Sister Schools: US—Pennsylvania State Univ, California State Univ; Japan—Tokyo College of Art and Design, Osaka Univ of Arts, Tokyo Univ of Arts; Norway—National School of Arts and Crafts at Oslo; Germany—Academy of Fine Arts at Stuttgart; India—National Inst of Design
Contact: Foreign Affairs Office, Central Academy of Fine Arts, 34 Donghuan North Rd., Dongcheng District, Beijing PRC

Central Conservatory of Music*
Responsible Bureau: Ministry of Culture
Departments: Composition, Piano, Wind Instruments, Chinese Traditional Instruments
Teachers and Students: facilities include 1.3 million vol library; music library with 1.4 million items
Contact: Foreign Affairs Office, Central Conservatory of Music, Xinwenhua St., Beijing PRC

Central Institute of Arts and Handicrafts
Responsible Bureau: Ministry of Light Industry
Departments: Special Arts and Handicrafts, Decorations, Ceramics, Dyes, Fashion Design, Industrial Planning, Interior Decorating, History of Arts and Handicrafts
Contact: Foreign Affairs Office, Central Institute of Arts and Handicrafts, Dong Huan Rd., Beijing PRC

China Conservatory of Music
Responsible Bureau: Ministry of Culture
Departments: Composition, Voice, Instruments, Opera, Musicology, Music Theory, Musical Technology
Sister Schools: Japan—Osaka School of Music; US—Chicago Conservatory of Music; Germany—Heidelberg Univ; Hong Kong—National Minorities School of Music
Teachers: can teach English, Western Culture and Western musical instruments
Students: can join any degree program
Contact: Foreign Affairs Office, China Conservatory of Music, 17 Qianhai West St., Beijing PRC

Chinese Central Institute of Drama/Opera
Responsible Bureau: Ministry of Culture
Departments: Composition, Operatic Culture, Stage Decoration, Acting, Directing
Contact: Foreign Affairs Office, Chinese Institute of Drama/Opera, Xuanwu District, Bejing PRC

Chinese Institute of Traditional Opera
Responsible Bureau: Ministry of Culture
Departments: Operatic Culture, Acting, Stage Decorating
Contact: Foreign Affairs Office, Chinese Institute of Traditional Opera, Dongcheng District, Beijing PRC

FINANCE/COMMERCE/ECONOMICS

Beijing Institute of Commerce
Responsible Bureau: Ministry of Commerce
Departments: Commercial Economics, Management, Accounting, Statistical Planning, Storage and Shipment
Teachers and Students: facilities include 300,000 vol library with 6,000 foreign language vols
Contact: Foreign Affairs Office, Beijing Institute of Commerce, 11 Fu Cheng Rd., Haidian District, Beijing PRC

Beijing Institute of Consumer Goods
Responsible Bureau: National Bureau of Consumer Goods
Departments: Consumer Goods Management, Finance and Accounting, Labor Economics
Contact: Foreign Affairs Office, Beijing Institute of Consumer Goods, Tong County, Beijing PRC

Beijing Institute of Economics
Responsible Bureau: City Bureau of Higher Education
Departments: Industrial Economics, Statistics, Labor Economics, Foreign Trade Economics, Finance and Accounting, Economics, Management, Security, Economic Mathematics
Contact: Foreign Affairs Office, Beijing Institute of Economics, Chaoyangmenwai, Beijing PRC

Beijing Institute of Finance and Trade
Responsible Bureau: City Bureau of Higher Education
Departments: Management, Accounting, Finance, Financial Management, Commercial Economics
Contact: Foreign Affairs Office, Beijing Institute of Finance and Trade, 68 Zao Ling Front Street, Xuanwu District, Beijing PRC

Central Institute of Finance and Economic Policy
Responsible Bureau: Ministry of Finance
Departments: Economic Planning, Finance, Accounting, Economic Management, Economics of Basic Construction
Contact: Foreign Affairs Office, Central Institute of Finance and Economic Policy, Xizhimenwai, Beijing PRC

University of International Business and Economics
Responsible Bureau: Ministry of Foreign Economic Relations and Trade
Departments: Foreign Trade Management, Foreign Languages, Foreign Trade, Customs Management, International Economic Cooperation, Economic Law
Foreign Students: several hundred enroll in different programs of study coordinated and conducted by the Department of Foreign Studies
Foreign Teachers: more than 30

Sister Schools: more than 100 institutions of higher learning and research in over 20 countries and areas, including the US, Canada, Japan, France, Britain, Germany, Italy, Portugal, Hungary, Russian Federation, Holland, Belgium, Yugoslavia, Finland, Poland, Czech, Slovakia, New Zealand, Australia, S. Korea, Headquarters of EEC, Hong Kong, Macao and Taiwan
Teachers: can teach English, Western Culture, technical subjects (business, management, economics); facilities include 2 English-language journals, 1 Japanese journal
Students: small number of students in degree program, but several hundred students on short-term study program of Chinese business and management
Contact: Department of Foreign Studies, P.O. Box 69, University of International Business and Economics (UIBE), Beijing 100029 PRC
∎ **Phone:** (86-10) 492-8099 or 422-552 ext. 2325, 2327 or 2329
Fax: (86-10) 492-8098   **e-mail:** dfsuibe@iuol.cn.net
URL: http://www.izad.com/dfsuibe/

BROADCASTING/FOREIGN LANGUAGES

Beijing Institute of Broadcasting
Responsible Bureau: Ministry of Radio and Television
Departments: Microwave Broadcasting, Radio Technology, Television, News, Cultural Editing, Broadcasting, Foreign Languages
Accommodations: nice; 2 rms for singles, 3 rms married teachers, w/ shared kitchen, relaxed visitor registration; but campus is "in the sticks," 45 mins by bike or bus from town
Contact: Foreign Affairs Office, Beijing Institute of Broadcasting, Chaoyang District, Beijing PRC

Beijing Institute of Languages
Responsible Bureau: State Education Committee
Departments: Foreign Languages, Languages and Literatures
Accommodations: pretty good, "but there are often little problems that take time to straighten out"
Teaching Conditions: "no materials are provided, no curriculum, and a lot of confusion"; can teach English, Literature, Journalism, Writing Skills, American Culture
Learning Conditions: 1st year program "rigid," but courses more flexible in second year
Contact: Foreign Affairs Office, Beijing Institute of Languages, Haidian District, Beijing PRC

Beijing Number 2 Institute of Foreign Languages
Responsible Bureau: National Bureau of Tourism
Departments: English, Slavic Languages, West European Languages, Asian and African Languages, Foreign Economic Cooperation
Foreign Students: 400
Accommodations: "the best living conditions for teachers in China"; large 3-rm apartments w/ kitchen, oven, TV, fridge, a/c, heating, 2 balconies; but campus 45 minutes from town, difficult to get to at night
Teaching Conditions: 8-16 hrs/wk; situations vary; some departments "are completely hands off the teachers, some provide some supervison, some control tightly"; students very bright, but lack ambition because "their job prospects are so dismal"; class size good, 18-20 students
Contact: Foreign Affairs Office, Beijing Number 2 Institute of Foreign Languages, Dingfuzhuang, Chaoyang District, Beijing 100024 PRC

Beijing University of Foreign Studies
Responsible Bureau: State Education Committee
Departments: English, Russian, Japanese, French, German, Spanish, Arabic, Slavic Languages, Asian and African Languages, Chinese
Accommodations: "Foreign Expert housing is very nice; Foreign Teacher housing is typical Chinese apartments, which are simple but adequate"
Teacher Salary/Benefits: varies
Teaching Conditions: 10-14 hrs/wk; English programs divided between 1st and 2nd English programs, and Training Center; 1st English Dept trains undergrads, 2nd English Dept trains Middle School teachers; Training Center trains workers from various *danwei* on short-term programs—"very little communication between the departments"; class size good, 15-20 students, + some larger lectures which break down into study groups
Learning Conditions: many foreign students—US, Canada, Japan, USSR; most in formal exchange programs, but "anyone with money can arrange something"
Contact: Foreign Affairs Office, Beijing Institute of Foreign Languages, Haidian District, Beijing PRC

NORMAL SCHOOLS

Beijing Normal School
Responsible Bureau: State Education Committee
Departments: Education, Psychology, Chinese, Economics, Philosophy, History, Library Science, Foreign Languages, Astronomy, Geology, Biology, Mathematics, Physics, Radio Technology, Chemistry, Physical Education, Art
Contact: Foreign Affairs Office, Beijing Normal School, 19 Xinjiekouwai St., Xinjiekouwai, Taiping Village, Beijing 100875 PRC

Beijing Teachers Institute
Responsible Bureau: City Bureau of Higher Education
Departments: Political Education, Chinese, History, Geology, Biology, Mathematics, Physics, Chemistry, Music, Art, Foreign Languages
Contact: Foreign Affairs Office, Beijing Teachers Institute, Haidian District, Beijing PRC

MEDICAL SCHOOLS

Beijing College of Traditional Chinese Medicine International
Responsible Bureau: Ministry of Sanitation and Hygiene
Departments: Chinese Medicine, Chinese Pharmacology, Acupuncture and Acupressure, Nursing and Care
Sister Schools: in US, UK, Japan, Australia, France, Canada, Germany, Italy
Teachers: can teach English, Western Medicine
Students: have special English-language training in Traditional Chinese Medicine
Contact: Foreign Affairs Office, Beijing College of Traditional Chinese Medicine International, 11 Beisanhuan E. Ave., Beijing PRC

Capital Institute of Medicine
Responsible Bureau: City Committee of Sanitation and Hygiene
Departments: Medicine, Pediatrics, Oral Medicine
Contact: Foreign Affairs Office, Capital Institute of Medicine, You'anmenwai, Beijing PRC

China Xiehe Medical University
  Responsible Bureau: Ministry of Sanitation and Hygiene
  Departments: Medical Practice, Nursing and Care
  Contact: Foreign Affairs Office, China Xiehe Medical University, Dongdan, Beijing PRC

TECHNICAL SCHOOLS

Beijing Aerospace University*
  Responsible Bureau: Aerospace Ministry
  Departments: Materials, Electronics, Automation and Control, Computer Science, Management, Applied Mathematics, Applied Physics, Mechanical and Electronic Equipment, Systems Engineering, Power Production
  Sister Schools: 16 in US, UK, Canada, Australia, Japan, France, Belgium
  Contact: Foreign Affairs Office, Beijing Aerospace University, 37 Xueyuan Rd., Haidian District, Beijing PRC

Beijing Agricultural University
  Responsible Bureau: Ministry of Agriculture, Livestock, and Fisheries
  Departments: Agriculture, Gardening, Crop Protection, Soil Chemistry, Livestock, Veterinary Medicine, Agricultural Meteorology, Nutrition, Biology, Agricultural Economics
  Contact: Foreign Affairs Office, Beijing Agricultural University, Western Suburbs, Beijing PRC
  URL: http://solar.rtd.utk.edu/~china/uni/BAU/agri.html

Beijing Institute of Architectural Engineering
  Responsible Bureau: City Architectural Committee
  Departments: Architecture, Urban Planning, Electronic Equipment, Civil Engineering
  Contact: Foreign Affairs Office, Beijing Institute of Architectural Engineering, Exhibition Rd., West City District, Beijing PRC

Beijing Institute of Computer Science
  Responsible Bureau: City Committee of Science
  Departments: Computer Science
  Contact: Foreign Affairs Office, Beijing Institute of Computer Science, Haidian District, Beijing PRC

Beijing Institute of Engineering
  Responsible Bureau: Ministry of Weapons and Military Equipment
  Departments: Mechanics, Radiation, Automation and Control, Electronics, Computer Science, Chemistry, Power, Vehicle Studies, Management, Foreign Languages, Mathematics, Physics, Industrial Planning
  Contact: Foreign Affairs Office, Beijing Institute of Engineering, Haidian District, Beijing PRC

Beijing Institute of Hydroelectricity, Electric Power, and Economic Management
  Responsible Bureau: Ministry of Water and Electricity
  Departments: Hydroengineering, Electric Power, Economics
  Contact: Foreign Affairs Office, Beijing Institute of Hydroelectricity, Electric Power, and Economic Management, Dingfu Village, Beijing PRC

Beijing Institute of Industrial and Chemical Fibers
Responsible Bureau: Ministry of Textiles
Departments: Industrial Chemistry, Gaofenzi, Chemistry, Electronic Equipment
Contact: Foreign Affairs Office, Beijing Institute of Industrial and Chemical Fibers, Andingmenwai, Beijing Special Zone, PRC

Beijing Institute of Industrial Chemistry
Responsible Bureau: Ministry of Industrial Chemistry
Departments: Chemistry, Mechanics, Automation, Radiation Physics
Contact: Foreign Affairs Office, Beijing Institute of Industrial Chemistry, Heping St., Andingmenwai, Beijing Special Zone, PRC

Beijing Institute of Information Engineering
Responsible Bureau: Ministry of Electronics
Departments: Computer Science, Management Engineering
Contact: Foreign Affairs Office, Beijing Institute of Information Engineering, Deshengmenwai, Beijing PRC

Beijing Institute of Light Industry
Responsible Bureau: Ministry of Light Industry
Departments: Mechanics, Industrial Chemistry, Automation, Management
Contact: Foreign Affairs Office, Beijing Institute of Light Industry, 3 Fucheng Rd., Haidian District, Beijing PRC

Beijing Institute of Meteorology
Responsible Bureau: National Bureau of Meteorology
Departments: Meteorology, Atmospheric Physics
Contact: Foreign Affairs Office, Beijing Institute of Meteorology, Haidian District, Beijing PRC

Beijing Institute of Post and Telecommunications*
Responsible Bureau: Ministry of Post and Telecommunications
Departments: Electronic Mail, Radio Technology, Mechanics, Management, Applied Physics
Sister Schools: France—Univ Pierre and Marie Curie; Ecole Nationale Superieure des Telecommunications de Bretagne; Univ of Brest; Inst Nationale des Telecommunications d'Evry; Ecole Nationale Superieure des Telecommunications de Paris
Contact: Foreign Affairs Office, Beijing Institute of Post and Telecommunications, 42 Xueyuan Rd., Haidian District, Beijing PRC

Beijing University of Agricultural Engineering
Responsible Bureau: Ministry of Agriculture, Livestock, and Fisheries
Departments: Electric Power, Hydrology and Hydroelectric Construction, Agricultural Equipment, Agricultural Mechanization, Animal Products Processing
Contact: Foreign Affairs Office, Beijing University of Agricultural Engineering, Haidian District, Beijing Special Zone, PRC

China University of Geosciences
Responsible Bureau: Ministry of Geology
Departments: Geology, Geography, Chemistry, Physics, Meteorology, Biology
Accommodations: reasonable; Chinese-style apartments w/ kitchen, balcony, simple furniture

Teaching Conditions: 8-14 hrs/wk, class size varies, 12-35 students; students "moderately well motivated"
Contact: Foreign Affairs Office, China University of Geosciences, Xueyuan Lu 29, Haidian District, Beijing 10083 PRC

Peking Union Medical College
Responsible Bureau: Ministry of Sanitation and Hygiene
Departments: Medicine, Sanitation and Hygiene, Oral Medicine, Pharmacology, Nursing and Care
Accommodations: Nice guest house, good hot showers
Library: Fairly good, access to books difficult.
Contact: Foreign Affairs Office, Peking Union Medical College, Haidian District, Beijing PRC

University of Northern Industry
Responsible Bureau: China National Non-Ferrous Metals Company
Departments: Industry, Architectural Engineering, Economic Management, Foreign Languages, Sociology
Contact: Foreign Affairs Office, University of Northern Industry, Shijingshan District, Beijing PRC

University of Science and Technology/Beijing
Responsible Bureau: Ministry of Industrial Metal Production
Departments: Mining, Industrial Metal Production, High Temperature Studies, Materials, Mechanics, Automation, Physics, Chemistry, Management, Sociology
Accommodations: poor, 1small rm, w/ shared bath and cooking facilities, w/ washer, TV; strict midnight curfew, visitor registration; location central to campus, 20-25 mins walk from shops and movies
Teaching Conditions: 14 hrs/wk, plus 2 office hours; good English reading room, but closed to students; no secretaries or photocopying
Contact: Foreign Affairs Office, University of Science and Technology/Beijing, Haidian District, Beijing PRC

FUJIAN — Closest of the mainland provinces to Taiwan, Fujian features extraordinary coastal military facilities, particularly near the commercial center at Xiamen. Fujianese is a distinct language, related more closely to native Taiwanese than to Mandarin. In all larger cities, however, fluent Mandarin speakers abound. An important center of foreign trade and ancient home to many of the world's Overseas Chinese, Fujian is wealthy by Chinese standards, particularly in Xiamen and in the capital, Fuzhou. Food is rich and varied, featuring plenty of fresh produce and seafood. Weather is mild most of the year, though broiling in summer. While air transport is convenient, it is expensive, and railways reach only to Fuzhou. Most ground transport in Fujian involves endless hours on creaking buses.

UNIVERSITIES

Fuzhou University*
Responsible Bureau: Provincial Higher Education Administration
Departments: Geology, Materials and Mining, Mechanical Engineering, Electrical Mechanics, Industrial Chemistry, Computer Science, Light Industry, Radio Technology, Agricultural Construction, Mathematics, Physics, Chemistry, Foreign Languages, Management, Economics, Statistics, Accounting
Contact: Foreign Affairs Office, Fuzhou University, Gongye Rd., Fuzhou, Fujian PRC

Overseas Chinese University
Responsible Bureau: State Council, Overseas Chinese Association
Departments: Mechanical Engineering, Electrical Engineering, Computer Science, Industrial Chemistry, Architecture, Civil Engineering, Chinese, Foreign Languages, Mathematics, Physics, Biology, Travel and Tourism, Management, Law, Industrial Arts
Teachers: univ privately funded by overseas Chinese benefactor; new accommodations and some flexible programs
Contact: Foreign Affairs Office, Overseas Chinese University, Chengdong, Quanzhou, Fujian PRC

Xiamen University*
Responsible Bureau: State Education Committee
Departments: Chinese, Journalism, History, Anthropology, Philosophy, Foreign Languages, Mathematics, Computer Science, Physics, Chemistry, Timing Equipment, Aquaculture, Biology, Economics, Management, Statistics, Accounting, Finance, Foreign Trade, Law
Sister Schools: relations w/ 12 schools in US, UK, Canada, Japan, Germany, Australia, Belgium
Teachers and Students: accepts foreign teachers of Western languages/cultures and technical subjects; has large program in Chinese Language and Culture for foreign students; facilities include Museum of Anthropology, Museum of Lu Xun, 1.5 million vol library; school has one of China's premier depts of Southeast Asian Studies (part of Anthropology)
Contact: Foreign Affairs Office, Xiamen University, Siming S. Rd., Xiamen, Fujian PRC

FINANCE/ECONOMICS

Xiamen Institute of Economics
Responsible Bureau: Provincial Government
Departments: International Economic Management
Contact: Foreign Affairs Office, Xiamen Institute of Economics, Gulang Island, Xiamen, Fujian PRC

NORMAL SCHOOLS

Fujian Normal School
Responsible Bureau: Provincial Higher Education Administration
Departments: Education, Political Education, Chinese, History, Library Science, Geology, Biology, Mathematics, Physics, Chemistry, Physical Education, Music, Art, Foreign Languages
Contact: Foreign Affairs Office, Fujian Normal School, Cangshan District, Fuzhou, Fujian PRC

MEDICAL SCHOOLS

Fujian College of Chinese Medicine
Responsible Bureau: Provincial Higher Education Administration
Departments: Medical Practice, Acupuncture, Chinese Pharmacology
Contact: Foreign Affairs Office, Fujian College of Chinese Medicine, Wusi N. Rd., Fuzhou, Fujian PRC

Fujian Medical College
Responsible Bureau: Provincial Higher Education Administration
Departments: Medicine, Oral Medicine, Stomatology, Sanitation and Hygiene, Medical Examination
Sister Schools: US—Univ of Minneapolis-St. Paul
Accommodations: very good; 5 rms w/ kitchen, washer, frig; no curfew; 25 min walk from downtown
Teaching Conditions: 12 hrs/wk; good teaching materials, library; school also open to new materials; some secretarial support
Contact: Foreign Affairs Office, Fujian Medical College, Chatingjiaotong Rd., Fuzhou, Fujian PRC

TECHNICAL SCHOOLS

Jimei Navigation Institute
Responsible Bureau: Ministry of Transportation
Departments: Aviation and Shipping, Boat Mechanics, Marine Engineering, Electrical Engineering, Basic Studies
Contact: Foreign Affairs Office, Jimei Navigation Institute, Jimei District, Xiamen, Fujian PRC

Xiamen Institute of Aquaculture
Responsible Bureau: Ministry of Agriculture, Livestock, and Fisheries
Departments: Fishery Mechanics, Aquaculture, Aquacultural Products Processing
Contact: Foreign Affairs Office, Xiamen Institute of Aquaculture, Jimei District, Xiamen, Fujian PRC

GANSU — Dry, dusty Gansu province stretches like a narrow bow between Inner Mongolia and Qinghai, reaching to Xinjiang in the far west and Sichuan and Shanxi in the east. Originally settled as part of the Silk Road trading route with the Near East, Gansu still displays her origins in the layout of her cities. From Tianshui in the east to Anxi and Dunhuang in the west, all line up along the ancient trade routes, most of which are now accessed by one of China's longest railways. Gansu's desert climate has preserved astonishing art and architecture, from the centuries of Buddhist grottoes at Dunhuang to the guard towers of the Great Wall's far western tip at Jiayuguan to Yellow Lamaseries and Buddhist caves near the capital at Lanzhou. Along with standard Han food, Gansu offers dishes of the Hui and Mongolian nationalities as well as many local specialties made with the honeydew and the white lily bud. Weather is high desert; language quite standard Mandarin outside minority areas.

UNIVERSITIES

Gansu Unified University
Responsible Bureau: Provincial Education Administration
Departments: Computer Science, Grains and Nutrition, Foreign Language, Finance and Accounting
Contact: Foreign Affairs Office, Gansu Unified University, Lanzhou, Gansu PRC

Gold City Unified University
Responsible Bureau: Provincial Education Administration
Departments: Agricultural Construction, Industrial Chemistry, Computer Science, Library Science, English, Accounting, Planning and Statistics
Contact: Foreign Affairs Office, Gold City Unified University, Dongfanghong Square, Lanzhou, Gansu PRC

Lanzhou University*
Responsible Bureau: State Education Committee
Departments: Mathematics, Mechanics, Physics, Electronics and Information Systems, Geography, Atmospheric Science, Geology, Chinese Language and Literature, History, Economics, Journalism, Philosophy, Legal Science, Administrative Management Information Science, Foreign Language and Literature
Chinese Students: 10,798   **Foreign Students:** 47   **Foreign Teachers:** 6
Accommodations: The Guesthouse and the Foreign Students Apartment
Teacher Salary/Benefits: 1700-2300¥   **Teaching Conditions:** 14-16 hrs/wk
Student Tuition/Expenses: USD$1,400/yr for Chinese Langauge, USD$2,000-4,000 for undergraduate, master, doctorate/year
Contact: Mr. Yang Shu, Foreign Affairs Office, Lanzhou University, Tianshui Rd., Lanzhou, Gansu 730000 PRC   ■ **Phone:** (86-931) 861-7355 or 891-2850
Fax: (86-931) 861-8777   **e-mail:** yangs@lzu.edu.cn or zhangzg@izu.edu.cn
URL: http://www.lzu.edu.cn

MINORITIES/POLITICS AND LAW

Gansu Institute of Politics and Law
Responsible Bureau: Provincial Justice Administration
Departments: Law
Contact: Foreign Affairs Office, Gansu Institute of Politics and Law, Anning W. Rd., Lanzhou, Gansu PRC

Northwest Minorities Institute
Responsible Bureau: National Minorities Committee
Departments: Livestock and Veterinary Medicine, Medical Practice, Languages and Literatures, History, Politics, Mathematical and Theoretical Chemistry, Industrial Arts, Trade
Contact: Foreign Affairs Office, Northwest Minorities Institute, Xibeixin Village, Lanzhou, Gansu PRC

COMMERCE

Lanzhou Institute of Commerce
Responsible Bureau: Ministry of Commerce
Departments: Commercial Economics, Financial Statistics, Finance
Contact: Foreign Affairs Office, Lanzhou Institute of Commerce, Duanjiawan, Lanzhou, Gansu PRC

NORMAL SCHOOL

Northwest Normal School
Responsible Bureau: Provincial Education Administration
Departments: Education, Politics, Telephone Education, Chinese, History, Geology, Biology, Mathematics, Physics, Computer Science, Physical Education, Chemistry, Music, Art, Foreign Languages
Contact: Foreign Affairs Office, Northwest Normal School, Shilidian, Lanzhou, Gansu PRC

MEDICAL SCHOOLS

Lanzhou Medical College
Responsible Bureau: Provincial Administration of Sanitation and Hygiene
Departments: Medicine, Pharmacology, Sanitation and Hygiene, Oral Medicine
Contact: Foreign Affairs Office, Lanzhou Medical College, Donggang W. Rd., Lanzhou, Gansu PRC

Gansu College of Chinese Medicine
Responsible Bureau: Provincial Administration of Sanitation and Hygiene
Departments: Acupuncture, Chinese Medicine, Chinese Pharmacology
Contact: Foreign Affairs Office, Gansu College of Chinese Medicine, Dingxi E. Rd., Lanzhou, Gansu PRC

TECHNICAL SCHOOLS

Gansu University of Technology
Responsible Bureau: Ministry of Mechanics
Departments: Mechanics, Automation and Control, Natural Products Architecture, Industrial Management
Contact: Foreign Affairs Office, Gansu University of Technology, Langongping, Lanzhou, Gansu PRC

Lanzhou Railway Institute
Responsible Bureau: Ministry of Railways
Departments: Mechanics, Environmental Engineering, Natural Products Architecture, Railway Shipping, Automation and Control
Chinese Students: 5,000 +
Contact: Foreign Affairs Office, Lanzhou Institute of Railways, Anning W. Rd., Lanzhou, Gansu PRC
URL: http://www.lzri.edu.cn/

GUANGDONG — Guangdong ranks as China's wealthiest province as well as her most Westernized. Deeply influenced by neighboring Hong Kong, particularly in the border town of Shenzhen, Guangdong displays a bustle and vivacity of capitalist enterprise which, while tame compared with Hong Kong, nevertheless far outstrips China's interior. Foreigners unable to give up Western import goods and dance halls that rock till dawn would do well to stay in Guangdong. "Teachers mean nothing here," writes one respondent. "The businessman is king." Foreigners are less of a rarity in Guangdong than in many other areas, and receive less deference and attention.

Guangzhou (Canton), the capital, hosts the majority of China's foreign trade, and offers many opportunities for moonlighting in business. Shenzhen is a world unto itself (Chinese nationals need special border passes to enter the city), dedicated largely to facilitating trade with Hong Kong. Smaller cities such as Shaoguan and Shantou offer more of a view into traditional Chinese life, but remain wealthier than more northern cities. Some of China's best cooking comes from Guangdong, for with her fertile land and relative wealth, the province produces epicureans alien to the poorer, more barren interior. Guangdong weather is steamy, and her language is Cantonese, not comprehensible to students of Mandarin.

UNIVERSITIES

Guangzhou University
Responsible Bureau: City Committee of Higher Education
Departments: Industrial Workers Construction, Electronics, Computer Science, English, Secretarial Science, Industrial Management, Accounting, Law, Highway Bridge Building, Speakers and Recording
Contact: Foreign Affairs Office, Guangzhou University, Xiaobeixiatang, Guangzhou, Guangdong PRC
URL: http://www.guangzu.edu.cn/

Jiaying University
Responsible Bureau: Provincial Bureau of Higher Education
Departments: Accounting, Economic Management, English, Applied Computer Science
Contact: Foreign Affairs Office, Jiaying University, Mazigang, Mei County, Guangdong PRC

Jinan University
Responsible Bureau: State Department, Overseas Chinese Association
Departments: Medicine, Literature, Theoretical Engineering, Economics, Liberal Arts, Journalism, History, Chemistry, Physics, Biology, Computer Science, Mathematics
Foreign Teachers: 10
Sister Schools: US—California State Univ, Texas Tech Univ, Miami Univ; UK—Simon Fraser Univ, Liverpool School of Tropical Medicine
Teachers and Students: school has strong focus on involving overseas Chinese in the PRC educational system; has various programs with sister schools
Contact: Foreign Affairs Office, The College of Chinese Language & Culture, Jinan University, Shougouling Road, Shahe, Guangzhou 510610 PRC
I Phone: (86-020) 8772-3598 or 8770-6866   **e-mail:** ohwy@jnu.edu.cn
URL: http://www.jnu.edu.cn

Shantou University
Responsible Bureau: Provincial Bureau of Higher Education
Departments: 7 colleges in university: Science, Engineering, Liberal Arts, Law, Business Management, Fine Arts and Medicine
Chinese Students: 5,000   **Foreign Students:** 54
Foreign Teachers: 9
Accommodations: rms, w/ kitchen, A/C, TV, washer, fridge, no curfew, very central location
Teacher Salary/Benefits: 2,600-3,000¥ RMB/mo; USD$800-1,600 for int'l airfare allowance per year

Teaching Conditions: Foreign Language Teachers - 16 hrs/wk, others 10-12 hrs/wk; excellent library, but not open to students; campus is beautiful
Student Tuition/Expense: USD$1,800/yr; accommodation - USD$3/a night (sharing a room w/2 beds)
Students: all studying Chinese
Contact: Foreign Affairs Office, Shantou University, Shantou, Guangdong 515063 PRC
I Phone: (86-754) 8851-0520   **Fax:** (86-754) 8851-0520
URL: http://www.stu.edu.cn/

Shenzhen University*
Responsible Bureau: Provincial Bureau of Higher Education
Departments: Mechanics, Electronics, Architecture, Chinese, English, Mathematics, Physics, Industrial Management, Finance and Accounting, Law, Computer Science
Accommodations: not bad; 1 or 2 rms, w/ shared kitchen and common rm, washer, TV, tape recorder, fridge, A/C, phone, plenty of hot water and no need for heat; use of car and driver for fee; foreigner compound somewhat isolated and campus 20-30 mins from downtown by bus, but visitor registration lax
Teaching Conditions: fairly good: 8-14 hrs/wk, excellent language lab, photocoping, and AV facilities (no secretarial help for teachers, but PCs available for use) "the library is one of the best I have seen," although may be closed stack for students
Learning Conditions: not bad; "learned a lot, wonderful cultural experience"
Contact: International Office, Shenzhen University, Guangdong Province, 518060 PRC
I Phone: (86-755) 8666-1940   **Fax:** (86-755) 8666-1940
e-mail: houmf@szu.edu.cn   **URL:** http://www.szu.edu.cn/

Wuyi University
Responsible Bureau: Higher Educatin Bureau of Guangdong Province
Departments: Management, Transportation Systems Engineering, Electronic & Information Engineering, Civil Engineering, Computer Science, Mechanical & Electrical Engineering, Chemical & Environmental Engineering, Mathematics, Physics, Textile & Clothing, Social Science, Physical Education
Chinese Students: 5,000   **Foreign Students:** 9   **Foreign Teachers:** 4
Sister Schools: US—SUNY College at Old Westbury, Maricopa Community College; Switzerland—Burgdort Institute of Technology; Canada—Univ. of Victoria
Accommodations: Apartments for foreign teachers; guest house rooms for foreign students
Teacher Salary/Benefits: 1,500-2,000¥ RMB/month **Teaching Conditions:** 12-14 hrs/wk
Student Tuition/Expense: USD$65 per credit; lodging USD$5-6 a day
Contact: Ms. Betty Song, Centre for International Academic Exchange, Wuyi University, Jiangmen, Guangdong 529020 PRC
I Phone: (86-750) 8335-2112 ext. 5112   **Fax:** (86-750) 8335-4323
e-mail: fa@wyu.edu.cn   **URL:** http://www.wuy.edu.cn/INTR1.HTML

Zhongshan University*
Responsible Bureau: Ministry of Education
Departments: Mathematics, Power Studies, Computer Science, Physics, Electronics, Chemistry, Biology, Geology, Geography, Meteorology, Chinese, History, Anthropology, Philosophy, Foreign Languages, Library Science, Economics, Management, Law
Foreign Students: 200   **Sister Schools:** many
Teachers: high-powered campus, many "children of elite"; campus has Museum of Anthropology, several English-language journals

Students: many good programs: Mandarin, Cantonese, business/economics; some "isolation from everyday life"
Contact: External Affairs Office, Zhongshan University, Guangzhou, 510275 PRC
I Phone: (86-20) 8418-5465 or 8418-5527   **Fax:** (86-20) 8418-4860
e-mail: adeao@zsulink.zsu.edu.cn   **URL:** http://www.zsu.edu.cn/

MINORITIES/POLITICS & LAW

Guangdong Institute of Minorities
Responsible Bureau: Provincial Bureau of Higher Education
Departments: Politics, Chinese, Mathematics, Economic Mathematics, Finance
Contact: Foreign Affairs Office, Guangdong Institute of Minorities, Shipai, Guangzhou, Guangdong PRC

ARTS/MUSIC

Guangzhou Academy of Fine Arts
Responsible Bureau: Provincial Bureau of Higher Education
Departments: Traditional Chinese Painting, Oil Painting, Printmaking, Industrial Arts, Sculpture, Design, Fine Arts Education
Students: study Chinese art/music; plan summer program as well as program for degree students
Contact: Foreign Affairs Office, Guangzhou Academy of Fine Arts, 257 Changgangdong Rd., Guangzhou, Guangdong PRC

Sea Star Music Institute
Responsible Bureau: Provincial Bureau of Higher Education
Departments: Voice, Minority Music, Wind and String Instruments, Piano, Composition Theory, Teaching
Contact: Foreign Affairs Office, Sea Star Music Institute, Xianliedongheng Rd., Guangzhou, Guangdong PRC

COMMERCE/FINANCE/ECONOMICS

Guangdong Commercial College
Responsible Bureau: Provincial Bureau of Higher Education
Departments: Commercial and Industrial Management, Finance and Accounting
Teachers: teach English, business/management
Contact: Foreign Affairs Office, Guangdong Commercial College, Chisha, Haizhu District, Guangzhou, Guangdong PRC

Guangzhou Institute of Foreign Trade
Responsible Bureau: Ministry of Foreign Trade
Departments: Foreign Trade Economics, Import and Export, Foreign Industrial Finance and Economics
Contact: Foreign Affairs Office, Guangzhou Institute of Foreign Trade, Northern Suburbs, Guangzhou, Guangdong PRC

FOREIGN LANGUAGES

Guangzhou Institute of Foreign Languages
Responsible Bureau: State Education Committee

Departments: English, French, German, Spanish, Russian, Japanese, Thai, Indonesian, Vietnamese
Sister Schools: UK—Murdoch Univ; Australia—Univ of Perth; Germany—Univ of Paderborn
Teachers: teach English, Western Culture
Students: huge complex for foreign students learning Chinese, especially for Chinese gov't scholarship students prior to entering Chinese-language degree programs; students in foreigners-only dorm
Contact: Foreign Affairs Office, Guangzhou Institute of Foreign Languages, Huangpodong, Northern Suburbs, Guangzhou, Guangdong PRC

NORMAL SCHOOLS

Guangzhou Teachers College
Responsible Bureau: City Education Committee
Departments: Chinese, History, Politics, English, Mathematics, Physics, Chemistry, Biology, Geology
Accommodations: very good; 2 rms, w/ washer, dryer, TV, tape recorder, space heater, fans; cafeteria food cheap and great; very central location; strict visitor registration
Teaching Conditions: 12-14 hrs/wk; materials and library very good
Contact: Foreign Affairs Office, Guangzhou Teachers College, Guihuagang, Guangzhou, Guangdong PRC

South China Normal School
Responsible Bureau: Provincial Bureau of Higher Education
Departments: Chinese, Foreign Languages, Politics, History, Education, Mathematics, Physics, Chemistry, Distance Education, Biology, Geology, Physical Education, Library Science
Contact: Foreign Affairs Office, South China Normal School, Shipai, Guangzhou, Guangdong PRC

MEDICAL SCHOOLS

Guangdong College of Medicine and Pharmacology
Responsible Bureau: Provincial Bureau of Higher Education
Departments: Medicine, Sanitation and Hygiene, Pharmacology, Nursing and Care
Teacher: rather isolated; "not a good place for young people just out of college—it's a rather lonely gig"
Accommodations: very good; 4 rms w/ kitchen, TV, tape recorder, washer, fridge; no curfew
Teaching Conditions: 18 hrs/wk; good students; library short on foreign-language materials
Contact: Foreign Affairs Office, Guangdong College of Medicine and Pharmacology, Baogang St., Guangzhou, Guangdong PRC

Guangzhou College of Medicine
Responsible Bureau: City Education Committee
Departments: Medicine
Contact: Foreign Affairs Office, Guangzhou College of Medicine, Dongfengxi Rd., Guangzhou, Guangdong PRC

Guangzhou College of Traditional Chinese Medicine
Responsible Bureau: Ministry of Sanitation and Hygiene
Departments: Medical Practice, Acupuncture, Chinese Pharmacology
Sister Schools: US—Univ of Illinois Medical Center at Chicago
Teachers and Students: accepts foreign teachers of English, technical subjects; has program in Chinese Medicine for foreign students
Contact: Foreign Affairs Office, Guangzhou College of Traditional Chinese Medicine, Guoji Rd., Guangzhou, Guangdong PRC

Zhanjiang Medical College
Responsible Bureau: Provincial Bureau of Higher Education
Departments: Medicine
Contact: Foreign Affairs Office, Zhanjiang Medical College, Wenming Rd., Zhanjiang, Guangdong PRC

Zhongshan Medical College
Responsible Bureau: Ministry of Sanitation and Hygiene
Departments: Medicine, Oral Medicine, Sanitation and Hygiene, Stomatology, Radiation Therapy, Nursing and Care, Nutrition
Accommodations: small but nice: kitchens, + excellent cafeteria (students 2/rm in dorms)
Teaching Conditions: 14 hrs/wk; school very open to new materials; huge campus— "easy to get lost"
Students: large number of Chinese gov't scholarship medical students; some self-paying acupuncture students
Contact: Foreign Affairs Office, Zhongshan Medical College, Zhongshan #2 Rd., Guangzhou, Guangdong PRC

TECHNICAL SCHOOLS

Guangdong Institute of Mechanical Engineering
Responsible Bureau: Provincial Mechanics Administration
Departments: Mechanics, Automation, Computer Science, Management, Foreign Trade
Contact: Foreign Affairs Office, Guangdong Institute of Mechanical Engineering, Wushan St., Guangzhou, Guangdong PRC

Guangdong Institute of Technology*
Responsible Bureau: Provincial Bureau of Higher Education
Departments: Mechanics, Materials, Automation, Electrical Equipment, Computer Science, Geology, Environmental Studies, Industrial Chemistry, Agricultural Construction, Management, Foreign Languages
Contact: Foreign Affairs Office, Guangdong Institute of Technology, Dongfengwu Rd., Guangzhou, Guangdong PRC

South China Agricultural University*
Responsible Bureau: Ministry of Agriculture, Livestock, and Fisheries
Departments: Agricultural Science, Crop Protection, Gardening, Silkworm and Mulberry Cultivation, Livestock and Veterinary Medicine, Agricultural Mechanics, Biology, Agricultural Education, Forestry, Agricultural Economics, Soil Chemistry
Sister Schools: US—Univ of Pennsylvania, UC-Davis, Silsoe College, Riverina-Murray Inst; Japan—Kyushu Univ; Australia—Univ of Sydney, Massey Univ; Germany—Univ of Kasetsart; Philippines—Univ of Philippines

Contact: Foreign Affairs Office, South China Agricultural University, Shipai, Guangzhou, Guangdong PRC

South China Institute of Technology*
Responsible Bureau: Ministry of Education
Departments: Mechanical Engineering, Architectural Engineering, Ships and Boating, Radio and Telecommunications Technology, Electric Power, Automation, Computer Science, Inorganic Materials, Chemistry, Papermaking, Nutrition, Mathematics, Power Studies, Physics, Engineering Management
Sister Schools: US—Texas Tech Univ, Univ of Pittsburgh, Edinboro Univ of PA, Georgia Inst of Tech, Southern Methodist Univ; UK—City Univ of London; Hong Kong—HK Polytechnique; Germany—Univ of Braunschweig
Teachers and Students: have various exchange programs with sister schools; also accept outside foreign teachers and students; Inst has large library (approx 1 million vols), and in-school publishing house (SCIT Press)
Contact: Foreign Affairs Office, South China Institute of Technology, Shipai, Guangzhou, Guangdong PRC

GUANGXI — Officially named the Guangxi Zhuang Autonomous Region, Guangxi is home to the Zhuang people, China's largest minority group, numbering just over 12 million. Lush and fertile, the province holds some of China's most fabulous natural wonders, from the stark karst mountains of Guilin to the echoing caverns of the Li River. Resident foreigners tend to congregate in the tourist capital at Guilin, but should not neglect the verdant beauty of Yangshuo or the palm-tree–lined beaches of the capital, Nanning.

UNIVERSITIES

Guangxi University*
Responsible Bureau: Regional Education Administration
Departments: Industrial Metals Mining, Industrial Metals Refinement, Electric Power, Mechanical Engineering, Industrial Chemistry, Light Industry, Civil Engineering, Law, Mathematics, Physics, Chemistry, Chinese, Philosophy, Foreign Languages, Economics
Contact: Foreign Affairs Office, Guangxi University, Xixiangtang Rd., Nanning, Guangxi PRC
URL: http://www.gxu.edu/cn/WWW/gxu/gxunet.html

Yongjiang University
Responsible Bureau: Regional Education Administration
Departments: English, Industrial Management, Applied Microcomputers, Livestock Feed Industry
Accommodations: 3 rms w/ kitchen, washer, TV, tape recorder, no curfew; but no heat or hot water. Campus is in Pu Miao, a tiny village about 45 mins from Nanning; univ provides foreign teacher w/ "weekend" rm in Nanning as well as 3 rms at Pu Miao campus
Teaching Conditions: 14 hrs/wk, facilities mediocre but "they try their best"; no secretaries or photocopying
Contact: English Dept, Yongjiang University, Pumiao, Nanning, Guangxi PRC
Minorities/Politics & Law

Guangxi Institute for Nationalities
  Responsible Bureau: Regional Minorities Committee
  Departments: Politics, History, Chinese, Mathematics, Physics, Chemistry, Foreign Languages, Minority Languages
  Teachers: teach English, Western Culture; opportunities for independent research on minorities
  Students: have programs in Chinese, Chinese Culture, "China's Minorities"
  Contact: Foreign Affairs Office, Guangxi Institute for Nationalities, Xixiangtang, 530006 Nanning, Guangxi PRC

ARTS/MUSIC

Guangxi Institute of Arts
  Responsible Bureau: Regional Education Administration
  Departments: Teaching, Art, Music
  Contact: Foreign Affairs Office, Guangxi Institute of Arts, Jiaoyu Rd., Nanning, Guangxi PRC

NORMAL SCHOOLS

Guangxi Normal Institute
  Responsible Bureau: Regional Education Administration
  Departments: Chinese, Political Education, English, Mathematics, Physics, Chemistry, Geology
  Contact: Foreign Affairs Office, Guangxi Normal Institute, Mingxiu Rd., Nanning, Guangxi PRC

Guangxi Normal School
  Responsible Bureau: Regional Education Administration
  Departments: Chinese, Politics, History, Foreign Languages, Education, Mathematics, Physics, Chemistry, Biology, Physical Education
  Contact: Foreign Affairs Office, Guangxi Normal School, Wangcheng, Guilin, Guangxi PRC

MEDICAL SCHOOLS

Guangxi College of Chinese Medicine
  Responsible Bureau: Regional Education Administration
  Departments: Chinese Medicine, Chinese Pharmacology, Acupuncture
  Contact: Foreign Affairs Office, Guangxi College of Chinese Medicine, Mingxiu, Nanning, Guangxi PRC

Guangxi Medical College
  Responsible Bureau: Regional Education Administration
  Departments: Medicine, Oral Medicine, Sanitation and Hygiene
  Contact: Foreign Affairs Office, Guangxi Medical College, Taoyuan Rd., Nanning, Guangxi PRC

You River Institute of Minority Medicine
  Responsible Bureau: Regional Education Administration
  Departments: Medicine
  Contact: Foreign Affairs Office, You River Institute of Minority Medicine, Baise, Guangxi PRC

TECHNICAL SCHOOLS

Guangxi Agricultural College
Responsible Bureau: Regional Education Administration
Departments: Agricultural Science, Gardening, Crop Protection, Agricultural Mechanics, Agricultural Economics, Livestock and Veterinary Medicine, Fresh Water Aquaculture
Contact: Foreign Affairs Office, Guangxi Agricultural College, Xuzhou Rd., Nanning, Guangxi PRC

Guangxi Institute of Industry
Responsible Bureau: Regional Education Administration
Departments: Mechanical Engineering, Civil Engineering, Economics, Chinese, Industrial Worker's Construction, Economic Management
Contact: Foreign Affairs Office, Guangxi Institute of Industry, Liuzhou, Guangxi PRC

Guilin Institute of Electronic Industry
Responsible Bureau: Ministry of Electronics
Departments: Mechanical Production, Equipment Design, Communications Engineering, Surveying Technology, Applied Computer Science, Automation and Control, Production, Finance and Accounting
Contact: Foreign Affairs Office, Guilin Institute of Electronic Industry, Liuhe Rd., Guilin, Guangxi PRC

Guilin Institute of Geology
Responsible Bureau: China National Non-Ferrous Metals Company
Departments: Geology, Materials Exploration, Chemical Exploration, Hydro-engineering, Surveying, Economic Management
Contact: Foreign Affairs Office, Guilin Institute of Geology, Pingfengshan, Guilin, Guangxi PRC

Guilin Institute of Technology
Responsible Bureau: China Non-Ferrous Metal Industry Co.
Departments: Natural Resource Engineering, Land Development and Surveying, Applied Chemistry, Business Management and Tourisn, Environmental Sciences, Foreign Languages, Basic Sciences, Social Science
Chinese Students: 3,200   **Foreign Students:** 8
Foreign Teachers: 3   **Sister Schools:** 2
Accommodations: Apartments
Teacher Salary/Benefits: 1,200¥ RMB/mo; 2,200¥ RMB yearly holiday bonus; free housing equipped appropriately, bicycle
Teaching Conditions: 12-16 hrs/wk; use of projector, Audio-Video Center, duplication machine and Chinese coordinator
Student Tuition/Expenses: USD$1,000 tuition plus living expenses; housing USD$20/wk
Teachers: aged 30-50 preferred; should have good rapport with students, healthy, and not quit halfway through semester
Students: Students who are interested in studying at our Institute should have a basic understanding of Chinese
Contact: Foreign Affairs Office, Guilin Institute of Technology, 12 Jiangan Rd., Guilin, Guangxi PRC
I Phone: (86-773) 581-5621 ext. 5600   **Fax:** (86-773) 581-2796

GUIZHOU — Deep in China's steamy south, Guizhou is far off the beaten tourist track. Known best for China's highest waterfall at Huangguoshu near Anshun, the province is also home to a bewildering variety of minorities, from the Miao and Buyi to the Hmong. While not so famous as neighboring Guangxi, Guizhou also offers some fabulous karst mountains and gorgeous jungle scenery. While all schools in Guizhou that accept foreigners are located in the capital at Guiyang or the industrial center at Zunyi, foreign residents have also gained permission to visit rarely accessible minority areas. Weather is warm to hot year-round, food spicy, and language in Han areas strongly influenced by Hunanese.

UNIVERSITIES

Guizhou People's University
Responsible Bureau: Provincial Government
Departments: Secretarial Science, Law, English, Industrial Management
Contact: Foreign Affairs Office, Guizhou People's University, Xiangshi Rd., Guiyang, Guizhou PRC

Guizhou University*
Responsible Bureau: Provincial Education Committee
Departments: Chinese, History, Philosophy, Foreign Languages, Mathematics, Computer Science, Physics   **Students:** 5,000
Teachers and Students: accepts foreign teachers of Western languages/cultures and technical subjects; has large program in Chinese Language/Culture for foreign students
Contact: Foreign Affairs Office, Guizhou University, South Huaxi Ave, Guiyang, Guizhou 550025 PRC
I Phone: (86-851) 385-1956 or 385-1010   **Fax:** (86-851) 385-5885
URL:http://www.gzu.edu.cn/english/gzgx/gzdx/indexen.html

MINORITIES/LAW

Guizhou Minorities Institute
Responsible Bureau: Provincial Education Committee
Departments: Mathematics, History, Physics, Chinese, Industrial Arts, Administrative Mangement, Language, Economic Administration, Sociology, Languages of Minority Nationalities
Contact: Foreign Affairs Office, Guizhou Minorities Institute, Huaxi District, Guiyang, Guizhou PRC
URL: http://www.gzu.edu.cn/english/gzgx/gzmzxyen.html

NORMAL SCHOOLS

Guiyang Normal School
Responsible Bureau: Provincial Education Committee
Departments: Chinese, Political Education, History, Foreign Languages, Education, Mathematics, Physics, Chemistry, Biology, Physical Education, Arts, Geology
Contact: Foreign Affairs Office, Guiyang Normal School, Waihuan E. Rd., Guiyang, Guizhou 550001 PRC

MEDICAL SCHOOLS

Guiyang College of Chinese Medicine
Responsible Bureau: Provincial Education Committee
Departments: Chinese Medicine, Chinese Pharmacology
Contact: Foreign Affairs Office, Guiyang College of Chinese Medicine, Dong Rd.,
Guiyang, Guizhou PRC

Guiyang College of Medicine
Responsible Bureau: Provincial Committee of Higher Education
Departments: Medicine, Pharmacology, Sanitation and Hygiene
Contact: Foreign Affairs Office, Guiyang College of Medicine, Beijing Rd..,
Guiyang, Guizhou PRC

Zunyi College of Medicine
Responsible Bureau: Provincial Education Committee
Departments: Medicine, Oral Medicine
Contact: Foreign Affairs Office, Zunyi College of Medicine, Waihuan Rd., Zunyi,
Guizhou PRC

TECHNICAL SCHOOLS

Guizhou Institute of Technology
Responsible Bureau: Provincial Education Committee
Departments: Geology, Mining, Industrial Metals, Mechanics, Electrical
Mechanics, Industrial Chemistry, Natural Products Architecture
Contact: Foreign Affairs Office, Guizhou Institute of Technology, Caijiaguan,
Guiyang, Guizhou PRC

HAINAN ISLAND — Only separated as a province from Guangdong in
1990, Hainan remains far poorer than her northern neighbor. Her miles
of beaches, fertile landmass, rich mineral deposits, wealth of minority
peoples, and strategic importance, however, all promise a stellar future.
Haikou, China's southernmost city and the gateway to the South China
Sea, is the island's economic and industrial center. Weather is tropical
and language a variant of Cantonese.

Hainan University
Responsible Bureau: Provincial Bureau of Higher Education
Departments: Electronics, Agricultural Construction, Law, Finance and Accounting,
Chinese, Mathematics, Chemistry, Agricultural Science, Physical Education, Political
History, English, Physics, Biology, Medicine, Veterinary Medicine
Contact: Foreign Affairs Office, Hainan University, Haikou, Hainan, PRC

HEBEI — Breadbasket of China, Hebei produces some of the finest wheat and corn in the country. The capital at Shijiazhuang houses several important agricultural research stations as well as a number of major schools and industries. Zhangjiakou on the Great Wall is home of some of the earliest archaeological finds in China, including the site of "Peking Man." Chengde (Jehol) in northern Hebei was the summer hunting lodge of the Qing Emperors, who had replicas of the most famous temples and towers of all China built in the Chengde hills for their amusement. Beidaihe on the coast is the summer resort of today's leaders, and many Chinese tourists to Beidaihe's beaches amuse themselves guessing which villa houses Deng Xiao-ping. Weather is hot in summer, cold in winter, and dry. Food is hearty, grain-based fare, featuring plenty of man-tou (steamed bread) and noodles. Language is remarkably standard Mandarin.

UNIVERSITIES

Handan University
Responsible Bureau: City Government
Departments: Secretarial Science, Management, Art, Mechanics, Computer Science, Agricultural Construction
Contact: Foreign Affairs Office, Handan University, Zhuhe Rd., Handan, Hebei PRC

Hebei University
Responsible Bureau: Provincial Education Committee
Departments: Education, Chinese, History, Library Science, Philosophy, Foreign Languages, Mathematics, Physics, Chemistry, Biology, Economics, Law
Sister Schools: US—CAEE
Teachers: can teach English, Western Culture, technical subjects
Students: has special program in Chinese Language and Culture
Contact: Foreign Affairs Office, Hebei University, Hezuo Rd., Baoding, Hebei PRC

Shijiazhuang University
Responsible Bureau: Provincial Education Committee
Departments: Computer Science, Agricultural Construction, Mechanics
Contact: Foreign Affairs Office, Shijiazhuang University, Xinhuaxi Rd., Shijiazhuang, Hebei PRC

Tangshan University
Responsible Bureau: City Government
Departments: Mechanics, Chemical Engineering, Agricultural Construction, Chinese, Economic Policy, Physics, Foreign Languages
Contact: Foreign Affairs Office, Tangshan University, Jianshe Rd., Tangshan, Hebei PRC

Zhangjiakou University
Responsible Bureau: City Government
Departments: Agricultural Science, English, Economic Policy
Contact: Foreign Affairs Office, Zhangjiakou University, Xihuozi St., Zhangjiakou, Hebei PRC

FINANCE/ECONOMICS

Hebei Institute of Finance and Economics
Responsible Bureau: Provincial Education Committee
Departments: Economic Policy, Finance, Planning, Statistics, Management
Accommodations: rms + bath, w/ TV, washer, fridge, A/C, no kitchen, no curfew; centrally located for campus, 20 min bike to downtown; special cook for foreign teachers
Teaching Conditions: 14 hrs/wk; good ditto machine but no secretaries or photocopies; library poor, not open to students and only unpredictably to teachers
Contact: Foreign Affairs Office, Hebei Institute of Finance and Economics, Hongqi Ave., Shijiazhuang, Hebei PRC

NORMAL SCHOOLS

Hebei Normal Institute
Responsible Bureau: Provincial Education Committee
Departments: Political Education, Chinese, History, Mathematics, Physics, Chemistry, Arts and Industries, Foreign Languages
Contact: Foreign Affairs Office, Hebei Normal Institute, Hongqi Ave., Shijiazhuang, Hebei PRC

Hebei Teachers University
Responsible Bureau: Provincial Education Commission
Departments: Political Education, Chinese Language and Literature, Geology, Education, Physics, Chemistry, Biology, Physical Education, Mathematics, Music, Art, Foreign Languages, Literature, History, Population Research, A-V Teaching Skills
Sister Schools: US—Univ of Northern Iowa, College of Staten Island (NY), City Univ of NY, Drake Univ (Iowa); Simpson College (Iowa); UK—York Univ; Australia—Univ of New South Wales
Teachers: teach English, Literature
Students: study in Chinese Language and Culture program (classes in Chinese Language/Literature, Landscape Painting, Folk Music, Martial Arts)
Contact: Foreign Affairs Office, Hebei Teachers University, Yuhuazhong Rd., Shijiazhuang, Hebei PRC

MEDICAL SCHOOLS

Chengde Institute of Medicine
Responsible Bureau: Provincial Education Committee
Departments: Medicine, Chinese Medicine, Nursing and Care
Contact: Foreign Affairs Office, Chengde Institute of Medicine, Cuiqiao Rd., Chengde, Hebei PRC

Hebei Institute of Chinese Medicine
Responsible Bureau: Provincial Administration of Sanitation and Hygiene
Departments: Chinese Medicine
Contact: Foreign Affairs Office, Hebei Institute of Chinese Medicine, Xinshinan Rd. Shijiazhuang, Hebei PRC

Hebei Institute of Medicine
Responsible Bureau: Provincial Education Committee
Departments: Medicine, Sanitation and Hygiene, Oral Medicine, Pharmacology

Contact: Foreign Affairs Office, Hebei Institute of Medicine, Chang'an Rd., Shijiazhuang, Hebei PRC

Zhangjiakou Institute of Medicine
Responsible Bureau: Provincial Education Committee
Departments: Medicine, Chinese Medicine, Medical Testing and Examination
Contact: Foreign Affairs Office, Zhangjiakou Institute of Medicine, Changqing Rd. Zhangjiakou, Hebei PRC

TECHNICAL SCHOOLS

Hebei Institute of Architectural Engineering
Responsible Bureau: Provincial Education Committee
Departments: Architectural Engineering
Contact: Foreign Affairs Office, Hebei Institute of Architectural Engineering, Jianguo Rd., Zhangjiakou, Hebei PRC

Hebei Institute of Chemical Engineering
Responsible Bureau: Provincial Education Committee
Departments: Chemical Engineering, Environmental Studies, Mechanics, Textiles, Light Industry
Contact: Foreign Affairs Office, Hebei Institute of Chemical Engineering, Yuhua Rd., Shijiazhuang, Hebei PRC

Hebei Institute of Coal Mining Architecture and Engineering
Responsible Bureau: Ministry of Coal Mining
Departments: Geology, Mining, Mechanics, Electrical Equipment, Natural Products Architecture and Engineering
Contact: Foreign Affairs Office, Hebei Institute of Coal Mining Architecture and Engineering, Guangming Rd., Handan, Hebei PRC

Hebei Institute of Engineering
Responsible Bureau: Provincial Education Committee
Departments: Automation, Mechanics, Chemistry, Agricultural Construction, Industrial Management, Computer Science
Contact: Foreign Affairs Office, Hebei Institute of Engineering, Hongqiao District, Tianjin, Hebei PRC

Hebei Institute of Geology
Responsible Bureau: Ministry of Geology and Mining
Departments: Geology, Water Engineering, Materials and Resources, Economic Management
Contact: Foreign Affairs Office, Hebei Institute of Geology, Yihua District, Zhangjiakou, Hebei PRC

Hebei Institute of Mechanical and Electrical Engineering
Responsible Bureau: Provincial Education Committee
Departments: Mechanics, Automation, Management
Contact: Foreign Affairs Office, Hebei Institute of Mechanical and Electrical Engineering, Xinhuaxi Rd., Shijiazhuang, Hebei PRC

North China Institute of Hydrology and Hydroelectricity
Responsible Bureau: Ministry of Hydroelectricity
Departments: Hydrology, Geology, Power Production, Mechanical Engineering
Sister School: UK—Univ of Warwick
Contact: Foreign Affairs Office, North China Institute of Hydrology and Hydro-electricity, Zhonghua Rd., Handan, Hebei PRC

North China Institute of Electronics
Responsible Bureau: Ministry of Water and Electricity
Departments: Power Production, Electric Power, Electronics, Mechanics
Contact: Foreign Affairs Office, North China Institute of Electronics, Qingnian Rd., Baoding, Hebei PRC

Shijiazhuang Railroad Institute
Responsible Bureau: Ministry of Railways
Departments: Railway Construction, Mechanical Engineering, Railroad Technology, Architecture
Contact: Foreign Affairs Office, Shijiazhuang Railroad Institute, Beihuandong Rd., Shijiazhuang, Hebei PRC

Tangshan Institute of Engineering Technology
Responsible Bureau: Provincial Education Committee
Departments: Mining and Materials, Industrial Metals Production, Mechanics, Automation, Industrial Chemistry, Agricultural Construction, Industrial Management
Contact: Foreign Affairs Office, Tangshan Institute of Engineering Technology, Xinhuadong District, Tangshan, Hebei PRC

HEILONGJIANG — China's northernmost province and home to the annual Ice Festival, Heilongjiang borders with Inner Mongolia, Siberia, and Jilin. Heavily influenced in architecture and culture by Russia, the province has a more European feel than most of China, with solid, granite-faced cities nestled in deep, virgin forests. Weather is a serious consideration; the province receives plentiful coal, so central heating is generous. But outdoors winter temperatures regularly drop to -50°F without the windchill factor. Summers are mild, and spring and fall cool. Heilongjiang cuisine is very hearty by Chinese standards, featuring large portions of meat and many potato dishes, as well as exotica of the northern forests, from bear's paw to pheasant. The capital, Harbin, is a major industrial and transportation center, and also the most important center for Soviet Studies in the PRC. Daqing houses China's premier oil fields, while Qiqiha'er and Mudanjiang offer important border region and minority studies. The border with Siberia is heavily patrolled, but foreign residents have gained access for camping and hiking to backcountry trails normally sealed off to foreigners. Language is fairly standard Mandarin.

UNIVERSITIES

Harbin University of Science and Technology*
Responsible Bureau: Ministry of Machine Industry
Departments: Electrical Machines, Electrical Materials, Electronics Engineering, Computer Engineering, Mechanics I, Mechanics II, Technical Physics,

Management Engineering, Social Sciences, Foreign Langauges (English, Japanese), Basic course teaching section
Chinese Students: 13,000   **Foreign Students:** 20   **Foreign Teachers:** 5
Accommodations: Free living in foreign expert building, restaurant or gas tank available
Teacher Salary/Benefits: 1,200-2,000¥ RMB/month, int'l r-t airfare may be available in regard to the specific background of the individual
Teaching Conditions: 16 hrs/wk; students are English majors, foreign trade majors and postgraduates
Other: The present HUST is a merger of former HUST and Harbin Institute of Electrical Technology and Harbin Mechanical Electrical College
Contact: Yu Xian Ying, Foreign Affairs Office, Harbin University of Science and Technology, Xuefu Rd., Harbin, Heilongjiang PRC
I Phone: (86-451) 668-2604 or 210-9549   **Fax:** (86-451) 668-2604 or 219-0549
e-mail: public@hubrst.edu.cn

Harbin University of Technology
Responsible Bureau: Aerospace Ministry
Departments: Precision Equipment Engineering, Power Production, Computer Science, Control, Industrial Workers Construction, Radio Technology, Electrical Equipment, Chemistry, Mechanics, Metallurgy, Management, Physics, Mathematics, Power Engineering
Contact: Foreign Affairs Office, Harbin University of Technology, Xidazhi St., Harbin, Heilongjiang PRC

Heilongjiang University
Responsible Bureau: Provincial Education Committee
Departments: Chinese, History, Philosophy, Foreign Languages, Mathematics, Physics, Chemistry, Computer Science, Library Investigation, Economics, Law
Accommodations: pretty good; 1-1/2 rms w/ kitchen, TV, tape recorder, fridge, plenty of heat, bus 2x/wk to downtown (else 1 hr on public bus)
Teaching Conditions: 14 hrs/wk; excellent language lab, great library but students have no access; also tendency to "isolate" foreign teachers from meetings and "the life of the department"—"it pays to fight for things around here"
Students: have program in Chinese Language/Culture
Contact: Foreign Affairs Office, Heilongjiang University, 24 Xuefu Rd., Harbin, Heilongjiang PRC

Jiamusi University
Responsible Bureau: City Government
Departments: Mechanical Arts, Chinese, Secretarial Arts, Russian
Sister School: US—Florida College
Teachers: can teach English, technical subjects
Contact: Foreign Affairs Office, Jiamusi University, Sifeng Rd., Jiamusi, Heilongjiang PRC

Jixi University
Responsible Bureau: City Government
Departments: Mechanical Electronics, Chinese, Computer Science, Industrial Management
Contact: Foreign Affairs Office, Jixi University, Jiguan District, Jixi, Heilongjiang PRC

Mudanjiang University
Responsible Bureau: City Government
Departments: Secretarial Science, Industrial Management, Commercial Management, Industrial Chemistry, Dyes, Industrial Workers Construction
Contact: Foreign Affairs Office, Mudanjiang University, Beishan, Mudanjiang, Heilongjiang PRC

University of Harbin
Responsible Bureau: City Government
Departments: Industrial Worker's Construction, Nutrition, Industrial Management, Chinese, Law, Packaging, Fashion
Contact: Foreign Affairs Office, University of Harbin, Daowai District, Harbin, Heilongjiang PRC

FINANCE/COMMERCE/ECONOMICS

Heilongjiang Institute of Commerce
Responsible Bureau: Ministry of Commerce
Departments: Oil Storage, Electronics, Mechanics, Nutrition, Commercial Goods Management, Chinese Pharmacological Production, Commercial Economics
Contact: Foreign Affairs Office, Heilongjiang Institute of Commerce, Tongda St., Harbin, Heilongjiang PRC

NORMAL SCHOOLS

Harbin Normal School
Responsible Bureau: Provincial Education Committee
Departments: Education, Politics, Chinese, History, Geology, Biology, Mathematics, Physics, Chemistry, Physical Education, Music, Art, Foreign Languages
Contact: Foreign Affairs Office, Harbin Normal School, Hexing Rd., Harbin, Heilongjiang PRC

Mudanjiang Normal School
Responsible Bureau: Provincial Education Committee
Departments: Politics, Chinese, Biology, Mathematics, Physics, Physical Education, English
Contact: Foreign Affairs Office, Mudanjiang Normal School, Dongjingchengzhen, Ning'an County, Heilongjiang PRC

Qiqiha'er Normal School
Responsible Bureau: Provincial Education Committee
Departments: Pre-education Training, Political Education, Chinese, History, Geology, Biology, Mathematics, Physics, Chemistry, Physical Education, Music, Foreign Languages
Contact: Foreign Affairs Office, Qiqiha'er Normal School, Xihongqiao, Qiqiha'er, Heilongjiang PRC

MEDICAL SCHOOLS

Harbin Medical College
Responsible Bureau: Provincial Education Committee
Departments: Medicine, Oral Medicine, Sanitation and Hygiene
Contact: Foreign Affairs Office, Harbin Medical College, Nangang District, Harbin, Heilongjiang PRC

Heilongjiang College of Traditional Chinese Medicine
  Responsible Bureau: Provincial Education Committee
  Departments: Acupuncture, Chinese Medicine, Chinese Pharmacology
  Contact: Foreign Affairs Office, Heilongjiang College of Traditional Chinese Medicine, Huhe Rd., Harbin, Heilongjiang PRC

Jiamusi College of Medicine
  Responsible Bureau: Provincial Education Committee
  Departments: Medicine, Oral Medicine, Pharmacology
  Contact: Foreign Affairs Office, Jiamusi College of Medicine, Dexiang St., Jiamusi, Heilongjiang PRC

TECHNICAL SCHOOLS

Daqing Petroleum Institute*
  Responsible Bureau: Ministry of Petroleum
  Departments: Oil Exploration, Oil Development, Oil Refinement, Oil Mechanics, Computers and Control, Industrial Management
  Contact: Foreign Affairs Office, Daqing Petroleum Institute, Anda, Heilongjiang PRC

Harbin Institute of Architectural Engineering
  Responsible Bureau: City Ministry of Architecture and Environmental Protection
  Departments: Architecture, Urban Planning, Architectural Materials, Mechanical and Electrical Management Engineering
  Contact: Foreign Affairs Office, Harbin Institute of Architectural Engineering, Xidazhi St., Harbin, Heilongjiang PRC

Harbin Institute of Electrical Engineering
  Responsible Bureau: Ministry of Mechanics
  Departments: Electrical Mechanics, Control, Electrical Engineering Materials, Mechanics, Management, Political Education
  Chinese Students: 1,500   **Sister School:** Japan—Chiba Univ
  Contact: Foreign Affairs Office, Harbin Institute of Electrical Engineering, Daqing St., Harbin, Heilongjiang PRC

Harbin Institute of Ship and Boat Engineering*
  Responsible Bureau: China General Ship and Boat Company
  Departments: Ships and Boats, Ship Engineering, Power Production, Automation and Control, Sonar, Mechanics, Electronics, Management, Political Education
  Sister Schools: US—Southern Louisiana Univ; Japan—Nagasaki Inst of Applied Sciences; Germany—Hamburg Univ
  Contact: Foreign Affairs Office, Harbin Institute of Ship and Boat Engineering, Wenmiao St., 11/F, Nangang District, Harbin, Heilongjiang PRC

Heilongjiang Institute of Mining
  Responsible Bureau: Ministry of Coal Mining
  Departments: Materials and Mining Engineering, Electrical Equipment and Resource Choice, Mechanical Engineering, Architectural Engineering
  Accommodations: not bad; 2 rms w/ bath, kitchen, TV, tape recorder, phone, plenty of hot water, occasional use of car and driver; dorm central to campus, 30 min walk from downtown
  Teaching Conditions: good; close cooperation between Chinese, foreign staff; school invites Russian teachers from Komsomolsk-on-Amur Polytechnical

Institute in Russia as well as English teachers, which provides interesting oppor-
tunities for cultural exchange; no photocopying or secretarial assistance
Contact: Foreign Affairs Office, Heilongjiang Institute of Mining, Jiguan District,
Jixi, Heilongjiang PRC

Jiamusi Institute of Industry
Responsible Bureau: Provincial Economic Committee
Departments: Mechanics, Power Production Mechanics, Agricultural Mechanics,
Computer Science, Industrial Management, Mechanical Electronics
Contact: Foreign Affairs Office, Jiamusi Institute of Industry, Xinangang, Jiamusi,
Heilongjiang PRC

Northeast Institute of Agriculture
Responsible Bureau: Provincial Administration of Agriculture, Livestock, and Fisheries
Departments: Agricultural Science, Gardening, Agricultural Industry, Livestock
and Veterinary Medicine, Agricultural Economics
Contact: Foreign Affairs Office, Northeast Institute of Agriculture, Gongbin Rd.,
Harbin, Heilongjiang PRC

Northeast Institute of Heavy Mechanics
Responsible Bureau: Ministry of Mechanics
Departments: Industrial Metals Mechanics, Mechanical Engineering, Automation
and Control, Management, Political Education
Contact: Foreign Affairs Office, Northeast Institute of Heavy Mechanics, Fula'erji,
Qiqiha'er, Heilongjiang PRC

Qiqiha'er Institute of Light Industry
Responsible Bureau: Provincial Economic Committee
Departments: Light Industry, Chemistry, Automation, Mechanics, Management
Engineering
Contact: Foreign Affairs Office, Qiqiha'er Institute of Light Industry, Wenhua St.,
Qiqiha'er, Heilongjiang PRC

HENAN — An important center of ancient Chinese culture, dry, dusty
Henan houses some of China's most important archaelogical treasures,
from the Buddhist grottoes at Longmen near Luoyang to Shang Dynasty
ruins in the capital at Zhengzhou. China's early Jewish community was
also centered in Henan, particularly in Kaifeng, whose people no longer
adhere to Judaism but eschew pork because "it is our tradition."
Language is fairly standard Mandarin and food is heavy by Chinese standards, and includes many wheat products. Henan weather features four
distinct seasons, but, away from the Yellow River valley and the rich agricultural lands near Zhengzhou, is dusty and windy year-round.

UNIVERSITIES

Henan University*
Responsible Bureau: Provincial Higher Education Committee
Departments: Chinese, Political Education, History, Education, Mathematics,
Physics, Chemistry, Geology, Physical Education, Art, Computer Science, Law,
Foreign Languages

Sister School: US—exchange program with Lee College, Cleveland, TN Comment: we received a letter which contained facts asked for in our survey but which read as though it had been copied by a non-native speaker. Therefore, we have not included some of the more dubious information.

Accommodations: 2 rms, hot water in the morning only, kitchen

Contact: Foreign Affairs Office, Henan University, Minglun St., Kaifeng, Henan PRC

Kaifeng University

Responsible Bureau: City Government

Departments: Politics, Industrial Management, Finance and Accounting, Chinese, Geology, Secretarial Science, Mechanics, Computer Software

Contact: Foreign Affairs Office, Kaifeng University, Xiangyang Rd., Kaifeng, Henan PRC

Luoyang University

Responsible Bureau: City Government

Departments: Mechanics, Computer Science, Management, Industrial Workers Construction, Finance and Accounting, Foreign Languages, Chinese, Archaeology

Contact: Foreign Affairs Office, Luoyang University, Tanggong W. Rd., Luoyang, Henan PRC

Pingyuan University

Responsible Bureau: City Government

Departments: Applied Micromechanics, Secretarial Science, Economics, Industrial Management, Physical Education, Statistics, Cotton Textiles

Contact: Foreign Affairs Office, Pingyuan University, Luotuowan, Xinxiang, Henan PRC

Zhengzhou University*

Responsible Bureau: Provincial Education Committee

Departments: Mathematics, Computer Science, Physics, Chemistry, Electronics, Chinese, Journalism, Foreign Languages, Philosophy, Politics, Law, Economics, History, Library Science

Contact: Foreign Affairs Office, Zhengzhou University, Daxue Rd., Zhengzhou, Henan PRC   **URL:** http:.//www.zzu.edu.cn/

FINANCE/ECONOMICS

Henan Finance and Economics University

Responsible Bureau: State Education Commission

Departments: International Economics, Accounting, Trade, Finance and Banking, Agricultural Economics, Labor and Personnel Economy Information, Secretary, Law, Trade and Finance, English

Chinese Students: 3,700   **Foreign Students:** 6

Foreign Teachers: 2   **Sister Schools:** 2

Accommodations: Free housing, cooking facilities, TV, fridge, etc.

Teacher Salary/Benefits: 1,500¥ RMB/month; travel allowances per year - 2,200¥ RMB/year

Teaching Conditions: 14-16 hrs/wk; access to audio-video equipment, computer, enough teaching materials

Student Tuition/Expense: USD$800/term; USD$1,600/yr

Contact: Foreign Affairs Office or International Culture and Education Exchange Center, Henan Finance and Economics University, No. 80 Wenhua Rd., Zhengzhou, Henan Province 450002 PRC

I Phone: (86-371) 394-1254   **Fax:** (86-371) 394-0714

Henan Institute of Economics and Finance
 Responsible Bureau: Provincial Education Committee
 Departments: Economics, Statistics, Trade, Economic Policy and Finance, Secretarial Science
 Contact: Foreign Affairs Office, Henan Institute of Economics and Finance, Nongye Rd., Zhengzhou, Henan PRC

NORMAL SCHOOLS

Henan Normal School
 Responsible Bureau: Provincial Higher Education Committee
 Departments: Mathematics, Physics, Chemistry, Biology, Political Education, Physical Education, Chinese, Education, Foreign Languages
 Contact: Foreign Affairs Office, Henan Normal School, Muye Village, Xinxiang, Henan PRC

MEDICAL SCHOOLS

Henan College of Chinese Medicine
 Responsible Bureau: Provincial Higher Education Committee
 Departments: Chinese Medicine, Chinese Pharmacology, Acupuncture
 Contact: Foreign Affairs Office, Henan College of Chinese Medicine, Jinshui Rd., Zhengzhou, Henan PRC

Henan College of Medicine
 Responsible Bureau: Provincial Education Committee
 Departments: Medicine, Sanitation and Hygiene, Oral Medicine, Pediatrics
 Contact: Foreign Affairs Office, Henan College of Medicine, Daxue Rd., Zhengzhou, Henan PRC

TECHNICAL SCHOOLS

Luoyang Institute of Industry
 Responsible Bureau: Ministry of Mechanics
 Departments: Mechanics, Agricultural Equipment, Electrical Equipment Automation, Management, Sociology
 Contact: Foreign Affairs Office, Luoyang Institute of Industry, Xiyuan Rd., Luoyang, Henan PRC

Zhengzhou Institute of Aviation Industry and Management
 Responsible Bureau: Ministry of Aviation
 Departments: Financial Management, Planning Management, Consumer Goods Management, Personal File Management
 Contact: Foreign Affairs Office, Zhengzhou Institute of Aviation Industry and Management, Hanghai Rd., Zhengzhou, Henan PRC

Zhengzhou Institute of Light Industry
 Responsible Bureau: Ministry of Light Industry
 Departments: Control Engineering, Nutritional Engineering, Industrial Chemistry, Mechanics, Finance and Accounting, Industrial Management
 Sister Schools: US—Univ of Kansas, Univ of Pittsburgh
 Contact: Foreign Affairs Office, Zhengzhou Institute of Light Industry, Wenhua Rd., Zhengzhou, Henan PRC

Zhengzhou Institute of Technology
  Responsible Bureau: Ministry of Industrial Chemistry
  Departments: Mechanical Engineering, Industrial Chemistry, Natural Products Engineering, Mechanical Electronics Engineering, Hydrology, Economic Management
  Sister Schools: US—Univ of Oakland, Univ of Delaware; UK—Worcester Polytechnic; Japan—Northeast Univ
  Contact: Foreign Affairs Office, Zhengzhou Institute of Technology, 52 Wenhua Rd., Zhengzhou, Henan PRC

HUBEI — China's industrial heartland, Hubei province produces much of the nation's steel and houses most of her heavy industry. The capital, Wuhan, is actually three closely interlinked cities—Wuchang, Hanyang, and Hankou. A key transportation center, Wuhan hosts excellent flight, water, and rail connections to most of China's major cities. As one respondent wrote, "it's hot as hell here in summer, and freezing in winter, but at least it's easy to escape." Where the Chang Jiang (Yangtze) flows through Hubei it has cut the spectacular "Three Gorges," beloved of Chinese poets and painters, and many river valley towns, such as tiny Yichang, back onto cliffs so sheer the towns are accessible only by water. Hubei food is hearty, her weather extreme (and no heating allowed in Wuhan and other south-of-the-Chiang-Jiang towns), and her language heavily accented Mandarin.

UNIVERSITIES

Huazhong University of Science and Technology*
  Responsible Bureau: State Education Commission
  Departments: Mathematics, Physics, Chemistry, Mechanical Science and Engineering, Materials Science and Engineering, Power Engineering, Electrical Power Engineering, Opto-Elecronics Engineering, Electronics and Information Engineering, Solid State Electronics, Automation Control Engineering, Computer Science & Engineering, Civil Structural Engineering, Architecture, Bioengineering, Chinese Language & Literature, Journalism, Political Science & Law, Sociology, Arts, Philosophy, Business Administration, Economics, Finance, Foreign Languages, Mechanics, Naval Architecture and Ocean Engineering, Automobile Engineering
  Students: 14,500   **Foreign Students:** 115
  Foreign Teachers: 8
  Contact: Zhou Shao Lin, Foreign Affairs Office, Huazhong University of Science and Technology, Wuhan, Hubei PRC
  I Phone: (86-27) 754-2457   **Fax:** (86-27) 754-7063
  e-mail: fso@blue.hust.edu.cn
  URL: http://sun200.whnet.edu.cn/enghust/enghome.htm

Hubei University
  Responsible Bureau: Provincial Education Committee
  Departments: Political Education, Education Management, Chinese, History, Geology, Physics, Biology, Mathematics, Chemistry, Physical Education, English, Economic Management
  Contact: Foreign Affairs Office, Hubei University, Wuchang, Baoji'an, Wuhan, Hubei PRC

Jianghan University
Responsible Bureau: City Education Committee
Departments: Economic Management, Political Law, Accounting and Statistics, Chinese and Secretarial Science, Foreign Languages, Mechanical Electronics, Urban Planning and Environmental Protection, Mathematical Statistics, Physical Education, Industrial Arts, Agricultural Science
Contact: Foreign Affairs Office, Jianghan University, Hankou, Zhaojiatiao, Wuhan, Hubei PRC

Wuhan University*
Responsible Bureau: Ministry of Education
Departments: Chinese, Journalism, History, Philosophy, Politics, Economics, Economic Management, Law, Library Science, Intelligence Gathering, Foreign Languages, Mathematics, Computer Science, Physics, Chemistry, Environmental Science, Biology, Water Resource Exploration, Atmospheric Physics, Epidemiology
Students: 15,000   **Foreign Students:** over 100   **Sister Schools:** many
Accommodations: excellent; 4 students each in 2br suites w/ central living space, own bathroom, no cooking facilities but hotplates OK, also cafeteria; "the food and service are both great if you treat the staff well, but bad if you are rude"; also good private restaurants on campus; dorms central to campus, 20 min bus ride from downtown
Contact: Foreign Affairs Office, Wuhan University, Wuchang, Luojiashan, Wuhan, Hubei PRC
URL: http://www.whu.edu/cn/

MINORITIES/POLITICS & LAW

South Central University of Nationalities
Responsible Bureau: State Nationalities Affairs Commission
Departments: Chinese History of Chinese Nationalities, Minority Cultures, Ethnology, Religions, Minorities Handicrafts, Law Science, Foreign Language, Education Management, Finance & Economy, Chemistry
Chinese Students: 7,000   **Foreign Students:** 5-20   **Foreign Teachers:** 5-10
Sister Schools: Canada—Univ. of Regina
Teacher Salary/Benefits: 1,000-3,000¥ RMB/month for foreign teachers
Teaching Conditions: 10-16 hrs/wk; an apartment is provided
Student Tuition/Expense: USD$200-250/month
Other: We welcome foreigners to teach and study at our university
Contact: Daly, Foreign Affairs Office, South Central Univeristy of Nationalities, Wuhan, Hubei PRC
I Phone: (86-27) 780-0443   **Fax:** (86-27) 780-0443

South Central Institute of Politics and Law
Responsible Bureau: Ministry of Justice
Departments: Law, Economic Law
Sister Schools: Australia—relations with Sydney University
Teachers: teach English, Western Politics, Law
Contact: Foreign Affairs Office, South Central Institute of Politics and Law, Wuchang District, Wuhan, Hubei PRC

ARTS/MUSIC

Hubei Academy of Fine Arts
  Responsible Bureau: Provincial Education Committee
  Departments: Arts, Industrial Arts, Teaching
  Contact: Foreign Affairs Office, Hubei Academy of Fine Arts, Wuchang, Huzhong Village, Wuhan, Hubei PRC

Wuhan Music Academy
  Responsible Bureau: Provincial Education Committee
  Departments: Composition, Voice, Minority Music, Piano, Wind and String Instruments, Music
  Contact: Foreign Affairs Office, Wuhan Music Academy, Wuchang, Jiefang Rd., Wuhan, Hubei PRC

FINANCE/COMMERCE/ECONOMICS

South Central University of Economics and Finance
  Responsible Bureau: Ministry of Finance
  Departments: Economics, Politics, Accounting, Finance, Statistics, Economic Information, Architecture
  Contact: Foreign Affairs Office, South Central University of Economics and Finance, Wuchang, Wuluo Rd., Wuhan, Hubei PRC

NORMAL SCHOOLS

Hubei College of Education
  Responsible Bureau: Provincial Education Committee
  Departments: Politics, Chinese, English, Mathematics, Physics, Chemistry, History
  Contact: Foreign Affairs Office, Hubei College of Education, 23 Wuluo Rd., Wuchang, Hubei PRC

Huazhong Normal School
  Responsible Bureau: State Education Committee
  Departments: Education, Politics, Telephone Education, Languages and Literatures, History, Library Science, Intelligence Gathering, Geology, Physics, Biology, Mathematics, Chemistry, Physical Education, Foreign Languages
  Contact: Foreign Affairs Office, Huazhong Normal School, Wuchang, Guizishan, Wuhan, Hubei PRC

MEDICAL SCHOOLS

Hubei Institute of Chinese Medicine
  Responsible Bureau: Provincial Education Committee
  Departments: Acupuncture, Chinese Medicine, Chinese Pharmacology
  Contact: Foreign Affairs Office, Hubei Institute of Chinese Medicine, Wuchang, Yunjiaqiao, Wuhan, Hubei PRC

Hubei Institute of Medicine
  Responsible Bureau: Provincial Higher Education Administration
  Departments: Medicine, Pediatrics, Oral Medicine, Population Planning, Management

Contact: Foreign Affairs Office, Hubei Institute of Medicine, Wuchang, Gaojiawan, Wuhan, Hubei PRC

Tongji College of Medicine
Responsible Bureau: Ministry of Sanitation and Hygiene
Departments: Medicine, Pediatrics, Sanitation and Hygiene, Environmental Health, Obstetrics and Gynecology, Stomatology, Pharmacology, Management
Contact: Foreign Affairs Office, Tongji College of Medicine, Hankou, Hangkong Rd., Wuhan, Hubei PRC

TECHNICAL SCHOOLS

China University of Geological Science*
Responsible Bureau: Ministry of Geography
Departments: Geology, Mining Production, Water Resource Management, Exploration, Exploration Engineering, Economic Management, Earth Chemistry, Computer Science
Sister Schools: Germany—Univ of Hanover, Univ of Clausthal
Contact: Foreign Affairs Office, China University of Geological Science, Wuchang, Yujiashan, Wuhan, Hubei PRC

Gezhouba Institute of Hydroelectrical Engineering
Responsible Bureau: Ministry of Hydroelectric Power
Departments: Hydrology and Hydroelectric Power, Shipping Mechanics, Electrical Equipment Automation
Contact: Foreign Affairs Office, Gezhouba Institute of Hydroelectrical Engineering, Wangzhougang, Yichang, Hubei PRC

Huazhong Institute of Technology
Responsible Bureau: State Education Committee
Departments: Mathematics, Chemistry, Physics, Power Studies, Biology, Radiation, Architecture, Mechanics, Electronics, Power Production, Solid State Electronics, Electric Power, Automation and Control, Computer Science, Ships and Boating, Management, Foreign Languages, Chinese, Information Science
Contact: Foreign Affairs Office, Huazhong Institute of Technology, Wuchang, Guanshankou, Wuhan, Hubei PRC

Hubei Institute of Technology
Responsible Bureau: Provincial Education Committee
Departments: Mechanical Engineering, Electrical Equipment, Papermaking, Plastics, Yeasts and Leavening, Arts, Industrial Workers Construction, Industrial Management
Contact: Foreign Affairs Office, Hubei Institute of Technology, Wuchang, Nanhu, Wuhan, Hubei PRC

Wuhan City Institute of Construction
Responsible Bureau: City Bureau of Construction and Environmental Protection
Departments: Urban Planning, Urban Construction, Environmental Engineering, Landscape Gardening
Contact: Foreign Affairs Office, Wuhan City Institute of Construction, Wuchang, Xujiashan, Wuhan, Hubei PRC

Wuhan Industrial University
Responsible Bureau: National Bureau of Architectural Materials
Departments: Silicon Processing, Automation, Mechanics, Non-metallic Mining, Construction, Management, English
Contact: Foreign Affairs Office, Wuhan Industrial University, Wuchang, Mafangshan, Wuhan, Hubei PRC

Wuhan Institute of Chemical Technology
Responsible Bureau: Ministry of Industrial Chemistry
Departments: Mining, Industrial Chemistry, Mechanics, Automation, Economic Management
Contact: Foreign Affairs Office, Wuhan Institute of Chemical Technology, Wuchang, Lujiaxiang, Wuhan, Hubei PRC

Wuhan Institute of Hydroelectrical Engineering
Responsible Bureau: Ministry of Hydroelectric Power
Departments: Chemistry, Environmental Engineering, Automation, Applied Computer Science, Hydrology, Mechanical Electronics, River Protection and Control, Industrial Workers Construction, Shipping, High Temperature Areas Theory, Mechanics
Contact: Foreign Affairs Office, Wuhan Institute of Hydroelectrical Engineering, Wuhan, Luojiashan, Wuhan, Hubei PRC

Wuhan Institute of Marine Shipping
Responsible Bureau: Ministry of Transportation
Departments: Ships and Boating, Power Production, Mechanics, Management
Contact: Foreign Affairs Office, Wuhan Institute of Marine Shipping, Wuchang, Yujiatou, Wuhan, Hubei, PRC

Wuhan Institute of Steel
Responsible Bureau: Ministry of Industrial Metals
Departments: Mine Site Choice, Industrial Metals, Industrial Chemistry, Materials, Mechanics, Automation, Management, Electrical Equipmentization
Contact: Foreign Affairs Office, Wuhan Institute of Steel Wuchang, Renjia Rd., Wuhan, Hubei PRC

Wuhan Institute of Technology
Responsible Bureau: China National Vehicle Company
Departments: Mechanics, Cars and Tractors, Electrical Engineering, Management Engineering
Contact: Foreign Affairs Office, Wuhan Institute of Technology, Wuchang, Mafangshan, Wuhan, Hubei PRC

Wuhan Institute of Textiles
Responsible Bureau: Ministry of Textiles
Departments: Textiles, Mechanical Electronics, Textile Chemistry Engineering
Contact: Foreign Affairs Office, Wuhan Institute of Textiles, Wuchang, Guanshan, Wuhan, Hubei PRC

HUNAN — Hunan, birthplace of Mao Ze-dong, remains a center of traditional agriculture. The province's rich alluvial flatlands host a farming life whose rhythms remain essentially what they were when the young Mao wrote his influential "Report on the Peasant's Movement of Hunan." The capital, Changsha, is an important center for education and medical research, while Mao's birthplace at Shaoshan hosts key study centers of Communist history. Hunan food is hearty and spicy, and her language is Mandarin, but with a thick accent. Weather can be extreme and heating is not allowed, so pack accordingly.

UNIVERSITIES

Changsha University
Responsible Bureau: City Government
Departments: Mechanical Control, Textiles, Industrial Workers Construction, Computer Science, Journalism, Secretarial Science, English, Industrial Management, Commercial Accounting, Political Propaganda, Law, Finance and Accounting
Contact: Foreign Affairs Office, Changsha University, Xining St., Changsha, Hunan PRC

Hunan University*
Responsible Bureau: Ministry of Mechanics
Departments: Natural Products Engineering, Mechanics, Electrical Equipment, Industrial Chemistry, Architecture, Environmental Design, Computer Science, Economic Management, Basic Science
Contact: Foreign Affairs Office, Hunan University, Yuelushan, Changsha, Hunan PRC

Hunan University of Science and Technology*
Responsible Bureau: Provincial Committee of Science
Departments: Life Science, Linguistics, Management Science, Information Science, Physics, Resource Science, Architecture, Nutrition, Travel and Tourism
Contact: Foreign Affairs Office, Hunan University of Science and Technology, Jinwanzi, Changsha, Hunan PRC

Xiangtan University
Responsible Bureau: Provincial Education Committee
Departments: Mechanics, Industrial Chemistry, History, Foreign Languages, Philosophy, Economics, Law, Computer Science, Mathematics, Physics, Chemistry
Accommodations: 2 or 3 rms, w/ TV, tape recorder, fridge, fan; no kitchen but can use hotplate; no curfew, relaxed visitor registration, central location
Contact: Foreign Affairs Office, Xiangtan University, Western Suburbs, Xiangtan, Hunan PRC

FINANCE/COMMERCE/ECONOMICS

Hunan Institute of Finance and Economics
Responsible Bureau: Chinese People's Bank
Departments: Finance, Economic Policy, Economics, Statistics, Information
Contact: Foreign Affairs Office, Hunan Institute of Finance and Economics, Shijiachong, Changsha, Hunan PRC

Hunan Technical School of International Economic Management
Responsible Bureau: Provincial Committee of Foreign Economic Relations
Departments: International Economics, International Trade
Contact: Foreign Affairs Office, Hunan Technical School of International Economic Management, Yuhua Rd., Changsha, Hunan PRC

NORMAL SCHOOLS

Hunan Normal University
Responsible Bureau: Provincial Education Committee
Departments: Chinese, Politics, History, Education, Foreign Languages, Industrial Arts, Mathematics, Physics, Chemistry, Biology, Geology, Physical Education
Accommodations: rms w/ shared bath, kitchen, washer, TV, tape recorder, fridge, oven, bike, VCR, A/C, fan; location central to campus but 30 min walk from downtown; strict 11 p.m. curfew, and Chinese students discouraged from visiting
Teaching Conditions: 6-10 hrs/wk; terrible materials, but good library and photocopy facilities
Learning Conditions: great teachers and materials
Contact: Foreign Affairs Office, Hunan Normal University, Hexi, Changsha, Hunan PRC

MEDICAL SCHOOLS

Hunan College of Traditional Chinese Medicine
Responsible Bureau: Hunan Provincial Education Commission
Departments: Traditional Chinese Medicine, Acupuncture, Pharmacology, Basic Science, Adult Education, Social Science
Chinese Students: 4,261   **Foreign Students:** 10   **Foreign Teachers:** 2
Teacher Salary/Benefits: around 800¥ RMB/month
Teaching Conditions: 15 hrs/wk; classroom, laboratory
Accommodations: 4 rms w/ kitchen, TV, washer, fridge, bike, A/C; overseas students apartment housing; no curfew, "lax" visitor registration, location central to campus and free market, 20 min. walk from downtown
Student Tuition/Expense: 2,800¥ RMB/academic year
Learning Conditions: "great" courses in Acupuncture/Accupressure, Traditional Chinese Medicine; but "don't bother with the library"
Contact: Foreign Affairs Office, Hunan College of Traditional Chinese Medicine, 107 Shaoshan Rd., 410007 Changsha, Hunan PRC
I Phone: (86-731) 555-6660   **Fax:** (86-731) 553-2948

Hunan Medical College
Responsible Bureau: Ministry of Sanitation and Hygiene
Departments: Medicine (Oncology, Pharmacology, Dentistry), Sanitation and Hygiene
Sister Schools: US—Yale Univ, Univ of Colorado, Harvard Univ, Iowa Univ, Univ of Nebraska, San Francisco State Univ, Univ of Washington; Hong Kong—Hong Kong Univ
Teachers and Students: very old college, w/ several long-standing exchange programs, including Yale-China (oldest continuing US-China exchange); has various programs w/ sister schools and also accepts outside foreign teachers
Contact: Foreign Affairs Office, Hunan Medical College, North District, Changsha, Hunan PRC

TECHNICAL SCHOOLS

Changsha Institute of Hydrology and Hydroelectric Power
Responsible Bureau: Ministry of Water and Electricity
Departments: Electric Power, Chinese, Mathematics, Physics, Chemistry, Foreign Languages, Finance and Economics
Contact: Foreign Affairs Office, Changsha Institute of Hydrology and Hydroelectric Power, Yaojin Rd., Changsha, Hunan PRC

Changsha Institute of Transportation
Responsible Bureau: Ministry of Transportation
Departments: Architectural Engineering, Civil Engineering, Mechanical Engineering, Management
Contact: Foreign Affairs Office, Changsha Institute of Transportation, Southern Suburbs, Changsha, Hunan PRC

Changsha Railway Institute
Responsible Bureau: Ministry of Railways
Departments: Mechanics, Vehicles, Electronics, Agricultural Construction, Shipping, Foreign Languages
Contact: Foreign Affairs Office, Changsha Railway Institute, Shaoshan Rd., Changsha, Hunan PRC

Hunan Institute of Agriculture
Responsible Bureau: Provincial Education Committee
Departments: Agricultural Science, Gardening, Livestock and Veterinary Medicine, Agricultural Equipment, Agricultural Economics, Examination
Contact: Foreign Affairs Office, Hunan Institute of Agriculture, Eastern Suburbs, Changsha, Hunan PRC

South Central University of Technology
Responsible Bureau: China National Non-Ferrous Metals Company
Departments: Geology, Materials and Mining, Industrial Metals, Mining Engineering, Materials, Metallurgy, Mechanics, Automation and Control, Computer Science, Chemistry, Management, Mathematical Theory, Politics, Foreign Languages
Teachers: teach English and/or technical subjects
Contact: Foreign Affairs Office, South Central University of Technology, Yuelushan, Changsha, Hunan PRC

Xiangtan Institute of Mining
Responsible Bureau: Ministry of Coal Mining
Departments: Materials and Mining, Geology, Mechanics, Automation
Contact: Foreign Affairs Office, Xiangtan Institute of Mining, Xiangtan, Hunan PRC

INNER MONGOLIA — Arching across China's northern border with the Mongolian People's Republic, Inner Mongolia was divided off as a Chinese province in 1947. The vast, windswept grasslands of the Mongolian steppes and the colorful Mongolian people, many of whom still follow traditional nomadic ways of life, make Inner Mongolia one of the PRC's most exotic destinations. Most foreign residents are concentrated in the capital at Hohot (Huhehaote), economic center of the region as well as home to Mongolia's Yellow Lamaist hierarchy. The industrial center at Baotou, however, and the grasslands town of Tongliao, offer isolated but fascinating destinations for those who want to get truly off the beaten track. Weather is chill and windy most of the year, food hearty but unvarying, consisting primarily of mutton, flatbreads, and powdered goat-cheese tea. Language is Mongolian, though in the cities Mandarin speakers predominate.

UNIVERSITIES

Fengzhou Unity University
  Responsible Bureau: Regional Education Administration
  Departments: Commercial Economic Management, Applied Computer Science
  Contact: Foreign Affairs Office, Fengzhou Unity University, Haila'er Elementary
  School, Hohot, Inner Mongolia PRC

Green Mountain University
  Responsible Bureau: Regional Education Committee
  Departments: Industrial Workers Construction, Chinese Language and Literature,
  English, Industrial Management, Electrical Power Plants and Electrical Systems
  Contact: Foreign Affairs Office, Green Mountain University, Bali Village, Hohot,
  Inner Mongolia PRC

University of Inner Mongolia*
  Responsible Bureau: Regional Education Administration
  Departments: Mongolian Language and Literature, Chinese Language and
  Literature, History, Philosophy, Economics, Law, Foreign Languages, Physics,
  Chemistry, Biology, Electronics
  Students: have student program in Mongolian language and culture
  Contact: Foreign Affairs Office, University of Inner Mongolia, Xincheng District,
  Hohot, Inner Mongolia PRC

FINANCE/ECONOMICS

Inner Mongolia Institute of Economic Policy
  Responsible Bureau: Regional Education Administration
  Departments: Finance, Economic Policy, Industrial Economics, Commercial
  Economics, Planning and Statistics, Industrial Management, Sales Finance
  Contact: Foreign Affairs Office, Inner Mongolia Institute of Economic Policy,
  Haila'er Rd., Hohot, Inner Mongolia PRC

NORMAL SCHOOLS

Inner Mongolia Minorities Normal School
  Responsible Bureau: Regional Education Administration
  Departments: History, Politics, Mathematics, Chinese Language and Literature,
  Mongolian Language and Literature, Physics, Chemistry, English, Geology
  Contact: Foreign Affairs Office, Inner Mongolia Minorities Normal School,
  Tongliao, Inner Mongolia, PRC

Inner Mongolia Normal School
  Responsible Bureau: Regional Education Administration
  Departments: Education and Schools, Mongolian Language and Literature,
  Chinese Language and Literature, Foreign Languages, Political Education,
  History, Music, Art, Mathematics, Physics, Chemistry
  Contact: Foreign Affairs Office, Inner Mongolia Normal School, Xincheng District,
  Hohot, Inner Mongolia PRC

MEDICAL SCHOOLS

Baotou Institute of Medicine
 Responsible Bureau: Regional Education Administration
 Departments: Medicine, Sanitation and Hygiene
 Contact: Foreign Affairs Office, Baotou Institute of Medicine, Gangtie Ave., Baotou, Inner Mongolia PRC

Inner Mongolia Institute of Medicine
 Responsible Bureau: Regional Education Administration
 Departments: Medicine, Pharmacology, Chinese Medicine, Mongolian Medicine, Medical Practice
 Contact: Foreign Affairs Office, Inner Mongolia Institute of Medicine, Xinhua St., Hohot, Inner Mongolia PRC

Inner Mongolia Institute of Minority Medicine
 Responsible Bureau: Regional Education Administration
 Departments: Medicine, Mongolian Medicine
 Contact: Foreign Affairs Office, Inner Mongolia Institute of Minority Medicine, Tongliao, Inner Mongolia PRC

TECHNICAL SCHOOLS

Baotou Institute of Steel
 Responsible Bureau: Ministry of Industrial Metals
 Departments: Materials and Mining Engineering, Industrial Metals, Mechanical and Electrical Engineering, Architecture
 Contact: Foreign Affairs Office, Baotou Institute of Steel, Kundulun District, Baotou, Inner Mongolia PRC

Inner Mongolia Institute of Agriculture and Livestock
 Responsible Bureau: Regional Education Administration
 Departments: Livestock, Grasslands, Veterinary Medicine, Agricultural Science, Crop Protection, Agricultural Economics, Vegetables
 Contact: Foreign Affairs Office, Inner Mongolia Institute of Agriculture and Livestock, Hohot, Inner Mongolia PRC

Inner Mongolia Institute of Industry
 Responsible Bureau: Regional Education Administration
 Departments: Material Arts, Chemistry, Power Production, Architecture, Electrical Equipment, Management, Industrial Workers Construction
 Contact: Foreign Affairs Office, Inner Mongolia Institute of Industry, Aimin Rd., Hohot, Inner Mongolia PRC

JIANGSU —Home of scenic Suzhou, Wuxi, Yangzhou, and Yixing as well as of bustling Nanjing, Jiangsu houses, according to one Chinese official, nearly a fifth of all foreign teachers and students in China. A major center of industry, transportation, and research, Nanjing also houses several of China's largest universities as well as beautiful temples and museums. Breathtaking Suzhou, replete with Ming and Qing gardens; Wuxi, home of Lake Tai; ancient Yangzhou, where Marco Polo once was mayor; and Yixing, cradle of Purple-Sand ceramics, offer some of the most gorgeous scenery in China. Jiangsu food is varied and delicious, featuring dozens of different dumplings and buns. Weather is mostly mild, though pollution in Nanjing is atrocious. Language is thickly accented Mandarin.

UNIVERSITIES

Jiangnan University
Responsible Bureau: City Government
Departments: Mechanics, Automation, Radio Technology, Computer Science, Chemistry, Textiles, Agricultural Construction, Management, Chinese, Foreign Languages, Medical Practice
Contact: Foreign Affairs Office, Jiangnan University, Yanxi Rd., Wuxi, Jiangsu PRC

Nanjing University*
Responsible Bureau: State Education Committee
Departments: Chinese, History, Philosophy, Library Science, Foreign Languages, Economics, Law, Computer Science, Mathematics, Physics, Chemistry, Environmental Studies, Geology, Geography, Atmosperic Studies, Astronomy, Biology
Foreign Teachers: 97   **Sister Schools:** US—CIEE, other schools
Accommodations: 1 lg rm, w/ TV, fridge, no kitchen, cafeteria food "inedible"; 10 min walk from downtown
Teaching Conditions: 12 hrs/wk; materials terrible, no language lab, library OK but no secretarial support
Students: very large programs in Chinese Language, Culture, some short term, organized through Sister Schools; others long term. Some foreign students able to share dorm rooms with Chinese students
Contact: Foreign Affairs Office, Nanjing University, 22 Hankou Rd., Nanjing, Jiangsu 210093 PRC
I Phone: (86-25) 332-5044   **Fax:** (86-25) 331-6747
URL: http://www.nju.edu.cn/

Pengcheng University
Responsible Bureau: City Government
Departments: Agricultural Construction, Mechanical Electronics, Industrial Management, Literature
Contact: Foreign Affairs Office, Pengcheng University, Southern Suburbs, Xuzhou, Jiangsu PRC

Suzhou University
Responsible Bureau: Provincial Bureau of Higher Education
Departments: Chinese, Politics, History, Foreign Languages, Physical Education, Mathematics, Physics, Chemistry, Economic Policy, Law
Contact: Foreign Affairs Office, Suzhou University, Shizi St., Suzhou, Jiangsu PRC

University of Rivers and Oceans
Responsible Bureau: Ministry of Water and Electricity
Departments: Hydroelectric Power, Marine Shipping and Aquaculture, Field Irrigation, Surveying, Power Studies, Automation, Agricultural Construction, Management
Foreign Students: many   **Foreign Teachers:** 10-15

Teachers: can teach English, Western Culture, technical subjects
Students: school formerly had 100+ Chinese gov't scholarship students; was site of 1989 anti-African student riots; number of foreign students currently in flux
Contact: Foreign Affairs Office, University of Rivers and Oceans, Xikang Rd., Nanjing, Jiangsu PRC

FINANCE/COMMERCE/ECONOMICS

Nanjing Institute of Finance and Trade
Responsible Bureau: City Government
Departments: Industrial Management, Foreign Trade, Accounting, Finance, Taxation
Contact: Foreign Affairs Office, Nanjing Institute of Finance and Trade, Fenhuang W. St., Nanjing, Jiangsu PRC

ARTS/MUSIC

Nanjing Academy of Arts
Responsible Bureau: Provincial Bureau of Higher Education
Departments: Arts, Music
Contact: Foreign Affairs Office, Nanjing Academy of Arts, Huju N. Rd., Nanjing, Jiangsu PRC

NORMAL SCHOOLS

Nanjing Normal University
Responsible Bureau: Jiangsu Education Bureau
Departments: Chinese Language and Literature, Education, Foreign Languages and Literature, History, Sociology, Mathematics, Computer Science, Biology, Physics, Chemistry, Geography, Music, Fine Arts, Physical Education
Chinese Students: over 7,000   **Foreign Students:** 306   **Foreign Teachers:** 1
Sister Schools: US—Union College; Korea—Sookinyang Women's Univ.
Accommodations: Foreign experts and students housed at Nan Shan Hotel and students' dorms
Teacher Salary/Benefits: Foreign teachers starting 1,500¥ RMB/month
Teaching Conditions: 12-16 hrs/wk
Student Tuition/Expense: Foreign student ranging from USD$1,800-2,500/year
Contact: Foreign Affairs Office, Nanjing Normal University, Ninghai Rd., Nanjing, Jiangsu PRC
Phone: (86-25) 372-8418   **Fax:** (86-25) 370-6565 or 771-8174

Xuzhou Railway Normal School
Responsible Bureau: Ministry of Railways
Departments: Chinese, Mathematics, Biology, History, Chemistry, English
Contact: Foreign Affairs Office, Xuzhou Railway Normal School, Renmin Rd., Xuzhou, Jiangsu PRC

Xuzhou Teachers College
Responsible Bureau: Provincial Education Commission
Departments: Chinese, History, Foreign Languages, Political Education, Mathematics, Physics, Chemistry, Physical Education, Geology, Biology
Sister School: Australia—University of Melbourne
Accommodations: great; 4 rms w/ kitchen (in cookhouse across courtyard) bath, washer, TV, tape recorder, plenty of hot water, A/C, vacuum cleaner, bike, use of

car and driver when needed, no curfew; cook provided if wish; dorm central to campus and 15 min walk from downtown

Teaching Conditions: workload heavy; 16-24 hrs/wk but students excellent; no photocopying, but secretarial assistance available, + foreign teachers get own office; excellent library, w/ subscriptions to many foreign magazines, including Time, Newsweek, Life, Harpers, Atlantic Monthly, etc.

Contact: Foreign Affairs Office, Xuzhou Teachers College, Heping Rd., Xuzhou, Jiangsu PRC

Yangzhou Normal School
Responsible Bureau: Provincial Bureau of Higher Education
Departments: Chinese, History, Politics, English, Mathematics, Physics, Chemistry, Physical Education, Commercial Economics
Contact: Foreign Affairs Office, Yangzhou Normal School, Western Suburbs, Yangzhou, Jiangsu PRC

MEDICAL SCHOOLS

Jiangsu College of Medicine
Responsible Bureau: Ministry of Atomic Industry
Departments: Medicine, Radiation Therapy, Politics
Contact: Foreign Affairs Office, Jiangsu College of Medicine, Renmin Rd., Suzhou, Jiangsu PRC

Nanjing College of Chinese Medicine
Responsible Bureau: Provincial Bureau of Higher Education
Departments: Chinese Medicine, Chinese Pharmacology, Acupuncture, Acupressure
Contact: Foreign Affairs Office, Nanjing College of Chinese Medicine, Hanzhong Rd., Nanjing, Jiangsu PRC

Nanjing College of Medicine
Responsible Bureau: Provincial Bureau of Higher Education
Departments: Medicine, Pediatrics, Oral Medicine, Sanitation and Hygiene, Nursing and Care
Contact: Foreign Affairs Office, Nanjing College of Medicine, Hanzhong Rd., Nanjing, Jiangsu PRC

Nanjing College of Pharmacology
Responsible Bureau: National Medical and Pharmacological Bureau
Departments: Pharmacology, Chinese Pharmacology; Pharmacological Production, Chemistry
Sister Schools: Japan—Gifu College of Pharmacology, US—Univ of Pittsburgh
Contact: Foreign Affairs Office, Nanjing College of Pharmacology, Tongjiagang, Nanjing, Jiangsu PRC

Nanjing Railway College of Medicine
Responsible Bureau: Ministry of Railways
Departments: Medicine, Sanitation and Hygiene
Contact: Foreign Affairs Office, Nanjing Railway College of Medicine, Dingjiaqiao Rd., Nanjing, Jiangsu PRC

Nantong College of Medicine
Responsible Bureau: Ministry of Transportation

Departments: Medicine, Aviation and Shipping Medicine
Contact: Foreign Affairs Office, Nantong College of Medicine, Qixiu Rd., Nantong, Jiangsu PRC

Suzhou Medical College
Responsible Bureau: Ministry of Education Commission
Departments: Preventative Medicine, Pediatrics, Basic Medical Science, Pharmacy Mediation Medicine, Medical Imaging
Chinese Students: 2,600   **Foreign Teachers:** 2
Sister Schools: US—Lema Linda University, Univ. of South Florida
Accommodations: house in good condition
Teacher Salary/Benefits: 1,700-2,000¥ RMB/month
Teaching Conditions: 12-14 hrs/wk; working in foreign language department and training center   **Student Tuition/Expense:** USD$2,500-3,000/yr
Contact: Shi Fu Xi, Director, Foreign Affairs Office, Suzhou Medical College, Suzhou, Jiangsu PRC
I Phone: (86-512) 519-0889   **Fax:** (86-517) 512-0889

Xuzhou College of Medicine
Responsible Bureau: Provincial Bureau of Higher Education
Departments: Medicine
Contact: Foreign Affairs Office, Xuzhou College of Medicine, Huaihai W. Rd., Xuzhou, Jiangsu PRC

Yangzhou College of Medicine
Responsible Bureau: Provincial Bureau of Higher Education
Departments: Medicine, Chinese Medicine, Obstetrics and Gynecology
Contact: Foreign Affairs Office, Yangzhou College of Medicine, Huaihai Rd., Yangzhou, Jiangsu PRC

Zhenjiang College of Medicine
Responsible Bureau: Provincial Bureau of Higher Education
Departments: Examination, Medicine
Contact: Foreign Affairs Office, Zhenjiang College of Medicine, Jiefang Rd., Zhenjiang, Jiangsu PRC

TECHNICAL SCHOOLS

Changzhou Institute of Industrial Arts
Responsible Bureau: City Government
Departments: Mechanics, Computer Science, Industrial Automation, Industrial Management, Foreign Languages, Secretarial Sciences, Agricultural Construction
Contact: Foreign Affairs Office, Changzhou Institute of Industrial Arts, Zhoujiaxiang, Changzhou, Jiangsu PRC

Chinese Institute of Mining
Responsible Bureau: Ministry of Coal Mining
Departments: Coal Field Geology, Resource Exploration and Surveying, Materials and Mining, Coal Mining Construction and Techniques, Mechanics, Unified Coal Theory and Use, Automation, Coal Industry Management
Contact: Foreign Affairs Office, Chinese Institute of Mining, Xuzhou, Jiangsu PRC

East China Institute of Industry
Responsible Bureau: Ministry of Weapons and Military Equipment
Departments: Mechanics, Industrial Chemistry, Electronics, Mechanical Control Arts, Computer Science, Radiation Electronics Technology, High Temperature Physics Engineering, Aviation Power Studies, Automation/Control, Management, Basic Sciences
Contact: Foreign Affairs Office, East China Institute of Industry, Xiaolingwei, Nanjing, Jiangsu PRC

Jiangsu Institute of Agriculture
Responsible Bureau: Provincial Bureau of Higher Education
Departments: Agricultural Science, Gardening, Livestock, Veterinary Medicine, Mechanical Electronics, Field Irrigation, Animal Products Processing, Livestock Feed and Nutrition, Nutrition and Hygiene, Village Construction
Contact: Foreign Affairs Office, Jiangsu Institute of Agriculture, Western Suburbs, Yangzhou, Jiangsu PRC

Jiangsu Institute of Industrial Chemistry
Responsible Bureau: Provincial Administration of Industrial Chemistry
Departments: Non-organic Industrial Chemistry, Industrial Chemistry Mechanics, Management Engineering
Contact: Foreign Affairs Office, Jiangsu Institute of Industrial Chemistry, Jichang Rd., Changzhou, Jiangsu PRC

Jiangsu Institute of Technology
Responsible Bureau: Ministry of Mechanics
Departments: Electrical Equipment, Power Production, Mechanics, Information, Management, Agricultural Mechanics, Agricultural Mechanization
Contact: Foreign Affairs Office, Jiangsu Institute of Technology, East Suburbs, Zhenjiang, Jiangsu PRC

Nanjing Aeronautical Institute
Responsible Bureau: Ministry of Aviation
Departments: Airplanes, Generators, Automation and Control, Electronics, Mechanics, Management, Wind Power Production, Computer Science
Sister Schools: US—Univ of New Mexico, Univ of Tennessee, Georgia Inst of Technology; UK—Univ of Glasgow, Univ of Nottingham, Oxford Univ, Manchester Univ; Japan—Kyushu Univ; Sweden—Univ of Stockholm
Contact: Foreign Affairs Office, Nanjing Aeronautical Institute, 29 Yudao St., Nanjing, Jiangsu PRC

Nanjing Agricultural University
Responsible Bureau: Ministry of Agriculture, Livestock, and Fisheries
Departments: Agricultural Sciences, Crop Protection, Soil Chemistry, Gardening, Livestock, Veterinary Medicine, Agricultural Economics, Agricultural Mechanization, Nutrition, Animal Products Processing
Contact: Foreign Affairs Office, Nanjing Agricultural University, Zhongshanmenwai, Nanjing, Jiangsu PRC

Nanjing College of Food Economics
Responsible Bureau: Ministry of Commerce
Departments: Planning and Statistics, Finance and Accounting, Economics, Grain and Oils Storage
Contact: Foreign Affairs Office, Nanjing College of Food Economics, Fujian Rd., Nanjing, Jiangsu PRC

Nanjing Institute of Architecture and Engineering
Responsible Bureau: City Ministry of Construction and Environmental Protection
Departments: Agricultural Construction, Mechanics, Geology of Rivers and Lakes, Water Surveying, Architectural Economic Management
Contact: Foreign Affairs Office, Nanjing Institute of Architecture and Engineering, Zhongshan N. Rd., Nanjing, Jiangsu PRC

Nanjing Institute of Industrial Chemistry
Responsible Bureau: Ministry of Industrial Chemistry
Departments: Industrial Chemistry, Mechanics, Applied Chemistry
Contact: Foreign Affairs Office, Nanjing Institute of Industrial Chemistry, Xinmofan Blvd., Nanjing, Jiangsu PRC

Nanjing Institute of Industry
Responsible Bureau: State Education Committee
Departments: Architectural Engineering, Mechanical Engineering, Power Production, Radio Technology, Civil Engineering, Environmental Studies, Electronics, Mathematical Power Studies, Automation and Control, Computer Science, Physical Chemistry, Biological Medicine, Materials, Sociology, Management
Contact: Foreign Affairs Office, Nanjing Institute of Industry, Sipai Building, Nanjing, Jiangsu PRC

Nanjing Institute of Meteorology*
Responsible Bureau: National Bureau of Meteorology
Departments: Weather-Driven Power Production, Weather, Meteorology, Atmospheric Exploration, Atmospheric Physics, Agricultural Meteorology
Sister School: UK—Univ of Edinburgh
Contact: Foreign Affairs Office, Nanjing Institute of Meteorology, Pukou District, Nanjing, Jiangsu PRC

Nanjing Institute of Post and Telecommunications
Responsible Bureau: Ministry of Post and Telecommunications
Departments: Electronic Mail, Radio Technology, Computer Science, Mail Routes
Contact: Foreign Affairs Office, Nanjing Institute of Post and Telecommunications, Guangdong Rd., Nanjing, Jiangsu PRC

Nanjing Institute of Resource Engineering
Responsible Bureau: Provincial Science Committee
Departments: High Temperature Studies, Electrical Equipment, Industrial Water Conservation, Nuclear Power Plants, Village Resources, Scientific Personal File Management
Contact: Foreign Affairs Office, Nanjing Institute of Resource Engineering, Jiangwangmiao, Nanjing, Jiangsu PRC

Nanjing University of Chemical Technology
Responsible Bureau: Chinese Ministry of Chemical Industry
Departments: Basic Sciences, Chemical Engineering, Silicate Engineering, Mechanical Engineering, Applied Chemistry, Automation & Computer Science, Social Science, High Polymer Science, Engineering Biochemical Science & Engineering, Trade & Economics
Chinese Students: 4,500
Foreign Teachers: 2 long-term teachers, 20 short-term teachers/yr
Sister Schools: Univ. of Ottawa, Univ. of Pittsburgh, Nagoya Inst. of Technology

Accommodations: Special living quarters for foreign teachers and students
Teacher Salary/Benefits: 1,200-2,500¥ RMB/month plus vacation subsidies, free lodging and medicare
Teaching Conditions: 12-14 hrs/wk; PhD or master degree holders in Biomedical Engineering, Chemical Engineering, Computer Science, English Language and Engineering
Student Tuition/Expense: USD$1,800-2,500/yr depending on the subject
Contact: Robin L. P. Han, Foreign Affairs Office, Nanjing University of Chemical Technology, Nanjing, Jiangsu PRC
I Phone: (86-25) 321-1323   **Fax:** (86-25) 321-1323
e-mail: Robin@dns.njuct.edu.cn

Nanjing University of Forestry
Responsible Bureau: Ministry of Forestry
Departments: Forestry, Forest Disease Prevention and Control, Park Forests, Forestry Management, Forest Products Chemistry, Lumber Processing, Lumber Water Shipment, Forestry Mechanics, Lumber Trade
Contact: Foreign Affairs Office, Nanjing University of Forestry, Shaoshan Rd., Nanjing, Jiangsu PRC

Nanjing University of Science & Technology
Responsible Bureau: Ministry of Machinery Industry
Departments: Chemical Engineering, Fine Chemical Technology, Applied Chemistry, Environmental Science & Engineering, Electrical Engineering, Communication Engineering, Optical Engineering, Photoelectric Tech., Applied Electronic Technology, Computer Science, Automatic Control (P.T.O.)
Chinese Students: 13,000   **Foreign Students:** 5   **Foreign Teachers:** 7
Sister Schools: Univ. of Taukuba, Fuknoka Institute of Technology
Accommodations: Zilu Guest House (with about 100 rooms)
Teacher Salary/Benefits: 1,800¥ RMB monthly salary; 2,000¥ RMB vacation allowance
Teaching Conditions: 12-14 hrs/wk; return int'l ticket; free housing
Contact: Division of International Exchange, Nanjing University of Science & Technology, Nanjing, Jiangsu PRC

Nantong Textiles Institute
Responsible Bureau: Provincial Bureau of Higher Education
Departments: Mechanical Electronics, Textiles, Economic Management
Contact: Foreign Affairs Office, Nantong Textiles Institute, Yijiaqiaodong, Nantong, Jiangsu PRC

Suzhou City Institute of Construction and Environmental Protection
Responsible Bureau: City Construction and Environmental Protection Ministry
Departments: Architecture, Urban Planning, Environmental Engineering, Environmental Planning and Management
Contact: Foreign Affairs Office, Suzhou City Institute of Construction and Environmental Protection, Fengqiao, Suzhou, Jiangsu PRC

Suzhou Silk and Brocade Institute
Responsible Bureau: China National Silks and Brocades Company
Departments: Silks and Brocades, Dye and Fiber Chemistry, Mechanics and Electrical Equipment, Industrial Management, Industrial Arts
Contact: Foreign Affairs Office, Suzhou Silk and Brocade Institute, Xiangmenwai, Suzhou, Jiangsu PRC

Wuxi Institute of Light Industry
Responsible Bureau: China National Council of Light Industry
Departments: Biotechnology, Food Science & Engineering, Automation, Mechanical Engineering, Chemical Engineering, Textile Engineering, Garmet Design, Industry Design, Business and Trade Management, Foreign Languages, Social Sciences, Mathematics, Physics
Chinese Students: 6,776   **Foreign Students:** 28   **Foreign Teachers:** 2
Sister Schools: US—Rutgers, UC-Davis, Kansas Univ; Japan—Kyushu Univ, Gifu Univ.; 2 universitities in Canada, and 2 universities in Russia
Accommodations: Single room w/bathroom, kitchen, cable TV, air-conditioning, IDD, fridge
Teacher Salary/Benefits: 3,000¥ RMB/month, travel allowance 2,200¥ RMB/year
Teaching Conditions: 12-14 hrs/wk; a tape recorder, a Chinese teaching assistant
Student Tuition/Expense: Undergraduate USD$2,000/yr, Postgraduates USD$2,500-3,000/yr, Advanced students for Chinese courses USD$1,200/yr
Contact: Yu Hua Ying, Director, Foreign Affairs Office, Wuxi Institute of Light Industry, No. 170 Huibe Road, Wuxi, Jiangsu 214036 PRC
I Phone: (86-510) 580-6751   **Fax:** (86-510) 580-7976
URL: http://www.wxuli.edu.cn/

Zhenjiang Institute of Ships and Boats
Responsible Bureau: China General Ships and Boating Company
Departments: Ships and Boats, Mechanics, Automation and Control, Management
Sister School: USSR—Nikclayev Shipbuilding Inst
Contact: Foreign Affairs Office, Zhenjiang Institute of Ships and Boats, Huancheng Rd., Zhenjiang, Jiangsu PRC

JIANGXI — Center since ancient times of China's porcelain industry, Jiangxi remains today the world's premier porcelain-producing region, from the ancient kilns at Jingdezhen to the "kaolin" trading centers in the capital at Nanchang. The province was also important in Repulican-era and revolutionary history, and towns such as Nanchang and Ganzhou house large historical collections. Weather is mild spring and fall, steamy in summer and cool in winter. Language is a mixture of thickly accented Mandarin and Fujianese, food richly varied with many dishes related to Guangdon cooking.

UNIVERSITIES

Jiangxi University*
Responsible Bureau: Ministry of Education
Departments: Chinese, Journalism, History, Philosophy, Library Science, Foreign Language, Mathematics, Information, Computer Science, Physics, Radio Technology, Chemistry, Nutrition, Biology, Microbiology, Fresh Water Aquaculture, Political Economics, Management, Law
Contact: Foreign Affairs Office, Jiangxi University, Disi Jiaotong Rd., Nanchang, Jiangxi, PRC

FINANCE/ECONOMICS

Jiangxi Institute of Economics and Finance
  Responsible Bureau: Ministry of Finance
  Departments: Statistics, Finance & Accounting, Finance, Basic Construction
  Econimics, Economics, Industrial Economics, Agricultural Economics, Commercial Economics
  Contact: Foreign Affairs Office, Jiangxi Institute of Economics and Finance,
  Xiaoluo, Nanchang, Jiangxi PRC

NORMAL SCHOOLS

Gannan Normal School
  Responsible Bureau: Provincial Higher Education Administration
  Departments: Chinese, Political Education, Foreign Languages, Mathematics, Physics, Chemistry, Physical Education, Music, Art
  Contact: Foreign Affairs Office, Gannan Normal School, Hongqi Blvd., Ganzhou,
  Jiangxi PRC

Jiangxi Normal University
  Responsible Bureau: Provincial Education Administration
  Departments: Chinese, History, Foreign Languages, Political Education, Education, Music, Art, Mathematics, Physics, Chemistry, Geology, Computer Science,
  Physical Education
  Contact: Foreign Affairs Office, Jiangxi Normal University, Disi Jiaotong Rd.,
  Nanchang, Jiangxi PRC

MEDICAL SCHOOLS

Jiangxi Institute of Chinese Medicine
  Responsible Bureau: Provincial Administration of Sanitation and Hygiene
  Departments: Chinese Medicine, Pharmacology
  Contact: Foreign Affairs Office, Jiangxi Institute of Chinese Medicine, Bayi Blvd.,
  Nanchang, Jiangxi PRC

Nanchang College of Medicine
  Responsible Bureau: Provincial Administration of Sanitation and Hygiene
  Departments: Medicine, Pediatrics, Oral Medicine, Sanitation and Hygiene
  Contact: Foreign Affairs Office, Nanchang College of Medicine, Bayi Blvd.,
  Nanchang, Jiangxi PRC

TECHNICAL SCHOOLS

East China Geological Institute
  Responsible Bureau: Ministry of Atomic Industry
  Departments: Geology, MaExperimentation, Water Exploration, Water Resource
  Management
  Sister School: US—Univ. of Texas, El Paso
  Teachers: can teach English, Geology, Hydrogeology
  Students: Geology Dept can accept foreign students
  Contact: Foreign Affairs Office, East China Geological Institute, Fuzhou, Jiangxi
  PRC

East China University of Transportation
  Responsible Bureau: Ministry of Railways
  Departments: Agriculture, Mechanics, Electrical Equipment, Economic Management
  Contact: Foreign Affairs Office, East China University of Transportation, Shuanggang, Nanchang, Jiangxi PRC

Jiangxi Industrial University
  Responsible Bureau: Provincial Education Administration
  Departments: Mechanics, Electrical Mechanics, Industrial Chemistry, Agricultural Construction, Nutrition
  Contact: Foreign Affairs Office, Jiangxi Industrial University, Disi Jiaotong Rd., Nanchang, Jiangxi PRC

Jiangxi Institute of Industrial Metals
  Responsible Bureau: China National Non-Ferrous Metals Company
  Departments: Mining, Mechanical Engineering, Industrial Metals, Automation, Management
  Contact: Foreign Affairs Office, Jiangxi Institute of Industrial Metals, Ganzhou, Jiangxi PRC

Jingdezhen Institute of Porcelain
  Responsible Bureau: Ministry of Light Industry
  Departments: Engineering, Mechanics, Industrial Management
  Contact: Foreign Affairs Office, Jingdezhen Institute of Porcelain, Eastern Suburbs, Jingdezhen, Jiangxi PRC

Nanchang Institute of Aviation Industry
  Responsible Bureau: Ministry of Aviation
  Departments: Materials, Industrial Chemistry, Mechanics, Electronics
  Contact: Foreign Affairs Office, Nanchang Institute of Aviation Industry, Shanghai Rd., Nanchang, Jiangxi PRC

JILIN — The center of Qing Dynasty Manchuria (colonial-era Manchukuo), Jilin today retains a split personality. At Changchun, the capital, the province seems a major center of science and technology, home to China's auto industry, one of her most famous film studios, and some of her top medical research. In border towns like Tonghua and Yanji, the province seems a small Korea, fortified against military crossings, but the site of much quiet small-scale trade (Tonghua is one of the few towns in the world where U.S. citizens can sample freshly made North Korean kim chee). In between lie the Changbaishan Mountains, dotten with ski resorts, hiking trails, winter-olympics training centers, and farmers searching for the almost unimaginably valuable wild Changbaishan Ginseng. Weather is far northern, food bland but hearty, and language fairly standard Mandarin.

UNIVERSITIES

Jilin City Unity University
Responsible Bureau: City Government
Departments: English, Law, Biology, High Temperature Engineering, Industrial Worker's Construction, Computer Science
Contact: Foreign Affairs Office, Jilin City Unity University, Jilin Ave., Jilin City, Jilin PRC

Jilin Industrial University
Responsible Bureau: Ministry of Mechanics
Departments: Agricultural Engineering, Vehicles, High Temperature Energy Production, Mechanics, Electronics, Computer Science, Materials, Mathematical Theory, Management Theory, Intelligence Gathering
Contact: Foreign Affairs Office, Jilin Industrial University, Stalin Ave., Changchun, Jilin PRC

Jilin University*
Responsible Bureau: Ministry of Education
Departments: Chinese, History, Politics, Library Science, Philosophy, Foreign Languages, Mathematics, Physics, Chemistry, Electronics, Computer Science, Biology, Law, Economics
Contact: Foreign Affairs Office, Jilin University, 77 Jiefang Ave., Changchun, Jilin PRC
I Phone: (86-431) 898-6373   **Fax:** (86-431) 892-3907   **URL:** http://www.jlu.edu.cn/

Jilin University of Science and Technology*
Responsible Bureau: Provincial Education Administration
Departments: Nursing, Political History, Mathematics, Japanese, Biology, Industrial Management, English, Library Science, Intelligence Gathering, Applied Computer Science, Law
Contact: Foreign Affairs Office, Jilin University of Science and Technology, Weixing Rd., Changchun, Jilin PRC

Yanbian University
Responsible Bureau: Provincial Education Committee
Departments: Mathematics, Chemistry, Physics, Geology, English, Politics, History, Foreign Languages, Industrial Arts, Physical Education
Contact: Foreign Affairs Office, Yanbian University, Yanji, Jilin PRC

ARTS/MUSIC

Jilin Academy of Arts
Responsible Bureau: Provincial Cultural Administration
Departments: Music, Opera, Art
Contact: Foreign Affairs Office, Jilin Academy of Arts, Ziyou Blvd., Changchun, Jilin PRC

FINANCE/COMMERCE

Jilin Institute of Finance and Trade
Responsible Bureau: Provincial Education Committee
Departments: Accounting and Statistics, Economic Policy and Finance, Trade Economics, Foreign Trade, Grains

Contact: Foreign Affairs Office, Jilin Institute of Finance and Trade, Stalin Ave., Changchun, Jilin PRC

FOREIGN LANGUAGES

Changchun Foreign Languages Technical College
Responsible Bureau: Provincial Education Committee
Departments: English, Russian, Japanese
Contact: Foreign Affairs Office, Changchun Foreign Languages Technical College, Hongqi St.k, Changchun, Jilin PRC

NORMAL SCHOOLS

Changchun Normal School
Responsible Bureau: China National Non-Ferrous Metals Company
Departments: Chinese, Foreign Languages, Mathematics, Physical Education, Political History, Chemistry, Physics, Music
Contact: Foreign Affairs Office, Changchun Normal School, Changjiu Highway, Changchun, Jilin PRC

Jilin Normal School
Responsible Bureau: Provincial Education Committee
Departments: Chinese, Mathematics, Politics, History, Physics, Chemistry, Foreign Languages
Contact: Foreign Affairs Office, Jilin Normal School, Jiangnan St., Jilin City, Jilin PRC

Northeast Normal University
Responsible Bureau: State Education Committee
Departments: Education, Political Education, History, Chinese, Foreign Languages, Music, Art, Mathematics, Physics, Chemistry, Biology, Geology, Physical Education, Library Science, Telephone Education
Sister Schools: US—Univ. of Wisconsin, Univ. of Mississippi, Univ. of California, Univ. of Michigan, S. Illinois Univ., Stanford; Japan—Univ. of Miyagi, Univ. of Okayawa, Obirin College; Canada—Univ. of Saskatchewan
Teachers and Students: facilities include 2.3 million vol library, Museum of Biology, Museum of Ancient Chinese History
Contact: Foreign Affairs Office, Northeastern Normal University, Stalin Ave., Changchun, Jilin PRC

Siping Normal School
Responsible Bureau: Provincial Education Administration
Departments: Chinese, Politics, History, Foreign Languages, Mathematics, Physics, Chemistry, Biology, Geology, Physical Education
Contact: Foreign Affairs Office, Siping Normal School, Tiexi District, Siping, Jilin PRC

Tonghua Normal School
Responsible Bureau: Provincial Education Committee
Departments: Politics, History, Chinese, Mathematics, Education, Physics, Chemistry, English, Biology, Physical Education
Contact: Foreign Affairs Office, Tonghua Normal School, Laozhan St., Tonghua, Jilin PRC

MEDICAL SCHOOLS

Bethune Institute of Medicine
  Responsible Bureau: Ministry of Sanitation and Hygiene
  Departments: Medicine, Pediatrics, Oral Medicine, Environmental Medicine, Nutritional Examination
  Sister Schools: Canada—Univ. of Saskatchewan; Japan—Kyushu Univ., Tohoku Univ.
  Contact: Foreign Affairs Office, Bethune Institute of Medicine, 6 Xinmin Ave., Changchun, Jilin PRC

Changchun Institute of Chinese Medicine
  Responsible Bureau: Provincial Sanitation and Hygiene Administration
  Departments: Chinese Medicine, Chinese Pharmacology
  Contact: Foreign Affairs Office, Changchun Institute of Chinese Medicine, Gongneng Blvd., Changchun, Jilin PRC

Jilin Institute of Medicine
  Responsible Bureau: Provincial Sanitation and Hygiene Administration
  Departments: Medicine, Examination
  Contact: Foreign Affairs Office, Jilin Institute of Medicine, Beijing Rd., Jilin City, Jilin PRC

Yanbian Medical College
  Responsible Bureau: Provincial Sanitation and Hygiene Administration
  Departments: Medical Practice, Pharmacology
  Accommodations: 5 rms for 2 people, w/kitchen, washer, TV, tape recorder, fridge, plenty of heat but no hot water; also special cook for foreign teachers; no curfew and lax visitor registration
  Teaching Conditions: 12 hrs/wk; materials and library poor; secretarial help available, but no photocopying
  Contact: Foreign Affairs Office, Yanbian Medical College, Yanji, Jilin PRC

TECHNICAL SCHOOLS

Changchun Institute of Geology
  Responsible Bureau: Ministry of Geology and Mineral Resources
  Departments: Geology, Hydroengineering, Materials Exploration, Timing Equipment, Mining Exploration, Equipment Management, Political Education
  Contact: Foreign Affairs Office, Changchun Institute of Geology, Geology Palace, Changchun, Jilin PRC

Changchun Institute of Post and Telecommunications
  Responsible Bureau: Ministry of Post and Telecommunications
  Departments: Electronic Mail, Radio Technology, Computer Science, Management
  Contact: Foreign Affairs Office, Changchun Institute of Post and Telecommunications, Nanhu Blvd., Changchun, Jilin PRC

Changchun Institute of Precision Radiation Mechanics
  Responsible Bureau: Ministry of Weapons and Military Equipment
  Departments: Radiation, Physics, Electronics, Materials, Mechanics, Management, Basic Science, Statistics
  Contact: Foreign Affairs Office, Changchun Institute of Precision Radiation Mechanics, Weixing Rd., Changchun, Jilin PRC

Jilin Institute of Architectural Engineering
   Responsible Bureau: Provincial and City Administrations of Environmental Protection
   Departments: Architecture, Construction Management, Labor Salaries
   Contact: Foreign Affairs Office, Jilin Institute of Architectural Engineering, Hongqi St., Changchun, Jilin PRC

Jilin Institute of Industrial Chemistry
   Responsible Bureau: Provincial Oil and Chemistry Administration
   Departments: Industrial Chemistry, Chemical Mechanics
   Contact: Foreign Affairs Office, Jilin Institute of Industrial Chemistry, Longtan District, Jilin City, Jilin PRC

Jilin Institute of Industry
   Responsible Bureau: Provincial Education Committee
   Departments: Mechanics, Materials, Electronics, Management, Light Industrial Chemistry
   Contact: Foreign Affairs Office, Jilin Institute of Industry, Yan'an Rd., Changchun, Jilin PRC

Northeast Institute of Electrical Power Engineering
   Responsible Bureau: Ministry of Water and Electricity
   Departments: Power Production, Electric Power, Architecture, Applied Chemistry
   Accommodations: 2 rms, w/TV, tape recorder, fridge, "inadequate" hot water and kitchen, some use of car and drive; central to campus and markets, but 30 mins by bus to downtown
   Contact: Foreign Affairs Office, Northeast Institute of Electric Power Engineering, Chanchun Rd., Jilin City, Jilin PRC

   LIAONING — Strategically crucial Liaoning province has changed ownership more often in the last 2 centuries than any other Chinese province, as the Russians battled for a warm-water port, the Japanese struggled for a foothold in Manchuria, the Europeans coveted rail lines, and the US searched for influence after Yalta. This importance is reflected still today. The capital, Shenyang, is the only mid-sized Chinese city with sizable numbers of foreign consulates and the port city of Dalian (Dairen) is the northernmost of China's Special Economic Zones and a major center of foreign trade. Weather is harsh in the province's northern end, more mild on the coast. Liaoning cuisine is rich in seafood but not overly varied in produce. Language is fairly standard Mandarin.

UNIVERSITIES

Anshan University
   Responsible Bureau: City Government
   Departments: Chinese, Finance, Mechanical Electronics, Medical Practice, Architecture
   Contact: Foreign Affairs Office, Anshan University, Shijiao, Anshan, Liaoning PRC

Benxi University
   Responsible Bureau: City Government
   Departments: Mechanical Control, Electrification, Industrial Management,

Industrial Worker's Construction, Financial Accounting, Statistics, Medical Practice
Contact: Foreign Affairs Office, Benxi University, Pingshan District, Benxi, Liaoning PRC

Dalian University
Responsible Bureau: City Government
Departments: 3 colleges; Medicine (Medicine, Nursing, Acupuncture, Stomatology and Medical Inspection); Teaching (General Liberal Arts); Engineering (Electrical Equipment, High Temperature Studies, Micromechanics, Agricultural Construction, Scientific Intelligence Gathering, Consumer Goods Management, Accounting, Packaging, Industrial Management, Mechanical Control, Statistics, Organic Chemical Engineering, Industrial Design)
Teachers: can teach English, Western Culture, technical subjects
Students: training center in Chinese Language and Culture, including classes in Calligraphy, Tai Chi Chuan, Chinese Cooking, and excursions
Contact: Foreign Affairs Office, Dalian University, 142 Sanyuan St., Xigang District, Dalian, Liaoning PRC

Dandong University
Responsible Bureau: City Government
Departments: Industrial Economics, Architectural Engineering, Textiles, Management Engineering, Finance and Accounting
Contact: Foreign Affairs Office, Dandong University, Zhenan District, Dandong, Liaoning PRC

Fushun University
Responsible Bureau: City Government
Departments: Industrial Chemistry, Textiles, Silicate Industry, Mechanical Weaving, Industrial Workers Construction, Environmental Engineering, Medical Practice, Industrial Management
Contact: Foreign Affairs Office, Fushun University, Xinfu District, Fushun, Liaoning PRC

Jinzhou University
Responsible Bureau: City Bureau of Education
Departments: Agricultural Economics, Secretarial Science, Industrial Chemistry, Industrial Management, Orchard Production, Livestock and Veterinary Medicine
Contact: Foreign Affairs Office, Jinzhou University, Shizhuan School, Jinzhou, Liaoning PRC

Liaoning University*
Responsible Bureau: Provincial Bureau of Higher Education
Departments: Chinese, Journalism, History, Personal File Management, Philosophy, Law, Political Economics, Finance, Statistics, Foreign Languages, Mathematics, Physics, Chemistry, Biology, Accounting, Insurance
Sister Schools: US—Southern Illinois Univ., Univ. of Denver; Japan—Kansai Univ., Toyana Univ.
Teachers and Students: facilities include 1.2 million vol. library, in-school publishing house (LU Press); has large program in Chinese Language and Culture
Contact: Foreign Affairs Office, Liaoning University, Chongshan W. Rd., Shenyang, Liaoning PRC

Shenyang University*
Responsible Bureau: Provincial Bureau of Higher Education
Departments: Industrial Automation, Mechanical Production, Environmental Protection, Industrial Workers Construction, Finance, Statistics, Industrial Economics
Accommodations: spacious, plenty of heat, flowering plum trees outside of windows
Contact: Foreign Affairs Office, Shenyang University, Dadong District, Shenyang, Liaoning PRC

ARTS/MUSIC

Lu Xun Academy of Fine Arts
Responsible Bureau: Provincial Bureau of Higher Education
Departments: Handicrafts and Arts, Teaching, Fashion, Photography, Arts Design
Contact: Foreign Affairs Office, Lu Xun Academy of Fine Arts, 1 Sanhao St., Shenyang, Liaoning PRC

FINANCE/COMMERCE/ECONOMICS

Northeast Institute of Finance and Economics
Responsible Bureau: Ministry of Finance
Departments: Economics, Planning and Statistics, Accounting, Foreign Trade, Finance, Industrial Management
Accommodations: 3 rms., some w/kitchen, fridge, TV; strict 11 p.m. curfew
Teaching Conditions: 12-14 hrs/wk; good language lab, reasonable materials, no secretarial support or photocopying
Contact: Foreign Affairs Office, Northeast Institute of Finance and Economics, Heishijiao, Dalian, Liaoning PRC

Shenyang Institute of Economics and Finance
Responsible Bureau: City Government
Departments: Labor Economics, Industrial Management, Accounting, Statistics, Commercial Management, Economic Policy, Foreign Trade Economic Management, Information Management
Contact: Foreign Affairs Office, Shenyang Institute of Economics and Finance, Beijing Ave., Shenyang, Liaoning PRC

FOREIGN LANGUAGES

Dalian Foreign Languages Institute
Responsible Bureau: Provincial Higher Education Committee
Departments: English, Russian, Japanese, French
Contact: Foreign Affairs Office, Dalian Foreign Languages Institute, Zhongshan District, Dalian, Liaoning 11601 PRC

NORMAL SCHOOLS

Jinzhou Normal Institute
Responsible Bureau: Provincial Bureau of Higher Education
Departments: Chinese, Political History, Mathematics, Physics, Chemistry, Foreign Languages
Contact: Foreign Affairs Office, Jinzhou Normal Institute, Anhe St., Jinzhou, Liaoning PRC

Liaoning Foreign Language Normal Institute
Responsible Bureau: Provincial Bureau of Higher Education
Departments: English, Russian, Japanese
Contact: Foreign Affairs Office, Liaoning Foreign Language Normal Institute, Qingnian St., Liaoyang, Liaoning PRC

Liaoning Normal School
Responsible Bureau: Provincial Bureau of Higher Education
Departments: Education and Schools, Political Education, Japanese, History, Library Science, Geology, Biology, Mathematics, Computer Science, Physics, Chemistry, Physical Education, Foreign Languages
Contact: Foreign Affairs Office, Liaoning Normal School, Shahekou District, Dalian, Liaoning PRC

Shenyang Normal Institute
Responsible Bureau: Provincial Bureau of Higher Education
Departments: Political Education, Education Management, Chinese, Foreign Languages, Biology, Mathematics, Physics, History of the Chinese Communist Party
Contact: Foreign Affairs Office, Shenyang Normal Institute, Huanghe Ave., Shenyang, Liaoning PRC

MEDICAL SCHOOLS

Chinese University of Medical Science
Responsible Bureau: Ministry of Sanitation and Hygiene
Departments: Medicine, Pediatrics, Oral Medicine, Sanitation and Hygiene, Stomatology, Registered Nursing
Contact: Foreign Affairs Office, Chinese University of Medical Science, Nanjing St., Shenyang, Liaoning PRC

Dalian Institute of Medicine
Responsible Bureau: Provincial Administration of Sanitation and Hygiene
Departments: Medicine, Oral Medicine, Sanitation and Hygiene Management
Sister Schools: US—Boston Univ. School of Medicine; Japan—Tokyo Medical Univ.
Contact: Foreign Affairs Office, Dalian Institute of Medicine, 220 Xinghai #3 Station, Dalian, Liaoning PRC

Jinzhou Institute of Medicine
Responsible Bureau: Provincial Administration of Sanitation and Hygiene
Departments: Medicine and Pharmacology
Contact: Foreign Affairs Office, Jinzhou Institute of Medicine, Le'an St., Jinzhou, Liaoning PRC

Liaoning Institute of Chinese Medicine
Responsible Bureau: Provincial Administration of Sanitation and Hygiene
Departments: Acupuncture, Chinese Bone Treatment, Chinese Pharmacology
Contact: Foreign Affairs Office, Liaoning Institute of Chinese Medicine, Beiling Ave., Shenyang, Liaoning PRC

Shenyang Institute of Medicine
Responsible Bureau: Provincial Bureau of Higher Education
Departments: Composition, Direction, Voice, Music, Instruments, Musical Education

Contact: Foreign Affairs Office, Shenyang Institute of Medicine, Sanhao St., Shenyang, Liaoning PRC

Shenyang Institute of Pharmacology
Responsible Bureau: National Medical and Pharmacological Bureau
Departments: Pharmacology, Japanese, Chinese Pharmacology, Chemical Pharmacological Production, Microproduction, Pharmacological Management
Contact: Foreign Affairs Office, Shenyang Institute of Pharmacology, Wenhua Rd., Shenyang, Liaoning PRC

TECHNICAL SCHOOLS

Anshan Institute of Steel
Responsible Bureau: Ministry of Industrial Metals
Departments: Materials and Metals, Industrial Metals, Mechanics, Automation and Control, Industrial Chemistry
Contact: Foreign Affairs Office, Anshan Institute of Steel, Zhonghua Rd., Anshan, Liaoning PRC

Chinese Institute of Xingshi Police
Responsible Bureau: Ministry of Public Security
Departments: Xingshi Intelligence, Clue Investigation, Document Investigation, Chemical Investigation, Photography, Police Medicine
Contact: Foreign Affairs Office, Chinese Institute of Xingshi Police, Houtawan St., Shenyang, Liaoning PRC

Dalian Institute of Aquaculture
Responsible Bureau: State Education Committee
Departments: Fishery Mechanics, Fishing Port Architecture, Aquaculture, Economic Management, Aquatic Breeding
Contact: Foreign Affairs Office, Dalian Institute of Aquaculture, Heishijiao Village, Dalian, Liaoning PRC

Dalian Institute of Industry
Responsible Bureau: State Education Committee
Departments: Mechanics, Materials, Shipbuilding, Electronics, Computer Science, Architecture, Hydrology, Industrial Chemistry, Management, Sociology, Mathematics, Physics, Power Science, Foreign Languages
Contact: Foreign Affairs Office, Dalian Institute of Industry, Luanjin Village, Dalian, Liaoning PRC

Dalian Institute of Light Industry
Responsible Bureau: Ministry of Light Industry
Departments: Chemistry, Mechanical Electronics, Nutrition, Textiles, Fashion
Contact: Foreign Affairs Office, Dalian Institute of Light Industry, Ganjingzi District, Dalian, Liaoning PRC

Dalian Institute of Marine Shipping
Responsible Bureau: Ministry of Transportation
Departments: Sailing, Steamer Mechanics, Computer Science, Electronics, Marine Shipping Management
Contact: Foreign Affairs Office, Dalian Institute of Marine Shipping, Lingshuiqiao, Dalian, Liaoning PRC

Dalian Railway Institute
Responsible Bureau: Ministry of Railways
Departments: Mechanical Cars and Vehicles, Materials, Mechanics, Electrical Equipment Engineering
Contact: Foreign Affairs Office, Dalian Railway Institute, Shahekou District, Dalian, Liaoning PRC

Fushun Institute of Petroleum
Responsible Bureau: China National Petroleum and Chemicals General Company
Departments: Mechanics, Automation, Oil Chemistry, Management
Contact: Foreign Affairs Office, Fushun Institute of Petroleum, Wanghua District, Fushun, Liaoning PRC

Fuxin Mining Institute
Responsible Bureau: Ministry of Coal Mining
Departments: Materials and Mining, Resource Exploration, Mechanical Electronics, Mechanics, Management, Automation and Control, Computer Science
Accommodations: 3-4 rooms w/cooking facilities (including toaster oven); no curfew
Teaching Conditions: 16 hrs/wk; library had good foreign-language books on mining and science but not much else
Learning Conditions: overall learning conditions petty good
Contact: Foreign Affairs Office, Fuxin Mining Institute, Fuxin, Liaoning PRC

Jinzhou Institute of Industry
Responsible Bureau: Provincial Mechanics Administration
Departments: Mechanics, Automation and Control, Management
Contact: Foreign Affairs Office, Jinzhou Institute of Industry, Jingye St., Jinzhou, Liaoning PRC

Northeast Institute of Technology
Responsible Bureau: Ministry of Industrial Metals
Departments: Mathematics, Physics, Materials and Mining, Mining Engineering, Industrial Metals, Non-ferrous Metals, Materials, Metals Processing, High Temperature Engineering, Mechanics, Automation and Control
Sister Schools: US—Univ. of Pittsburgh, Appalachian State Univ; Japan—Tohoku Univ., Nagoya Univ., Kansai Univ.; Australia—Univ. of Wollongong; Sweden —Royal Inst. of Tech., Lingkoping Univ.
Contact: Foreign Affairs Office, Northeast Institute of Technology, Wenhua Rd., Shenyang, Liaoning PRC

Shenyang Agricultural University
Responsible Bureau: Ministry of Agriculture, Livestock, and Fisheries
Departments: Agricultural Science, Gardening, Soil Chemistry, Crop Protection, Agricultural Economics, Livestock and Veterinary Medicine, Agricultural Engineering, Forestry
Contact: Foreign Affairs Office, Shenyang Agricultural University, Dongling District, Shenyang, Liaoning PRC

Shenyang Institute of Architectural Engineering
Responsible Bureau: City Ministry of Architecture and Environmental Protection
Departments: Automation and Control, Architectural Engineering, Mechanics
Contact: Foreign Affairs Office, Shenyang Institute of Architectural Engineering, Wenhua Rd., Shenyang, Liaoning PRC

Shenyang Institute of Industrial Chemistry
Responsible Bureau: Ministry of Industrial Chemistry
Departments: Mechanics, Computer Science, Industrial Chemistry, Applied Chemistry
Contact: Foreign Affairs Office, Shenyang Institute of Industrial Chemistry, Tiexi District, Shenyang, Liaoning PRC

Shenyang Institute of Industry
Responsible Bureau: Ministry of Weapons and Military Equipment
Departments: Mechanics, Electrical Engineering, Industrial Management
Contact: Foreign Affairs Office, Shenyang Institute of Industry, Wenhua Rd., Shenyang, Liaoning PRC

Shenyang Institute of Aeronautical Engineering
Responsible Bureau: Ministry of Aviation
Departments: Aviation engineering, Security, Mechanics, Electronics
Contact: Foreign Affairs Office, Shenyang Institute of Aeronautical Engineering, Huanghe Ave., Shanyang, Liaoning PRC

Shenyang Polytechnical University
Responsible Bureau: Ministry of Mechanics
Departments: Mechanics, Electronics, Electrical Equipment, Computer Science, Management Engineering
Contact: Foreign Affairs Office, Shenyang Polytechnical University, Xinghua St., Shenyang, Liaoning PRC

NINGXIA — Home to the Muslim Hui people, tiny Ningxia offers foreigners a view into a tightly knit traditional culture. In the capital at Yinchuan, veiled Hui women, and men in white caps, pray daily to Mecca and sell mutton and flatbreads. The Yellow River winds through the region, past largely unexplored Buddhist grottoes and ancient fortresses. Resident foreigners have floated the province's length in traditional Hui sheepskin-bladder rafts! Weather is dry but temperate, with harsh winds in winter, language fairly standard Mandarin.

Ningxia College of Medicine
Responsible Bureau: Regional Administration of Sanitation and Hygiene
Departments: Medical Practice, Sanitation and Hygiene, Medical Examination Technology
Contact: Foreign Affairs Office, Ningxia College of Medicine, Southern Suburbs, Yinchuan, Ningxia PRC

Ningxia Institute of Industry
Responsible Bureau: Regional Economic Committee
Departments: Industrial Workers Construction, Mechanical Control, Industrial Management
Contact: Foreign Affairs Office, Ningxia Institute of Industry, Xinshi District, Yinchuan, Ningxia PRC

Ningxia University* (formerly Ningxia Techer's College)
Responsible Bureau: Regional Education Administration
Departments: Foreign Languages, Politics & Law, History, Chinese, Mathematics, Physics, Chemistry, Economics, Accounting, Engineering, Physical Education
Contact: Foreign Affairs Office, Ningxia University, No. 21, Wenchui Bei Road, Xinshi District, Yinchuan, 750021 Ningxia PRC
I Phone: (86-951) 207-7800
URL: http://www.xanet.edu.cn/xiju/newxjtu/xbu/html/nx/nd.html

QINGHAI — Once largely part of Tibet, Qinghai retains much of the varied culture of that region. The capital at Xining offers study of dozens of minority cultures, from tiny Bayi villages to the Tibetan Yellow Lamaists at the Ta'ersi Lamasery. Qinghai Lake, China's largest salt lake, offers fabulous bird-watching, while the region's immensely varied topography provides constant photo opportunities. the soft, temperate green hills of Xining give way to frozen crags in the south at Geladaintong, the headwaters of the Yellow, Yangtze, and Mekong rivers, and to harsh salt flats in the west. Ge'ermu (Golmud) in the west is the overland gateway to Tibet as well as supply station for most of the labor camps in China's vast gulag system. Language is fairly standard Mandarin among Han residents, varied among minorities. Food is varied among minority regions, with lots to chose from in Xining. Weather in Xining offers four distinct seasons, none especially harsh, but gets fiercer in higher-altitude regions.

Qinghai College of Medicine
Responsible Bureau: Provincial Education Administration
Departments: Medicine, China Medicine, Rodent Control
Contact: Foreign Affairs Office, Qinghai College of Medicine, 84 Kunlun Rd., Xining, Qinghai PRC

Qinghai College of Nationalities
Responsible Bureau: Provincial Minorities Committee
Departments: Political Education, Languages and Literature, Law, Mathematics, Theoretical Chemistry
Teachers and Students: excellent ethnology programs; many opportunities for field study of minority groups; reasonable library
Contact: Foreign Affairs Office, Qinghai College of Nationalities, 25 Bayi Rd., Xining, Qinghai PRC

Qinghai Institute of Engineering and Agriculture
Responsible Bureau: Provincial Education Administration
Departments: Mechanics, Industrial Chemistry, Natural Products Architecture, Hydroelectricity, Agricultural Science, Plant Protection
Teachers and Students: school emphasizes science and technology teaching
Contact: Foreign Affairs Office, Qinghai Institute of Engineering and Agriculture, North Suburbs, Xining, Qinghai PRC

Qinghai Normal School
Responsible Bureau: Provincial Education Administration
Departments: Political Education, Chinese, History, Geology, Biology, Mathematics, Physics, Education, Chemistry, Foreign Languages, Physical Education, Industrial Arts

Contact: Foreign Affairs Office, Qinghai Normal School, Wusi Ave., Xining, Qinghai PRC

SHAANXI — Shaanxi, and particularly the capital at Xi'an, is one of China's most popular tourist destinations. Xi'an houses some of China's most famed cultural and historical treasures, from the terra-cotta warriors of Qinshihuangdi to the Ming Dynasty Drum Tower and City Walls, and is one of the mainland's most international cities. Yan'an in the north was the endpoint of Mao's Long March and remains a mecca for historians of Chinese communism. Shaanxi summers are hot and dry, and winters cold and windy, particularly in the Western Hills at Baoji. Food is hearty, greasy, and mildly spiced, featuring many thick noodle soups and buns. Language is heavily accented Mandarin. While many of the region's archaeological treasures have yet to be excavated, and others remain under wraps for lack of funds for adequate display, resident foreigners have gained superb access to documents and artifacts for study and research.

UNIVERSITIES

Baoji University
  Responsible Bureau: City Bureau of Education
  Departments: Mechanical Production, Computer Science, Industrial Automation, Management
  Contact: Foreign Affairs Office, Baoji University, Gongyuan Rd., Baoji, Shaanxi PRC

Northwest University*
  Responsible Bureau: Provincial Bureau of Higher Education
  Departments: Chinese, History, Philosophy, Foreign Languages, Mathematics, Computer Science, Physics, Chemistry, Industrial Chemistry, Geography, Geology, Biology, Economics
  Teachers and Students: accepts foreign teachers of both English and technical subjects; has large program in Chinese culture
  Contact: Foreign Affairs Office, Northwest University, Xiaonanmenwai, Xi'an, Shaanxi PRC
  URL: (in Chinese only) http://www.nwu.edu.cn/

Shaanxi Teachers University
College of Xian International Chinese Studies for International Students
  Responsible Bureau: State Education Commission
  Departments: Chinese, Chinese Literature
  Sister Schools: numerous universities abroad
  Students: have long term and short term Chinese language and cultural classes
  Other: also offers non-major courses in Chinese Calligraphy, Chinese History, QiGong, Translation, Chinese Painting, Chiense Kong Fu, Chinese Newspaper Reading and Chinese Customs and Habits in Western Areas
  Contact: The International Students Office, College of Xian International Chinese Studies, Shaanxi Teachers University, Xi'an, Shaanxi 710062 PRC
  I Phone: (86-29) 523-5942   **Fax:** (86-29) 526-1212 or 526-1391
  URL: http://www.buffalo.edu/~yaopu/a.html

Agricultural Construction, Mathematics, Power Studies, Physics, Foreign Languages, Library Science, Intelligence Gathering
Sister Schools: relations with 21 schools in Canada, France, Germany, Italy, UK and US
Teacher Accommodations: 3 rms, w/TV, fridge, cooking facilities; strict 11 p.m. curfew; location central to campus, 45 min walk from downtown
Teaching Conditions: 14 hrs/wk; no secretarial help or photocopying
Students: have large programs in Chinese Language and Culture, students housed in dorms
Contact: Foreign Affairs Office, Xi'an Transportation University, 26 Xianning Road, Xi'an, Shaanxi PRC

Yan'an University
Responsible Bureau: Provincial Bureau of Higher Education
Departments: Political Education, Chinese, Mathematics, Physics, Chemistry, English
Teachers: school very eager to have foreign teachers; will be very generous
Teacher Accommodations: 4 rms, w/kitchen, TV, tape recorder, fridge, use of car and driver, no curfew, liberal on student visits
Teaching Conditions: 8-9 hrs/wk; both photocopying and secretaries available
Contact: Foreign Affairs Office, Yan'an University, Yangjialing, Yan'an, Shaanxi PRC

ARTS/MUSIC

Xi'an Academy of Art
Responsible Bureau: Provincial Bureau of Higher Education
Departments: Chinese Traditional Painting, Oil Painting, Woodblock Painting
Contact: Foreign Affairs Office, Xi'an Academy of Art, Southern Suburbs, Xi'an, Shaanxi PRC

Xi'an Music Academy
Responsible Bureau: Provincial Bureau of higher Education
Departments: Composition, Voice, Instrumental Music, Wind and String Instruments, Piano, Accordion
Contact: Foreign Affairs Office, Xi'an Music Academy, Chang'an Central Rd., Xi'an, Shaanxi PRC

MINORITIES/POLITICS AND LAW

Northwest Institute of Politics and Law
Responsible Bureau: Ministry of Justice
Departments: Philosophy, Political Economics, Law, Economic Law, Labor Reform Management
Contact: Foreign Affairs Office, Northwest Institute of Politics and Law, Chan'an S. Rd., Xi'an, Shaanxi PRC

Tibetan Minority Institute
Responsible Bureau: District Education Administration
Departments: Politics, Languages and Literature, History, Physical Education, Medicine, Economics
Contact: Foreign Affairs Office, Tibetan Minority Institute, Chengyang, Shaanxi PRC

FINANCE/ECONOMICS/COMMERCE

Shaanxi Institute of Finance and Economics
  Responsible Bureau: People's Bank, Central Branch
  Departments: Industrial Economics, Trade Economics, Consumer Goods, Statistics, Accounting, Finance
  Contact: Foreign Affairs Office, Shaanxi Institute of Finance and Economics, Cuihua Rd., Xi'an, Shaanxi PRC

FOREIGN LANGUAGES

Shaanxi Province Technical Normal Institute of Foreign Languages
  Responsible Bureau: Provincial Education Administration
  Departments: English, Russian
  Contact: Foreign Affairs Office, Shaanxi Province Technical Normal Institute of Foreign Languages, Zhenhua N. Rd., Xi'an, Shaanxi PRC

Xi'an Foreign Languages Institute
  Responsible Bureau: Provincial Bureau of Higher Education
  Departments: English, Russian, Japanese, German, French, Spanish, Travel and Tourism
  Teachers: teach English and other Western languages, Western Culture, some teacher-training
  Students: large program in Chinese Language and Culture
  Contact: Foreign Affairs Office, Xi'an Foreign Languages Institute, Southern Suburbs, Xi'an, Shaanxi PRC

NORMAL SCHOOLS

Baoji Normal School
  Responsible Bureau: Provincial Bureau of Higher Education
  Departments: Political Education, Chinese, Mathematics, Physics, Chemistry, English, History
  Contact: Foreign Affairs Office, Baoji Normal School, Shibahe, Baoji, Shaanxi PRC

Shaanxi Normal School
  Responsible Bureau: State Education Committee
  Departments: Education, Political Education, Chinese, History, Biology, Geology, Mathematics, Physics, Chemistry, Physical Education, Foreign Languages, Distance Education
  Accommodations: 4 rms w/kitchen, bath, TV, fridge, A/C; fairly strict 10:30 p.m. curfew; location on edge of campus, 1 hr. walk to downtown
  Teaching Conditions: 8-10 hrs/wk; photocopying available, students good
  Contact: Foreign Affairs Office, Shaanxi Normal School, Chang'an S. Rd., Xi'an, Shaanxi PRC

MEDICAL SCHOOLS

Xi'an Medical College
  Responsible Bureau: Ministry of Sanitation and Hygiene
  Departments: Medicine, Oral Medicine, Sanitation and Hygiene, Stomatology, Pharmacology

Teachers and Students: accepts foreign students in all degree programs; accepts foreign teachers of English, technical subjects. Foreigners have also helped edit school's foreign-language publications; *Acta Academiae Medicinae Xian* (Quarterly); *Medical Education Study*; and *Medical Geography Abroad*
Contact: Foreign Affairs Office, Xi'an Medical College, Southern Suburbs, Xi'an, Shaanxi PRC

Yan'an Medical College
Responsible Bureau: Provincial Bureau of Higher Education
Departments: Medicine
Contact: Foreign Affairs Office, Yan'an Medical College, Dufuquan, Yan'an, Shaanxi PRC

TECHNICAL SCHOOLS

Northwest Institute of Architectural Engineering
Responsible Bureau: City Ministry of Architecture and Environmental Protection
Departments: Natural Products Architecture, Mechanical Electronics Engineering
Contact: Foreign Affairs Offfice, Northwest Institute of Architectural Engineering, Xiaozhai, Xi'an, Shaanxi PRC

Northwest Institute of Telecommunications Engineering
Responsible Bureau: Ministry of Electronics
Departments: Information, Electronics, Computer Science, Physics, Management Engineering, Mathematics, Foreign Languages
Sister Schools: US—Univ. of Wisconsin
Teachers: accepts foreign teachers of both English and technical subjects
Contact: Foreign Affairs Office, Northwest Institute of Telecommunications Engineering, Taibai Rd., Xi'an, Shaanxi PRC

Northwest Institute of Textile Science and Technology
Responsible Bureau: Ministry of Textiles
Departments: Textiles, Mechanical Electronics, Fashion, Textile Chemistry, Industrial Management
Contact: Foreign Affairs Office, Northwest Institute of Textile Science and Technology, Jinhua S. Rd., Xi'an, Shaanxi PRC

Shaanxi Institute of Mechanical Engineering
Responsible Bureau: Ministry of Mechanics
Departments: Materials Engineering, Mechanical Engineering, Precision Engineering, Printing Technology, Automation and Control, Hydrology and Hydraulic Engineering, Industrial Management and Economic Engineering
Sister Schools: US—Rochester Inst. of Technology, Northern Illinois Univ.; Japan —Kyoto Univ., Fukui Univ., Italy—Univ. of Rome
Teachers: accepts foreign teachers in both English and technical subjects
Contact: Foreign Affairs Office, Shaanxi Institute of Mechanical Engineering, Jinhua S. Rd., Xi'an, Shaanxi PRC

Xi'an Institute of Geology
Responsible Bureau: Ministry of Geography and Mining Products
Departments: Geological Exploration, Surveying
Contact: Foreign Affairs Office, Xi'an Institute of Geology, Yanta Rd., Xi'an, Shaanxi PRC

Xi'an Institute of Metallurgy and Construction Engineering
Responsible Bureau: Ministry of Industrial Metals
Departments: Architecture, Environmental Studies, Industrial Metals, Materials and Mining, Mechanical Electronics, Management
Sister Schools: Australia—Univ. of Wollongong; Japan—Kyushu Univ.; US—Old Dominion Univ.
Teachers and Students: accepts teachers of both English and technical subjects
Contact: Foreign Affairs Office, Xi'an Institute of Metallurgy and Construction Engineering, Hepingmenwai, Xi'an, Shaanxi PRC

Xi'an Institute of Mining
Responsible Bureau: Ministry of Coal Mining
Departments: Materials and Mining, Mechanical Electronics, Geology
Contact: Foreign Affairs Office, Xi'an Institute of Mining, Yanta Rd., Xi'an, Shaanxi PRC

Xi'an Institute of Petroleum
Responsible Bureau: Ministry of Petroleum
Departments: Mechanical Engineering, Timing Equipment and Automation, Industrial Economics, Petroleum Development, Computer Science
Contact: Foreign Affairs Office, Xi'an Institute of Petroleum, Lingyuan Rd. S. Section, Xi'an, Shaanxi PRC

Xi'an Institute of Technology
Responsible Bureau: Ministry of Engineering and Electronics Industry
Departments: Computer Science, Finance, Economics, Radiation, Precision Mechanics, Electronics
Chinese Students: 5,000
Teachers: opportunities for English teachers and tech experts
Contact: Foreign Affairs Office, Xi'an Institute of Technology, 7 Jinhua N. Rd., Eastern Suburbs, Xi'an, Shaanxi PRC
URL: http://www.xanet.edu.cn/xjtu/newxjtu/xbu/html/sx/xgy.html

Xi'an University of Industry
Responsible Bureau: Ministry of Aviation
Departments: Mathematical Theory of Power Studies, Mechanics, Materials, Shipping, Electronics, Military Engineering, Automation and Control, Computer Science, Management, Natural Products Architecture, Sociology
Contact: Foreign Affairs Office, Xi'an University of Industry, Youyi W. Rd., Xi'an, Shaanxi PRC

SHANDONG — Birthplace of Confucius and center of Yellow River culture, Shandong is rich with historical and architectural treasures, from the ancient tombs at Zibo to the Buddhist temples and caverns at Lingyansi near Jinan. For more recent history the port city of Qingdao, built largely during the German occupation and resembling a "little Bavaria," offers many insights into Republican-era struggles, while industry in the capital at Jinan has been important to the economic development of "New China." Language is heavily accented Mandarin, and food richly varied during most of the year, featuring much seafood and reduced to white-cabbage blandness only in the depths of winter. Weather in the interior is broiling in summer, freezing in winter; along the coast mild most of the year but with harsh winter blasts.

UNIVERSITIES

Qingdao University
Responsible Bureau: Provincial Higher Education Administration
Departments: Mathematics, Industrial Management, Foreign Languages, Physics, Chemistry, Environmental Protection, Electrical Equipment, Chinese, History
Sister School: US—Connecticut College
Accommodations: 2-4 rms, w/ kitchen, TV, fridge, shared washer, bikes; little heat and hot water; central to campus and freemarket, but 45 min. bus ride from downtown
Teaching Conditions: 10-16 hrs/wk; class size good, excellent language lab, good library but tight on student access; foreign teachers have set up "student library;" "Qingdao U. is a new school still very much under construction; lots of flexibility, but many things still 'to be worked out'"
Student Tuition/Expenses: varied, starting at approx US$800/semester
Learning Conditions: all student programs individualized; work closely w/ FAO before and after arrival to see your needs are met
Contact: Foreign Affairs Office, Qingdao University, Shinan District, Qingdao, Shandong PRC

Shandong University*
Responsible Bureau: State Education Committee
Departments: Chinese, History, Philosophy, Law, Foreign Languages, Library Science, Mathematics, Computer Science, Physics, Radio Technology, Radiation, Chemistry, Biology, Microbiology, Scientific Socialism
Sister Schools: US—Harvard Univ, Indiana Univ, City College of NY; Japan—Yamaguchi Univ; UK—Univ of Regina; Australia—Univ of Adelaide
Accommodations: 2-3 rms, but pleasant, w/ kitchen, washer, tape recorder, TV, shared bikes; in walled compound on leafy campus
Teaching Conditions: 12-18 hrs/wk, great students—Key Univ w/ good facilities (library 1.7 million vol, in-school publishing house [SU Press])
Student Tuition/Expenses: vary by program
Learning Conditions: many programs (esp Chinese Language/Culture) set curricula, fairly inflexible; if want to design own curricula, be in touch early and often w/ waiban
Contact: Foreign Affairs Office, Shandong University, Jinan, Shandong, PRC

Shandong University of Oceanography
Responsible Bureau: State Education Committee
Departments: Physics, Aquaculture, Chemistry, Oceanology, Geology, Aquatic Products, Aquatic Breeding, Mathematics, Marine Engineering, Foreign Languages
Accommodations: very good in some ways, but small; nice old bldg w/ wood paneling in the interior; plentiful heat, cooking facilities, TV, bike
Teaching Conditions: 14 hrs/wk; "at first I was required to correct 100 writing essays per week, but when I complained about this the English Dept was quite flexible about dropping this requirement"
Students: no foreign students now, school trying to set up exchange program
Contact: Foreign Affairs Office, Shandong University of Oceonography, Yushan Rd., Qingdao, Shandong PRC

Yantai University
Responsible Bureau: Provincial Education Administration
Departments: Architecture, Mechanics, Chemistry, Foreign Languages, Mathematics, Physics, Law, Industrial Workers Construction

Accommodations: very good; 6 rms w/ balconies, kitchen, view of sea, shared washer, TV, fridge, bike; cafeteria "cheap but sloppy;" dorm central to campus, 20 min from downtown by bus; strict visitor registration

Teaching Conditions: 12 hrs/wk; good language lab and library; secretarial support

Contact: Foreign Affairs Office, Yantai University, Qingquanzhai, Yantai, Shandong PRC

ARTS/MUSIC

Shandong Academy of Fine Arts
Responsible Bureau: Provincial Cultural Administration
Departments: Music, Arts, Opera, Applied Arts, Arts Education
Contact: Foreign Affairs Office, Shandong Academy of Fine Arts, Wenhua E. Rd., Jinan, Shandong PRC

FINANCE/ECONOMICS

Shandong Institute of Economics
Responsible Bureau: Provincial Economic Committee
Departments: Accounting, Statistics, Economic Policy, Finance, Economics, Foreign Trade, Teaching
Chinese Students: 1,700
Contact: Foreign Affairs Office, Shandong Institute of Economics, Yanzishan E. Alley, Jinan, Shandong PRC

NORMAL SCHOOLS

Qufu Teachers University
Responsible Bureau: Provincial Higher Education Administration
Departments: Chinese, Politics, History, Foreign Languages, Education, Mathematics, Physics, Industrial Arts, Physical Education, Chemistry, Biology, Geology
Sister Schools: US—Skidmore College; Canada—McGill Univ
Accommodations: pretty good; 2-4 rms w/ kitchen,TV, tape recorder, washer, bike; no curfew, fairly lax visitor registration; location central to campus, easy bike ride from downtown
Teaching Conditions: 10-16 hrs/wk, dedicated students, poor materials but reasonable library, school "very helpful" (e.g., aided 1 foreign teacher to make nationwide contact with Chinese Shakespeare scholars)
Contact: Foreign Affairs Office, Qufu Teachers University, Xiguan, Qufu, Shandong PRC

Shandong Normal School
Responsible Bureau: Provincial Education Administration
Departments: Education, Politics, History, Chinese, Foreign Languages, Mathematics, Computer Science, Physics, Chemistry, Biology, Moral Education, Geology, Industrial Arts, Physical Education
Contact: Foreign Affairs Office, Shandong Normal School, Wenhua E. Rd., Jinan, Shandong PRC

Shandong Teachers University
Responsible Bureau: Shandong Provincial Education Commission
Chinese Students: 8,000   **Foreign Students:** 80
Foreign Teachers: 13   **Sister Schools:** 30 in over 10 countries
Teacher Salary/Benefits: 1,400-2,000¥ RMB/month, one-way or return air ticket, shipment of one-cubic meter crate; Foreign Teacher, expert status: 2,200¥ RMB/

month, vacation allowances, free medical care, free accommodations
Teaching Conditions: 8-14 hrs/wk
Contact: Mr. Cheng Biao, Chief of Foreign Teachers Program, or Mr. Li Jie, Chief of Foreign Students Program, Shandong Teachers Univeristy, 88 E. Wenhua Rd., Jinan, Shandong 250014 PRC
I Phone: (86-531) 296-6954   **Fax:** (86-531) 296-6954
e-mail: oipstu@public.jn.sd.cn

Victory Oil Field Normal School
Responsible Bureau: Ministry of Petroleum
Departments: Chinese, Mathematics, Physics, Chemistry, Foreign Languages, Political History, Industrial Arts, Physical Education
Teachers: teach English; "pretty lonely, but the terms are very generous"
Contact: Foreign Affairs Office, Victory Oil Field Normal School, Dongying, Shandong PRC

Yantai Teachers College
Responsible Bureau: Provincial Higher Education Administration
Departments: Chinese, Politics, English, Mathematics, Physics, Chemistry, Physical Education, Biology
Contact: Foreign Affairs Office, Yantai Teachers College, Southern Suburbs, Yantai, Shandong PRC

MEDICAL SCHOOLS

Changwei Medical College
Responsible Bureau: Provincial Administration of Sanitation and Hygiene
Departments: Medicine, Sanitation and Hygiene Management
Contact: Foreign Affairs Office, Changwei Medical College, Shengli Ave., Weifang, Shandong PRC

Qingdao Medical College
Responsible Bureau: Shandong Education Government
Departments: Medicine, Pediatrics, Notation, Medical Imaging, Nursing, Traditional Chinese Medicine, Chinese Studies, History
Chinese Students: 4,000   **Foreign Students:** 26
Foreign Teachers: 4   **Sister Schools:** 3 in Korea, 1 in Israel, 3 in US
Accommodations: Visitor hotel in college
Teacher Salary/Benefits: 1,500-2,300¥ RMB/month
Teaching Conditions: 13-16 hrs/wk
Teachers: teach English, Western Culture; nice accommodations and pleasant students; campus in downtown Qingdao
Student Tuition/Expense: USD$1,500/yr for Chinese Study; USD$2,500 for TCM and medicine
Contact: Foreign Affairs Office, Qingdao Medical College, Huangtai Rd., Qingdao, Shandong PRC
I Phone: (86-532) 380-1449   **Fax:** (86-532) 380-1449

Shandong College of Chinese Medicine
Responsible Bureau: Provincial Administration of Sanitation and Hygiene
Departments: Medicine, Chinese Pharmacology
Contact: Foreign Affairs Office, Shandong College of Chinese Medicine, Jingshi Rd., Jinan, Shandong, PRC

Shandong College of Medicine
  Responsible Bureau: Ministry of Sanitation and Hygiene
  Departments: Medicine, Oral Medicine, Sanitation and Hygiene, Pharmacology
  Contact: Foreign Affairs Office, Shandong College of Medicine, Wenhua W. Rd., Jinan, Shandong PRC

Shandong Medical University
  Responsible Bureau: Ministry of Public Health
  Departments: School of Pre-clinical Medicine, School of Public Health, Nursing, Pharmacology, Stomatology
  Chinese Students: 519/163
  Foreign Teachers: 3 long-term English teachers every year
  Sister Schools: Niaka Ya Ma Medical Univ., Univ. of Utah
  Accommodations: available in expert rooms
  Teacher Salary/Benefits: Depending on the qualifications and experience, the salary varies from 1,200-2,000¥ RMB/month
  Teaching Conditions: 12-15 hrs/wk; teaching materials, tapes, lap machines are provided
  Student Tuition/Expense: Five year program of medicine: USD$3,000/year; books & accommodations: USD$4-6 a day
  Contact: Foreign Affairs Office, Shandong Medical University, 5/F, Dental Hospital Building, 44 Wenhua Rd., Jinan, Shandong 250012 PRC
  I Phone: (86-531) 295-2424 ext. 221   **Fax:** (86-531) 295-3813
  e-mail: sdvd@public.jn.sd.cn

Tai'an College of Medicine
  Responsible Bureau: Provincial Administration of Sanitation and Hygiene
  Departments: Medicine, Radiation Therapy, Nursing and Care
  Contact: Foreign Affairs Office, Tai'an College of Medicine, Taishan W. Rd., Tai'an, Shandong PRC

TECHNICAL SCHOOLS

Qingdao Institute of Architecture and Engineering
  Responsible Bureau: Ministry of Metallurgical Industry
  Departments: Architecture, Architectural Engineering, Environmental Engineering, Mechanical Engineering, Management, Economics, Computer Science, Foreign Languages, Social Science, Mining Engineering
  Chinese Students: 5,000   **Foreign Teachers:** 4
  Sister Schools: Sweden—Royal Institite of Technology; US—Illinois Institute of Technology
  Accommodations: 2-3 rms in nice old bldg, w/ kitchen, shared bath, TV, tape recorder, bike; central location and reasonable doorman
  Teacher Salary/Benefits:
  Teaching Conditions: 12-14 hrs/wk   **Student Tuition/Expense:** USD$1,500
  Other: Foreign students can choose either double rooms or single rooms, which are about USD$3-4 a day
  Contact: Lin Xuming, Foreign Affairs Office, Qingdao Institute of Architecture and Engineering, 11 Fushun Rd., Qingdao, Shandong 266033 PRC
  I Phone: (86-532) 562-5598   **Fax:** (86-532) 562-3639

Shandong Agricultural University
Responsible Bureau: Provincial Agricultural Administration
Departments: Agricultural Science, Crop Protection, Soil Chemistry, Forestry, Gardening, Livestock and Veterinary Medicine, Agricultural Equipment, Agricultural Economics
Contact: Foreign Affairs Office, Shandong Agricultural University, Tai'an, Shandong PRC

Shandong College of Light Industry
Responsible Bureau: State Education Bureau of Shandong Province
Departments: Mechanical & Electrical Engineering, Chemical Engineering, Food Engineering, Inorganic Material, Industrial Design, Industrial Economics and Trade
Chinese Students: 2,977   **Foreign Students:** 0
Foreign Teachers: 3   **Accommodations:** college hotel
Teacher Salary/Benefits: 1,200-2,000¥ RMB/month
Teaching Conditions: 14 hrs/wk; two main teaching buildings and two buildings for experiments
Student Tuition/Expenses: 324-1,600¥ RMB/year
Contact: Foreign Affairs Office, Shandong College of Light Industry, No. 23 N. Huang Tai Road, Jinan, Shandong PRC
I Phone: (86-531) 896-4221 ext. 217   **Fax:** (86-531) 896-8495

Shandong Institute of Architectural Engineering and Materials
Responsible Bureau: National Bureau of Architectural Materials
Departments: Material Science, Applied Chemistry, Automation, Non-metallic Mining
Contact: Foreign Affairs Office, Shandong Institute of Architectural Engineering and Materials, Baihushan Rd., Zhibo, Shandong, PRC

Shandong Institute of Architectural Engineering
Responsible Bureau: Provincial, City, and County Construction Committees
Departments: Architecture, Mechanical Electronics, Urban Planning, Architectural Engineering
Contact: Foreign Affairs Office, Shandong Institute of Architectural Engineering, Heping Rd., Jinan, Shandong PRC

Shandong Institute of Light Industry
Responsible Bureau: Provincial Number One Light Industrial Administration
Departments: Mechanical Electronics, Light Industrial Chemistry, Silicate Industry, Art Design
Contact: Foreign Affairs Office, Shandong Institute of Light Industry, Huangtai N. Rd., Jinan, Shandong PRC

Shandong Institute of Mining
Responsible Bureau: Ministry of Coal Mining
Departments: Geology, Coal Mine Architecture and Construction, Coal Exploration, Electrical Equipment, Coal Mine Mechanics, Computer Center
Contact: Foreign Affairs Office, Shandong Institute of Mining, Tai'an, Shandong PRC

Shandong Petroleum Institute
Responsible Bureau: Ministry of Petroleum
Departments: Basic Science, Exploration, Resource Development, Oil Refinement, Mechanics, Automation, Management, Computer Science

Teachers: considering setting up exchange programs w/ several US and Canadian universities
Contact: Foreign Affairs Office, Shandong Petroleum Institute, Dongying, Shandong PRC

Shandong Polytechnical University
Responsible Bureau: Provincial Bureau of Higher Education
Departments: Mechanical Engineering, Electrical Engineering, Power Production, Electric Power, Electric Equipment, Electronics, Computer Science, Chemistry, Hydrology, Management Engineering, Basic Studies
Sister School: Coventry Polytechnic
Contact: Foreign Affairs Office, Shandong Polytechnical University, Jingshi Rd., Jinan, Shandong PRC

Shandong Textile Engineering College
Responsible Bureau: Provincial Textile Administration
Departments: Textile Engineering, Mechanical Electronic Engineering, Textile Chemistry, Management Engineering, Applied Arts
Accommodations: pretty good; 2-3 rms, w/ kitchen, TV, tape recorder, bike; central location; major curfew and visitor registration problems ("doorkeeper was nasty ogre")
Teaching Conditions: 14 hrs/wk; good students but poor materials
Contact: Foreign Affairs Office, Shandong Textile Engineering College, Fushun Rd., Qingdao, Shandong PRC

SHANGHAI — The largest city in China and the second largest in the world, the Shanghai Special Zone houses nearly 20 million people. This vibrant, bustling city is one of the most modern and international in China, with tremendous cultural and economic opportunities. The Bund, built during the colonial era, and the city's other commercial centers offer unparalleled shopping. Transport is convenient, and foreign residents have many opportunities to moonlight in business and journalism. Foreigners are no rarity in Shanghai, and will rarely receive special attention, for better or worse. Many foreign residents compare Shanghai with New York—"the people have a hard edge," wrote one respondent. "It can be abrasive, but it's very exciting." Shanghai cuisine is one of the finest in China, though sweeter and more oily than many foreign palates prefer. Weather is chilly and damp in winter, mild spring and fall, and suffocating in summer. The Shanghainese language is not comprehensible to Mandarin speakers, but nearly everyone in the city speaks Mandarin if pushed.

UNIVERSITIES

Fudan University*
Responsible Bureau: State Education Committee
Departments: Languages and Literatures, Journalism, History, Economics, Philosophy, International Politics, World Economics, Law, Mathematics, Physics, Atomic Science, Electronics, Chemistry, Biology, Management, Power Studies, Materials, Radiation Physics, Statistics, Mathematical Operational Research, Foreign Languages

Foreign Students: 600 long term & 500 short-term overseas students
Sister Schools: US—State Univ of New York x at Albany, St. Mary's College, MD, Univ of Southern Maine, UC Fullerton, many others
Accommodations: all foreigners in walled compound; teachers 2-3 rms w/ kitchen, TV, tape recorder; students 2 per rm; rather cut off from campus life
Teaching Conditions: 12-16 hrs/wk; great facilities, but students "discouraged from too much contact." Fudan is one of China's top schools—many students children of elite
Student Tuition/Expenses: variable; many students enroll through univs in home country
Learning Conditions: few opportunities to practice Chinese within compound: "English, French, and Japanese prevail"; libraries "excellent," but card catalogs all in Chinese
Contact: Admission Office, International Cultural Exchange School, Fudan University, 280 Zhen Tong Rd., Shanghai 200433 PRC
❚ **Phone:** (86-21)6548-3962or 6549-2222   **Fax:** (86-21) 6549-1669
URL: http://www.fudan.edu.cn/

Shanghai Polytechnical University*
Responsible Bureau: City Bureau of Higher Education
Departments: Mechanics, Electrical Mechanics, Industrial Automation, Industrial Metallurgy, Computer Science, Industrial Chemistry, Management
Contact: Foreign Affairs Office, Shanghai Polytechnical University, Yanchang Rd., Shanghai PRC

Shanghai Transportation University*
Responsible Bureau: State Education Committee
Departments: Shipping and Marine Aquaculture, Power Production Mechanics, Electric Power, Automation and Control, Computer Science, Electronic Communication, Materials, Mechanical Mathematics, Precision Engineering, Applied Physics, Power Studies, Applied Chemistry, Management, Foreign Trade, Scientific Foreign Languages, Sociology
Teachers: teach English, Western Culture, variety of technical subjects; "Jiaoda" is a Key Univ, one of China's most famous
Students: various programs in Chinese Language/Culture, as well as degree programs
Contact: Foreign Affairs Office, Shanghai Transportation University, Huashan Rd., Shanghai PRC

Shanghai University
Responsible Bureau: City Bureau of Higher Education
Departments: Chinese, History, Law, Library Science, Sociology, Mechanics, Electronics, Microelectronics and Automation, Radio Technology, Foreign Languages, Art Design, Oil Painting, Chinese Painting, Sculpture, Politics
Chinese Students: 17,400   **Foreign Students:** over 200
Sister Schools: Australia—Sydney Institute of Language and Commerce
Contact: Foreign Affairs Office, Shanghai University, 149 Yanchang Rd., Shanghai 200072 PRC
❚ **Phone:** (86-21) 5663-1515 ext. 2846   **URL:** http://www.shu.edu.cn/

Tongji University*
Responsible Bureau: State Education Committee
Departments: Architecture, Agricultural Construction Design, Highways and Transportation, Minerology, Surveying, Materials, Environmental Studies, Mechanics, Electronics, Management, Economic Information, Marine Aquaculture and Geology, Foreign Languages, Mathematics, Power Studies, Physics, Chemistry

Students: 15,000   **Foreign Students:** over 200
Teachers and Students: one of China's premier institutions with very large programs for foreign teachers and students
Contact: Ms. Yan Yujin, Foreign Affairs Office, Tongji University, Siping Rd., Shanghai PRC
Phone and Fax: (86-21) 6502-8933   **URL:** http://www.tongji.edu.cn/

ARTS/MUSIC

Shanghai Conservatory of Music
Responsible Bureau: Ministry of Culture
Departments: Composition, Direction, Voice, Wind and String Instruments, Minority Instruments, Piano, Musicology
Chinese Students: 800+   **Foreign Students:** 20-25
Foreign Teachers: 5-8
Teachers: can teach English, Western Culture
Students: can study Chinese Language, Culture, traditional musical instruments; school "very flexible"
Contact: Foreign Affairs Office, Shanghai Conservatory of Music, 20 Fenyang Rd., Shanghai PRC

Shanghai Drama/Opera Institute
Responsible Bureau: Ministry of Culture
Departments: Acting, Stage Decoration, Operatic Culture, Directing
Contact: Foreign Affairs Office, Shanghai Drama/Opera Institute, Jing'an District, Shanghai PRC

POLITICS AND LAW

East China Institute of Politics and Law
Responsible Bureau: Ministry of Justice   **Departments:** Law
Accommodations: 2-4 rms in quiet area of campus, w/ TV, tape recorder, shared bike, kitchen; campus 2 min walk from Zhongshan Park, 20 min bus ride from Bund
Teaching Conditions: 12-14 hrs/wk; students very sharp
Learning Conditions: "lots of good teachers, but the program is pretty unstructured, so you have to be self-motivated"
Contact: Foreign Affairs Office, East China Institute of Politics and Law, Wanhangdu Rd., Shanghai PRC

FINANCE/COMMERCE/ECONOMICS

China Europe International Business School (CEIBS)
Responsible Bureau: Shanghai Municipal Government (through Shanghai Jiaotong Univ.)
Departments: Executive Department (International Management; Senior Management; Functional Management; Junior Managment; Seminars); Full-time MBA; Part-time Executive MBA
Chinese Students: (MBA program) 120
Foreign Students: (MBA program) 10 allowed/year
Teachers and Students: MBA program accepts qualified students who have a university degree and at least two yrs. prior work experience; open to young managers normally under age 35 (max. age 40); 1997 tuition USD$15,000; non-refundable application fee for int'l students USD$100

Contact: Admissions Office, China Europe International Business School, 800 Dongchuan Rd., Minhang, Shanghai 200240 PRC
l Phone: (86-21) 6463-8462 or 6463-0200 ext. 2052
Fax: (86-21) 6435-8928 or 6463-8470   **e-mail:** svhooydonk@ceibs.sjtu.edu.cn
URL: http://www.ceibs.edu/

Shanghai College of Economics and Finance
Responsible Bureau: Ministry of Finance
Departments: Economics, Industrial Economics, Trade Economics, Economic Information, Statistics, Accounting, Finance, World Economics
Contact: Foreign Affairs Office, Shanghai College of Economics and Finance, Hongkou District, Shanghai PRC

Shanghai Institute of Foreign Trade*
Responsible Bureau: Ministry of Foreign Trade
Departments: Foreign Trade Economics, Foreign Trade Foreign Languages, International Economic Law, Industrial Management
Sister Schools: US—Univ of San Francisco, Univ of Lincoln, Eastern Washington Univ, Columbia Univ; Ausrtalia—Univ of Sydney; Japan—Univ of Tokyo, Southwestern College
Accommodations: bedrm, shared kitchen and bath, Western toilet and "10 sq. meter bathtub," washer, dryer, TV, tape recorder, fridge; heat and A/C "great when they turn it on"
Teaching Conditions: 10-12 hrs/wk; students great, "love 'em to death!" little photocopying, but secretarial assistance available; library "fairly well equipped," including subscriptions to Time, Newsweek, etc., but closed to undergrads
Contact: Foreign Affairs Office, Shanghai Institute of Foreign Trade, 620 Gubei Rd., Shanghai PRC

FOREIGN LANGUAGES

Shanghai Foreign Languages Institute*
Responsible Bureau: State Education Committee
Departments: English, German, Foreign Trade, French, Arabic, Russian, Japanese, Spanish, Chinese
Teachers: can teach Western Culture, languages
Students: study Chinese Language, Culture; many Chinese government scholarship students learning Chinese prior to entering Chinese-language degree programs; large foreigner compound, "it can be hard to practice Chinese"
Contact: Foreign Affairs Office, Shanghai Foreign Languages Institute, 119 Tiyuhui Rd., Shanghai PRC

NORMAL SCHOOLS

East China Normal University*
Responsible Bureau: State Education Committee
Departments: Education, Political Education, Chinese, History, Geology, Mathematics, Physics, Chemistry, Biology, Library Sciences, Foreign Languages, Electronic Education, Industrial Arts, Physical Education, Psychology, Computer Science, Mathematical Theory, Statistics, Electronic Science and Technology, Economics
Contact: Foreign Affairs Office, East China Normal University, 3663 Zhongshan N. Rd., Shanghai PRC

Shanghai Normal School
Responsible Bureau: City Bureau of Higher Education
Departments: Political Education, Chinese, History, Mathematics, Physics, Chemistry, Foreign Languages, Industrial Arts, Physical Education, Geology, Computer Science
Contact: Foreign Affairs Office, Shanghai Normal School, Xuhui District, Shanghai PRC

Shanghai Teachers College of Technology
Responsible Bureau: City Bureau of Higher Education
Departments: Chinese, English, Political Education, Mathematics, Physics, Chemistry, Biology, Mechanics, Architecture
Sister School: US—Glendale Community College
Contact: Foreign Affairs Office, Shanghai Teachers College of Technology, Fengxian County, Shanghai 201418 PRC

Shanghai Teachers University
Responsible Bureau: Shanghai Municipal Government Education Commission
Departments: Education Administration, Mathematics, Chemistry, Biology, Geography, Physical Education, College of International Cultural Exchange, College of Foreign Languages, College of Vocational & Technological Education, College of Adult Education, College of Art, College of Liberal Arts, College of Technology & Information, College of Law, Political Science, Business
Chinese Students: 7,968
Foreign Students: 214 long-term students, including 7 studying for masters degrees and 4 studying for doctorates
Foreign Teachers: 4
Sister Schools: US—Ball State Univ.; Australia—Univ. of Southern Queensland; Korea—Jeonju Univ.; Japan—Kyoto Education Univ.
Accommodations: Two well-equipped guest houses on campus, with restaurants and a dining hall inside
Teaching Conditions: New classrooms with air conditioners, new language laboratory
Students: 20 periods for foreign students taking language courses; 26 periods for foreign students studying for undergraduate degree
Student Tuition/Expense: USD$2,000/yr for undergraduate courses; USD$1,800/yr, USD$900/semester for language courses
Contact: Ms. Li Mei Zhen, Director, International Exchange Division (Foreign Affairs Office), Shanghai Teachers University, Shanghai PRC
I Phone: (86-21) 6470-1661   **Fax:** (86-21) 6470-1661

MEDICAL SCHOOLS

Shanghai College of Traditional Chinese Medicine
Responsible Bureau: City Bureau of Higher Education
Departments: Chinese Medicine, Chinese Pharmacology, Acupuncture and Acupressure
Sister Schools: US—Harvard Medical School, Univ of San Francisco; Japan—Kawasaki Medical School, Showa Univ; Germany—Univ of Groningen
Students: has program in Traditional Chinese Medicine for foreign students
Contact: Foreign Affairs Office, Shanghai College of Traditional Chinese Medicine, 539 Lingling Rd., Xuhui District, Shanghai PRC

Shanghai Number One College of Medicine*
Responsible Bureau: Ministry of Sanitation and Hygiene
Departments: Medicine, Sanitation and Hygiene, Pharmacology
Contact: Foreign Affairs Office, Shanghai Number One College of Medicine, Yixueyuan Rd., Shanghai PRC

Shanghai Number Two College of Medicine
Responsible Bureau: City Bureau of Higher Education
Departments: Medicine, Pediatrics, Oral Medicine, Medical Examination, Biological Medicine
Sister Schools: US—Univ of Missouri (Kansas City), UC San Francisco; Japan—Osaka Univ; France—Univ of Rene Descartes, Univ d'Aix-Marseilles; Belgium—Univ of Antwerp
Contact: Foreign Affairs Office, Shanghai Number Two College of Medicine, 280 Chongqing S. Rd., Luwan District, Shanghai PRC

Shanghai Railway School of Medicine
Responsible Bureau: Ministry of Railroads
Departments: Medicine, Oral Medicine
Contact: Foreign Affairs Office, Shanghai Railway School of Medicine, Zhabei District, Shanghai PRC

TECHNICAL SCHOOLS

Chinese University of Textiles
Responsible Bureau: Ministry of Textiles
Departments: Textiles, Mechanics, Automation, Textile Chemistry, Management, Fashion, Chemical Fibers
Contact: Foreign Affairs Office, Chinese University of Textiles, Yan'an W. Rd., Shanghai PRC

East China Institute of Technology
Responsible Bureau: State Education Committee
Departments: Chemistry, Industrial Chemistry, Biological Chemistry, High Radiation Materials, Organic Materials, Automation and Control, Mechanics, Environmental Studies, Mathematics, Physics, Management, Foreign Languages, Sociology, Computer Science
Accommodations: good; 2 rms, w/ washer, TV, tape recorder, fridge, shortwave radio, no kitchen but cafeteria cheap and good; no curfew, lax visitor registration; central to campus (east side by Sun Yat-sen tomb—pretty countryside, 45 min by bus to Bund)
Teaching Conditions: 15 hrs/wk, + 8 office hrs; classes include International Trade; language lab excellent; library and materials so-so
Contact: Foreign Affairs Office, East China Institute of Technology, Meilung Rd., Shanghai PRC

Shanghai City Institute of Construction
Responsible Bureau: City Construction Committee
Departments: Architecture, Management, Urban Planning, Heating and Air Conditioning, Architectural and Construction Mechanics
Contact: Foreign Affairs Office, Shanghai City Institute of Construction, Yangpu District, Shanghai PRC

Shanghai Fisheries University

Responsible Bureau: Ministry of Agriculture, Livestock, and Fisheries
Departments: Aquaculture, Marine Products Processing, Aquatic Breeding, Aquaculture Economics and Management
Chinese Students: 3,000   **Foreign Teachers:** 2-3
Sister Schools: Japan—Mie Univ.; S. Korea—Yosu National Fisheries Univ.
Accommodations: Guest house   **Teacher Salary/Benefits:** 2,000-2,500¥ RMB
Teaching Conditions: 12-14 hrs/wk   **Student Tuition/Expense:** 2,000-3,000¥ RMB
Contact: Wang Jixiang, International Exchange Center, Shanghai Fisheries University, 334 Jungong Rd., Shanghai PRC
Phone: (86-21) 6543-1090   **Fax:** (86-21) 6543-4287
e-mail: Walt@public.sta.net.cn

Shanghai Institute of Agriculture

Responsible Bureau: City Agricultural Committee
Departments: Agricultural Science, Crop Protection, Livestock and Veterinary Medicine, Gardening, Agricultural Economics
Sister School: Japan—Univ of Osaka
Contact: Foreign Affairs Office, Shanghai Institute of Agriculture, Shanghai County, Qibao Hamlet, Shanghai PRC

Shanghai Institute of Architectural Engineering and Materials

Responsible Bureau: National Bureau of Architectural Materials
Departments: Materials, Mechanical Electronics, Industrial Management
Contact: Foreign Affairs Office, Shanghai Institute of Architectural Engineering and Materials, Jiangwanwu E. Rd., Shanghai PRC

Shanghai Institute of Electric Power

Responsible Bureau: Ministry of Water and Electricity
Departments: Power Production, Electric Power, Management
Contact: Foreign Affairs Office, Shanghai Institute of Electric Power, Pingliang Rd., Shanghai PRC

Shanghai Institute of Mechanical Engineering

Responsible Bureau: Ministry of Mechanics
Departments: Timing Mechanisms and Devices, Power Production Mechanics, Systems Engineering and Automation, Computer Science, Scientific and Technological Foreign Languages
Sister Schools: US—MIT, Indiana Univ; Hong Kong—Hong Kong Polytechnic; Japan—Univ of Tokyo; Switzerland—Federal Inst of Technology; Germany—Univ of Stuttgart
Contact: Foreign Affairs Office, Shanghai Institute of Mechanical Engineering, 516 Jungong Rd., Shanghai PRC

Shanghai Institute of Railways

Responsible Bureau: Ministry of Railways
Departments: Railway Shipping, Mechanics, Electrical Equipment, Natural Materials Engineering, Electronic Mail and Computer Science
Contact: Foreign Affairs Office, Shanghai Institute of Railways, 1 Zhennan Rd., Shanghai PRC

Shanghai Maritime University
Responsible Bureau: Ministry of Transportation
Departments: Maritime Boats, Ship Mechanics, Mechanics, Computer Science, Water Transport Management, International Marine Shipping, Foreign Languages
Accommodations: rms, w/ kitchen, TV, fridge, tape recorder, bike; 11:30p.m. curfew, but flexible; visitors must register; SMU is in Pudang, an isolated area by Shanghai standards
Teaching Conditions: 16-18 hrs/wk; school materials poor, but open to new; library good and open to students
Contact: Foreign Affairs Office, Shanghai Maritime University, 1550 Pudong Rd., Shanghai PRC

Shanghai Science and Technology Cadres Institute
Responsible Bureau: City Bureau of Higher Education
Departments: Materials, Physics, Radio Electronics, Mathematics, Micromechanics, Computer Science, Chemistry, Biology
Accommodations: rms, w/ kitchen, TV; 10 p.m. curfew; bold new location is fairly isolated, too far from Shanghai for a day trip, but cooler and cleaner than the city
Teaching Conditions: 15 hrs/wk, students great (older cadres); no language lab
Contact: Foreign Affairs Office, Shanghai Science and Technology Cadres Institute, Jiading County, Shanghai Special Zone, PRC

Shanghai University of Engineering Technology
Responsible Bureau: City Economic Committee
Departments: Mechanics, Electronics and Electrical Equipment, Management, Industrial Chemistry, Materials, Vehicle Studies, Textiles, Mechanical Electronics, Textile Chemistry
Contact: Foreign Affairs Office, Shanghai University of Engineering Technology, Xianxia Rd., Shanghai PRC

SHANXI — Heavily hit by cutbacks in government subsidies to mining, Shanxi is one of China's poorest regions. The capital at Taiyuan offers dozens of lovely temples and several fine museums, and the Buddhist grottoes at Datong rank among China's finest. Mt. Wutai, one of China's holiest Buddhist mountains, offers centuries of temples and shrines, including the oldest extant Buddhist temple in China. However, due to the region's poverty, the local government tends to be leery of outside eyes. Even Mt. Wutai is officially a closed area, and while travel permits are routinely granted, foreigners are closely tracked. Foreign residents have much better access to the region than travelers, and one Datong teacher reported studying ancient sutras found at Lianyungang with some local scholars. Still, this is not a region for those who want free access to nightclubs. Food is bland but hearty, with many noodle dishes; weather dry, dusty, and harsh in winter; and language thickly accented Mandarin.

UNIVERSITIES

Shanxi University
Responsible Bureau: Provincial Education Administration
Departments: Chinese, Law, Library Science, History, Education, Philosophy, Politics, Foreign Languages, Mathematics, Computer Science, Physics, Chemistry, Biology, Environmental Protection, Economics, Law, Physical Education, Art/Music
Sister Schools: UK—Sussex Univ; US—Univ of South Carolina, Connecticut College
Teachers: teach English language and/or technical subjects
Students: have large program in Chinese Language/Culture
Contact: Foreign Affairs Office, Shanxi University, Wucheng Rd.,Taiyuan, Shanxi 030006 PRC

Taiyuan University
Responsible Bureau: City Government
Departments: Mechanics, Steel and Iron Patternmaking, Computer Software, Industrial Chemistry, Industrial Workers Construction, Crop Protection, Nursing and Care, Chinese, Politics, History, Planning and Statistics, Finance
Contact: Foreign Affairs Office, Taiyuan University, Jingangli, Taiyuan, Shanxi PRC

Yunzhong University
Responsible Bureau: City Government
Departments: Coal and Industrial Chemistry, Sanitation and Hygiene, Industrial Management, Education Management
Contact: Foreign Affairs Office, Yunzhong University, Xinjian S. Rd., Datong, Shanxi PRC

FINANCE/COMMERCE/ECONOMICS

Shanxi Institute of Economic Policy
Responsible Bureau: Ministry of Commerce
Departments: Commercial Economics, Statistics, Accounting, Finance
Contact: Foreign Affairs Office, Shanxi Institute of Economic Policy, Nanneihuan St., Taiyuan, Shanxi PRC

NORMAL SCHOOLS

Shanxi Normal School
Responsible Bureau: Provincial Education Administration
Departments: Chinese, Political Education, History, Geology, Biology, Mathematics, Chemistry, Physical Education, Foreign Languages
Contact: Foreign Affairs Office, Shanxi Normal School, Linfen, Shanxi PRC

MEDICAL SCHOOLS

Shanxi Institute of Medicine
Responsible Bureau: Provincial Education Administration
Departments: Medicine, Sanitation and Hygiene
Contact: Foreign Affairs Office, Shanxi Institute of Medicine, Xinjian S. Rd., Taiyuan, Shanxi PRC

TECHNICAL SCHOOLS

Shanxi Agricultural University*
Responsible Bureau: Provincial Education Administration
Departments: Agricultural Science, Crop Protection, Soil Chemistry, Gardening, Forestry, Livestock, Veterinary Medicine, Agricultural Mechanics, Agricultural Economics, Nutrition
Contact: Foreign Affairs Office, Shanxi Agricultural University, Taigu County, Taiyuan, Shanxi PRC

Shanxi Institute of Mining
Responsible Bureau: Ministry of Coal Mining
Departments: Materials and Mining, Geology, Mining Construction and Techniques, Mechanics, Electrical Equipment
Contact: Foreign Affairs Office, Shanxi Institute of Mining, Yingzexi Ave., Taiyuan, Shanxi PRC

Taiyuan Institute of Heavy Mechanics
Responsible Bureau: Ministry of Mechanics
Departments: Mechanics, Library Science
Contact: Foreign Affairs Office, Taiyuan Institute of Heavy Mechanics, Taiyuan, Shanxi PRC

Taiyuan Institute of Mechanics
Responsible Bureau: Ministry of Weapons and Military Equipment
Departments: Mechanics, Automative Control, Industrial Chemistry
Contact: Foreign Affairs Office, Taiyuan Institute of Mechanics, Shanglan Village, Taiyuan, Shanxi PRC

Taiyuan University of Technology*
Responsible Bureau: Provincial Education Commission
Departments: Mechanics, Electrical Machinery, High Temperature Studies, Information Control and Engineering, Computer Science, Agricultural Construction, Industrial Chemistry, Applied Chemistry, Hydrology, Mathematics, Power Science
Sister Schools: UK—Univ of Liverpool, Polytechnic of Newcastle-upon-Tyne; US—Univ of South Carolina, Oberlin College
Teachers: can teach English, Western Culture, technical subjects
Contact: Foreign Affairs Office, Taiyuan University of Technology, 11 Yingzexi Ave., Taiyuan, Shanxi PRC

SICHUAN — Lush and steamy Sichuan, irrigated by the Chang Jiang (Yangtze), Yalong, and Jialing Rivers, is China's most populous province and one of her most fertile areas. Ranging from the subtropics at Dukou to dry, temperate weather at Se'erxu, Sichuan never offers freezing conditions (except on her mountaintops), and her farmers harvest some of China's finest produce year-round. Sichuan cuisine is spicy, her people almost exclusively Han in the East and North, mixing with Shani in the South and Tibetan and Chang in the West. Two of China's most famous mountains (holy Buddhist Mt. Emei and the Giant Buddha Mountain at Leshan) tempt climbers, and the province offers unparalleled wildlife viewing activities, including the only preserve in the world offering a fair shot at seeing giant pandas in the wild. Millennia of Buddhist and secular art and architecture grace Sichuan, particularly in the temples of the capital at Chengdu, of Qingchengshan, and of Emei Shan, and in the caves at Dazu. Near Qingchengshan ancient Dujiangyan, the world's oldest man-made irrigation project, still stands in tribute to China's ancient technology. The mighty Chang Jiang (Yangtze) is the province's main transportation artery, and the lifeblood of Chongqing, the province's largest city and key commercial center. Language is thickly accented Mandarin.

UNIVERSITIES

Chengdu University of Science and Technology*
Responsible Bureau: Ministry of Education/Provincial Government
Departments: Mechanical Engineering, Electrical Engineering, Chemistry, Hydrology, Metallurgy, High Energy Radiation Materials, Computer Science, Power Studies, Mathematics, Physics, Management, Politics
Teachers and Students: accepts foreign teachers of English, scientific English, and technical subjects; accepts foreign students in Chinese Language and degree programs; excellent waiban, good financial packages, large libraries and good facilities
Contact: Foreign Affairs Office, Chengdu University of Science and Technology, #24, Secion 1, Renmin Nanlu, Chengdu, Sichuan 610065 PRC

Chengdu University
Responsible Bureau: City Government
Departments: Industrial Management, Mechanics, Electrical Equipment Engineering and Chemistry, Mathematical Theory, Chinese, Foreign Languages
Contact: Foreign Affairs Office, Chengdu University, Renmin N. Rd., Chengdu, Sichuan PRC

Chongqing University*
Responsible Bureau: State Education Committee
Departments: Mechanical Engineering, Radiation, Precision Equipment Engineering, High Temperature Studies, Radio and Telecommunications Technology, Computer Science, Management, Mathematics, Applied Physics, Applied Chemistry
Chinese Students: 13,000
Sister Schools: US—Univ of California, Western Washington State Univ, Univ of San Diego, Univ of Virginia; also universities in Canada, Japan, France, Great Britain, Germany, Russia, Azerbaijian, and Hong Kong
Accommodations: 1-2 rms w/ kitchen, A/C, washer, TV, no curfew, central location
Teaching Conditions: 14 hrs/wk, terrible materials; library well equipped but a "state secret" and tough to get into
Contact: Foreign Affairs Office, Chongqing University, Shazheng St., Chongqing, Sichuan 630031 PRC
URL: http://www.cqu.edu.cn/

Hanzhihua University
Responsible Bureau: City Government
Departments: Industrial Worker's Construction, Computer Science, Mechanical Control, Chinese, Political Management, Teaching, Secretarial Science
Contact: Foreign Affairs Office, Hanzhihua University, Bingcaogang, Dukou, Sichuan PRC

Sichuan University*

Responsible Bureau: State Education Committee
Departments: Chinese, Journalism, History, Personal Files, Philosophy, Foreign Languages and Literatures, Library Science, Mathematics, Physics, Radio Technology, Chemistry, Biology, Computer Science, Economics, Management, Commerce, Trade, Law
Accommodations: -5 rms w/ kitchen, TV, tape recorder, bike, A/C; but in walled compound and very strict about Chinese visitors
Teacher Salary/Benefits: varied; many Fulbright Experts—individuals generally get poor contracts here
Teaching Conditions: Key University with top-notch students, good facilities—but staff tends toward inflexibility
Learning Conditions: students in foreign compound; "I felt I had to go off campus to practice my Chinese"
Contact: Foreign Affairs Office, Sichuan University, Wangjianglou, Jiuyanqiao, Chengdu, Sichuan 61004 PRC

Yuzhou University

Responsible Bureau: City Bureau of Education
Departments: Mechanics, Electronics, Economic Management, Chemistry, Biology, Chinese, Mathematics, Physics, Foreign Languages, Physical Education, Statistics
Contact: Foreign Affairs Office, Yuzhou University, Xianfeng St., Chongqing, Sichuan PRC

MINORITIES/POLITICS AND LAW

Southwest Institute of Politics and Law*

Responsible Bureau: Ministry of Justice
Departments: Law, Economic Law, Criminal Investigation, Administrative Management, Labor Reform Management
Contact: Foreign Affairs Office, Southwest Institute of Politics and Law, Shapingba District, Chongqing, Sichuan PRC

Southwest Minorities Institute

Responsible Bureau: National Bureau of Minorities
Departments: Livestock and Veterinary Medicine, Politics, History, Chinese, Minority Languages, Mathematics, Theoretical Chemistry
Teacher Accommodations: 2 rms, w/ kitchen, TV, tape recorder, bike; strict curfew and registration of visitors
Teaching Conditions: 14 hrs/wk; students great; materials provided bad, but library good
Learning Conditions: fairly good; library resources limited and teaching methods and materials traditional
Contact: Foreign Affairs Office, Southwest Minorities Institute, Qinglong Village, Chengdu, Sichuan PRC

ARTS/MUSIC

Sichuan Academy of Arts

Responsible Bureau: Provincial Bureau of Higher Education
Departments: Industrial Arts, Painting, Plastics, Decoration Design
Contact: Foreign Affairs Office, Sichuan Academy of Arts, Jiulongbo District, Chongqing, Sichuan PRC

Sichuan Conservatory of Music
Responsible Bureau: Provincial Bureau of Higher Education
Departments: Voice, Musical Instruments, Wind and String Instruments, Composition, Minority Music
Contact: Foreign Affairs Office, Sichuan Conservatory of Music, Xinnanmenwai, Chengdu, Sichuan PRC

FINANCE/COMMERCE/ECONOMICS

Southwest Institute of Finance and Economics
Responsible Bureau: Chinese People's Bank
Departments: Finance, Political Economics, Agricultural Economics, Accounting, Statistics, Economic Policy, Economic Management
Contact: Foreign Affairs Office, Southwest Institute of Finance and Economics, Xiguanghua Village, Chengdu, Sichuan, PRC

FOREIGN LANGUAGES

Sichuan Foreign Language Institute
Responsible Bureau: Bureau of Higher Education
Departments: English, Russian, Japanese, French, German
Teachers and Students: accepts foreign teachers of Western languages/cultures; has large Chinese Language program for foreign students
Contact: Foreign Affairs Office, Sichuan Foreign Language Institute, Lieshi Rd., Chongqing, Sichuan 630031 PRC

NORMAL SCHOOLS

Chongqing Normal School
Responsible Bureau: Provincial Bureau of Higher Education
Departments: Chinese, History, Foreign Languages, Mathematics, Physics, Chemistry, Biology, Geology, Chinese
Contact: Foreign Affairs Office, Chongqing Normal School, Tianchen Rd., Chongqing, Sichuan PRC

Nanchong Normal School
Responsible Bureau: Provincial Bureau of Higher Education
Departments: Chinese, Foreign Languages, Politics, History, Mathematics, Physics, Chemistry, Biology
Contact: Foreign Affairs Office, Nanchong Normal School, Renmin N. Rd., Nanchong, Sichuan PRC

Sichuan Normal School
Responsible Bureau: Provincial Bureau of Higher Education
Departments: Chinese, Political Education, Foreign Languages, History, Education, Mathematics, Physics, Chemistry, Biology, Geology
Contact: Foreign Affairs Office, Sichuan Normal School, Dongcheng District, Chengdu, Sichuan 610066 PRC

Southwest Normal School
Responsible Bureau: State Education Committee
Departments: History, Music, Art, Mathematics, Physics, Chemistry, Biology, Geology, Physical Education, Telephone Technology, Pre-education Training,

Politics, Chinese, Library Management, Foreign Languages, Political Education
Contact: Foreign Affairs Office, Southwest Normal School, Beipei, Chongqing, Sichuan PRC

MEDICAL SCHOOLS

Chengdu College of Chinese Medicine
Responsible Bureau: Provincial Bureau of Higher Education
Departments: Chinese Medicine, Acupuncture, Chinese Pharmacology, Western Medicine
Contact: Foreign Affairs Office, Chengdu College of Chinese Medicine, Xiluo Rd., Chengdu, Sichuan PRC

Chongqing College of Medicine
Responsible Bureau: Provincial Bureau of Higher Education
Departments: Medicine, Pediatrics, Medical Examination, Population Planning
Contact: Foreign Affairs Office, Chongqing College of Medicine, Shapingba District, Chongqing, Sichuan PRC

Sichuan Medical College
Responsible Bureau: Ministry of Sanitation and Hygiene
Departments: Medicine, Stomatology, Oral Medicine, Sanitation and Hygiene Inspection, Pharmacology, Pharmacological Chemistry, Nutrition
Sister Schools: US—Univ of Washington; Canada—Univ of British Columbia, Univ of Toronto
Teachers and Students: accepts foreign teachers of English, technical subjects; has program for foreign students in Chinese Medicine
Contact: Foreign Affairs Office, Sichuan Medical College, Chengdu, Sichuan PRC

West China University of Medical Sciences
Responsible Bureau: Ministry of Health
Departments: Basic Medical Sciences, Clinical Medicine, Stomatology, Pharmacy, Public Health, Foreign Languages, Social Science, Continuing Education Faculty of Forensic Medicine
Chinese Students: 5,700   **Foreign Teachers:** 4
Sister Schools: US—Univ. of Washington, Seattle
Contact: Office for International Cooperation, West China University of Medical Sciences, Sichuan PRC   **e-mail:** dff@iris.imicams.ac.cn

TECHNICAL SCHOOLS

Chengdu College of Geology
Responsible Bureau: Ministry of Geology
Departments: Geology, Mining Production and Exploration and Research, Applied Chemistry, Water Resource Geology, Global Physics, Nuclear Materials, Mining Exploration, Applied Mathematics, Sociology
Sister Schools: Australia—Univ of Adelaide; France: Univ of Lower Saxony
Contact: Foreign Affairs Office, Chengdu College of Geology, Northeast Suburbs, Chengdu, Sichuan PRC

Chengdu Institute of Meteorology
Responsible Bureau: National Bureau of Meteorology

Departments: Meteorology, Exploration and Surveying, Electronics, Finance and Economics
Contact: Foreign Affairs Office, Chengdu Institute of Meteorology, Renmin S. Rd., Chengdu, Sichuan PRC

Chengdu Institute of Radio Engineering
Responsible Bureau: Ministry of Electronic Industry
Departments: Radio and Telecommunications Technology, Electromagnetic Fields, Electronics, Applied Chemistry, Mechanics, Computer Science, Social Science, Mathematics, Physics
Sister Schools: Japan—Keio Univ; Germany—Fachhochschule Aachen
Contact: Foreign Affairs Office, Chengdu Institute of Radio Engineering, Eastern Suburbs, Chengdu, Sichuan PRC

Chengdu Institute of Technology
Responsible Bureau: The Ministry of Geology and Mineral Resources
Departments: Geology, Applied Chemistry, Hydrogeology & Engineering, Geology, Petroleum, Information Engineering of Applied Geophysics, Nuclear Resource & Technology, Applied Mathematics, Mechanical Engineering, Social Sciences, Scientific Management, Computer Engineering, Resources & Economics, Civil Engineering, Foreign Langauges
Chinese Students: 6,400   **Foreign Students:** 10 (in 1996)
Foreign Teachers: 6
Sister Schools: US—Moscow State Univ., Univ. of Oklahoma, Colubmia Univ.; Europe—Technische University Branschweig
Accommodations: furnished air-conditioned apartment is provided free to teachers; dining room available
Teacher Salary/Benefits: 1,500-2,500¥ RMB/month; travel allowance of 2,200¥ RMB per academic year
Teaching Conditions: 14-20 hrs/wk; neccesary materials and equipment are available
Student Tuition/Expense: USD$800-1,500/semester
Other: Chinese language training classes have been offered to foreign students since 1984
Contact: Foreign Affairs Office, Changdu Institute of Technology, Chengdu, Sichuan 610059 PRC
I Phone: (86-28) 407-8960   **Fax:** (86-28) 334-1229
e-mail: ynhd@cdit.edu   **URL:** http://www.cdit.edu

Chongqing Institute of Architectural Engineering*
Responsible Bureau: City Ministry of Construction and Environmental Protection
Departments: Agricultural Construction, Electronics, Automation, Mechanics, Management, Secretarial Sciences, Politics
Sister Schools: US—Univ of Minnesota, Univ of Washington, Univ of Tennessee, Univ of Michigan; Canada—Univ of Manitoba; Japan—Univ of Waseda
Contact: Foreign Affairs Office, Chongqing Institute of Architectural Engineering, Shapingba District, Chongqing, Sichuan PRC

Chongqing Institute of Post and Telecommunications
Responsible Bureau: Ministry of Post and Telecommunications
Departments: Electronic Mail, Radio Technology, Management
Accommodations: not very good, 4 rms, cooking facilities, appliances didn't always work
Teaching Conditions: 15 hrs/wk; teaching materials terrible, but school open to new materials
Contact: Foreign Affairs Office, Chongqing Institute of Post and Telecommunications, Nan'an District, Chongqing, Sichuan PRC

Chongqing Institute of Transportation
Responsible Bureau: Ministry of Transportation
Departments: Highways and Bridges, Management, Mechanics, Marine Shipping Ports
Contact: Foreign Affairs Office, Chongqing Institute of Transportation, Dahuang Rd., Chongqing, Sichuan PRC

Southwest Institute of Petroleum
Responsible Bureau: Ministry of Petroleum
Departments: Resource Exploration, Mechanics, Applied Chemistry, Management, Petroleum Geology
Contact: Foreign Affairs Office, Southwest Institute of Petroleum, Shiyou E. Rd., Nanchong, Sichuan PRC

Southwest University of Agriculture
Responsible Bureau: Ministry of Agriculture, Livestock, and Fisheries
Departments: Agricultural Science, Gardening, Crop Protection, Soil Chemistry, Nutrition, Silkworm and Mulberry Cultivation, Agricultural Mechanics, Agricultural Economics, Aquatic Products, Agricultural Education, Livestock and Veterinary Medicine, Finance and Accounting, Statistics
Accommodations: 6 rms for 2 people, w/ kitchen, TV, tape recorder, bike, shared washer; cafeteria food inedible
Teaching Conditions: 12-15 hrs/wk; shortage of materials
Contact: Foreign Affairs Office, Southwest University of Agriculture, Beipei, Chongqing, Sichuan PRC

Sichuan Institute of Technology
Responsible Bureau: Provincial Bureau of Higher Education
Departments: Mechanical Engineering, Vehicles, Power Production, Nutrition, Architectural Engineering, Materials
Contact: Foreign Affairs Office, Sichuan Institute of Technology, Bi County, Chengdu, Sichuan PRC

Southwest University of Transportation*
Responsible Bureau: Ministry of Railways
Departments: Agricultural Construction, Mechanics, Mechanical Cars and Vehicles, Electrical Equipment, Computer Science, Shipping, Materials, Mathematics, Management, Power Studies, Finance and Accounting, Sociology, Foreign Languages
Contact: Foreign Affairs Office, Southwest University of Transportation, Emei County, Sichuan PRC

TIANJIN — China's third largest city, Tianjin (the Tianjin Special Zone) connects Bejing with the Bohai Gulf, forming a crucial economic corridor. One of China's most important centers of foreign trade, the zone offers resident foreigners excellent moonlighting opportunities in business, finance, and trade. The zone also has spectacular shopping opportunities in the new Fashion District, Food District, and indoor freemarkets downtown as well as a wealth of cultural activities. Too far from Beijing for a convenient day trip, the city is very accessible to the capital for weekend visits. Several important museums grace Tianjin, as do a number of important historic districts, particularly those reflecting the city's treaty port years and those important in the life of Zhou En-lai. Weather is temperate, though windy in winter. Food is excellent and quite varied. Language is standard Mandarin.

UNIVERSITIES

Nankai University*
Responsible Bureau: State Education Committee
Departments: Chinese, History, Philosophy, Library Science, Sociology, Economics, International Economics, Law, Foreign Languages, Finance, Mathematics, Physics, Biology, Chemistry
Sister Schools: US—Temple Univ, Univ of Minnesota, Kansas Univ, State Univ of NY, Indiana Univ; Japan—Ritsumeikan Univ; Australia—Univ of Melbourne, Australian National Univ, Laval Univ; Canada—McGill Univ, McMasters Univ
Teachers: Nankai is one of China's premier univs; accepts foreign teachers and experts in various fields; facilities include 1.9 million vol library, 2 English-language quarterly journals, 2 in-school publishing houses (NU Press, NU Publishing House)
Students: has special programs in Chinese Canguage/Culture, as well as students in degree programs; students in walled compound
Contact: Office for International Academic Exchanges, Nankai University, Tianjin 300071 PRC
I Phone: (86-22) 350-8229 or 350-2990 (Office); (86-22) 350-8632 (International Program); (86-22) 350-8686 (International Students Admission)
Fax: (86-22) 350-2990 (Office)   **e-mail:** zhangmz@sun.nankai.edu.cn
URL: http://www.nankai.edu.cn/

Tianjin University*
Responsible Bureau: State Education Committee
Departments: Mechanics, Microengineering, High Temperature Physical Engineering, Electrical Engineering, Water Power, Ships and Boats, Management, Chemical Engineering, Applied Chemistry, Architecture, Computer Science, Physics
Sister Schools: Canada, Japan, France, Germany, US
Teachers and Students: facilities 1.1 million vol library
Contact: Foreign Student Office, Tianjin University, 92 Wei Jin Rd., Tianjin 300072 PRC
I Phone: (86-022) 335-0835   **Fax:** (86-022) 335-0853
e-mail: intstudy@tju.edu.cn   **URL:** http://www.tju.edu.cn/

ARTS/MUSIC

Tianjin Institute of Art
Responsible Bureau: City Bureau of Higher Education
Departments: Teaching, Painting, Handicraft Arts, Pattern Design, Fashion, Dyes
Contact: Foreign Affairs Office, Tianjin Institute of Art, Tianwei District, Tianjin PRC

Tianjin Institute of Music
Responsible Bureau: City Bureau of Higher Education
Departments: Composition Theory, Voice, Minority Instruments, Wind and String Instruments, Teaching
Contact: Foreign Affairs Office, Tianjin Institute of Music, Hedong District, Tianjin PRC

FINANCE/COMMERCE/ECONOMICS

Tianjin Institute of Commerce
Responsible Bureau: Ministry of Commerce
Departments: Packaging Engineering, Nutrition Engineering, Management Engineering, Frozen Goods Engineering, Industrial Management

Contact: Foreign Affairs Office, Tianjin Institute of Commerce, Northern Suburbs, Tianjin PRC

Tianjin Institute of Finance and Economics
Responsible Bureau: City Bureau of Higher Education
Departments: Foreign Trade, Finance, Economic Policy and Accounting, Industrial Management, Commercial Economics
Contact: Foreign Affairs Office, Tianjin Institute of Finance and Economics, Hexi District, Tianjin PRC

Tianjin Institute of Foreign Trade
Responsible Bureau: Ministry of Foreign Trade and Economics
Departments: Foreign Trade and Economics, Foreign Trade English
Contact: Foreign Affairs Office, Tianjin Institute of Foreign Trade, Hebei District, Tianjin PRC

FOREIGN LANGUAGES

Tianjin Foreign Languages Institute
Responsible Bureau: City Bureau of Higher Education
Departments: English, Japanese, Western Languages
Contact: Foreign Affairs Office, Tianjin Foreign Languages Institute, Hexi District, Tianjin PRC

NORMAL/MEDICAL SCHOOLS

Tianjin College of Chinese Medicine
Responsible Bureau: City Bureau of Higher Education
Departments: Chinese Medicine, Acupuncture, Chinese Pharmacology, Chinese Bone Treatment, Chinese External Medicine
Contact: Foreign Affairs Office, Tianjin College of Chinese Medicine, Nankai District, Tianjin Special Zone PRC

Tianjin Institute of Medicine
Responsible Bureau: City Bureau of Higher Education
Departments: Medicine, Oral Medicine, Sanitation and Hygiene, Nursing and Care, Precision Medical Timing Equipment
Contact: Foreign Affairs Office, Tianjin Institute of Medicine, 62 Qi Xiang Tai Rd., Heping District, Tianjin PRC

Tianjin Normal School
Responsible Bureau: City Bureau of Higher Education
Departments: Political Education, Chinese, History, Education, Mathematics, Physics, Chemistry, Biology, Geology, Foreign Languages
Contact: Foreign Affairs Office, Tianjin Normal School, Hexi District, Tianjin PRC

TECHNICAL SCHOOLS

Civil Aviation Institute of China
Responsible Bureau: National Bureau of Civil Aviation
Departments: Aviation Management, Aviation Mechanics, Aviation Timing Control Electronics, Aviation Radio
Accommodations: 4 rms w/ kitchen, washer, TV, phone, fan, A/C, plenty of heat/hot

water, use of car and driver Saturday a.m.; location central to campus and markets but 2 hrs from downtown by public bus; 30 min by school shuttle—last shuttle leaves downtown 5:40 p.m.—to have evening downtown must take taxi, approx 40¥
Teaching Conditions: 8 hrs/wk; good students, excellent library; staff very sophisticated; CAIC is specialized training school for civil aviation, run by CAAC; students mix of trainees and professionals; in addition to 2 long-term foreign English teachers, have frequent short-term foreign technical experts
Contact: Foreign Affairs Office, Civil Aviation Institute of China, Zhanggui Village, East Suburbs, Tianjin PRC

Tianjin Institute of Light Industry
Responsible Bureau: Ministry of Light Industry
Departments: Mechanical Engineering, Nutritional Engineering, Chemical Engineering, Electrical Equipment Technology and Automation, Organic Chemistry, Heavy Transport and Mechanics
Contact: Foreign Affairs Office, Tianjin Institute of Light Industry, 1486 Da Gu S. Rd., Hexi District, Tianjin PRC

Tianjin Institute of Technology
Responsible Bureau: City Bureau of Higher Education
Departments: Radio Technology, Automation, Mechanics, Microengineering, Chemical Engineering, Computer Science, Mathematics, Physics, Foreign Languages, Management Engineering
Contact: Foreign Affairs Office, Tianjin Institute of Technology, Hexi District, Tianjin PRC

Tianjin Textiles Institute
Responsible Bureau: Ministry of Textiles
Departments: Textile Engineering, Fashion, Mechanics, Automation, Industrial Management
Contact: Foreign Affairs Office, Tianjin Textiles Institute, Hedong District, Tianjin PRC

TIBET — Surely one of the most exotic of study/teaching abroad destinations, Tibet University offers some excellent programs in Tibetan language and culture and invites up to 10 foreign teachers a year. The program is often suspended due to political difficulties, however, and even at the best of times, foreigners admit to many difficulties, from coping with altitude sickness to nightly curfews and house-to-house searches. Not for the faint of heart!

Tibet University*
Responsible Bureau: District Educational Administration
Departments: Mathematical Theory, Politics, Languages and Literatures, Music and Art, Tibetan Language and Literature, History, Chemistry, Biology, Geology
Teachers: accepts foreigners as English/Western-culture teachers; "fascinating, but lots of strict curfews, and they keep pretty close tabs on us"
Contact: Foreign Affairs Office, Tibet University, Lhasa, Tibet PRC

XINJIANG — China's northwesternmost province, Xinjiang is a land of extremes, from the lowest desert basin in the world to the massive peaks of the Altan mountains, from the howling Gobi and Taklamakan deserts "of no return" to the gracious, shaded oases of Turpan and Kashgar. Most famous for the architectural and sculptural wonders remaining from her Silk Road history, Xinjiang is also rich with minority cultures, particularly that of the Uighurs, a central Asian people closer in language and custom to the Arab nations than to the Han Chinese. Major cities are Urumqi, the bustling capital; Kashgar, on the border of Pakistan (from which enterprising tourists can apply to enter Soviet Central Asia or to travel the Karakoram highway); and Turpan, where resident foreigners can watch Uighur dancers under grape trellises in the shadow of Suleiman's Minaret. Food is Central Asian—mutton, beef, flatbreads, noodles, and lots of raisins, melons, and dried peaches and plums. Weather throughout Xinjiang is high desert: broiling in the day, freezing at night, wind-swept year-round, and searingly dry. Language is fairly standard Mandarin in Han areas, variable among minorities.

Kashgar Normal School
Responsible Bureau: Regional Education Administration
Departments: Political Education, Languages and Literatures, Mathematics, Physical Chemistry, Physical Education
Contact: Foreign Affairs Office, Kashgar Normal School, Kashgar, Xinjiang PRC

Xinjiang College of Chinese Medicine
Responsible Bureau: Regional Administration of Sanitation and Hygiene
Departments: Chinese Medicine, Acupuncture
Accommodations: spacious, tree-lined campus; rare in Urumqi
Contact: Foreign Affairs Office, Xinjiang College of Chinese Medicine, Beijing Rd., Urumqi, Xinjiang PRC

Xinjiang Institute of Economics and Finance
Responsible Bureau: Regional Economics Commission
Departments: Finance and Economics, Planning and Statistics, Finance and Accounting, Finance
Contact: Foreign Affairs Office, Xinjiang Institute of Economics and Finance, Ergong, Urumqi, Xinjiang PRC

Xinjiang Institute of Industry
Responsible Bureau: Regional Education Administration
Departments: Mechanics, Electrical Mechanics and Electrical Equipment Timing Devices, Industrial Chemistry, Light Industry, Civil and Architectural Engineering
Contact: Foreign Affairs Office, Xinjiang Institute of Industry, Youhao Rd., Urumqi, Xinjiang PRC

Xinjiang Institute of Petroleum
Responsible Bureau: Regional Petroleum Bureau
Departments: Geology, Mechanics, Management Engineering
Contact: Foreign Affairs Office, Xinjiang Institute of Petroleum, Mingyuan, Urumqi, Xinjiang PRC

Xinjiang Medical College
Responsible Bureau: Regional Education Administration
Departments: Medical Practice, Pharmacology, Public Sanitation and Hygiene, Rodent Control
Contact: Foreign Affairs Office, Xinjiang Medical College, Xinyi Rd., Urumqi, Xinjiang PRC

Xinjiang Normal School
Responsible Bureau: Regional Education Administration
Departments: Political Education, Languages and Literatures, Foreign Languages, Education, Mathematics, Physics, Chemistry
Contact: Foreign Affairs Office, Xinjiang Normal School, Kunlun Rd., Urumqi, Xinjiang PRC

Xinjiang University
Responsible Bureau: Regional Education Administration
Departments: Chinese, History, Politics, Foreign Languages, Mathematics, Physics, Chemistry, Biology, Geology, Law
Sister Schools: more than 1- foreign university and research institute
Contact: Foreign Affairs Office, Xinjiang University, 14 Shengli Rd., Urumqi, Xinjiang 830046 PRC
I Phone: (86-991) 286-2753   **URL:** http://xju1.xju.edu.cn/

Yili Normal School
Responsible Bureau: Regional Education Administration
Departments: Languages and Literatures, Mathematics, Physics, Chemistry, Foreign Languages, Physical Education
Contact: Foreign Affairs Office, Yili Normal School, Jiefang Rd., Yining, Xinjiang PRC

YUNNAN — Bordered by Burma, Vietnam, and Laos as well as by Sichuan, Guizhou, and Guangxi, Yunnan is peopled with a greater variety of minorities than any other Chinese province. Deep in the southern jungles of Xishuangbanna foreigners can eat fried bumblebees while howler monkeys shriek from the banyan trees. In the capital at Kunming, the "City of Eternal Spring," traders from the border regions meet on gracious, tree-lined avenues near Dianchi, the "Inland Sea." Ancient ocean floors cracked into a fairy tale "Stone Forest" in Lunan County's "Valley of the Gods." Dali in the lush green Erhai Valley, nestled against the blue Cangshan mountains, surely ranks among the world's remaining paradises. Climate throughout the province is mild (tending toward steamy in Xishuangbanna), and the area traditionally relaxed about foreigners. Food is rich and varied, including many tropical fruit dishes. Language is fairly standard Mandarin in Han areas, variable among minorities.

UNIVERSITIES

Kunming University
Responsible Bureau: City Government
Departments: Mechanical Production, Electrical Mechanics and Electrical Equipment, Industrial Worker's Construction, Rubber Arts, Chinese Language and Literature, Industrial Finance and Accounting, Industrial Management
Contact: Foreign Affairs Office, Kunming University, Cuihu N. Rd., Kunming, Yunnan PRC

Yunnan University*
Responsible Bureau: Provincial Education Administration
Departments: Chinese Language and Literature, Journalism, History, Personal File Studies, Philosophy, Foreign Languages, Mathematics, Computer Science, Physics, Radio Technology, Chemistry, Meteorology, Biology, Economics
Teaching Conditions: 10-12 hrs/wk; school "very open to new ideas"
Learning Conditions: fairly progressive teachers; small, but very pretty; campus, overall quite beautiful
Contact: Foreign Affairs Office, Yunnan University, Cuihu N. Rd., Kunming, Yunnan 650091 PRC
URL: http://www.ynu.edu.cn/html/yund.html

MINORITIES/POLITICS AND LAW

Yunnan Institute of Nationalities
Responsible Bureau: Provincial Minority Committee
Departments: Politics, Chinese Language and Literature, Minority Languages and Literatures, History, Foreign Languages
Contact: Foreign Affairs Office, Yunnan Institute of Nationalities, Lianhuachi, Kunming, Yunnan PRC

ARTS/MUSIC

Yunnan Academy of Art
Responsible Bureau: Provincial Education Administration
Departments: Art, Industrial Arts, Composition, Minority Music, Voice, Wind Instruments, Opera
Contact: Foreign Affairs Office, Yunnan Academy of Art, Mayuan, Kunming, Yunnan PRC

FINANCE/COMMERCE

Yunnan Institute of Finance and Trade
Responsible Bureau: Provincial Economic Committee
Departments: Finance, Commercial Economics, Economic Policy, Basic Construction Finance and Credit, Planning and Statistics
Accommodations: 1 rm + bath, no kitchen; has TV, washer, fairly stiff 11:30 p.m. curfew; location central to campus, 30 min from downtown by bike; cafeteria cheap and good
Teaching Conditions: 16 hrs/wk, excellent language lab, no photocopying or secretaries; library easily accessible, lots of economy books
Contact: Foreign Affairs Office, Yunnan Institute of Finance and Trade, Shangma Village, Kunming, Yunnan PRC

NORMAL SCHOOLS

Yunnan Normal School
Responsible Bureau: Provincial Education Administration
Departments: School Education, Chinese, History, English, Physical Education, Physics, Chemistry, Biology
Contact: Foreign Affairs Office, Yunnan Normal School, Xizhan, Kunming, Yunnan PRC

MEDICAL SCHOOLS

Dali College of Medicine
Responsible Bureau: Provincial Education Administration
Departments: Medical Practice
Sister Schools: US—China Institute of Chinese Medicine
Teacher Accommodations: excellent; 1 large rm, w/ washer, dryer, TV, tape recorder; no kitchen, but cafeteria cheap and good; no guest rooms
Teaching Conditions: 12-14 hrs/wk; staff pleasant, although sometimes "slowness of bureaucracy made it difficult to get things done"
Contact: Foreign Affairs Office, Dali College of Medicine, Xiaguan, Dali, Yunnan PRC

Kunming College of Medicine
Responsible Bureau: Provincial Education Administration
Departments: Clinical Medicine, Preventive Medicine, Stomatology, Forensic Medicine
Sister Schools: France—Ecole Parisien; Australia: Univ of Sydney Medical School; US—Washington Univ
Teacher Accommodations: New dorm completed in 1992; 1 rm/teacher w/ shared bath, TV, tape recorder, fridge, bike, space heater, typewriter; dorm central to campus, 30 min walk from downtown
Teaching Conditions: 14 hrs/wk; good variety of courses, excellent students; no secretarial help or photocopies; library good for medical materials, poor for general reading
Students: some short courses in Chinese Medicine available
Contact: Foreign Affairs Office, Kunming College of Medicine, Renminxi Rd., Kunming, Yunnan 650031 PRC

Yunnan College of Traditional Chinese Medicine
Responsible Bureau: Provincial Education Administration
Departments: Chinese Herbs, Chinese Medicine, Chinese Pharmacology
Chinese Students: 1,041   **Foreign Students:** 6
Accommodations: housing is free, with TV and bathroom; Students: USD$180/month with telephone, TV and bathroom
Teacher Salary/Benefits: 1,200¥ RMB/month   **Teaching Conditions:** 20 hrs/wk
Student Tuition/Expense: Study in the college: USD$2,000/yr; Practice in the hospital: USD$400/month
Contact: Foreign Affairs Office, Yunnan College of Traditional Chinese Medicine, 6 Bai Ta Rd., Kunming, Yunnan 650011 PRC
I Phone: (86-871) 715-0981   **Fax:** (86-871) 715-0983

TECHNICAL SCHOOLS

Kunming Institute of Technology
Responsible Bureau: China National Non-Ferrous Metals Company
Departments: Geology, Materials and Mining, Metallurgy, Metallurgical Materials and High Temperature Control, Mechanical Engineering, Automation and Control, Environmental Engineering, Foreign Languages, Architectural Engineering and Power Studies
Sister Schools: US—South Dakota School of Mines and Technology, Lehigh Univ, Colorado State Univ; France—Inst Nationale de Science Appliques de Lyon; Germany—Univ of Karlsruhe

Teachers and Students: accepts foreign teachers in both English and technical subjects; has large library (approx 650,000 vols) and Museum of Geology
Contact: Foreign Affairs Office, Kunming Institute of Technology, Lianhuachi, Kunming, Yunnan PRC

Yunnan Institute of Technology
Responsible Bureau: Provincial Education Administration
Departments: Mechanical Engineering, Vehicle Engineering, Electrical Equipment Engineering, Architectural Engineering, Glue and Paper Manufacturing, Chemical Engineering, Nutrition Engineering
Contact: Foreign Affairs Office, Yunnan Institute of Technology, Huancheng Donglu, Xizi, Kunming, Yunnan PRC

ZHEJIANG — "Heaven," claims the old Chinese saying, "has paradise. The earth has Suzhou and Hangzhou." Home of West Lake with its dozens of spectacular temples, mountains, and groves, Hangzhou, the capital of Zhejiang, ranks among China's most beloved tourist destinations. The ancient port city of Wenzhou, now a bustling mercantile center; the charming temples and lively intellectual life of Ningbo; Shaoxing, home of one of China's finest traditional liquors; and proximity to Shanghai and to Jiangsu Province (home of Suzhou) complete the region's charms. Resident foreigners have been able to explore every crag around West Lake and gain access to Putuoshan, the only of China's major Buddhist mountains not regularly open to foreigners. Zhejiang weather is mild, and food is rich and varied with much seafood and produce. Language is a variant of Fujianese, but Mandarin speakers abound.

UNIVERSITIES

Hangzhou University
Responsible Bureau: Provincial Bureau of Education
Departments: Philosophy, Economics, Law, Chinese, History, Education, Foreign Languages, Psychology, Geology, Mathematics, Statistical Mechanics, Physics, Chemistry, Biology, Physical Education
Sister Schools: relations w/ 17 schools in US, Canada, Australia, Germany, Belgium, Japan
Teachers and Students: has various exchange programs w/ sister schools
Contact: Foreign Affairs Office, Hangzhou University, Tianmushan Rd., Hangzhou, Zhejiang PRC

Ningbo University
Responsible Bureau: City Government
Departments: Art, Computer Science, History, Foreign Languages, Chemistry, Physics
Foreign Students: 0   **Foreign Teachers:** 3-5
Teachers: can teach English, Western Culture; Ningbo is still under construction; lots of carpentry going on, but setting lovely
Contact: Foreign Affairs Office, Ningbo University, Ningbo, Zhejiang PRC

Wenzhou University
Responsible Bureau: City Government
Departments: Industrial Management, Secretarial Science, Foreign Trade Economics, Electronics, Nutrition, Agricultural Construction
Contact: Foreign Affairs Office, Wenzhou University, Jiaoxiangxiang, Wenzhou, Zhejiang PRC

Zhejiang University*
Responsible Bureau: State Education Committee
Departments: Mathematics, Physics, Chemistry, Power Studies, Geology, Electrical Equipment, Industrial Chemistry, Agricultural Construction, Mechanics, Radio Electronics, Radiation Timing Equipment, Materials, High Temperature Physics, Scientific Experimentation Timing Equipment, Computer Science, Management, Languages, Sociology
Sister Schools: US—Univ of Utah, Univ of Massachussetts, Rochester Inst of Technology, Rutgers, Georgia Inst of Technology, Univ of Maryland, California State Univ, Northridge Univ; Germany—Berlin Tech Univ, Univ of Wurzburg; Belgium—Univ of Ghent, Univ of Lund
Teachers and Students: has various short-term study and other programs w/ sister schools, also small program in Chinese Language and Culture for long-term foreign students; facilities include 1.1 million vol library
Contact: Foreign Affairs Office, Zhejiang University, Yuquan, Hangzhou, Zhejiang PRC

ARTS/MUSIC

Zhejiang Academy of Fine Arts
Responsible Bureau: Ministry of Culture
Departments: Chinese Traditional Painting, Oil Painting, Woodblock Painting, Plastics, Industrial Arts
Contact: Foreign Affairs Office, Zhejiang Academy of Fine Arts, Nanshan Rd., Hangzhou, Zhejiang PRC

FINANCE/COMMERCE/ECONOMICS

Hangzhou Institute of Commerce
Responsible Bureau: Ministry of Commerce
Departments: Management, Planning and Statistical Financial Accounting, Nutrition, Electronics, Information
Sister Schools: US—Univ of South Florida
Contact: Foreign Affairs Office, Hangzhou Institute of Commerce, Jiaogong Rd., Hangzhou, Zhejiang PRC

NORMAL SCHOOLS

Hangzhou Normal School
Responsible Bureau: City Committee of Humanities Education
Departments: Chinese, Political History, Foreign Languages, Mathematics, Physics, Chemistry, Biology, Music, Physical Education
Contact: Foreign Affairs Office, Hangzhou Normal School, Wenyi Rd., Hangzhou, Zhejiang PRC

Ningbo Normal School
  Responsible Bureau: City Bureau of Higher Education
  Departments: Chinese, Mathematics, Physics, Chemistry, Political History, English, Physical Education, Geology
  Contact: Foreign Affairs Office, Ningbo Normal School, Sanguantang, Ningbo, Zhejiang PRC

Zhejiang Normal University
  Responsible Bureau: Zhejiang Provincial Education Commission
  Departments: Chinese, Mathematics, Politics and Law Education, History, Foreign Languages, Biology, Geography, Physics, Chemistry, Physical Education, Music, Arts, Computer Science
  Chinese Students: 1,000   **Foreign Students:** 20   **Foreign Teachers:** 6
  Sister Schools: Bethany College, Univ. of Guam, Kiw International Univ. of Civil Aviation
  Accommodations: well-equipped apartments
  Teacher Salary/Benefits: 2,200-3,200¥ RMB/month
  Foreign-teacher status: 1,000-2,000¥ RMB/month
  Teaching Conditions: 14-16 hrs/wk; standard facilities
  Student Tuition/Expenses: USD$1,700/year
  Contact: Mr. Su Jinzin, Mr. Yu Zechuo, or Mr. Zhuang Yao, Foreign Affairs Office, Zhejiang Normal University, Gao Village, Jinhua, Zhejiang PRC
  I Phone: (86-579) 234-1801 ext. 2380   **Fax:** (86-579) 234-2323

MEDICAL SCHOOLS

Wenzhou College of Medicine
  Responsible Bureau: Provincial Administration of Sanitation and Hygiene
  Departments: Medicine, Pediatrics
  Contact: Foreign Affairs Office, Wenzhou College of Medicine, Wenzhou, Zhejiang PRC

Zhejiang College of Traditional Chinese Medicine
  Responsible Bureau: Provincial Administration of Sanitation and Hygiene
  Departments: Chinese Medicine, Acupuncture
  Chinese Students: 500
  Contact: Foreign Affairs Office, Zhejiang College of Traditional Chinese Medicine, Qingchun St., Hangzhou, Zhejiang PRC

Zhejiang University of Medicine
  Responsible Bureau: Provincial Government
  Departments: Medicine, Pharmacology, Stomatology, Biomedical Engineering, Infectious Diseases, Cardiology, Demography
  Sister Schools: US—Stanford Univ, Missouri Univ; Japan—Gifu Univ, Yamagata Univ; Germany—Univ of Mons, Univ of Lubeck
  Contact: Foreign Affairs Office, Zhejiang University of Medicine, Hanzhou, Zhejiang PRC

TECHNICAL SCHOOLS

China Institute of Measurement and Surveying
  Responsible Bureau: National Bureau of Measurement and Surveying
  Departments: Surveying, Power Measurement and Surveying, High Temperature Measurement, Electromagnetic Measurement, Radio Measurement
  Contact: Foreign Affairs Office, China Institute of Measurement and Surveying, Jiaogongsan Rd., Hangzhou, Zhejiang PRC

Hangzhou Institute of Electronics and Industry
Responsible Bureau: Ministry of Electronics
Departments: Mechanics, Industrial Economics, Management, Electronics
Contact: Foreign Affairs Office, Hangzhou Institute of Electronics and Industry, Wenyi Rd., Hangzhou, Zhejiang PRC

Zhejiang Forestry College
Responsible Bureau: Provincial Education Bureau
Departments: Forestry, Landscaping and Architecture, Foresty Products Processing, Economic Management
Chinese Students: 1,250   **Foreign Students:** 15   **Foreign Teachers:** 2
Accommodations: a building for experts (or foreign teachers or students)
Teacher Salary/Benefits: Expert salary: 2,200-3,000¥ RMB/month plus int'l travel expense; Teacher salary: 1,200-2,200¥ RMB/month
Teaching Conditions: 10-14 hrs/wk; a flat with special teaching room, dormitory and dining room
Student Tuition/Expense: short program: USD$1,500/month (includes tuition, room, boarding and application fee)
Other: Zhejiang Forestry college is situated in the city of Lin-an, 50 kilometers west of Hangzhou. Lin-an has a total population of 0.5 million, an annual percipitation of 1740.5 mm, and an average temperature of 15.8°C.
Contact: Foreign Affairs Office, Zhejiang Forestry College, Lin-an, Zhejiang 311300 PRC
I Phone: (86-571) 372-3544 ext. 2008   **Fax:** (86-571) 371-1464

Zhejiang Institute of Aquaculture
Responsible Bureau: Provincial Aquaculture Administration
Departments: Mechanics, Aquaculture, Aquatic Breeding, Marine Products, Nutrition
Contact: Foreign Affairs Office, Zhejiang Institute of Aquaculture, Pingyangpu, Putuo County, Zhejiang PRC

Zhejiang Institute of Silk and Brocade Industry
Responsible Bureau: China National Silk and Brocade Company
Departments: Silks and Brocades, Fashion, Mechanical Electronics, Dyes
Accommodations: good; 3 rms w/ kitchen, bath, TV, fridge, no curfew, occasional use of car and driver; location central to campus, 90 min walk from downtown
Teaching Conditions: moderate course load, good students but terrible language lab, library; some photocopying, secretaries provided
Contact: Foreign Affairs Office, Zhejiang Institute of Silk and Brocade Industry, Wenyi Rd., Hangzhou, Zhejiang PRC

Zhejiang Institute of Technology
Responsible Bureau: Provincial Education Committee
Departments: Industrial Chemistry, Mechanical Engineering, Electrical Engineering, Management, Civil Engineering, Light Industry
Sister Schools: Japan—Ashikaga Inst of Engineering
Contact: Foreign Affairs Office, Zhejiang Institute of Technology, Mishixiang, Hangzhou, Zhejiang PRC

Zhejiang University of Agriculture*
Responsible Bureau: Ministry of Agriculture, Livestock, and Fisheries/ Provincial Government

Departments: Agricultural Science, Gardening, Crop Protection, Soil Chemistry, Mulberry and Silkworm Cultivation, Livestock and Veterinary Medicine, Tea Cultivation, Agricultural Economics, Agricultural Mechanics, Environmental Protection, Agricultural Education, Nutrition
Sister Schools: US—Univ of Maryland, Oregon State Univ, Virginia Polytechnic Inst, State Univ of Virginia; Japan—Tokyo Univ, Shimane Univ; UK—Univ of Newcastle-upon-Tyne; Germany—Univ of Berlin
Contact: Foreign Affairs Office, Zhejiang University of Agriculture, Huajiachi, Hangzhou, Zhejiang PRC

TAIWAN — Also called "Formosa," (from a Portugese phrase meaning "Beautiful Island"), Taiwan is a semi-tropical jewel in the South China Sea, some 100 miles off the coast of Fujian Province. Ruled since 1949 by the Nationalist Party (Kuomintang, or KMT), the island suffered for nearly 40 years under martial law as KMT leaders insisted the island would one day "take back" the mainland. Though Taiwan's government lifted martial law in 1987, and declared peace with the mainland in 1991, relations between the two areas remain tense.

Taiwan has a modern, international economy, and her shops, at least in the cities, carry everything you might desire. In rural areas you can also see something of traditional culture. Most of the island's cultural and economic resources are centered in the capital at Taipei, though Kaohsiung in the south is a major center of heavy industry. Excellent scenery abounds throughout the island, particularly at the Sun-Moon Lake resort and the Hualien Gorge in the island's center, and at Kenting National Park in the South. Weather is broiling and humid in the summer, mild spring and fall, and damp and occasionally chill in the winter. Food is international, featuring cuisines from throughout China as well as many international restaurants. Indigenous Taiwanese cuisine is very light, focusing on seafood and heavily influenced by Japanese style. For more on these topics, see Chapter 2.

Chang Gung Institute of Nursing
Departments: full nursing program
Teachers and Students: school has excellent internship and training programs in cooperation w/ Linkou Chang Gung Memorial Hospital; no special programs for foreigners
Contact: Personnel Office, Chang Gung Institute of Nursing, 261 Wen-hwa #1 Rd., Kwei-shan, Tauyuan, Taiwan

Chang Gung Medical College
Departments: Medicine, Medical Technology, Nursing, Pathology
Teachers and Students: school offers graduate programs in medicine only, in association w/ Chang Gung Memorial Hospital; no special programs for foreigners
Contact: Personnel Office, Chang Gung Medical College, 259 Wen-hwa #1 Rd., Kwei-shan, Taoyuan, Taiwan

Chen-Hsiu Junior College of Technology
Departments: Chemical Engineering, Electrical Engineering, Civil Engineering, Electronic Engineering, Industrial Engineering and Management, Mechanical Engineering, Architectural Engineering

Teachers and Students: private college training technicians for industry; has some programs for Overseas Chinese
Contact: Personnel Office, Chen-Hsiu Junior College of Technology, 840 Cheng-Ching Rd., 83305 Niaau-sung Village, Kaohsiung County, Taiwan

Chih-Lee College of Business
Departments: International Trade, Business Administration, Accounting and Statistics, Secretarial Science, Banking and Insurance
Teachers and Students: private, comprehensive business school; no special programs for foreigners
Contact: Personnel Office, Chih-Lee College of Business, 313 Wen-hwa Rd., Section 1, Panchiao City, Taiwan

China Junior College of Technology
Departments: Mechanical Engineering, Electrical Engineering, Electronic Engineering
Teachers and Students: school has excellent technical facilities; no special programs for foreigners, but does provide adviser to help foreigners with cultural/ other difficulties; can arrange language tutoring
Contact: Personnel Office, China Junior College of Technology, 245 Yanchiuyuan Rd., Section 3, Nankang District, Taipei, Taiwan

China Junior College of Marine Technology
Departments: Navigation, Marine Engineering, Fisheries, Marine Products Processing, Shipping and Management, Electronic Communications
Teachers and Students: school focuses on providing trained technical personnel for the marine and aquaculture industries; no special programs for foreigners
Contact: Personnel Office, China Junior College of Marine Technology, 212 Yen-ping N. Rd., Section 9, Shih-lin District, Taipei, Taiwan

China Medical College
Departments: 9 depts including Chinese Traditional Medicine, Chinese Pharmaceutical Science
Teachers and Students: accepts foreign teachers in Western Medicine depts, and foreign students, especially in Chinese Medicine
Contact: Personnel Office, China Medical College, 91 Hsueh-shih Rd., Taichung, Taiwan

Chinese Culture University
Departments: 52 depts in 9 colleges: Liberal Arts, including Chinese Literature (classic and modern), History, Philosophy; Foreign Languages, including Oriental Languages, Western Languages; Law, including Political Science, Sino-American Relations, Dr. Sun Yat-Sen's Thought; Journalism and Communication; Arts, including Music (Western and Chinese), Fine Arts, Drama (Chinese Opera and Film); Science; Engineering; Agriculture; Business, including Int'l Trade, Tourism
Teachers and Students: has several programs for foreign students in various depts. Accepts teachers in several depts; campus on beautiful mountainside, close to Taipei and bordering the National Palace Museum
Contact: Personnel Office, Chinese Culture University, Hwa Kang, Yang Ming Shan, Taipei, Taiwan
▌**Phone:** (886-02) 861-1138   **Fax:** (886-02) 312-0089

Chin-Yi Institute of Technology
Departments: Mechanical Engineering, Electrical Engineering, Electronic Engineering, Chemical Engineering, Industrial Engineering and Management, Business Management
Teachers and Students: school trains technical personnel; no special programs for foreigners
Contact: Personnel Office, Chin-Yi Institute of Technology, 35 Lane 215, Chung Shan Rd., Section 1, 41111 Taipin, Taichung, Taiwan

Chung Hwa Junior College of Medical Technology
Departments: Nursing, Midwifery, Food and Nutrition, Medical Technology, Hospital Administration
Teachers and Students: school prepares students for technical medical positions; no special programs for foreigners
Contact: Personnel Office, Chung Hwa Junior College of Medical Technology, 31 Lane 373, Chung Sheng Rd., Jen Te Village, Tainan County, Taiwan

Chung Shan Medical and Dental College
Departments: Dental Medicine, Medicine, Medical Technology, Nursing, Nutrition, Rehabilitation
Contact: Personnel Office, Chung Shan Medical and Dental College, 113 Tachin St., Section 2, Taichung, Taiwan

Chung Yuan Christian University
Departments: 19 departments in 3 colleges: Engineering, Science, Business (including International Trade, Business Administration)
Contact: Personnel Office, Chung Yuan Christian University, 32023 Chung Li, Taiwan

Chung-Yu College of Business Administration
Departments: Business Administration, Accounting and Statistics, Banking and Insurance, International Trade, Secretarial Science
Teachers and Students: comprehensive business school; no special programs for foreigners
Contact: Personnel Office, Chung-Yu College of Business Administration, 40 Yi Rd., 7 Keelung, Taiwan

Deh Yu Nursing Junior College
Departments: Midwifery and Nursing, Food Health
Teachers and Students: no special programs for foreigners
Contact: Personnel Office, Deh Yu Nursing Junior College, 336 Fu Hsing Rd., Keelung, Taiwan

Far East Engineering College
Departments: Chemical Engineering, Electrical Engineering, Mechanical Engineering, Electronic Engineering, Industrial Engineering
Teachers and Students: school grants associate's degrees only; no special programs for foreigners
Contact: Personnel Office, Far East Engineering College, 49 Chung-hwa Rd., Hsi-chih Town, Tainan, Taiwan

Feng Chia University
Departments: 27 depts in 4 colleges: Engineering; Business (including Int'l Trade); Science; Management; also program in Chinese Literature

Sister Schools: has exchanges with 12 institutions in US, Belgium, Philippines, Thailand, Korea, Japan
Teachers and Students: cooperative programs w/ sister schools include exchanges of faculty, students, and publications. Also has Chinese Language Teaching Center
Contact: Personnel Office, Feng Chia University, 100 Wenhwa Rd., Seatwen District, Taichung, Taiwan

Foo Yin Junior College of Nursing and Medical Technology

Departments: Basic Nursing, Maternity Nursing, Pediatric Nursing, Surgical Nursing, Public Health Nursing, Psychiatric Nursing
Teachers and Students: comprehensive nursing program with good labs and other facilities; no special programs for foreigners
Contact: Personnel Office, Foo Yin Junior College of Nursing and Medical Technology, 151 Chin-hsueh Rd., 83101 Ta-liao Village, Kaohsiung County, Taiwan

Fu Jen Catholic University

Departments: 35 depts in 6 colleges: Liberal Arts (Chinese Literature, History, Philosophy); Art; Foreign Languages (English, German, French, Spanish, Japanese, Translation and Interpretation, Linguistics); Science and Engineering; Law; Management (Int'l Trade, Business Administration)
Sister Schools: in several countries
Teachers and Students: has Chinese Language Program for foreign students and accepts many foreign teachers in several depts
Contact: Personnel Office, Fu Jen Catholic University, 510 Chung Tsung Rd., Taipei, Hsinchuang District, Taiwan
❚ **Phone:** (886-02) 908-6220   **Fax:** (886-02) 904-4750

Hsing Wu College of Commerce

Departments: Accounting, Business Administration, International Trade, Tourism, Banking and Insurance
Teachers and Students: comprehensive business program; no special programs for foreigners
Contact: Personnel Office, Hsing Wu College of Commerce, Shieh Yang, Kang Linkou, Taipei County, Taiwan

Hung-Kuang Junior College of Nursing

Departments: Nursing and Midwifery, Food Science and Nutrition, Nursing, Industrial Safety and Health
Teachers and Students: school has excellent lab facilities, many extracurricular clubs, some sister relationships with foreign schools; no special programs for foreigners
Contact: Personnel Office, Hung-Kuang Junior College of Nursing, 34 Chung-chie Rd., 43309 Sha-lu, Taichung County, Taiwan

Hwa Hsia College of Technology

Departments: 5 depts, all Engineering related   **Chinese Students:** 3,700
Contact: Personnel Office, Hwa Hsia College of Technology, 111 Hun-Hsin St., 23557 Chung-Ho City, Taipei County, Taiwan

Kaohsiung Medical College

Departments: 10 depts, all related to Medicine or Nursing
Contact: Personnel Office, Kaohsiung Medical College, 100 Shih-chuan First Rd., Kaohsiung, Taiwan

Kouchi Junior College of Commerce
Departments: Accounting and Statistics, Banking and Insurance, Business Administration, International Trade, Finance and Taxation, Tourism
Teachers and Students: comprehensive business school; no special programs for foreigners
Contact: Personnel Office, Kouchi Junior College of Commerce, 84 Sang Do 2 Rd., 80223 Kaohsiung, Taiwan

Kuang Shan Institute of Technology
Departments: Chemical Engineering, Textile Engineering, Mechanical Engineering, Electrical Engineering, Electronic Engineering, Industrial Engineering and Management, Environmental Engineering
Teachers and Students: school trains technicians and professional engineers; no special programs for foreigners
Contact: Personnel Office, Kuang Shan Institute of Technology, 94 Da Wan Rd., Yung Kang Village, Tainan County, Taiwan

Kuang Wu Junior College of Technology
Departments: Mechanical Engineering, Electrical Engineering, Electronic Engineering, Chemical Engineering
Contact: Personnel Office, Kuang Wu Junior College of Technology, 151 I-Te St., 11271 Peito, Taipei County, Taiwan

Lienho Junior College of Technology
Departments: Electrical Engineering, Electronic Engineering, Chemical Engineering, Architectural Engineering, Industrial Engineering, Management, Ceramic Engineering, Industrial Design, Optical Engineering, Environmental Engineering
Teachers and Students: school is technical college preparing skilled personnel for industry; dept of industrial design is particularly well known for designing footwear; no special programs for foreigners
Contact: Personnel Office, Lienho Junior College of Technology, Miao Li, Taiwan

Ling Tung College
Departments: 13 depts including Int'l Trade and Business Administration
Contact: Personnel Office, Ling Tung College, 1 Ling Tung Rd., Nantun Taichung, Taiwan

Lung-hwa Junior College of Technology and Commerce
Departments: Mechanical Engineering, Electrical Engineering, Electronic Engineering, Chemical Engineering, Industrial Management
Teachers and Students: school is on south face of Long-Shou mountain; grants associate's degrees only, prepares skilled technicians for industry; no special programs for foreigners
Contact: Personnel Office, Lung-hwa Junior College of Technology and Commerce, Tao-yuan, Taiwan

Mei-Ho Junior College of Nursing
Departments: full Nursing program
Teachers and Students: school provides 5-year program for middle-school graduates, equivalent to high school + 2-year nursing degree; no special programs for foreigners
Contact: Personnel Office, Mei-Ho Junior College of Nursing, 23 Ping-kung Rd., Mei-Ho District, Nei-pu Village, Pingtung, Taiwan

Ming Chuan College
Departments: 9 depts, all business related, including Int'l Trade andTourism
Teachers and Students: accepts foreign teachers, particularly in dept of Tourism,
as teachers of English, Japanese, Spanish
Contact: Personnel Office, Ming Chuan College, 250 Chung Shan N. Rd., Section
5, Taipei, Taiwan
■ **Phone:** (886-02) 827-7413   **Fax:** (886-02) 312-0089

Nan-Tai Junior College of Technology
Departments: Electronic Engineering, Electrical Engineering, Mechanical
Engineering, Chemical Engineering, Industrial Engineering and Management,
Automobile Engineering, Int'l Trade, Business Administration
Contact: Personnel Office, Nan-Tai Junior College of Technology, 1 Nan-tai St.,
Yung Kung Village, Tainan County, Taiwan

Nanjeon Junior College of Technology
Departments: 7 depts, all Engineering related
Contact: Personnel Office, Nanjeon Junior College of Technology, 178 Chiao Chin
Rd., 73701 Yenshui Chen, Tainan County, Taiwan

National Central University
Departments: 14 depts in 4 colleges: Liberal Arts, including Chinese Literature,
Philosophy; Science; Engineering; Management, including Business Adminis-
tration, Financial Management
Chinese Students: 3,323
Teachers and Students: school accepts foreign teachers of English, technical sub-
jects, and foreign students in all depts; no special programs for foreigners; cam-
pus dominates lovely hill in small town, called "Garden of Chungli City"
Contact: Personnel Office, National Central University, 38 Wu Chuan Li, Chung-
Li, Taiwan
■ **Phone:** (886-02) 422-7151   **Fax:** (886-02) 392-2607

National Changhua University of Education
Departments: 9 depts including English and Business
Teachers and Students: accepts foreign teachers in English and Business depts and
foreign students; campus located on mountainside
Contact: Personnel Office, National Changhua University of Education, 1, Chin-
Teh Rd., Pai Sha Village, 50058 Changhua City, Taiwan
■ **Phone:** (886-04) 723-2105 ext. 212 (Foreign Student Affairs)
Fax: (886-04) 724-3074

National Chengchi University
Departments: 27 depts in 5 colleges, Liberal Arts and Sciences, including Chinese
Literature, Education, History; Foreign Languages, including Oriental Languages and
Cultures, Western Languages and Literature, Arabic Language and Literature; Commu-
nication; Law, including East Asian Studies and China Border Area Study; Commerce
Teachers and Students: Chengchi accepts more foreign students in degree pro-
grams than any other Taiwan univ, as well as 20-25 foreign teachers in Western
Languages and Culture; Chengchi is in mountainous picturesque suburb of Taipei
and is one of the most prestigious univs in Taiwan
Contact: Personnel Office, National Chengchi University, 64 Chih-nan Rd., Section
2, Taipei, Taiwan
■ **Phone:** (886-02) 939-8335 (for foreign students, ext. 301) **Fax:** (886-02) 939-8043

National Cheng Kung University

Departments: 30 depts in 5 colleges, Liberal Arts, including Chinese Literature, Foreign Languages and Literature, History; Science; Engineering; Management Science; Medicine

Teachers and Students: NCKU is most famous for its medical research, but accepts foreigners as teachers in the Foreign Languages and Literature Dept, and as students

Contact: Personnel Office, National Cheng Kung University, 1 Ta-hsueh Rd., 70101 Tainan, Taiwan

■ **Phone:** (886-06) 236-1111 ext. 205   **Fax:** (886-06) 236-8660

National Chiao Tung University

Departments: 12 depts in 3 colleges: Engineering; Science; Management

Teachers and Students: NCTU is a science-focused univ which cooperates with the Hsinchu Science Industrial Park; no special programs for foreigners

Contact: Personnel Office, National Chiao Tung University, 101, Kuang-Fu Rd., Sec. 2, Hsinchu, Taiwan

■ **Phone:** (886-03) 571-5130   **Fax:** (886-03) 572-2467

National Chiayi Institute of Agriculture

Departments: 13 depts all Agricultural Science related, including aquaculture

Teachers and Students: one of Taiwan's major agricultural schools, with cooperative extension program and active student clubs; no special programs for foreigners

Contact: Personnel Office, National Chiayi Institute of Agriculture, 84 Horng Mau Bei, Luh Lau Li 60083, Chiayi, Taiwan

National Chung Cheng University

Departments: 10 depts in 5 Colleges (Liberal Arts, including Chinese Literature and Foreign Language; Sciences; Social Sciences; Engineering; Management)

Contact: Personnel Office, National Chung Cheng University, 160, San Hsing, Ming-hsiung, 62117 Chiayi, Taiwan

■ **Phone:** (886-05) 272-0411   **Fax:** (886-05) 272-0408

National Chung Hsing University

Departments: 48 depts in 7 colleges: Agriculture; Science; Engineering; Liberal Arts, including Chinese Literature, History, Foreign Languages and Literature; Evening School, including all Liberal Arts depts plus Business and Accounting; plus 2 schools of law and commerce at Taipei campus; see following listing

Teachers and Students: accepts foreign teachers in Western Languages and Culture and foreign students (majority at Taipei campus)

Contact: Personnel Office, National Chung Hsing University, 250, Kuo-Kuong Rd., Taichung, Taiwan

■ **Phone:** (886-04) 287-3181   **Fax:** (886-04) 287-0925

National Chung Hsing University, College of Law and Commerce

Departments: 10 depts in both day and evening schools including Law, Business Administration, Cooperative Economics, Land Economics and Administration

Teachers and Students: accepts foreigners as both teachers and students in various departments

Contact: Personnel Office, National Chung Hsing University, College of Law and Commerce, 69 Chien Kuo North Rd., Section 2, Taipei, Taiwan

National I-lan Institute of Agriculture and Technology
Departments: 10 depts in 2 colleges: Agriculture, including aquaculture; Technology
Teachers and Students: accepts foreigners
Contact: Personnel Office, National I-Ian Institute of Agriculture and Technology, 1 Shang Nung Rd., I-Ian City, Taiwan

National Institute of the Arts
Departments: 4 depts including Music, Fine Arts, Theater, Dance; also has research center in traditional and folk arts and traditional theater and music
Teachers and Students: campus in wooded area at edge of Taipei
Contact: Personnel Office, National Institute of the Arts, 1 Hsueh-Yuan Rd., Peitou, Taipei, Taiwan
■ **Phone:** (886-02) 896-1000   **Fax:** (886-02) 893-8704

National Kaohsiung Institute of Marine Technology
Departments: 16 depts including Fisheries, Aquaculture, Seafood Technology, and other marine-related sciences
Teachers and Students: no special programs for foreigners
Contact: Personnel Office, National Kaohsiung Institute of Marine Technology, 142 Hai-chuan Rd., Nan-tzu District, 81105 Kaohsiung, Taiwan

National Kaohsiung Institute of Technology
Departments: 7 depts, all in Engineering
Teachers and Students:
Sister-school relations with: US— Univ of Akron, Tri-County Technology, Texas State Technical Inst; Korea—Daelim Inst of Technology; important industrial-related scientific inst
Contact: Personnel Office, National Kaohsiung Institute of Technology, 415 Chieh-kung Rd., 80782 Kaohsiung, Taiwan

National Kaohsiung Normal University
Departments: 7 depts including Chinese, English, Education
Teachers and Students: accepts several foreign teachers, especially in graduate inst of English Education; has program in Chinese for foreign students at graduate inst of Chinese Language and Literature
Contact: Personnel Office, National Kaohsiung Normal University, 116 Ho-Ping First Rd., Kaohsiung, Taiwan
■ **Phone:** (886-07) 751-7161 ext. 214   **Fax:** (886-07) 711-0315

National Open University
Departments: Business, Humanities, Social Sciences
Teachers: open univ offers televised continuing-education courses; foreigners have occasionally taught English through Open Univ
Contact: Personnel Office, National Open University, 172 Chung-Cheng Rd., 24702 Lu Chow, Taipei, Taiwan
■ **Phone:** (886-02) 282-9355   **Fax:** (886-02) 283-1721

National Pingtung Institute of Agriculture
Departments: 14 depts, all focused on Agriculture and Aquaculture
Teachers and Students: lovely rural setting, w/ largest campus in Taiwan, including model livestock and crop farms, aquaculture ponds, gardens; offers 1-½ yr training programs for foreign students, mostly from Southeast Asia

Contact: Personnel Office, National Pingtung Institute of Agriculture, 1 Hsueh-fu Rd., 91207 Nei-pu Village, Ping Tung County, Taiwan

National Sun Yat-Sen University
Departments: 14 depts in 5 colleges, Liberal Arts, including Chinese Literature, Foreign Language and Literature, Music; Science; Engineering; Management; Marine Science
Teachers and Students: accepts foreign teachers in Western Languages and Culture, and foreign students
Contact: Personnel Office, National Sun Yat-Sen University, 70, Lien-Hai Rd., Kaohsiung, Taiwan
▮ **Phone:** (886-07) 531-6170 ext. 2501   **Fax:** (886-07) 531-3603

National Taipei College of Business
Departments: Accounting, Statistics, Banking, Insurance, Business Administration, Finance and Taxation, Computer Science, Secretarial Science, International Trade
Teachers and Students: NTCB is one of the island's premier business schools; often accepts foreign teachers for Language, International Trade classes
Contact: Personnel Office, National Taipei College of Business, 321 Chi-nan Rd., Section 1, Taipei, Taiwan

National Taipei College of Nursing
Departments: full Nursing program
Teachers and Students: NTCN is a fully accredited nursing school, including large program in midwifery
Contact: Personnel Office, National Taipei College of Nursing, 365 Ming-te Rd., Peitou, Taipei, Taiwan
▮ **Phone:** (886-02) 822-7101   **Fax:** (886-02) 820-5680

National Taipei Institute of Technology
Departments: Mechanical Engineering, Electrical Engineering, Chemical Engineering, Materials and Minerals Resources Engineering, Civil Engineering, Electronic Engineering, Textiles, Industrial Design
Teachers and Students: accepts foreign teachers of technical subjects; student courses include internships in factories and other workplaces
Contact: Personnel Office, National Taipei Institute of Technology, 1 Chung-hsiao East Rd., Section 3, 10643 Taipei, Taiwan
▮ **Phone:** (886-02) 771-4800   **Fax:** (886-02) 751-8845

National Taiwan Academy of Arts
Departments: 10 depts including Chinese Music, Traditional Chinese Dance
Teachers and Students: accepts foreign students in all depts
Contact: Personnel Office, National Taiwan Academy of Arts, 59 Tah Kuan Rd., Section 1, Pan Chiao, Taipei, Taiwan

National Taiwan Institute of Technology
Departments: Industrial Management, Electronic Engineering, Mechanical Engineering, Textile Engineering, Construction Engineering, Electrical Engineering, Chemical Engineering, Business Administration, Information Management
Teachers and Students: NTIT has excellent computer and other technical facilities
Contact: Personnel Office, National Taiwan Institute of Technology, 43 Keelung St., Section 4, Taipei, Taiwan

■ Phone: (886-02) 733-3141   **Fax:** (886-02) 733-1044

National Taiwan Normal University
Departments: 22 depts in 4 colleges: Education; Liberal Arts, including Chinese, English, History; Science; Fine and Applied Arts; also has large Mandarin Training Center
Teachers: accepts teachers of Western Languages/Literature/Culture and of technical subjects
Students: accepts foreigners in all depts, and at MTC; MTC offers no dorms, but assists with finding local housing; class load is normally 2 hrs/day for regular or 4 hrs/day for intensive enrollment, and focuses on straight language instruction; MTC can assist, however, in finding tutors for martial arts, Chinese Music, etc.
Contact: Personnel Office, National Taiwan Normal University, 162 Ho-ping E. Rd., Section 1, 10610 Taipei, Taiwan
■ Phone: (886-02) 362-5621   **Fax:** (886-02) 392-2607

National Taiwan Ocean University
Departments: 15 depts in 3 colleges: Maritime Science; Fisheries Science; Science and Engineering
Teachers and Students: school on Taiwan's north coast, w/ excellent technical and aquaculture research facilities; close to several fisheries and shipbuilding firms, w/ which able to arrange internships; no special programs for foreigners
Contact: Personnel Office, National Taiwan Ocean University, 2 Pei-ning Rd., Keelung, Taiwan
■ Phone: (886-02) 462-2192   **Fax:** (886-02) 462-0724

National Taiwan University
Departments: 47 depts in 7 colleges: Liberal Arts, including Chinese Literature, Foreign Languages and Literature, History, Philosophy; Sciences; Law, including Political Science and 3 Principals of the People Studies; Medicine; Engineering; Agriculture; Management
Contact: Personnel Office, National Taiwan University, Main Campus: Section 4, Roosevelt Rd., (College of Law, College of Management: Hsu Chow Rd.), (College of Medicine: Jen Ai Rd.), Taipei, Taiwan
■ Phone: (886-02) 314-6960

National Tsing Hua University
Departments: 12 depts in 4 colleges: Science; Engineering; Nuclear Science; Humanities and Social Sciences, including Foreign Languages, Chinese Literature and Linguistics, Economics, History, Linguistics, Sociology and Anthropology, Literature
Teachers and Students: school emphasizes basic and applied sciences, works closely with Hsinchu Science and Industrial Park; often accepts foreign teachers for Humanities classes; no special programs for foreign students
Contact: Personnel Office, National Tsing Hua University, 101 Kuang Fu Rd., Section 2, Hsinchu City, Taiwan
■ Phone: (886-03) 571-5130   **Fax:** (886-03) 572-2467

National University Preparatory School for Overseas Chinese Students
Departments: 28 classes in 4 "groups": Science and Engineering; Liberal Arts; Medicine and Agriculture; Law and Commerce
Teachers and Students: school established by government to prepare "returning overseas Chinese students" for enrolling in Taiwan univs; includes intensive

Mandarin training, basic skills, "Living Guidance," many extra- curricular activities and clubs; rarely accepts foreign teachers
Contact: Personnel Office, National University Preparatory School for Overseas Chinese Students, 46 Hsin Liau Rd., Lin Kou, Taipei County, Taiwan

National Yang Ming Medical College
Departments: Medicine, Dentistry, Medical Technology, Neuroscience, Microbiology and Immunology, Biochemistry, Medical Engineering, Physiology, Pharmacology, Public Health, Nursing, Clinical Medicine, Rehabilitation Medicine, Anatomical Sciences, Genetics, Hospital Administration
Teachers and Students: comprehensive medical school; no special programs for foreigners
Contact: Personnel Office, National Yang Ming Medical College, 155 Li-nung Rd., Section 2, Shih-pai District, Taipei, Taiwan

National Yunlin Institute of Technology
Departments: Mechanical Engineering, Manufacturing, Mechanical Design, Electrical Engineering, Optical Engineering, Automation
Teachers and Students: small school w/ strong industrial focus, including large program in automobile design; no special programs for foreigners
Contact: Personnel Office, National Yunlin Institute of Technology, 123 University Rd., Sect. 3, Touliu, Yunlin, Taiwan
■ **Phone:** (886-05) 534-2601   **Fax:** (886-05) 532-1719

Overseas Chinese College of Commerce
Departments: 5 depts including Int'l Trade and Business Administration
Teachers and Students: private college that stresses Foreign Language Education, especially English
Contact: Personnel Office, Overseas Chinese College of Commerce, 100 Chiao Kwang Rd., 40721 Taichung, Taiwan

Private Chung Chou Junior College of Technology
Departments: Mechanical Engineering, Electrical Engineering, Electronic Engineering
Teachers and Students: school trains professional engineers; no special programs for foreigners
Contact: Personnel Office, Private Chung Chou Junior College of Technology, 6 Lane 2, Shan Chiao Rd., Section 3, Yuanlin, Changhua, Taiwan

Providence University
Departments: 18 depts divided between day and evening, undergrad and grad schools, including Western Languages and Literature, Chinese Literature, Tourism, Business
Contact: Personnel Office, Providence University, 200 Chungchi Rd., 43309 Shalu, Taichung County, Taiwan

Shih Chien College
Departments: 12 depts including Int'l Trade, Business Administration, Communication Design
Contact: Personnel Office, Shih Chien College, 3 Alley 62, Ta-chi St., Taipei, Taiwan

Shu-Ten Junior College of Technology
Departments: Mechanical Engineering, Electrical Engineering, Chemical Engineering, Industrial Engineering and Management

Contact: Personnel Office, Shu-Ten Junior College of Technology, 11 Taching St., Section 2, 40202 Taichung, Taiwan

Soochow University
Departments: 22 depts in 3 colleges: Arts (Chinese Literature, History, Philosophy); Foreign Languages and Literatures (English, Japanese, German); Science; Law; Business (Int'l Trade, Business Administration)
Sister Schools: US— UCLA; St. Olaf's College (MN), Univ of Wisconsin at Stevens Point; Japan—Takushoku Univ
Teachers and Students: has various exchange programs w/ sister schools; also has large Chinese Studies Program for foreign students; accepts foreign teachers in various depts, especially as language teachers
Contact: Personnel Office, Soochow University, Main Campus: 70 Lin-hsi Rd., Wai-shuang-hsi, Shihlin, 11102, (Downtown Campus: 56 Kueiyang St., Sec. 1, 10001) Taipei, Taiwan
∎ Phone: (886-02) 375-4337   Fax: (886-02) 356-0649

Tahan Junior College of Engineering and Business
Departments: Mechanical Engineering, Civil Engineering, Mining and Metallurgical Engineering, International Trade, Taxation and Finance, Accounting and Statistics
Teachers and Students: school prepares skilled technicians and workers for business and industry
Contact: Personnel Office, Tahan Junior College of Engineering and Business, 1 Sujen St., Peipu, Hualien, Taiwan

Ta Hwa Junior College of Technology
Departments: Chemical Engineering, Electrical Engineering, Industrial Engineering and Management, Mechanical Engineering, Electronic Engineering and Computer Science
Teachers and Students: school has sister relationships with several schools in Korea and the US, and occasionally sets up programs with these schools; excellent facilities in peaceful rural setting, with opportunities for cooperation with Hsinchu Science and Industrial Park
Contact: Personnel Office, Ta Hwa Junior College of Technology, 1 Ta-hwa Rd., Chunglin, Hsinchu, Taiwan

Tainan Junior College of Home Economics
Departments: Home Economics, Accounting and Statistics, Fashion Design, Arts and Crafts, Music, Interior Design
Teachers and Students: students primarily women; school prepares students for technical business positions and for "family education"
Contact: Personnel Office, Tainan Junior College of Home Economics, 529 Chung Cheng Rd., Yung Kang, Tainan, Taiwan

Taipei Medical College
Departments: Medicine, Pharmacy, Dentistry, Medical Technology, Nursing, Nutrition and Health, Graduate Institute of Pharmaceutical Sciences
Teachers and Students:
omprehensive medical school
Contact: Personnel Office, Taipei Medical College, 250 Wu-hsing St., Taipei, Taiwan

Taipei Municipal Teachers College
Departments: 8 depts including Languages and Literature Education and Music Education
Contact: Personnel Office, Taipei Municipal Teachers College, 1 Ai-Kuo W. Rd., Taipei, Taiwan
▌Phone: (886-02) 331-3040   **Fax:** (886-02) 381-4067

Taipei Physical Education College
Departments: 21 professional athletic programs, including Judo, Karate, Taekwon Do, and "Chinese Fencing"
Teachers and Students: school trains physical educators and professional athletes
Contact: Personnel Office, Taipei Physical Education College, 5 Tun Hwa N. Rd., 10590 Taipei, Taiwan

Taiwan Provincial Chiayi Teachers College
Departments: 4 depts including Languages Education
Chinese Students: 900
Contact: Personnel Office, Taiwan Provincial Chiayi Teachers College, 151 Lin-sen E. Rd, 60059 Chiayi City, Taiwan

Taiwan Provincial Hsin-chu Teachers College
Departments: Elementary Education, Languages and Literature Education, Social Studies Education, Mathematics and Science Education, Fine Arts Education
Teachers and Students: school trains elementary school teachers; no special programs for foreigners
Contact: Personnel Office, Taiwan Provincial Hsin-chu Teachers College, 521 Nan Dah Rd., Hsin-chu, Taiwan

Taiwan Provincial Hualien Normal College
Departments: Elementary Education, Language Education, Science and Mathematics Education, Social Studies Education
Teachers and Students: school trains elementary and secondary school teachers
Contact: Personnel Office, Taiwan Provincial Hualien Normal College, Hualien, Taiwan

Taiwan Provincial Pingtung Teachers College
Departments: Elementary Education, Chinese Language and Literature Education, Social Studies Education, Mathematics and Science Education, Early Childhood Development
Teachers and Students: strong teacher-training programs and good facilities (including ERIC research files on CD-ROM); accepts many foreign teachers in Languages and Literature, has some short-term Chinese Language and Culture programs for foreign students; campus on outskirts of the lovely Kenting National Park (tropical rainforest/wildlife preserve)
Contact: Personnel Office, Taiwan Provincial Pingtung Teachers College,   1 Lin Sen Rd., Pingtung, Taiwan

Taiwan Provincial Taichung Teachers College
Departments: 4 depts including Linguistics and Literary Education
Contact: Personnel Office, Taiwan Provincial Taichung Teachers College, 140 Min-sheng Rd., Taichung City West, Taiwan

Taiwan Provincial Tainan Teachers College
Departments: 5 depts including Languages and Literature Education
Contact: Personnel Office, Taiwan Provincial Tainan Teachers College, 33 Su Lin St., Section 2, Tainan, Taiwan

Taiwan Provincial Taipei Teachers College
Departments: 5 depts including Languages and Literature Education and Music Education
Contact: Personnel Office, Taiwan Provincial Taipei Teachers College, 134 Ho-ping East Rd., Section 2, Taipei, Taiwan

Taiwan Provincial Taitung Teachers College
Departments: 5 depts including Chinese Language Education
Teachers and Students: has program in Chinese Language for foreign students; local student population includes members of several aboriginal tribes
Contact: Personnel Office, Taiwan Provincial Taitung Teachers College, 684 Chunghua, Section 1, 95004 Taitung, Taiwan

Tajen Pharmaceutical College
Departments: 5 depts including Pharmacy, Industrial Safety and Health, Food Sanitation, Pollution Control
Contact: Personnel Office, Tajen Pharmaceutical College, 20 Wei-hsin Rd., 90703 Hsin-erh Village, Yen-pu Hsiang, Pingtung County, Taiwan

Tamkang University
Departments: 31 depts in 5 colleges: Liberal Arts (Chinese, English, Spanish, German, French, Japanese, History, European Studies, American Studies, Latin American Studies, Western Languages and Literature); Science; Engineering; Business (Int'l Trade, Economics); Management (Int'l Affairs and Strategic Studies, Information Management)
Teachers and Students: several exchange programs w/ sister schools; also large Chinese Language and Culture program for foreign students; accepts foreign teachers in many depts, especially languages and Western Area Studies
Contact: Personnel Office, Tamkang University, Main Campus: 151 Ying-chuan Rd., Tamsui, 25137, (City Campus: 18 Li-shui St., 10620) Taipei, Taiwan
■ **Phone:** (886-02) 621-4794   **Fax:** (886-02) 623-2154

Tamsui Oxford College
Departments: 9 depts including Tourism, Int'l Trade, Business Management
Contact: Personnel Office, Tamsui Oxford College, 32 Chen Li St., Tamsui, Taipei County, Taiwan

Tatung Institute of Technology
Departments: Mechanical Engineering, Electrical Engineering, Chemical Engineering, Business Management, Industrial Design, Information Engineering, Materials Engineering, Biological Engineering, Applied Mathematics
Teachers and Students: private college, founded and run by the Tatung Corporation; school conducts extensive research for corporation, provides excellent hand-on experience for students
Contact: Personnel Office, Tatung Institute of Technology, 40 Chung Shan N. Rd., Section 3, Taipei, Taiwan

Tung Fang Junior College of Technology
Departments: Food Engineering, Chemical Engineering, Industrial Engineering and Management, Industrial Arts, Electrical Engineering, Electronic Engineering
Teachers and Students: sister college relations w/: Japan—Bunri College; US—Pacific Union College; has various student exchanges w/ sister schools
Contact: Personnel Office, Tung Fang Junior College of Technology, 61 Lane 301, Chung Shan Rd., Section 1, 82901 Hu-nei Village, Kaohsiung County, Taiwan

Tunghai University
Departments: 29 depts in 7 colleges: Liberal Arts (Chinese Literature, Foreign Languages and Literature, History, Music, Philosophy); Science; Engineering; Management (International Trade); Law (Social Work, Public Administration); Agriculture; Evening School (Liberal Arts and Accounting)
Sister Schools: relations with sister schools in the US, Canada, England, Ireland, Finland, Germany, Japan, Korea
Teachers and Students: has many exchange programs with sister schools and also accepts independent foreign teachers; over 1/5 of Tunghai faculty are foreign appointees; Tunghai also has large program in Chinese Language and Culture for foreign students
Contact: Personnel Office, Tunghai University, Taichung, Taiwan
■ **Phone:** (886-04) 359-2977   **Fax:** (886-04) 359-2977

Tung Nan Junior College of Technology
Departments: 6 depts, all Engineering related
Contact: Personnel Office, Tung Nan Junior College of Technology, 92 Wan Shun Hamlet, Shen Kun Village, Taipei County, Taiwan

Van Nung Institute of Technology
Departments: 9 depts, most Engineering related including Int'l Trade and Business Administration
Contact: Personnel Office, Van Nung Institute of Technology, 63-1 Shui-wei Li, Chungli, Taoyuan, Taiwan

Wen Tzao Ursuline Junior College of Modern Languages
Departments: English, French, German, Spanish
Teachers and Students: accepts foreign language teachers
Contact: Personnel Office, Wen Tzao Ursuline Junior College of Modern Languages, 900 Mintsu 1 Rd., 80760 Kaohsiung, Taiwan

World College of Journalism, The
Departments: Newspaper Administration, News Editing and Reporting, Broadcasting and Television, Public Relations, Library Science, Motion Picture Production, Printing and Photography, Tourism Promotion
Teachers and Students: one of Taiwan's premier schools of Journalism; runs 2 college dailies and produces many films and promotional videos; school frequently accepts foreign teachers in Language, Communication, Journalism, and Broadcasting
Contact: Personnel Office, The World College of Journalism, 1 Lane 17, Mushan Rd., Section 1, 11603 Taipei, Taiwan

Wu Feng Industrial Junior College
Departments: Electrical Engineering, Electronic Engineering, Mechanical Engineering, Chemical Engineering

Teachers and Students: school trains technicians and professional engineers for industry; has arrangements w/ many businesses for internships
Contact: Personnel Office, Wu Feng Industrial Junior College, 117 Chien Kuo Rd., Section 2, Min Hsiung, Chia Yi, Taiwan

Yan Ya Junior College of Technology

Departments: Chemical Engineering, Textile Engineering, Civil Engineering, Mechanical Engineering, Architectural Engineering
Teachers and Students: school prepares skilled technicians for industry
Contact: Personnel Office, Yan Ya Junior College of Technology, 414 Chung Shan East Rd., Section 3, 32034 Chungli, Taiwan

Yuanpei Junior College of Medical Technology

Departments: Medical Administration, Medical Technology, Radiological Technology
Teachers and Students: school trains medical technicians; no special programs for foreigners
Contact: Personnel Office, Yuanpei Junior College of Medical Technology, 306 Yuanpei St., Hsin-chu, Taiwan

Yung Ta Junior College of Technology

Departments: Chemical Engineering, Electronic Engineering, Mechanical Engineering, Electrical Engineering, Industrial Engineering and Management
Teachers and Students: school trains skilled workers for industry; provides in-service training in many businesses; no special programs for foreigners
Contact: Personnel Office, Yung Ta Junior College of Technology, 316 Chung Shan Rd., Lin Lo District, 90902 Ping Tung, Taiwan

Teacher Sending Organizations

This directory lists organizations which recruit, send or place foreign teachers for posts in the PRC or Taiwan (we have also included a few listings for posts in Hong Kong). All listings are alphabetical by name of program. Please note that each listing represents a separate program, and that therefore some of the largest sending organizations have more than one listing.

PLEASE NOTE: A number of large organizations have specifically requested NOT to be listed in our directory. These are primarily religious organizations with a strong missionary focus. Should you wish to participate in such an organization, inquire about it carefully. Should you encounter members of such organizations in China, be aware of their agenda.

American Council of Learned Societies—US-China Exchange Program

The ACLS exchange program sends high school teachers to key secondary schools; Chinese teachers come teach in schools of American counterparts

Positions Available: 24 positions for secondary school teachers

Requirements for Teachers: Willing to teach English to Chinese students in grades 7-12 and also to Chinese teachers of English

Duration: One year

Salary: US home school continues to pay salary

Benefits: Health insurance if necessary; r-t economy airfare

Academic Calendar: Sep–Jun or Jul

Training and Support Services: Orientation before departure; ongoing support provided by New York and Beijing offices of Committee on Scholarly Communication with China; mid-year conference

Application Deadline: Jan 15

Special Focus/Affiliation: Schools in Chengdu, Beijing, Hohhot, and Suzhou

Contact: Margot E. Landman, Director, US-China Teachers Exchange, American Council of Learned Societies, 228 East 45th Street, New York, NY 10017-3398

■ **Phone:** (212) 697-1505 ext. 131

Fax: (212) 949-8058

e-mail: margot@acls.org

URL: http://www.acls.org/pro-ched.html

Amity Foundation

The Amity Foundation, an independent Chinese voluntary organization, was created in 1985 by Chinese Christian leaders

Positions Available: Language teachers

Requirements for Teachers: University degree and native or near-native command of the language they will teach; medical clearance is required; all candidates must be recommended by an overseas sponsoring agency (church-related organizations which support the goals of the Amity Foundation)

Duration: Two years (extendable)

Salary: Monthly stipend; yearly travel allowance

Benefits: Health care; housing

Academic Calendar: Begins in Sep

Training and Support Services:
Summer training program; orientation conference in Nanjing each summer; annual winter conference; regular workshops during the year

Special Focus/Affiliation: Amity is an independent Chinese organization, non-government and non-church; established by leaders of the China Christian Council; Christian leaders make up the majority of the Board of Directors

Contact: Ting Yen Ren, Educational Consultant, Amity Foundation, 17 Da Jian Yin Xiang, Nanjing 210029
■ **Phone:** (86-25) 774-1354
Fax: (86-25) 774-1053

Appalachians Abroad—Marshall University

Positions Available: English as a foreign language in K-12, college/university, and corporate settings

Requirements for Teachers: B.A.; TEFL certification (provided by Marshall University)

Duration: One year

Salary: Varies according to qualifications

Benefits: Free accommodations; airfare; travel stipend

Academic Calendar: Beginning Sep and Mar

Training and Support Services: 15-week training program in Sep; four-week intensive program in May; training includes 45 hours of Mandarin language training; 45 hours ESL methods

Application Deadline: Two weeks before program

Contact: Clark Egner, Center for International Programs, Marshall University, 212 Old Main, Huntington, WV 25755
■ **Phone:** (304) 696-6265
Fax: (304) 696-6353
e-mail: cip@marshall.edu **URL:** http://www.marshall.edu/esli/apa.htmlx

Association/International Teaching, Educational and Cultural Exchange

AITECE currently sponsors teachers at tertiary institutions in China and tries to maintain on-going contracts with these schools in order to place a consistent number of teachers

Positions Available: 50 language teachers; open placement

Requirements for Teachers: M.A.; preferably in TESL or language-related field; strong, active Christian commitment

Duration: Minimum one year; preferably two or three years

Salary: Negotiated with school in China

Benefits: Housing; overseas travel reimbursement

Academic Calendar: Late Aug–mid-Jan (Chinese New Year) and mid-Feb–early Jul

Training and Support Services:
Screening and interviews prior to departure to China; Hong Kong group orientation before first semester; winter break seminar in Hong Kong; regular visits by Hong Kong-based staff.

Application Deadline: Six months prior to semester placement

Special Focus/Affiliation: Roman Catholic NGO (Registered in PRC); focus on giving authentic Christian witness through professional service (strictly non-evangelical); compliance with PRC religious laws and policy.

Contact: USA Liaison Office: US Catholic China Bureau, Seton Hall University, China House, South Orange, NJ 07079-2689
■ **Phone:** (201) 761-9785
Fax: (201) 275-2223
e-mail: chinabur@lanmail.shu.edu

China Educational Exchange

Founded in 1981, CEE is a program of Mennonite church agencies; three Mennonite mission boards and the Mennonite Central Committee cooperate to provide opportunities to serve in China; candidates are approved and funded by one of these supporting agencies

Positions Available: English teachers

Requirements for Teachers: B.A.; Christian commitment; native English speech

Duration: Two year terms
Salary: Volunteer positions; Chinese salary of approximately 1500¥/month
Benefits: Medical coverage; chance for travel during summer and Chinese New Year breaks.
Academic Calendar: Standard Chinese academic year
Training and Support Services: One-month language training/cultural orientation in China prior to each year of service; Mid-year conference in Hong Kong; in-country pastoral/counselor support; twice per year visits from North American based staff
Application Deadline: Rolling; by Apr 2 for placements beginning same summer
Special Focus/Affiliation: CEE is an Inter-Mennonite program; placements tend to be at smaller, less prestigious institutions in Sichuan, Henan or Liaoning provinces
Contact: Myrrl Byler, China Educational Exchange, 1251 Virginia Ave., Harrisonburg, VA 22801
▌**Phone:** (540) 432-6983
Fax: (540) 434-5556
e-mail: chinaedex@aol.com

Colorado China Council

Positions Available: 25-30 for fall and spring; ten for spring only; some teach history, culture, law, politics if qualified
Requirements for Teachers: B.A./B.S. in any field; good health, flexibility, humor; Third-world travel; minimum 2.5 GPA; some teaching helpful; Chinese language not necessary by helpful; first 25-30 qualified applicants accepted; people then wait listed
Requirements for Administrators/Others: Established professionals considered on a per-need basis
Duration: One year and six months possible
Salary: 1,500-3,000¥ depending on academic background
Benefits: Housing; medical benefits; one month paid vacation, airfare home (reimbursed) in some cases
Academic Calendar: Sep 1–Jul 15 or Feb 15–Jul 15

Training and Support Services: Two-week summer training institute in Boulder, Colorado; appropriate support while in China; all materials supplied
Application Deadline: Nov 15 for spring; Feb 15 for fall and spring
Special Focus/Affiliation: China Teachers Consortium; founded by Yale-China in 1990; Princeton, Stanford, Oberlin, Western Washington University, and China Educational Exchange
Contact: Alice Renouf, Executive Director, 4556 Apple Way, Boulder, CO 80301
▌**Phone:** (303) 443-1108
Fax: (303) 443-1107
URL: http://www.asiacouncil.org

ELS International

ELS is a placement agency for ESL teachers; takes fee in form of percentage of first month's wages
Positions Available: EFL teachers and occasionally academic directors
Requirements for Teachers: B.A. and TEFL certificate
Duration: One year contract
Training and Support Services: Four-week intensive TEFL certificate program
Special Focus/Affiliation: Centers located in Shantou, Shanghai, Guangzhou, Taipei, Taichung, and Kaohsiung
Contact: ELS Language Centers, International Division, 5761 Buckingham Parkway, Culver City, CA 90230
▌**Phone:** (310) 342-4100
Fax: (310) 649-5231
e-mail: international@els.com
URL: http://www.els.com/intlhome.htm

International School of Beijing

ISB is a private co-ed primary school, founded in 1980
Requirements for Teachers: Two years-plus experience; at least B.A. and teaching certificate
Requirements for Administrators/Others: M.A. in Administration or related field; two years administrative

experience; international experience required
Duration: Two years initially; annual renewal
Salary: US$29,800-35,200
Benefits: Housing; r-t airfare annually; health insurance; shipping allowance
Academic Calendar: Aug–Jun
Training and Support Services: Two-week orientation on-site
Special Focus/Affiliation: Western Association of Schools and Colleges (WASC)
Contact: Alex Horsley, Director, International School of Beijing, c/o American Embassy, Beijing, PRC
■ **Phone:** (86-10) 6437-7119
Fax: (86-10) 6437-6989
e-mail: ahorsley@isb.bj.edu.cn
URL: http://www.isb.bj.edu.cn

International Scientific and Information Service, Inc.

This is a not-for-profit, tax-exempt organization that has been placing English teachers in China since 1983
Positions Available: English teachers at several universities located in major cities; positions available vary from year to year
Requirements for Teachers: TESOL training and experience preferred but will consider others; previous living/working/travels abroad highly desirable
Duration: One year (extendable)
Salary: According to current government regulation
Benefits: Free housing and health care; one-month vacation between semesters and vacation allowance; possible o-w or r-t int'l airfare
Academic Calendar: Sep 1–Jul 31; occasionally mid-Feb to mid-Jan
Training and Support Services: Works closely with accepted applicants one-on-one and guides them through paper work of obtaining visas to China; puts applicants in touch with others who have taught at Chinese institutions recently
Application Deadline: None

Contact: Dr. Tun-Hsu McCoy, Executive Director, 49 Thompson Hay Path, Setauket, NY 11733-1330
■ **Phone:** (516) 751-6437
e-mail: tmccoy@suffolk.lib.ny.us

The Morrison Christian Academy

Private, co-ed, primary/secondary school; current enrollment 610; 85% of faculty US nationals; most of faculty come from church-affiliated missions
Positions Available: Teachers; school administrators; school support staff; boarding parents
Requirements for Teachers: Christian commitment; teacher certification; two years teaching experience
Duration: Two year contract
Salary: Contact school
Benefits: Housing allowance; travel; taxes; retirement; medical; dependent allowance; dependent's tuition waived
Academic Calendar: Aug–early Jun
Training and Support Services: Professional development opportunities available; pre-field orientation required; survival Chinese course required
Application Deadline: Revolving
Special Focus/Affiliation: Evangelical Christian school focused on the needs of children of missionaries
Contact: Superintendent, Morrison Christian Academy, 136-1 Shui Nan Road, Taichung, Taiwan 406 Republic of China
■ **Phone:** (886-4) 292-1171 ext. 101
Fax: (886-4) 292-1174
e-mail: mca@ms8.hinet.net
URL:
http://www.xc.org/mk/schools/morrison/

The National Council of the Churches of Christ, USA

The NCCCUSA works in partnership with the Amity Foundation in the PRC
Positions Available: Teaching English in schools provided by The Amity Foundation
Requirements for Teachers: B.A. minimum; teaching experience, ESL training, or graduate degree desired; flexibility and openness; Christian faith and commitment

Duration: Two year contract with possible extension
Salary: Monthly stipend; room (or apartment) provided; some vacation bonus
Benefits: Basic health insurance; r-t airfare at start and end of contract
Academic Calendar: End of Aug–end of Jun
Training and Support Services: One-week US orientation in Jun; four weeks of language study and teacher training in PRC in Aug; continued support through the Amity Foundation network and the NCCCUSA
Application Deadline: See participating denominations list obtained through NCCCUSA
Special Focus/Affiliation: Affiliation is through communion members of the NCCCUSA; teachers are not missionaries even though sponsored by churches
Contact: Rev. Krystin Granberg, China Program Coordinator, NCCCUSA, 475 Riverside Drive Room #616, New York, NY 10115-0050
■ Phone: (212) 870-2630
Fax: (212) 870-2055
e-mail: krystin@ncccusa.org
URL: http://www.hk.super.net/~amityhk or http://www.seanet.com/~petash/re-echo.htm

Princeton-in-Asia

PIA acts as a placement agency for recent grads seeking teaching positions in Chinese universities; interns pay $20 (Princeton grads) or $30 (non-Princeton) application fee plus $300 program contribution upon acceptance of position
Positions Available: 25-40 intern teachers at approximately nine institutions throughout China, including People's Univ (Beijing) and Fudan Univ (Shanghai)
Requirements for Teachers: Young interns (recent college graduates) recruited primarily from Princeton Univ; must also interview and submit writing samples
Duration: One year renewable
Salary: 650-800¥/month (PRC schools);

US$384/month (Hong Kong schools)
Benefits: o-w int'l airfare (one-year contract); r-t int'l airfare (two-year contract); housing; health insurance; vacation bonus; excursions; terms vary among institutions
Academic Calendar: Sep–Jul
Training and Support Services: Interns can take optional TEFL preparation class for a $100 fee; comprehensive orientation prior to departure
Application Deadline: Dec 2
Contact: Carrie Gordon, Executive Director, Princeton-in-Asia, 224 Palmer Hall, Princeton University, Princeton, NJ 08544
■ Phone: (609) 258-3657
Fax: (609) 258-5300
e-mail: pia@phoenix.princeton.edu

Shanghai American School

Shanghai American School, grades pre-K-12, is a private, co-ed growing school, currently enrolling 650 students from 32 nations; WASC accreditation
Positions Available: Elementary classroom; guidance counselor; elementary art; ESOL teacher(s); numerous openings at both secondary and elementary levels
Requirements for Teachers: Current certification; two years exemplary prior experience; no dependents; teaching spouses preferred
Requirements for Administrators: Same as requirements for teachers
Salary: Highly competitive
Benefits: Furnised housing; retirement stipend
Academic Calendar: Sep–Jun
Training and Support Services: Extensive staff development including on campus M.A. program with Michigan State Univ international conference site in 1998
Application Deadline: May for following academic year
Special Focus/Affiliation: Academic program of high expectations and standards for all
Contact: Mr. Ron Montgomery, Superintendent or Dr. Rob Leveillee, Assistant Superintendent for Instruc-

tion, 50 Ji Di Lu, Zhu Di Township, Shanghai, 201106, PRC
▮ Phone: (86-21) 6221-1446
Fax: (86-21) 6221-1269

Skidmore College China Exchange Program

Positions Available: Six positions/year teaching ESL and Western culture at Qufu Teachers Univ; the Univ of Petroleum (Dongying);and Shengli Oilfields Teacher's College
Requirements for Teachers: B.A. required; Skidmore alums preferred, others considered
Durations: One year; renewable
Salary: Contact school
Benefits: o-w airfare back from China; housing; health insurance
Academic Calendar: Sep–Jul
Training and Support Services: Orientation for Skidmore alums in US
Special Focus/Affiliation: Academic
Contact: Dr. Murray Levith, Coordinator, Skidmore College Teach-In-China Program, Department of English, Skidmore College, Saratoga Springs, NY 12866
▮ Phone: (518) 584-5000 ext. 2307
Fax: (518) 584-3023
e-mail: mlevith@skidmore.edu

Taipei American School

Private primary/secondary school
Positions Available: General: 25-35 full-time positions for teachers of all subjects and special education; Administrators: less than one position/year
Requirements for Teachers: B.A.; one or two years full-time primary or secondary experience; teaching certificate required; M.A. and international experience preferred
Requirements for Administrators: M.A.; three years administrative experience and administrative certificate required; Ph.D. preferred
Duration: Two years; renewable indefinitely
Salary: Teachers: US$32,000-$50,000 starting; administrators: US$52,000-$84,000 starting

Benefits: r-t airfare from US for appointee and dependents; housing allowance; paid home leave every year; health, life, disability insurance; retirement plan; tuition for children enrolled at this school
Academic Calendar: Aug–Jun
Training and Support Services: Seven days on-site orientation
Application Deadline: Jan 1
Contact: Director of Human Resources, Taipei American School, #800 Chung Shan N. Rd., Sec. 6, Shih Lin, Taipei, Taiwan 11135, ROC
▮ Phone: (886) 2-873-9900
Fax: (886) 2-873-1641
e-mail: 101400.1052@compuserve.com

Tamkang University, Graduate Institute of American Studies

Private co-ed university, founded in 1971; current enrollment 10,000; 50% of GIAS faculty US nationals
Positions Available: Four-five full and part-time positions for teachers of political science, economics, sociology, history, and law
Requirements for Teachers: Ph.D. in subject taught required; teaching experience and language proficiency in Chinese preferred
Duration: One-two years; renewable
Salary: Negotiable
Benefits: o-w airfare from US for appointee only; housing sometimes provided or university assists in locating housing
Academic Calendar: Sep–Jun
Training and Support Services: None
Application Deadline: None
Any Special Focus/Affiliation: Academic
Contact: Dr. Lin Yun-shan, Tamkang University, Graduate Institute of American Studies, Main Campus, 151 Ying Chuan Rd., Tamsui, Taipei County, Taiwan 25137
▮ Phone: (02) 621-5656 ext. 716 or 705
Fax: (02) 620-9895
e-mail: tamerica@mail.tku.edu.tw

United Board for Christian Higher Education in Asia

Positions Available: ESL instructors; humanities/social sciences visiting professors; approximately 20 positions/year at various Chinese universities
Requirements for Teachers: To teach ESL: M.A.; visiting professor program: Ph.D.
Duration: One semester or one academic year
Salary: Negotiable
Benefits: r-t airfare for appointee; housing; health insurance
Academic Calendar: Sep 1–Jul 15
Application Deadline: Nov 30
Special Focus/Affiliation: Christian association
Contact: Anne Ofstedal, China Program Coordinator, United Board for Christian Higher Education in Asia, 475 Riverside Dr., Rm. 1221, New York, NY 10115
▌**Phone:** (212) 870-3113
Fax: (212) 870-2322
e-mail: anne@ubchea.org

United States Peace Corps

Positions Available: English as a foreign language teachers; teacher trainees
Requirements for Teachers: B.A. preferably in English education or related fields; M.A. in TEFL and related fields highly sought
Duration: Two years
Salary: Living allowance commensurate with local teachers
Benefits: Travel; full medical coverage; readjustment allowance after completion of service, approximately $5,400
Academic Calendar: Sep–Jul
Training and Support Services: 8-12 weeks of pre-service training; periodic in-service training; support from full-time program officer
Application Deadline: On-going
Contact: Peace Corps, Room 8500, 1990 K Street, NW, Washington, DC 20526
▌**Phone:** (800) 424-8580
URL: http://www.peacecorps.gov

Volunteers in Asia

Positions Available: Six-ten/year
Requirements for Teachers: B.A.
Duration: One-two years
Salary: Stipend
Benefits: Travelers health insurance
Academic Calendar: Sep–Jun
Training and Support Services: Non-intensive training goes from Mar–Jun; six training days and 13 day retreat; participants must take TESL class and language class
Application Deadline: Feb 7
Contact: Volunteers in Asia (VIA), PO Box 4543, Stanford, CA 94309
▌**Phone:** (415) 723-3228
Fax: (415) 725-1805
e-mail: volasia@volasia.org
URL: http://www.volasia.org

Western Washington University— China Teaching Program

The CTP offers training and placement for teaching posts in China; tuition: WA resident: $940, non-resident: $1,100; placement only option for those with both teaching and China experience, spring term start only: $520.
Positions Available: Teachers are trained the US and placed at schools and universities throughout China
Requirements for Teachers: Foreign teachers: B.A.; foreign experts: M.A. and teaching experience
Duration: One year; may be renewable
Salary: Foreign teacher: 1,200-1,800¥/month; foreign experts: 2,000-3,000¥/month
Benefits: Housing; health care; vacation; travel allowance; foreign experts also receive int'l air fare
Academic Calendar:
Training: Six weeks in US in Jul and Aug; teaching: Sep–Jul; placement only: Feb–Jan
Training and Support Services: Summer training includes TESOL, Chinese language, geography and history, cultural adaptation; support includes placement, assistance with visa, insurance, flight reservations
Application Deadline: Jan 31 for sum-

mer training program; Oct 31 for spring placement only
Special Focus/Affiliation: An academic program affiliated with Western Washington University Contact: Erica Littlewood Work, Director, China Teaching Program, Western Washington University, Old Main 530, Bellingham, WA 98225-9047
▌ Phone: (360) 650-3753
Fax: (360) 650-2847
e-mail: ctp@cc.wwu.edu

WorldTeach—Shanghai Summer Teaching Program (SSTP)

WorldTeach places young volunteers in Shanghai for a $3,850 fee which includes r-t airfare, health insurance, orientation and training, Chinese language lessons, weekend activities (such as calligraphy, trips to nearby cities, martial arts); financial aid for up to half of program cost available
Positions Available: Volunteer educators
Requirements for Teachers: B.A.; no experience necessary; applicants must be enrolled students and don't need to have earned a B.A. by application time.
Duration: One summer
Salary: None
Benefits: Housing; all meals
Academic Calendar: Depends on program
Training and Support Services: Orientation programs; on-site field coordinator
Application Deadline: Varies according to program
Special Focus/Affiliation: Affiliated with Harvard Institute for International Development
Contact: Anthony Meyer, Director of Admissions and Recruitment, WorldTeach, Harvard Institute for International Development, 1 Eliot Street, Cambridge, MA 02138-5705
▌ Phone: (617) 495-5527
Fax: (617) 495-1599
e-mail: info@worldteach.org
URL: http://www.igc.org/worldteach

Yale-China Association

The Yale-China program is the oldest continuously operating US-China teaching exchange

Positions Available: 10-14 positions for ESL teachers at Hunan Medical Univ; Yali Middle School (Changsha); Chinese Univ of Hong Kong; Zhongshan Univ; and Huizhen Academy (Ningbo)
Requirements for Teachers: Must be Yale senior; recent Yale graduate; or Yale graduate/professional student
Duration: Two years
Salary: Contact association
Benefits: r-t airfare from US for appointee; housing; insurance
Academic Calendar: Aug–Jul
Training and Support Services: Two-week orientation; annual teaching conference; periodic site visits by Hong Kong office director
Application Deadline: Contact sponsor for info
Contact: Program Manager, Yale-China Association, Box 208223, New Haven, CT 06520
▌ Phone: (203) 432-0881
Fax: (203) 432-2746
e-mail: ycassoc@pantheon.cis.yale.edu
URL: http://www.yale.edu/yalechin

YMCA Overseas Service Corps

Positions Available: ESL teachers for adults and children at associations throughout Taiwan
Requirements for Teachers: B.A. required; teaching experience and/or TESL training preferred
Duration: One year; renewable for one year
Salary: 16,000-18,000NTS/month
Benefits: o-w airfare to US on completion of assignment; housing; health insurance; one-week paid vacation; bonus
Academic Calendar: Oct–Oct
Training and Support Services: None
Application Deadline: Apr 15
Contact: USA/OSCY Taiwan, YMCA Overseas Service Corps, Int'l Division, YMCA of the U.S.A., 101 N. Wacker Dr., Chicago, IL 60606
▌ Phone: (312) 977-0031 ext 343
Fax: (312) 977-0884

Sending Organizations for Students

This directory lists organizations which send students to China. The directory is divided by home nation of the sending organization, and listings are alphabetical by name of organization. Please note that each listings is a separate rogram, and tht therefore some of the larger sending organizations have several listings.

TAIWAN SENDING ORGANIZATIONS

These organizations are recruitment centers for foreign students. They are not themselves schools. For schools in Taiwan, see listings in Directory 1.

Foundation for Scholarly Exchange
Program Description: Administrative organization (final selection and placement of 8-10 students/yr) for Fulbright exchange program sent through Institute of Int'l Education
Site(s) in Taiwan: Various institutions in Taiwan. May spend up to two months in mainland China
Dates: Sept–June
Eligibility: Graduate students; non-academic rofessionals in government, business or performing arts who have a bachelor's degree with at least 2 years full-time work experience
Subjects Taught: Students propose a study plan in the area in which they are interested
Cost: Program provides a monthly stipend of US$1,382 for ten mos, plus an incidental allowance; int'l travel and baggage allowances will be provided in the form of a fixed sum for grantee; air ticket provided; grantee will also be covered under a group health and accident insurance policy
Housing: Not provided
Application Deadline: Varies, but usually is the Sept. or Oct. before the grant year
Number of Students Sent/Yr Average: 8-10
Other: Preliminary section and screening is through IIE (Institute of International Education) in New York. Enrolled students must apply through their campus Fulbright reps. At-large students must request applications fom U.S.I.A. Fulbright. The Foundation only cosiders applicants whose dossiers are sent to it through IIE.
Contact: Campus Fulbright Rep., or U.S.I.A. Fulbright, US Student Program, 809 United Nations Plaza, New York, NY 10017-3580
∎ **Phone:** (212) 984-5330

U.K. Sending Organizations

These sending organizations arrange study programs in China primarily for UK and Commonwealth students.

University of Cambridge

Program Description: Students enrolled in Chinese Studies program spend a period of at least 6 months in East Asia during their third year
Site(s) in China: usually a university
Dates: Lent and Easter terms of third year
Eligibility: Third year
Subjects Taught: Chinese Studies
Number of Students Sent/Yr Average: 5-20
Contact: Secretary, Faculty of Oriental Studies, University of Cambridge, Sidgwick Avenue, Cambridge, CB3 9DA
■ **Phone:** (01223) 335108
Fax: (01223) 335110

University of Durham

Program Description: In their second year of East Asian Studies Program, approx. 20 Durham students spend a year in China
Site(s) in China: Renmin University of China, Beijing
Eligibility: Must be a Durham student enrolled in East Asian Studies
Credits Granted: Equivalent to student's second academic year
Subjects Taught: All class work is in Chinese; focus is on developing fluency in spoken and written Chinese
Contact: Registrar, Old Shire Hall, University of Durham, Durham DH1 3HP United Kingdom

■ **Phone:** (0) 191 374-3231
Fax: (0) 191 374-3242
e-mail: E.A.Studies@durham.ac.uk

University of Edinburgh—Department of East Asian Studies

Program Description: University of Edinburgh's second-year East Asian Studies students are sent to Taiwan
Site(s) in Taiwan: Mandarin Training Centre
Dates: August– May
Eligibility: Second year Chinese Honours students
Credits Granted: Record of study supplied. Credits not required by Edinburgh.
Subjects Taught: Mandarin, Calligraphy, Classical chinese
Cost: Fees paid by local education authority in Britain
Housing: Students make their own arrrangements
Application Deadline: June 1
Number of Students Sent/Yr Average: 8
Contact: Dept. of East Asian Studies, 8 Buccleuch Place, The University of Edinburgh, Edinburgh, EH8 9LW
■ **Phone:** (0131) 650-4227
Fax: (0131) 651-1258
e-mail: scot.chinese.centre@ed.ac.uk
URL: http://www.ed.ac.uk.~etev05/Chinese_at_Edinburgh.html

U.S. and Canadian Sending Organizations

These organizations arrange study programs in China primarily for US and Canadian students.

American Institute of Foreign Study (AIFS)

Program Description: AIFS students may take virtually any course offered at the university as long as they meet prerequisites and space is available. Normal medium of instruction is English but Cantonese may occasionally be used in class to clarify matters for some students
Site(s) in Hong Kong: City University of Hong Kong
Dates: Fall: Sept 11–Dec 20; Spring: Jan 22–May 9

Eligibility: College sophomores, juniors, seniors and graduate students; 2.5 minimum GPA
Credits Granted: Full course=4 courses worth; 12 credits
Subjects Taught: Business & Management, Economics & Finance, Law, Social Science and Chinese
Cost: Fall: $9,395; Spring: $9,395 — includes tuition, housing, meals, resident director
Housing: Homestay
Application Deadline: Fall: May 15; Spring: Nov. 1
Other: They also offfer fall, spring & summer programs in Czech Republic, England, France, Italy, Japan, Mexico, Russia, Spain, Argentina, Austria and Australia, and travel programs though Southeast Asia.
Contact: Yesenia Garcia, AIFS College Division, 102 Greenwich Avenue, Greenwich, CT 06830
■ **Phone:** (800) 727-2437 x 6084
Fax: (203) 869-9615
e-mail: aifs@aifs.org
URL: http://www.aifs.org

AFS Intercultural Programs
Program Description: Educator program—4 weeks in China to learn about the education system and also about Chinese culture
Site(s) in China: Beijing and Tianjing—2 weeks each
Dates: mid July–mid August
Eligibility: For educators
Cost: $1,000 not including domestic travel
Housing: dormitories
Application Deadline: March 17
Additional Comments: This program is a special 2 year grant program that will run only in 1997 and 1998. However, we will be running other programs. Call for more details.
Contact: Kirsten Faurot, AFS Intercultural Programs, 313 E. 43rd St., New York, NY 10017
■ **Phone:** (212) 299-9000 ext. 365
Fax: (212) 299-9093
e-mail: kfaurot@afs.org
URL: http://AFS.org

American University World Capitals Program
Program Description: Intensive Chinese language and business oriented program at the University of International Business and Economics at Beijing. Internships available. Field trip to southern China and Hong Kong
Site(s) in China: Beijing
Dates: Late August–early December
Eligibility: Second semester sophomores or above; 2.75 GPA
Credits Granted: 12-17
Subjects Taught: Intensive Chinese language—all levels, Chinese Economic Cooperation, Chinese History
Cost: Internship or Independent Study
Housing: Residential Hotel accommodations on or near campus
Application Deadline: May 1
Number of Students sent/Yr Average: 15
Contact: Katharine Kravetz, Director, World Capitals Program, The American University, 4400 Massachusetts Ave. NW, Washington, DC 20016
■ **Phone:** (800) 424-2600
Fax: (202) 895-4960
e-mail: kkravet@american.edu
URL: http://www.american.edu.otherdepts.washsem_worldcaps

Associated Colleges in China (ACC)
Program Description: Where language, culture and society are combined in one intensive study program
Site(s) in China: Beijing (Capital University of Business and Economics [CUEB])
Dates: Fall: Sept 1–Dec 6; Summer: June 27–Aug 23
Eligibility: Intermediate and advance students
Credits Granted: 10 credits for summer; 18-20 credits for fall from Hamilton College
Subjects Taught: Chinese Language
Cost: Summer: $3,950 (not including airfare); Summer & Fall: $12,900 (including airfare)
Housing: Foreign students' dorm. Double rooms with a/c, private baths & 24 hr. hot water supply
Application Deadline: March 1

Number of Students sent/Yr Average: 30
Contact: Director, Associated Colleges in China, Hamilton College, 198 College Hill Road, Clinton, NY 13323
∎ Phone: (315) 859-4771 or 859-4778
Fax: (315) 859-4687
e-mail: acchina@hamilton.edu
URL:http://www.hamilton.edu/html/academic/eal/Abroad-Link.html

Brethren Colleges Abroad
Program Description: The BCA Program in Dalian, China, is a one or two-semester program at the Dalian University of Foreign Languages for students from all US colleges and universities. the on-site director is Tamula Drumm. Field trips and an extensive study tour are included in the program — to Beijing, Mongolia and southern China.
Site(s) in China: Dalian University of Foreign Languages
Dates: Mid-August–January and/or February–July
Eligibility: Sophomores, Juniors, Seniors, Graduates; B- or above average; references
Credits Granted: 16-20 hours per semester, transcript provided
Subjects Taught: Chinese language (beg/int/adv), Calligraphy, Civilization/Culture, Chinese Literature, Chinese Film, Intercultural Studies, Chinese Music, Independent Studies
Cost: $12,545 ('95-'96 academic year); $7,245 ('95 to '96 semester) - includes international transportation, tuition, room, board, travel
Housing: Residence halls—arranged by program
Application Deadline: April 15 for fall and year; Nov 1 for spring
Number of Students Sent/Yr Average: 4
Additional Comments: Many internships, practica, and volunteer opportunities are available for BCA students in and near Dalian. This is a model program for practical experience, since there is an on-site director
Contact: Beverly S. Eikenberry, Brethren Colleges Abroad,   605 College Ave., North Manchester, IN 46962

∎ Phone: (219) 982-5238
Fax: (219) 982-7755
e-mail: BCA@manchester.edu
URL: http://studyabroad.com/BCA

Boston University
Program Description: 20 credit–20 week academic program, including a 4 credit internship component in Arts, Media, Law, Business, Advertising, Marketing, PR and Politics
Site(s) in China: Beijing and Harbin
Dates: Fall: July 21–Dec 15; Spring: Dec 31–June 1
Eligibility: Students who have completed 2 years of college level Chinese
Credits Granted: 20 credits
Subjects Taught: see above
Cost: Approx. $13,260—includes airfare, tuition, housing, board, books, study trips and internship
Application Deadline: Fall: March 15; Spring: Oct 15
Number of Students Sent/Yr Average: 15 per semester
Contact: Ned Quigley, Director, Boston University, International Programs, 232 Bay State Road, Boston, MA 02215
∎ Phone: (617) 353-9888
Fax: (617) 353-5402
e-mail: abroad@bu.edu
URL: http://web.bu.edu/abroad

California State University—CSU
International Programs in Taiwan
Program Description: Academic year program in Chinese culture for advanced students w/solid language background
Site(s) in Taiwan: Nationalal Chengchi University, Taipei, Taiwan
Dates: Sept–June (full period only)
Eligibility: Must be CSU student, junior or above, w/min. 3.0 GPA
Credits Granted: Undergrad credit available
Subjects Taught: Art History/ Appreciation, Chinese Language (Mandarin: int/adv), Chinese Studies
Cost: $9,360, including tuition, housing, all meals, int'l airfare, fees, excursions, books/materials

Housing: Apartments/homestay
Application Deadline: Feb 1
Number of Students Sent/Yr Average: varies
Other: Sponsor accredited in US; activities include excursions, field trips, program travel; some scholarships available
Contact: CSU International Programs in Taiwan, International Programs, Office of the Chancellor, California State University, 400 Golden Shore, Long Beach, CA 90802-4275
▐ **Phone:** (310) 985-2831

Chinese Language Education and Research Center (CLERC)—Peking University Summer Langauge Program

Program Description: A six week language course, run in cooperation with Peking University's Center for Teaching Chinese to Foreigners; includes two weeks of travel to some of China's most beautiful locations after completion of study.
Site(s) in China: Peking University, Beijing
Dates: Study begins first Monday of first week in July, yearly. 6 weeks of study, 2 weeks of travel
Eligibility: 18 years or older, 55 years max.; college enrollment preferred but not required
Credits Granted: 12 units credit, recognized by most US universitites and colleges. Certificate awarded upon successful completion of program.
Subjects Taught: Chinese Language (Mandarin) at all levels.
Cost: Approx. $3,800; includes tuition, room and board, books, visa fees, hotels, meals, and travel for two-week tour. Does not include international airfare.
Housing: Foreign Students Dormitory, Peking University campus. Two persons per room.
Application Deadline: May 12
Number of Students Sent/Yr Avg: 15
Other: Additional activities (calligraphy, T'ai Chi, cooking etc.) available for a small additional fee.

Contact: Program Coordinator, CLERC Summer Program, Chinese Language Education and Research Center, 510 Broadway, Suite 300, Millbrae, CA 94030
▐ **Phone:** (415) 259-2100
Fax: (415) 259-2108
URL: http://www.nanhai.com

The Chinese University of Hong Kong—The International Asian Studies Program (IASP)

Program Description: The 1997, International Asian Studies Program at the Chinese University of Hong Kong celebrates 20 years of providing a multidisciplinary curriculum of East Asian Studies and Chinese Language to students from all over the world.
Site(s) in Hong Kong: Shatin, New Territories, Hong Kong
Dates: (1997-1998) Fall: Sept 3–Dec 15; Spring: Jan 5–May 15
Eligibility: Sophomore and above, graduate & research students; 3.0 GPA
Credits Granted: Maximum 18, minimum 12
Subjects Taught: Chinese Language (Mandarin and Cantonese). Courses taught in English include: Accountancy, Anthropology, Architecture, Biology, Chemistry, Computer Science, Decision Sciences and Managerial Economics, Economics, Engineering, English, Fine Arts, Finance, Geography, German Studies, Government and Public Administration, History, International Business, Japanese Studies, Journalism and Communication, Management, Marketing, Music, Philosophy, Psychology, Religion and Theology, Sociology
Cost: (1997–1998) Year: $17,350; Term: $11,200
Housing: Included in program fee, in dormitories, with Chinese roommates
Application Deadline: Year and fall: March 15; Spring: Oct 1
Number of Students Sent/Yr Average: 100+
Other: IASP participants are encouraged to participate in student clubs, intramural athletics, varsity competitions, local cultural events and a host

family program. Scholarships available.
Contact: In North America: Judith Collins, International Asian Studies Program, Box 208223, 442 Temple Street, New Haven, CT 06520-8223
■ **Phone:** (203) 432-0850
Fax: (203) 432-7246
e-mail: iasp@minerva.cis.yale.edu
Outside North America: Office of International Studies Programmes, The Chinese University of Hong Kong, Shatin, New Territories, Hong Kong
■ **Phone:** (852) 2609-7597
Fax: (852) 2603-5045
e-mail: oisp@cuhk.edu.hk
URL: http://www.cuhk.edu.hk/oisp/

Colegate Study Abroad

Program Description: This Chinese study group is designed to give Colgate students in general and Asian/IR/POSC majored students in particular the opportunity to acquire an extensive knowledge of modern China and develop proficiency in Chinese language
Site(s) in China: Nanjing University
Dates: Spring term (biennial—1997, 1999)
Eligibility: Open to all Colgate students. Must have equivalent of 1 yr. Chinese language
Subjects Taught: Chinese language— all levels, Foreign Policy
Cost: Regular semester tuition and fes, books, supplies, + $3,780 which includes r-t airfare, housing, fees and excursions
Housing: Nanjing Univ. Foreign Students dorm
Application Deadline: Feb 1
Contact: Prof. Yufan Hao, Political Sciences Dept., 138 Persson Hall, Colgate Univ.
URL: http://149.43.1.8/ocstudy/asia/chinadesc.html

College of Saint Benedict/St. John's University

Program Description: 1 semester program in Chinese language/culture; some religious orientation
Site(s) in China: Chongqing (Southwest China Teachers University)
Dates: January–April
Eligibility: Must be sophomore or above, w/min. 2.5 GPA, good academic standing, current enrollment at accredited college
Credits Granted: Undergrad credit available
Subjects Taught: Chinese Language (Mandarin: beg/int/adv), Chinese Studies, Martial Arts
Cost: $9,200, excluding airfare ('96-'97)
Housing: Apartments
Application Deadline: March 1
Contact: Center for International Education, College of St. Benedict/St. John's University, Collegeville, MN 56321
■ **Phone:** (320) 363-2082
Fax: (320) 363-2013
e-mail: intleduc@csbsju.edu
URL: http://www.users.csbsju.edu/~globaled/

Duke University—Asian/Pacific Studies Institute

Program Description: 6 month study program in China including approximately 3 weeks of travel in China. Additional association members include Western Washington University-St. Louis, Wesleyan University and Smith College.
Site(s) in China: Capital Normal University in Beijing; Nanjing University in Nanjing
Dates: approximately June 19–Dec 19 each year
Credits Granted: 6 course credits
Subjects Taught: Chinese language/literature; history/anthropology; directed research project
Cost: $14,900 in 1997
Housing: College dormitories (Chinese roommates in Nanjing)
Application Deadline: March 1
Number of Students Sent/Yr Average: 20-25
Contact: Duke Study in China Program, Duke University, 2111 Campus Drive, Box #90411, Durham, NC 27708-0411
■ **Phone:** (919) 684-2604

Fax: (919) 681-6247
e-mail: ddhunt@acpub.duke.edu
URL: http://www.duke.edu

Duke University "Mini-Dragon" Program in Taiwan & Korea

Program Description: 6-week summer program with 3 weeks in Taipei, Taiwan and 3 weeks in Seoul, Korea, studying the political, economic and social developments in those two young democracies. Taught by US and foreign faculty.
Site(s) in China: Taipei, Taiwan; also Seoul, Korea (Academia Since & Yensei University)
Dates: May 16–June 27
Eligibility: undergraduate student in good academic standing
Credits Granted: 2 course credits (8 semester hours) undergraduate
Subjects Taught: Comparative Analysis of Democratic Institutions in East Asia; East Asian Political Economy
Cost: approx. $6,000, includes tuition, room, board, airfare, excursions
Housing: Guest houses at the hosting universities
Application Deadline: February 28
Number of Students Sent/Yr Average: 12
Other: Weekly excursions will include visits to government bodies, the DME, an automobile complex, a nuclear power plant and factories
Contact: Prof. Emerson Niou, "Mini-Dragon" Program in Taiwan & Korea, Duke University, 121 Allen Bldg., Durham, NC 27706
■ Phone: (919) 660-4307
Fax: (919) 660-4330
e-mail: niou@aepub.duke.edu

Friends World Program, Long Island University, Southampton China Program

Program Description: 1 or 2 semester program in Chinese language, culture; program prepares students to teach abroad; some religious orientation
Site(s) in China: Hangzhou (Zhejiang University)
Dates: Sept–Jan and/or Feb–May
Eligibility: Must be sophomore or above, min. age 18
Credits Granted: 15 credit hours undergrad per semester, no grad credit available
Subjects Taught: Agriculture, Chinese Language (Mandarin: beg/int/adv), Chinese Studies, Internships, Liberal Arts, Student Teaching, Arts & Traditional Chinese Medicine
Cost: $8,500 per semester, including tuition, housing, all meals, insurance, fees, books/materials
Housing: Apartments and dorms
Application Deadline: June 1 for fall; Nov 1 for spring
Other: Sponsor accredited in US; activities include excursions, field trips, grad students and adults may be accepted as auditors; program provides for individual field study
Contact: Jamie Howard, Friends World Admissions, Long Island University, 239 Montauk Highway, Southampton, NY 11968
■ Phone: (516) 287-8475
Fax: (516) 287-8463
e-mail: fw@southampton.livnet.edu
URL: http://www.southampton.livnet.edu/academic/fr_world/program.htm

Guilford College

Program Description: Conducted by China Educational Travel
Site(s) in China: Beijing (Beijing Normal College)
Dates: Spring and fall semesters
Housing: Multi-occupancy suites in the college's new international students residence hall
Contact: Miriam Collins, Guilford College, 5800 W. Friendly Ave., Greensboro, NC 27410
e-mail: collinsmn@rascal.guilford.edu
URL: http://www.guilford.edu/Study Abroad/China.html

International Honors Program on Global Ecology

Program Description: Around the world study and travel focused on comparative international study of ecology, environmental issues and anthropology
Site(s) in China: Itinerary varies each year

Dates: September–May (two semesters)
Eligibility: College age or older
Subjects Taught: Global ecology/environmental studies
Cost: $20,700 plus airfare
Housing: Homestays
Application Deadline: March 15
Number of Students Sent/Yr Average: 28
Contact: International Honors program on Global Energy, 19 Braddock Park, Boston, MA 02116
∎ **Phone:** (617) 267-0026
Fax: (617) 262-9299
e-mail: info@ihp.edu

Lock Haven University/Beijing Institute of Business
Program Description: 1 term or academic year in Chinese studies. BIB has foreign students from: Canada, United Kingdom, Finland, Russia, New Zealand and other countries
Site(s) in China: Beijing Institute of Business (BIB), Beijing
Dates: September–January
Eligibility: Sophomore or above; 2.5 QPA or above
Credits Granted: 12 to 15 credit hours per semester (undergraduate)
Subjects Taught: Chinese Studies—Chinese language (Mandarin: beg/int), Civilization & Culture, History, Social Science
Cost: $4,900 Pennsylvania resident; $6,300 non-resident. $150 non-refundable application fee is due on or before the application deadline
Housing: In dormitory facilities built especially for foreign students with meal plan that caters to the European and American needs
Application Deadline: Fall: March 15; Spring: October 15
Number of Students Sent/Yr Average: 2 to 3
Contact: Kendall Brostuen, Director, Institute for International Studies, Lock Haven University, Lock Haven, PA 17745
∎ **Phone:** (717) 893-2140
Fax: (717) 893-2537
e-mail: kbrostue@eagle.lhup.edu

URL: http://www.lhup.edu/intl_studies/going2.htm

Lock Haven University/Nanjing University
Program Description: 1 term or academic year in Chinese studies
Site(s) in China: Nanjing University, Nanjing
Dates: September–January
Eligibility: Sophomore or above; 2.5 QPA or above
Credits Granted: 12 to 15 credit hours per semester (undergraduate)
Subjects Taught: Chinese Studies—Chinese language (Mandarin: beg/int), Chinese Civilization & Culture, History, Social Science
Cost: $4,900 Pennsylvania resident; $6,300 non-resident. $150 non-refundable application fee is due on or before the application deadline
Housing: In dormitory facilities for foreign students
Application Deadline: Fall: March 15; Spring: Oct. 15
Number of Students Sent/Yr Average: 2 to 3
Contact: Kendall Brostuen, Director, Institute for International Studies, Lock Haven University, Lock Haven, PA 17745
∎ **Phone:** (717) 893-2140
Fax: (717) 893-2537
e-mail: kbrostue@eagle.lhup.edu
URL: http://www.lhup.edu/intl_studies/going2.htm

Lock Haven University/Changsha University of Electric Power
Program Description: 1 term or academic year in Chinese studies
Site(s) in China: Changsha University of Electric Power, Changsha
Dates: September–January
Eligibility: Sophomore or above, 2.5 QPA or above
Credits Granted: 12 to 15 credit hours per semester (undergraduate)
Subjects Taught: Chinese Studies—Chinese language (Mandarin: beg/int), Chinese Civilization & Culture, History, Social Studies, Fine Art

Cost: $4,900 Pennsylvania resident; $6,300 non-resident. $150 non-refundable application fee is due on or before the application deadline
Housing: In dormitory facilities for foreign students
Application Deadline: Fall: March 15; Spring: Oct. 15
Number of Students Sent/Yr Average: 2 to 3
Contact: Kendall Brostuen, Director, Institute for International Studies, Lock Haven University, Lock Haven, PA 17745
■ Phone: (717) 893-2140
Fax: (717) 893-2537
e-mail: kbrostue@eagle.lhup.edu
URL: http://www.lhup.edu/intl_studies/going2.htm

Miami University—Shanghai Political Economy Seminar

Program Description: Basic and practical introduction to China's economy and society
Site(s) in China: Shanghai, Suzhou, Ningbo
Dates: (1997) May 12–June 20—six weeks every year
Eligibility: Both undergraduates and graduates
Credits Granted: 6 credit hours—Political Science; 3 credit hours—Chinese
Subjects Taught: Political Economy, Chinese Language (Mandarin)
Cost: Approx. $2,800 (Ohio residents); $3,850 (non-Ohio residents)
Housing: Included, dormitory style and hotels
Application Deadline: March 10
Other: No language requirement; most suitable for business majors
Number of Students Sent/Yr Average: 15 per year since 1990
Contact: Dr. Walter Arnold, Dept. of Political Science, Miami University, Oxford, OH 45056
■ Phone: (513) 529-6386
Fax: (513) 523-2893
e-mail: arnoldw@casmail.muohio.edu

National Registration Center for Study Abroad (NRCSA)—Study Abroad-Taipei

Program Description: NRCSA is a consortium of 86 universities world-wide; students can register for study at any of these institutions: Taipei Language Institute is a member school, and students can apply, pay and receive US credit through NRCSA
Site(s) in China: Taipei
Dates: Year round
Eligibility: Must be a college student
Subjects Taught: Mandarin
Cost: $1,070 for 4 weeks
Housing: Homestay
Application Deadline: 40 days prior to start of program
Contact: Study Abroad–Taipei, National Registration Center for Study Abroad (NRCSA), PO Box 1393, Milwaukee, WI 53201
■ Phone: (414) 278-0631
Fax: (414) 271-8884
e-mail: ask@nrcsa.com
URL: http://www.nrcsa.com

Northern Illinois University—Business and Culture in China & Korea

Program Description: To provide students with the opportunity to be exposed to the international business environment in Asia and to management practices outside of the US. Participants will, in addition, have the opportunity to gain insights into cultural, social and political environments in each country
Site(s) in China: Shanghai, China; Seoul, Korea
Dates: May 13–June 21
Eligibility: Must be sophomore or above, with good academic standing
Credits Granted: 3-6 hour undergrad or graduate
Subjects Taught: Topics in Business; independent study project optional
Cost: $3,950 in 1996
Housing: Double rooms at Shanghai University of Finance and Kyung Hee University
Application Deadline: March 15
Number of Students Sent/Yr Average: 10

Contact: Anne Seitzinger, Study Abroad Office, Williston Hall 417, Northern Illinois University, DeKalb, IL 60115
■ Phone: (815) 753-0700
Fax: (815) 753-0825
e-mail: aseitz@niu.edu
URL: http://www.niu.edu/depts/intl_prgrm/ intl.html

Princeton University—Princeton in Beijing

Program Description: A high-quality intensive program in elementary, intermediate and advanced Chinese language study for the serious language student
Site(s) in China: Beijing Normal University, Beijing
Dates: June–August; 8 week session, equivalent of one academic year of Chinese language study
Credits Granted: Eight credits from Princeton Univesity and a certificate from Beijing Normal University
Subjects Taught: Chinese
Cost: $3,500 includes tuition, room, "Chinese table" meals, textbooks and audio tapes, lectures and excursions
Housing: Students live with their teachers in well-equipped dormitories on campus. Double rooms with a/c, telephones, TV and some have private bathrooms
Application Deadline: Feb. 1
Other: Financial aid available
Contact: Princeton in Beijing, 211 Jones Hall, Princeton University, Princeton, NJ 08544-1008
■ Phone: (609) 258-4269
Fax: (609) 258-6984
e-mail: pib@princeton.edu

St. Cloud State University—Study Center in Tianjin, China

Program Description: 1 semester program for beginning students in Chinese language, area studies
Site(s) in China: Tianjin (Nankai Univ)
Dates: Jan–May
Eligibility: Must be college student, min. age 18, w/min. 2.25 GPA

Credits Granted: 32 credit hours undergrad
Subjects Taught: Chinese Language (Mandarin: beg), Chinese Studies
Cost: $6,500, including tuition, housing, meals, int'l airfare, fees, excursions
Housing: Int'l student dorm
Application Deadline: Sept. 15
Number of Students Sent/Yr Average: 15
Contact: Study Center in Tianjin, China, Center for International Studies, St. Cloud State University, 720 4th Ave. S., St. Cloud, MN 56301-4498
■ Phone: (320) 255-4287
Fax: (320) 255-4223
e-mail: intstudy@stcloud.msus.edu

School for International Training (SIT)—Academic Semester Abroad

Program Description: Academic semester abroad program focusing on intensive Mandarin language learning and minority cultures; emphasis on independent field study project; homestays; 2 week study tour to Dali and Lijiang
Site(s) in China: Kunming based
Dates: Fall or Spring semesters
Eligibility: Sophomore or above; min. 2.5 GPA
Credits Granted: 16 undergrad credits
Subjects Taught: Mandarin (beg/int/adv), History, Politics, Economics, Geography, Social Anthropology, Field Studies, Independent Project
Cost: $9,300 for Academic year '96-'97, includes tuition, room, board, international travel, excursions, insurance
Housing: University dorms, homestays, small hotels
Application Deadline: Fall: June 15; Spring: Nov. 15
Number of Students Sent/Yr Average: 25
Other: 16 credit hours transferrable to home institution
Contact: CSA Admissions, School for International Training, Kipling Road, Brattleboro, VT 05301-0676
■ Phone: (800) 336-1616

Slippery Rock University—SRU/Shanghai International Studies University Exchange

Program Description: Since 1987. Program is exclusively for langauge accusation

Site(s) in China: Shanghai—Shanghai International Studies University

Dates: Sept–Jan.; Feb–June

Eligibility: Sophomore or Junior; min. 2.50 QPA; min. 1 year of Chinese

Credits Granted: 12-14 semester credits

Subjects Taught: Chinese language (beg/int/adv)

Cost: SRU tuition, room, meals

Housing: at SISU dorms

Application Deadline: April 15; Oct. 15

Number of Students Sent/Yr Average: 2-4

Contact: Stan Kendziorski, SRU/ Shanghai International Studies University Exchange, International Studies, Slippery Rock University, Slippery rock, PA 16057

■ **Phone:** (412) 738-2052

Fax: (412) 738-2959

e-mail: stanley.kendziorski@sru.edu

URL: http://www.sru.edu

Stanford University—Inter-University Board for Chinese Language Studies

Program Description: Full academic year program for intermediate and advanced Mandarin study in small classes and tutorials. Summer intensive program as well.

Site(s) in China: Tsinghua University, Beijing, PRC; National Taiwan University, Taipei, Taiwan

Dates: June–August

Eligibility: Minimum 2 years prior college Mandarin

Credits Granted: None. Students receive quarterly reports to seek credit from their home institutions

Subjects Taught: Mandarin Chinese

Cost: Beijing: $13,600 includes campus housing; Taipei: $10,500 housing not included

Housing: Students must arrange their own housing

Application Deadline: Feb. 1 for academic year

Number of Students Sent/Yr Average: 70-80

Contact: Elizabeth Benskin, Inter-University Program for Chinese Language Studies, Littlefield Center, Stanford University, Rm. 14, 300 Lausen St., Stanford, CA 94305-5013

■ **Phone:** (510) 642-3873

Fax: (510) 642-3873

e-mail: IUB@violet.berkeley.edu

URL: http://www-leland.stanford.edu/dept/IUB/

SUNY College at Cortland—Program at CNU

Program Description: Chinese language and culture at Capital Normal University

Site(s) in China: Capital Normal University (CNU), Beijing

Dates: Fall: Sept 1–mid Jan; Spring: mid Feb–late June; Academic year: Sept 1–late June

Eligibility: 2.5 GPA, at least junior standing, 1 yr. Mandarin recommended

Credits Granted: 12-16/semester

Subjects Taught: all levels of Mandarin, Chinese culture (in English), traditional paiting, calligraphy, music, plus other subjects

Cost: contact for details

Housing: Foreign guest house on campus. Meals in cafeteria on campus or in kitchen in guest house.

Application Deadline: March 7 for Fall & Academic year; Oct. 1 for Spring

Number of Studentes sent/Yr Average: 1-4

Contact: International Programs, Suny Cortland, PO Box 2000, Cortland, NY 13045

■ **Phone:** (607) 753-2209

Fax: (607) 753-5989

e-mail: studyabroad@snycorva.cortland.edu

URL: http://www.studyabroad.com/suny/cortland

SUNY College at Cortland—Program at BTC

Program Description: Physical Education at Beijing Teacher's College of Physical Education

Site(s) in China: Beijing Teachers College of Physical Education (BTC)

Dates: Fall: Sept 1–mid Jan; Spring: mid Feb–late June; Academic year: Sept 1–late June

Eligibility: 2.5 GPA, at least junior standing, 1 yr. Mandarin recommended
Credits Granted: 12-16/semester
Subjects Taught: BTCPE: physical education, martial arts, teaching methods
Cost: contact for details
Housing: Foreign guest house on campus. Meals in cafeteria on campus or in kitchen in guest house.
Application Deadline: March 7 for Fall & Academic year; Oct. 1 for Spring
Number of Studentes sent/Yr Average: 1-4
Contact: International Programs, Suny Cortland, PO Box 2000, Cortland, NY 13045
■ **Phone:** (607) 753-2209
Fax: (607) 753-5989
e-mail: studyabroad@snycorva.cortland.edu
URL: http://www.studyabroad.com/suny/cortland

SUNY University at Albany— China/SUNYA Exchange Program

Program Description: Exchange program emphasizing development of Chinese language skills above first-year level, with direct enrollment available to fluent/literate students. Univ. of Albany also offers a combined B.A. in Chinese/M.B.A. program with junior year spent in China
Site(s) in China: Beijing, Nanjing, Shanghai, Tianjin
Dates: Sept 1–June 30 (fall/ spring/ academic year)
Eligibility: Sophomores or above; good academic standing; min. 1 year Mandarin
Credits Granted: 24-30 undergrad
Subjects Taught: Chinese language (Mandarin), Chinese Studies; others for students with more advanced skills
Cost: $3,703 semester (New York residents; $5,902 semester (non-New York residents), includes tuition, fees, housing, meals, insurance
Housing: Dorms, residence halls
Application Deadline: Fall/academic year: Feb. 15; Spring: Oct. 1
Number of Students Sent/Yr Average: 10

Contact: Dr. Alex M. Shane, Director, China/SUNY Exhange Program, LI-84, SUNY University at Albany, International Programs, Albany, NY 12222
■ **Phone:** (518) 442-3525
Fax: (518) 442-3338
e-mail: oipua@csc.albany.edu
URL: http://www.albany.edu/~oipwebua
Dept. of East Asian Studies for info on M.B.A.: http://www.albany.edu/eas/easindex.html

Thunderbird—The American Graduate School of International Management

Program Description: Master of International Management (MIM) degree program, Certificate of Advance Study with a summer semester offered in China. Program is in International Business with focus on Asia. Summer program open to graduate level students, primary focus on business and management in Asia.
Site(s) in China: Beijing (Univ. of Int'l Business and Economics); Shanghai (Shanghai Univ. of Finance and Economics)
Dates: 10 weeks, late May to early August
Eligibility: Graduate level, must have Bachelor's degree
Credits Granted: 9-12 credits in business, international studies, Chinese
Subjects Taught: Chinese language (Mandarin), business, economics, international studies
Cost: $785 per credit hour, plus housing, meals, travel
Housing: Furnished rooms
Application Deadline: March 1
Number of Students Sent/Yr Average: 20
Contact: Overseas Programs Office, American Graduate School of International Management, Thunderbird Campus, Glendale, AZ 85306
■ **Phone:** (602) 978-7252
Fax: (602) 547-1356
e-mail: HAYTOND@t-bird.edu
URL: http://www.t-bird.edu/overs

US-China People's Friendship Association—Chinese Language Study
Program Description: 4 weeks to 1 semester of Chinese Language study; 5 days a week, 4 hours a day. All levels.
Site(s) in China: Beijing Language & Culture University, Beijing
Dates: Spring, summer & fall
Eligibility: College, pre-college, adults; min. age 16; max age 60; must be in good health
Credits Granted: None. Certificate of successful completion awarded
Subjects Taught: Chinese Language (Mandarin). Optional classses: Preparation of HSK (Chinese Proficiency Test), Business Conversation, Calligraphy, Painting, Written Chinese, Taiji and Chinese Songs
Cost: Approx. $2,350 for 4 weeks to $3,660 for 1 semester. Includes application fee, tuition, room, local sightseeing, field trips, int'l airfare
Housing: Campus dormitory
Application Deadline: 80 days prior to scheduled departure date
Number of Students Sent/Yr Average: 16 students
Other: Sponsor is not US accredited; sponsor is a non-profit organization. Chinese Language Study program is on-going since 1983.
Contact: Ruby M. Fong, USCPFA Chinese Language Study, 1175 Volz Dr., Sacramento, CA 95822
▮ Phone: (916) 447-3313
Fax: (916) 444-2288

University of Colorado at Boulder
Site(s) in China: Beijing, Nanjing and Shanghai
Eligibility: Must be at least a second semester freshman
Credits Granted: CU-Boulder credit "in-residence" for courses
Cost: CIEE program fees, CU-Boulder fee and in some cases, a fee for health insurance
Application Deadline: Spring: Oct. 1; Summer or Fall: March 1
Contact: Office of International Education, University of Colorado at Boulder
▮ Phone: (303) 492-7741
e-mail: studyabr@colorado.edu
URL: http://www.colorado.edu/OIE/Study Abroad/china.html

University of Hawaii at Manoa—Pacific Asian Management Institute (PAMI)
Program Description: Annual field study abroad to Asia
Site(s) in China: Beijing and/or Guangzhou; possibly Shenzhen
Dates: end of June–mid-July
Eligibility: Graduate or undergraduate student
Credits Granted: 6
Subjects Taught: Business Economics, Business
Cost: Approx. $3,750, plus tuition and campus housing for orientation and wrap-up sessions
Housing: Hotel costs on tour included; campus housing before and after trip for additional cost
Application Deadline: mid-March each year
Number of Students Sent/Yr Average: 25
Other: Accredited course (AACSB)
Contact: Associate Director, Pacific Asian Management Institute (PAMI), University of Hawaii at Manoa, 2404 Maile Way, C-202, Honolulu, HI 96822
▮ Phone: (808) 956-8041
Fax: (808) 956-9685
e-mail: pami@pami.cba.hawaii.edu
URL: http://www.cba.hawaii.edu/pami/

University of Massachusetts at Amherst—Shaanxi Normal University Exchange
Program Description: 1 or 2 term program in Chinese language, area studies for advance students
Site(s) in China: Xi'an (Shaanxi Normal Univ)
Dates: fall and/or spring terms
Eligibility: must be junior or above, w/2 yrs. Mandarin, good academic standing, current enrollment in degree program
Credits Granted: 30-32 credit hours undergrad per year

Subjects Taught: Chinese Language (Mandarin: int/adv), Chinese Studies
Cost: $4,400 per semester; $7,750 per year
Housing: Share rooms with international students in dorm
Application Deadline: March 15
Other: Sponsor accredited in US; activities include excursions
Contact: Prof. Shen Zhongwei, Director, Asian Languages & Literatures Dept., Thompson Hall, Box 37505, University of Massachusetts, Amherst, MA 01003-7505
∎ Phone: (413) 545-4350
Fax: (413) 545-4975
e-mail: kcroke@acad.umass.edu

University of Massachusetts at Amherst—Intensive Chinese Language Program—Summer

Program Description: Summer program in Chinese language, literature
Site(s) in Taiwan: Taichung, Taiwan (Tunghai Univ)
Dates: 8 weeks, July–August
Eligibility: must be sophomore or above, w/min B average, 1 year intensive Mandarin
Credits Granted: 10 credit hours undergrad; no grad credit
Subjects Taught: Chinese Language (Mandarin: beg/int), Chinese Literature
Cost: $2,400 (1997)
Housing: Dorms; share w/Chinese roommates
Application Deadline: March 15
Other: Activities include excursions
Contact: Prof. Shen Zhongwei, Director, Asian Languages & Literatures Dept., Thompson Hall, Box 37505, University of Massachusetts, Amherst, MA 01003-7505
∎ Phone: (413) 545-4350
Fax: (413) 545-4975
e-mail: kcroke@acad.umass.edu

University of Massachusetts at Amherst—Program in Taiwan

Program Description: Both a semester and an academic year program focusing on Chinese language studies at Tunghai University are offered.

Site(s) in Taiwan: Taichung, Taiwan (Tunghai University)
Dates: fall and/or spring terms
Eligibility: must be junior or above, w/min. 1 year college Mandarin, good academic standing, current enrollment in degree program
Credits Granted: 15 credit hours undergrad per semester
Subjects Taught: Chinese Language (Mandarin: int/adv), Chinese Culture
Cost: $6,750 for in-state Univ. of Massachusetts students; $7,750 for out-of-state students, $8,750 for all other students. Semester fees are $3,750, $4,250, and $4,850 respectively. Includes tuition and fees, infirmary health care, field trips and lodging.
Housing: Dorms with Chinese roommates
Application Deadline: Academic year/fall semester: March 15; Spring: Oct. 15
Other: Activities include excursions
Contact: Prof. Shen Zhongwei, Director, Asian Languages & Literatures Dept., Thompson Hall, Box 37505, University of Massachusetts, Amherst, MA 01003-7505
∎ Phone: (413) 545-4350
Fax: (413) 545-4975
e-mail: kcroke@acad.umass.edu

Whitworth College—Whitworth/Jilin Teachers College Exchange Program

Program Description: 1 or 2 semester program in Chinese language and area studies
Site(s) in China: Jilin Teachers College, Jilin
Dates: Aug–June (1 or 2 terms)
Eligibility: Must be junior or senior
Credits Granted: 15 credit hours undergrad per semester
Subjects Taught: Chinese Language (Mandarin: beg/int/adv), Civilization/Culture
Cost: $9,650 per semester, including tuition, housing, all meals
Housing: Dorms, homestay
Application Deadline: Fall: Feb. 1; Spring: Oct. 1
Number of Students Sent/Yr Average: 2

Contact: Sue Jackson, Whitworth/Jilin Teachers College Exchange Program, Center for International and Multicultural Education, Whitworth College, Spokane, WA 99251
■ **Phone:** (509) 466-1000
Fax: (509) 466-3723
e-mail: sjackson@whitworth.edu
URL: http://www.whitworth.edu

Whitworth College—
Whitworth/Nanjing University
Exchange Program

Program Description: 1 or 2 semester program in Chinese language and culture
Site(s) in China: Nanjing University, Nanjing
Dates: Sept–June (1 or 2 terms)
Eligibility: Must be Whitworth student, junior or senior year, w/min. 2.5 GPA and 1 year of college Mandarin

Credits Granted: 12-15 credit hours undergrad/semester
Subjects Taught: Chinese Language (Mandarin: beg/int/adv), Civilization/Culture
Cost: $9,650 per semester, including tuition, housing, all meals
Housing: Dorms
Application Deadline: Fall: Feb. 1; Spring: Oct. 1
Number of Students Sent/Yr Average: 1
Other: Sponsor accredited in the US
Contact: Sue Jackson, Whitworth/ Nanjing University Exchange Program, Center for International & Multicultural Education, Whitworth College, Spokane, WA 99251
■ **Phone:** (509) 466-1000
Fax: (509) 466-3723
e-mail: sjackson@whitworth.edu
URL: http://www.whitworth.edu

APPENDIX A

Chinese Language

This appendix includes a pronunciation guide for Chinese in both Pinyin and Wade-Giles; a glossary of Chinese terms of particular interest to students and teachers; a list of Chinese language preparatory programs; and a bibliography of Chinese-language study aids.

I Pronunciation Guide

(all English phonemes according to standard US English)

Pinyin	Wade Giles	Equivalent English Phoneme
a	a	"a" as in "mama"
b	p	"b" as in "boy"
c	ts	"ts" as in "cats"
d	t	"d" as in "radar"
e	er	no English phoneme; "oe" as in French "oevre"
f	f	"f" as in "father"
g	k	"g" as in "got"
h	h	"h" as in "hot"
i (before n)	i or ih	"i" as in "pin"
i (after sh)	ih	"ur" as in "cur"
i (after other consonants)	i or ee	"ee" as in "week"
j	ch	"j" as in "jump"
k	k'	"k" as in "kite"
l	l	"l" as in "lump"
m	m	"m" as in "mud"
n	n	"n" as in "nut"
o	aw	"o" as in "dog"
p	p'	"p" as in "pig"
q	ch'	"ch" as in "chat"
r	j	"j" as in "jump"

(Chinese has a second "r"-like sound as well with no equivalent English phoneme)

Pinyin	Wade Giles	Equivalent English Phoneme
s	s	"s" as in "sat"
t	t'	"t" as in "toy"
u	eu	"oo" as in "loon"
w	w	"w" as in "wand"
x	hs	"sh" as in "she"

y	io	"y" as in "young"
z	tz	"dz" as in "adze"
ai	i	"y" as in "fly"
ao	au	"ou" as in "loud"
ei	ay or ai	"ay" as in "pay"
ia	ya or ia	"ya" as in "yard"
iao	yao or iao	"eow" as in "meow"
iu	iu	"yo" as in "yo-yo"
ui	uay or uai	"way" as in "sway"
uo	aw	"aw" as in "paw"
ng	ng	"ng" as in "hang"
sh	shr	"shr" as in "shroud"
zh	dz, tz, or dh	no equivalent phoneme; halfway between "dr" as in "drop" and "dz" as in "adze"

II Glossary of Terms for Teachers/Students

Materials and Equipment

blackboard	*hēibǎn*	黑板
chalk	*fěnbǐ*	粉笔
ditto	*yóuyìn*	油印
ditto master	*yóuyìnjī*	油印机
marker	*cǎisèbǐ*	彩色笔
notebook	*bǐjìběn*	笔记本
overhead projector	*fàngyìngjī*	放映机
photocopier	*fùyìnjī*	复印机
photocopy	*fùyìn*	复印
tape recorder	*lùyīnjī*	录音机
slide projector	*huàndēngjī*	幻灯机
video/VCR	*lùxiàng/lùxiàngjī*	录象/录象机
white board	*báibǎn*	白板

Classroom Terms

class (academic)	*kè*	课
class ("class of 1997")	*bān*	班
class monitor	*bānzhǎng*	班长
department/major	*xì*	系
exam	*kǎoshì*	考试
final exam	*dàkǎo/qīmòkǎoshì*	大考/期末考试
grades	*fēnshu*	分数
homework	*gōngkè*	功课
midterm	*qīzhōngkǎoshì*	期中考试
paper/article	*lùnwén/wénzhāng*	论文/文章
quiz	*cèyàn/xiǎokǎo*	测验/小考
research paper	*yánjiūbàogào*	研究报告

School Terms

dean's office	*jiàowùchù*	教务处
doorkeeper (ogre)	*kānménde*	看门的
foreign affairs office	*wàibàn*	外办
foreign expert	*wàiguózhuānjiā*	外国专家
foreign teacher	*wàijiào*	外教
personnel office	*rénshìchù*	人事处
professor	*jiàoshòu*	教授
assistant professor/lecturer	*fùjiàoshòu/jiǎngshī*	副教授/讲师
president (of school)	*xiàozhǎng*	校长
vice president	*fùxiàozhǎng*	副校长
responsible person	*fùzérén*	负责人
school shuttle	*bānchē*	班车
service person	*fúwùyuán*	服务员
teacher	*lǎoshī/jiàoshī*	老师/教师
work unit	*dānwèi*	单位

Market Terms

Weights and Measures:
(1 jin = .5 kilogram = 1.1 lbs; 1 liang = .1 kilo = .22 lbs)

	gōngjīn (kilo)	公斤
	jīn	斤
	liǎng	两
	bàng (pound)	磅
Arts and Crafts Store	*gōngyìměishùdiàn*	工艺美术店
Department Store	*bǎihuòdiàn*	百货店
freemarket	*zìyóu shìchǎng*	自由市场
Friendship Store	*yǒuyì shāngdiàn*	友谊商店
NT$	*táibì*	台币
private store	*sīyíngshāngdiàn*	私营商店
RMB	*rénmínbì*	人民币
state store	*guóyíngdiàn*	国营店
yuan	*yuán*	元

Non-Chinese herbs & spices sold in China as herbal medicine

cinnamon	*guìpí*	桂皮
coriander	*yánsuì*	芫荽
cumin	*xiǎohuíxiāng*	小茴香
parsley	*ōuqín*	欧芹
rosemary	*míshùxiāng*	迷树香
saffron	*zànghónghuā*	藏红花
sage	*shùwěicǎo*	鼠尾草
thyme	*báilǐxiāng*	百里香

III Chinese Language Preparatory Programs

The following schools and institutions have major programs in Chinese language. Starred (*) schools have summer programs as well as semester classes:

UNITED STATES

CALIFORNIA:
City College of San Francisco
Los Angeles City College
Monterey Institute of International Studies
Pomona College
San Francisco State University
Scripps College
Stanford University
University of California (Berkeley, Los Angeles, San Diego, Santa Barbara, Santa Cruz)

COLORADO:
University of Colorado (Boulder)

CONNECTICUT:
Connecticut College
Yale University*

DISTRICT OF COLUMBIA:
Georgetown University
George Washington University

FLORIDA:
University of Miami

ILLINOIS:
University of Chicago*

INDIANA:
Indiana University (Bloomington)

MARYLAND:
University of Maryland (College Park)

MASSACHUSETTS:
Harvard University
Tufts University
University of Massachusetts (Amherst)
Wellesley College

MICHIGAN:
Michigan State University
Oakland University

MINNESOTA:
St. John's University*
University of Minnesota (Twin Cities)

MISSOURI:
Washington University

NEW JERSEY:
Douglass College
Livingston College
Princeton University
Rutgers
The State University of New Jersey
University College (New Brunswick)

NEW YORK:
City College of New York
Cornell University*
Hunter College
Queens College
Skidmore College
St. John's University
State University of New York (Albany, Binghamton, Buffalo, Cortland, New Paltz, Oswego)
University of Rochester

OHIO:
Oberlin College
Ohio State University (Columbus)
Wittenberg University

OREGON:
University of Oregon (Portland) *

PENNSYLVANIA:
Pennsylvania State
University of Pennsylvania
University of Pittsburgh

UTAH:
Brigham Young University

VERMONT:
School for International Training*
Middlebury College*

WISCONSIN:
Beloit College*
University of Wisconsin (Madison)

CANADA:
BRITISH COLUMBIA:
University of British Columbia
(Vancouver)

ONTARIO:
University of Toronto

SASKATCHEWAN:
St. Thomas More College

IV Bibliography for Chinese Language Study

Business Chinese 500. Beijing Language Institute. San Francisco: China Books & Periodicals, Inc., 1982. Excellent glossary of business terms, with exercises and tape set.

Chinese for Today. Beijing Language Institute. San Francisco: China Books & Periodicals, Inc., 1996. Newest series with simple texts and glossaries.

Chinese in Ten Minutes a Day. Kristine Kershul, ed. Seattle: Bilingual Books, 1988. Surprisingly useful for basic communications.

Practical Chinese Reader. Beijing Language Institute. San Francisco: China Books & Periodicals, Inc. 1986. Good intermediate reading series with glossaries.

Spoken Standard Chinese. Hugh M. Stimson and Parker Po Fei Huang. New Haven, CT: Yale Far Eastern Publications, 1976. Good 3-book series each for spoken/written skills.

Strange Stories from a Chinese Studio. Linda Hsia and Roger Yue, eds. New Haven, CT: Yale Far Eastern Publications, n.d. Traditional stories in simple Chinese with glossaries and study guide.

DICTIONARIES

A Chinese-English Dictionary and

An English-Chinese Dictionary. Beijing: Commercial Press, 1988. Distributed in the US by China Books & Periodicals, Inc. (San Francisco); very easy to use and remarkably complete dictionaries of modern Chinese arranged in alphabetical order of Pinyin romanization; simplified characters only.

Continental's English-Chinese Dictionary. Hong Kong: Hong Kong Press, n.d. One of the best pocket-sized English-Chinese dictionaries; complex characters only.

Matthew's Chinese-English Dictionary (13th Edition). Taipei: Dunhuang Press, 1975. Too basic for serious study of classical Chinese, Matthew's is still simple enough to use for introductory *wenyan* study or for reading modern literature, but too complex for a purely *baihua* dictionary; complex characters only, organized by alphabetical order of Wade-Giles romanization.

A New Practical Chinese-English Dictionary. Taipei: The Far East Book Company, 1971. A good pocket-sized dictionary of complex characters, organized by radical and stroke order.

Xinhua Zidian. Beijing: Xinhua Press, 1975. Excellent pocket-sized Chinese-Chinese dictionary, with both complex and simplified characters.

Publications on China-Related Topics

FUNDING SOURCES AND OTHER GUIDES

Directory of Publishers in China. Beijing: Foreign Languages Press, 1992. Publishers may be looking for English language polishers or editors, so don't forget this possible source of income while in China.

Funding for Research, Study, and Travel: The People's Republic of China. Denise Wallen and Karen Cantrell, eds. Phoenix: Oryx Press, 1987. A very complete list of all kinds of grants, scholarships and financial aid available to researchers, organizations, and students going to China. Also included is an index arranged by subject (e.g. International Relations, Calligraphy).

International Institute of Education Publications: *The Learning Traveler; Academic Year Abroad; Teaching Abroad; Vacation Study Abroad; Teaching in China Preparation Series*. For publications write 809 United Nations Plaza, New York, NY 10017 Phone: 212-984-5412

Financial Resources for International Study. Institute of International Education (New York). Princeton, N. J.: Peterson's Guides, 1989.

Teaching English in Asia: Finding a Job and Doing It Well. Galen Harris Valle. Berkeley, Pacific View Press, 1995. Guide to finding jobs as an English teacher in China, Japan, Indonesia, South Korea, and other East Asian Countries.

TOURIST AND BUSINESS GUIDEBOOKS

Beijing: Lonely Planet City Guide. Robert Storey. Oakland: Lonely Planet, 1996.

China, A Travel Survival Kit. Alan Samagalski. Berkeley: Lonely Planet Publications, 1991.

China: Business Strategies for the '90s. Arne J. DeKeijzer. Berkeley: Pacific View Press, 1992.

China Guide. Ruth Lor Malloy. New York: Open Road, 1996. Ninth edition of the popular one-volume guide to China.

China Off the Beaten Track. Brian Schwartz. New York: St. Martin's Press, 1983; Hong Kong: South China Morning Post, 1982.

Hong Kong Handbook including Macau and Guangzhou. Chico: Moon Publications, 1995.

Tibet Handbook: a Pilgrimage Guide. Victor Chan. Chico: Moon Publications, 1994. More than a guidebook, this is an encyclopedic reference to Tibet, with many maps, diagrams, and trekking itineries.

Tibet: Travel Survival Kit. Michael Buckley. Berkeley; South Yarra, Victoria, Australia: Lonely Planet Publications, 1986.

Visitor's Guide to Historic Hong Kong. Sally Rodwell. Hong Kong: Odyssey Guides, 1991. Guide to walking tours as a way of appreciating Hong Kong's unique history and culture.

CHINESE HISTORY AND POLITICS

Born Red. Gao Yuan. Stanford, Ca.: Stanford University Press, 1987. A chronicle of the Cultural Revolution.

Broken Portraits: Personal Encounters with Chinese Students. Michael David Kwan. San Francisco: China Books & Periodicals, Inc., 1990. A teacher's intimate account of the thoughts and motives of students in Beijing during 1989.

China, Alive in the Bitter Sea. Fox Butterfield. New York: Bantam, 1982.

China: a Macro History. Ray Huang. Armonk, N.Y., M.E. Sharpe, 1997. Highly readable survey of Chinese history, revised in 1997 to reflect recent research.

China on the Edge: The Crisis of Ecology and Development. He Bochuan. Berkeley: Pacific View Press, 1991. An analysis of China's environmental and population problems by a leading Chinese intellectual.

China Rising: The Meaning of Tiananmen. Lee Feigon. Chicago: I. R. Dee, 1990.

China Wakes. Nicholas D. Kristof and Sheryl WuDunn. New York: Vintage, 1995. Excellent report on China today by the award-winning journalists.

Chinese Profiles. Zhang Xinxin and Sang Ye. Beijing: Panda Books, 1986. Oral histories of ordinary Chinese people.

The China Reader. D. Milton, N. Milton, and Franz Schurman. New York: Random House, 1966–1972. A 4-volume history which includes: 1. Imperial China: decline of the last dynasty and the origins of modern China; the 18th and 19th centuries. 2. Republican China: nationalism, war, and the rise of Communism, 1911–1949. 3. Communist China: revolutionary reconstruction and international confrontation;1949–present. 4. People's China: social experimentation, politics, entry onto the world scene, 1966 through 1972.

Chinese Roundabout. Jonathan Spence. New York: Norton, 1992. Wonderful collection of essays by the famous historian.

Crisis at Tiananmen. Yi Mu and Mark Thompson. San Francisco: China Books, 1990. A Chinese journalist's view of the 1989 events at Tiananmen.

A Daughter of Han: the Autobiography of a Chinese Working Woman. Ida Pruitt, ed. Stanford, Ca.: Stanford University Press, 1967. The autobiography of Ning Lao T'ai-t'ai as told to Pruitt by Ning Lao.

The Death of Woman Wang. Jonathan Spence. New York: Viking Press, 1979.

Fanshen. William Hinton. New York: Vintage, 1966. A documentary of revolution in a Chinese village by an American who served as an agricultural adviser to the Chinese government. See also *Shenfan.*

Making Revolution: The Communist Movement in Eastern and Central China. Yung-Fa Chen. Berkeley: University of California Press, 1986.

The Memory Palace of Matteo Ricci. Jonathan Spence. New York: Penguin, 1985.

Monarchs and Minsters: The Grand Council in Mid-Ch'ing Ching. Beatrice S. Bartlett. Berkeley: University of California Press, 1990.

Life and Death in Shanghai. Nien Cheng. New York: Grove, 1986. An account of the experience of an upper-class Chinese woman during the Cultural Revolution. Provides the reader with a good understanding of the nature of the Cultural Revolution.

One Billion: A China Chronicle. Jay and Linda Mathews. New York: Ballantine, 1985.

Popular Protest and Political Culture in Modern China (Learning from 1989). Elizabeth Perry and Jeffrey Wasserstein: Boulder: Westview Press, 1991.

Red Star Over China. Edgar Snow. New York: Grove Press, 1967. A classic though somewhat naive account of the struggles and accomplishments of Chinese Communism during the early decades of the People's Republic of China.

The Search for Modern China. Jonathan Spence. New York: Norton, 1990.

Seven Years in Tibet. Heinrich Harper, trans. by Richard Graves. New York: Dutton, 1954. An account of an Austrian mountain climber's escape from a British internment camp in India during World War II and his 21-month journey through the Himalayas to safety in the Forbidden City of Lhasa in Tibet.

Shark's Fins and Millet. Ilona Ralf Sues. Boston: Little, Brown, 1944.

Shenfan. William Hinton. New York: Random House, 1983. A post-revolution documentary of the same village covered in *Fanshen.*

Son of the Revolution. Liang Heng and Judith Shapiro. New York: Knopf, 1983.

The Soong Dynasty. Sterling Seagrave. New York: Harper & Row, 1985.

Stillwell and the American Experience in China, 1911–1945. Barbara Tuchman. New York: Bantam, 1972. A fascinating account of American General Stillwell's experience in China.

U.S. Crusade in China. Michael Schaller. New York: Columbia University Press, 1979. Discussion of American policy toward China during World War.

CHINESE ART, LITERATURE AND PHILOSOPHY

Chinese Art. Daisy Lion-Goldschmidt. New York: Rizzoli, 1980.

A Connoisseur's Guide to Chinese Ceramics. Cecile and Michel Beurdeley. New York: Harper &Row, 1974. Excellent guide to Chinese ceramics through the dynasties.

The Dream of the Red Chamber. Hsueh-Chin Tsao, trans. by Florence and Isabel McHugh. New York: Pantheon, 1958.

My Land and My People. Bstan-dzin-rgya-mtsho, Dalai Lama XIV. New York: McGraw-Hill, 1962.

Outlines of Chinese Symbolism and Art Motives. Charles A. S. Williams. New York: Dover, 1990. A straightforward handbook for understanding Chinese symbolism and art.

Religion in China Today. Foster Stockwell. Beijing: New World Press, 1993. Good survey of the six major religions active in China today.

A Source Book in Chinese Philosophy. Chan Wing-Tsit. Princeton: Princeton University Press, 1964.

Sources of Chinese Tradition. William T. DeBary. New York: Columbia University Press, 1964.

The Story of the Stone. Hsueh-Chin Tsao, trans. by David Hawkes. Middlesex, U.K. Penguin, 1973–1982.

Tao Te Ching: The Classic Book of Integrity and the Way. Lao Tzu, trans. by Victor Mair. New York: Bantam, 1990.

GENERAL

All Under Heaven. Pearl S. Buck. New York: John Day Co., 1973.

China through My Window. Naomi Woronov. Armonk, NY: M. E. Sharpe, 1988. An account of life in China through the eyes of an American teacher.

A Day in the Life of China. David Cohen: San Francisco: Collins, 1985. A book of excellent photographs taken in different places throughout China on exactly the same day.

The Heart of the Dragon. Alasdar Clayre. Boston: Houghton Mifflin, 1985.

In China. Eve Arnold. New York: Knopf, 1980.

Iron and Silk. Mark Salzman. New York: Vintage, 1987.

Spring Moon. Bette Bao Lord. New York: Harper & Row, 1981. A work of fiction that gives a romanticized glimpse of life of affluent Chinese in traditional China.

CULTURAL ADAPTATION AND ADJUSTMENT

Beijinger in New York. Glen Cao. San Francisco: Cypress Book Co, 1993. This potboiler was enormously popular in China, and the basis for a big TV series. The depiction of life in the U.S. for a Chinese immigrant may be sensationalized, but reflects many current Chinese perceptions of the West, and may lead to a good discussion of cultural differences in the classroom.

Culture Shock: China. Kevin Sinclair with Iris Wong Po-yee. Portland: Graphic Arts, 1996.

Culture Shock: Taiwan. Chris and Ling-li Bates. Portland: Graphic Arts, 1995. With the above title, good preparation for the many practical changes of living in a Chinese society.

The Joy of Getting Along with the Chinese. Fred Schneiter. Long Beach: Heian International, 1994. Written by a long-time Hong Kong resident, and especially good for those living and working there.

The Travelers' Guide to Asian Customs and Manners. Nancy L. Braganti and Elizabeth Devine. New York: St. Martin's Press, 1988.

Teaching China's Lost Generation. Tani E. Barlowe and Donald M. Lowe. San Francisco: China Books & Periodicals, Inc., 1987.

Two Years in the Melting Pot. Liu Zongren. San Francisco: China Books & Periodicals, Inc., 1988.

MATERIALS FOR TEACHING ORAL AND LISTENING SKILLS

Many of the activities in these books (particularly *Action Plans, Keep Talking,* and *Recipes*) don't require the students to have written material in front of them, making these texts ideal for teachers without easy access to copying facilities.

Action Plans: 80 Student-Centered Language Activities. Marion Macdonald and Sue Rogers-Gordon. Rowley, MA: Newbury House, 1984.

Can't Stop Talking: Discussion Problems for Advanced Beginners and Low Intermediates. George Rooks. Rowley, MA: Newbury House, 1983.

Games for Language Learning. Andrew Wright, David Betteridge & Micahel Buckby, (Cambridge Handbooks for Language Teachers Series)

Great Ideas Listening and Speaking Activities for Students of American English. Leo Jones and Victoria Kimbrough. New York: Cambridge University Press, 1987. (Also buy tape and teacher's manual).

Idiomatic American English: A Step-by-Step Workbook for Learning Everyday American Expressions. Barbara K. Gaines. New York: Kodansha International, 1986. Students love idioms and this book contains about 900 of them (in context), along with exercises.

Keep Talking: Communicative Fluency Activities for Language Teaching. Fredericke Klippel. New York: Cambridge University Press, 1984.

Look Again Pictures: For Language Development and Lifeskills. Judy Winn-Bell Olson. Hayward: The Alemany Press, 1984. Contains material that "points out the 8 differences between the top picture and the bottom picture"; good for teaching prepositions, present progressive tense, or simply to make students speak. Overhead transparencies of the illustrations make effective teaching tools.

The Non-Stop Discussion Workbook: Problems for Intermediate and Advanced Students. George Rooks. Rowley, MA: Newbury House, 1981.

Recipes for Tired Teachers: Well-Seasoned Activities for the ESOL Classroom. Christopher Sion. Reading, MA: Addison-Wesley, 1985.

MATERIALS FOR TEACHING WRITING

From Process to Product: Beginning-Intermediate Writing Skills for Students of ESL. Natalie Lefkowitz. Englewood Cliffs, NJ: Prentice-Hall, 1988. Takes students through the writing process, from brainstorming to organizing ideas in a logical way. Contains ideas useful for any level, but more appropriate for beginning to intermediate.

Idea Exchange: Writing What You Mean. Linda Lonon-Blanton. Rowley, MA: Newbury House, 1988. Contains some of the traditional rhetorical forms (comparison and contrast, classification, etc.) but presents them in an innovative way. There are 2 books: Level 1 for beginning-intermediate and Level 2 for intermediate-advanced.

Practical Guide for Advanced Writers in English as a Second Language. Paul Munsell and Martha Clough. New York: MacMillan,1984. More of a traditional writing text which contains examples of and explanations for all of the major expository writing forms (contrast, classification, etc.).

Writer's Companion. Marcella Frank. Rowley, MA: Newbury House, 1983. Small, very useful book which contains an excellent, clear and concise explanation of the most common grammatical mistakes.

APPENDIX C

China-Related Resource Organizations

Embassies/Consulates/Government Representatives

AUSTRALIA

EMBASSY OF THE PRC
14 Federal Highway
Watson, A.C.T. 2602
(062) 412-446

CONSULATES-GENERAL OF THE PRC IN AUSTRALIA:
539 Elizabeth St.
Surry Hills
Sydney, N.S.W. 2010
(02) 698-7929

75-77 Irving Rd.
Toorak, VIC 3142
(03) 882-0604

TAIWAN

FAR EASTERN TRADING CORPORATION
P.O. Box 148
World Trade Center
Melbourne, VIC 3005
(03) 611-2988

FAR EASTERN TRADING CORPORATION,
SYDNEY BRANCH
Room 1902, Level 19
MLC Center, King St.
Sydney, N.S.W. 2000
(02) 223-3207

Cultural Division
Taipei Economic & Cultural Office in Australia
Unit 8, Tourism House
40 Blackall Street, Barton
Canberra Act 2600
Phone: (6)273-4904
Fax: (6)273-5209

CANADA

EMBASSY OF THE PRC
515 St. Patrick's St.
Ottawa, ON KIN 5H3
(613) 789-3434
URL: http://www.buildlink.com/embassy/

CONSULATES-GENERAL OF THE PRC
IN CANADA:

Toronto–
240 St. George St.
Toronto, ON M5R 2P4
Phone: (416) 964-7260
Fax: (416) 324-6468

Vancouver–
3380 Granville St.
Vancouver, BC V6H 3K3
Phone: (604) 734-7492
Fax: (604) 737-0154

TAIWAN

TAIPEI ECONOMIC & CULTURAL OFFICES:

Ottawa–
45 O'Connor St., Ste. 1960
Ottawa, ON K1P 1A4
Phone: (613) 231-5080
Fax: (613) 231-7112
DISCTRICTS: ON (Ottawa), PQ, MB

Toronto–
151 Yonge St., Ste. 1202
Toronto, ON M5C 2W7
Phone: (416) 369-9030
Fax: (416) 369-1473
Districts: ON (Toronto), PQ, NF, NS, NB, PE

Vancouver–
2008 Cathedral Place
925 W. Georgia St.
Vancouver, BC V6C 3L2
Phone: (604) 689-4111
Fax: (604) 689-0101
Districts: BC, SK, AB, NT, YT

NEW ZEALAND

EMBASSY OF THE PRC
6 Glenmore St.
Wellington
(64-04) 636-5197

TAIWAN

East Asian Trading Center
P.O. Box 10-250
The Terrace
Wellington
(614) 736-474

PARIS

TAIWAN

Service Culturel
Bureau De Representation De Taipei en France
78 Rue de L'Universite, 75007
Paris, France
Tel:(01)44398844-47
Fax:(01)44398873

UK

EMBASSY OF THE PRC
49-51 Portland Pl.
London, WIN 3AH
(071) 636-5197

TAIWAN

Free Chinese Center
4th Floor, Dorland House
14-16 Regent St.
London, SWEY 4PH
(071) 930-5767

British Taiwan Cultural Institute
6 Cork Street
London W1X 1PB, U.K.
Phone: (171)494-2500
Fax: (171)494-2520

US

EMBASSY OF THE PRC
2300 Connecticut Ave. NW
Washington, DC 20008
Phone: (202) 338-6688
Fax: (202) 588-9760
URL: http://www.china-embassy.org/
Districts: States other than those mentioned below

CONSULATES-GENERAL OF THE PRC IN THE UNITED STATES

Chicago–
104 S. Michigan Ave.
Chicago, IL 60603
Phone: (312) 803-0098
Fax: (312) 803)-0122
Districts: CO, IL, IN, IA, KS, MI, MN, MO, WI

Houston–
3417 Montrose Blvd
Houston, TX 77006
Phone: (713) 524-4311
Fax: (713) 524-7656
Districts: AL, AR, FL, GA, LA, MS, OK, TX

Los Angeles–
501 Shatto Pl.
Los Angeles, CA 90020
Phone: (213) 380-2506
Fax: (213) 380-1961
Districts: AZ, HI, NM, CA (Southern)

New York–
520 Twelth Ave.
New York, NY 10036
Phone: (212) 330-7409
Fax: (212) 502-0245
Districts: CT, ME, MA, NH, NJ, NY, OH, PA, RI, VT

San Francisco—
1450 Laguna St.
San Francisco, CA 94115
Phone: (415) 563-4857
Fax: (415) 563-0494
Districts: AK, NV, CA (Northern), OR, WA

TAIWAN

TAIPEI ECONOMIC & CULTURAL OFFICES:

Atlanta—
2 Midtown Plaza, Suite 1290
1349 West Peachtree St. NE
Atlanta, GA 30309
Phone: (404) 872-0123
Fax: (404) 873-3474
Districts: AL, GA, KY, NC, SC, TN

Boston—
99 Summer St., Ste. 801
Boston, MA 02102
Phone: (617) 737-2050
Fax: (617) 951-1684
Districts: ME, MA, NH, RI, VT

Chicago—
2 Prudential Plaza, 57-58th Floors
180 N. Stetson Ave.
Chicago, IL 60601
Phone: (312) 616-0100
Fax: (312) 616-1490
Districts: IL, IN, IA, MI, MN, OH, WI

District of Columbia—
4201 Wisconsin Ave., N.W.
Washington, DC 20016-2137
Phone: (202)895-1918
Fax: (202)895-1922

Guam—
PO Box 3416
Agana, Guam 96910
Phone: (617) 472-5865
Fax: (617) 472-5869
Districts: Caroline Island, Guam, Mariana Islands, Marshall Islands

Honolulu—
2746 Pali Highway
Honolulu, HI 96817
Phone: (808) 595-6347
Fax: (808) 595-6542
Districts: HI

Houston—
11 Greenway Plaza, Suite 2006
Houston, TX 77046
Phone: (713) 626-7445
Fax: (713) 626-1202
Districts: AR, LA, MS, OK, TX

Kansas City—
Penntower Office Center
3100 Broadway, Ste. 1001
Kansas City, MO 64111
Phone: (816) 531-1298
Fax: (816) 531-3066
Districts: CO, KS, MO, NE, ND, SD

Los Angeles—
3731 Wilshire Blvd., Suite 700
Los Angeles, CA 90010
Phone: (213) 389-1215
Fax: (213) 383-3245
Districts: AZ, CA (Southern), NM, Mexico

Miami—
The Colonnade
2333 Ponce de Leon Blvd., Suite 610
Coral Gables, FA 33134
Phone: (305) 443-8917
Fax: (305) 444-4796
Districts: FL, Puerto Rico, Virgin Islands, Bermuda

New York—
885 Secons Ave., 47th Floor
New York, NY 10017
Phone: (212) 317-7300
Fax: (212) 754-1549
Districts: CT, NJ, NY, PA

San Francisco—
555 Montgomery St., Ste. 501
San Francisco, CA 94111
Phone: (415) 362-7680
Fax: (415) 362-7680
Districts: CA (Northern), NV, UT

Seattle—
Suite 2410, Westin Bldg.
2001 6th Ave.
Seattle, WA 98121
Phone: (206) 441-4586
Fax: (206) 441-4320
Districts: ID, MT, OR, WA, WY

US GOVERNMENT OFFICES IN CHINA

Embassy
3 Xiushui Bei Jie
Jianguomenwai, Beijing PRC100600
Phone: (86-10) 532-3178
Fax: Ambassador/Economic:
     (86-10) 532-6422
Commercial: (86-10) 532-3178
Visas: (86-10) 532-3178

Chengdu Consulate General
4 Lingshiguan Lu
Chengdu, Sichuan Province PRC 610042
Phone: (86-28) 558-9642
Fax: (86-28) 558-3520

Guangzhou Consulate General
1 Shamian Nan Jie
Guangzhou, Guangdong Province
510133
Phone: (86-20) 888-8911
Fax: (86-20) 886-2341

Shanghai Consulate General
1469 Huaihai Zhong Lu
Shanghai, PRC 200031
Phone: (86-21) 433-6880
Fax: (86-21) 433-1476

Shengyang Consulate General
No. 52, Shi Si Wei Lu
Heping District
Shenyang, Liaoning Province 110003
Phone: (86-24) 282-0057

Hong Kong Consulate General
26 Garden Road
Hong Kong
Phone: (852) 2523-9011
Fax: (852) 2845-9800

Sister-City Programs

US–PRC:

Baltimore, MD (Xiamen)
Boston, MA (Hangzhou)
Boulder, CO (Lhasa)
Charlotte, NC (Baoding)
Chattanooga, TN (Wuxi)
Chicago, IL (Shenyang)
Cincinnati, OH (Liuzhou)
Columbus, OH (Hefei)
Denver, CO (Kunming)
Des Moines, IA (Shijiazhuang)
Erie, PA (Zibo)
Flint, MI (Changchun)
Harrisburg, PA (Luoyang)
Honolulu County, HI (Hainan Island)
Houston, TX (Shenzhen)
Joliet, IL (Liaoyang)
Kansas City, MO (Xi'an)
Long Beach, CA (Qingdao)
Los Angeles, CA (Guangzhou)
Midland, TX (Dongying)
New York, NY (Beijing)
Oakland, CA (Dalian)
Orlando, FA (Guilin)
Philadelphia, PA (Tianjin)
Phoenix, AZ (Chengdu)
Pittsburgh, PA (Wuhan)
Portland, OR (Suzhou)
Sacramento, CA (Jinan)
San Diego, CA (Yantai)
San Francisco, CA (Shanghai)
Seattle, WA (Chongqing)
Spokane, WA (Jilin)
St. Louis, MO (Nanjing)
St. Paul, MN (Changsha)
Tempe, AZ (Zhenjiang)
Titusville, FA (Yueyang)
Toledo, OH (Qinhuangdao)
Tulsa, OK (Beihai)
Washington, D.C. (Beijing)
Wilmington, DE (Ningbo)
Wilmington, NC (Dandong)
Witchita, KS (Kaifeng)

US–TAIWAN

Addison, TX (Panchiao City)
Albuquerque, NM (Hualien City)
Alhambra, CA (Hsinchu County)

Americus, GA (Yungho City)
Atlanta, GA (Taipei)
Austin, TX (Taichung)
Baton Rouge, LA (Taichung)
Beaverton, OR (Hsinchu County)
Bellevue, WA (Hualien City)
Bloomington, IN (Luchou Township)
Brunswick, GA (Ilan County)
Campbell, CA (Keelung City)
Casper, WY (Hsichih Township)
Charleston, IL (Fengshan City)
Cheyenne, WY (Taichung)
Cleveland, OH (Taipei)
Clallam County, WA (Miaoli County)
Colorado Springs, CO (Kaohsiung)
Columbus, OH (Tainan City)
Corpus Christi, TX (Keelung City)
East Orange, NJ (Chiayi County)
Enfield, CT (Chung Li City)
Flagstaff, AZ (Hsintien City)
Grover, CA (Tamsui Township)
Guam (Taipei)
Hawaii County, HI (Hualien County)
Holtville, CA (Chiangchung Hsiang)
Honolulu County, HI (Kaohsiung)
Houston, TX (Taipei)
Indianapolis, IN (Taipei)
Jackson, MS (Chiayi County)
Kansas City, MO (Tainan City)
King County, WA (Kaohsiung County)
Kissimee, FA (Miaoli Township)
Knoxville, TN (Kaohsiung)
Little Rock, AR (Kaohsiung)
Los Angeles, CA (Taipei)
Macon, GA (Kaohsiung)
Mankato, MN (Tamsui Township)
Marshall, TX (Taipei)
Maui County, HI (Pingtung County)
Miami, FA (Kaohsiung)
Mobile, AL (Kaohsiung)
Monterey Park, CA (Yungho City)
Morgantown, WV (Mucha District)
Muncie, IN (Changhua County)
New Haven, CT (Taichung)
Oklahoma City, OK (Taipei)
Orlando, FA (Tainan City)
Pensacola, FA (Kaohsiung)

Phoenix, AZ (Taipei)
Plains, GA (Kaohsiung)
Portland, OR (Kaohsiung)
Prince George's County, MD (Nantou County)
Reno, NV (Taichung)
Richland County, OH (Taipei County)
Salt Lake City, UT (Keelung City)
San Antonio, TX (Kaohsiung)
San Diego, CA (Taichung)

San Francisco, CA (Taipei)
San Gabriel, CA (Changhua City)
San Jose, CA (Tainan City)
Sumter, SC (Fengyuan City)
Tucson, AZ (Taichung)
Tulsa, OK (Kaohsiung)
Wildwood, NJ (Hsinchu County)
Williamsport, PA (Neipu Hsiang, Pingtung City)
Yakima, WA (Keelung City)

China-Related Associations, Organizations, and Foundations

This list reprinted with permission from the National Committee on US-China Relations' China Resource List

(see also listings in Directories 2 & 3 under Sending Organizations: the following have no formal sending programs, but can provide information)

US

American Bar Association's Law Committee on the PRC
Inernational Programs Coordination Office
750 North Lake Shore Dr.
Chicago, IL 60611

The Asia Society
725 Park Ave.
New York, NY 10021
(212) 288-6400
(regional Asia Societies in: Houston, Los Angeles, and Washington, DC)

The China Council of the Asia Society
725 Park Ave.
New York, NY 10021
(regional China Councils in Athens, GA; Austin, TX; Boulder, CO; Columbus, OH; East Lansing, MI; Milwaukee, WI; Portland, OR; Seattle, WA; St. Louis, MO; St. Paul, MN; Tucson, AZ)

Association for Asian Studies
1 Lane Hall
University of Michigan
Ann Arbor, MI 48109
(313) 665-2490

Center for Chinese Legal Studies Committee for Legal Exchange with China
Columbia University School of Law
435 W. 116th St.
New York, NY 10027
(212) 280-3422

Center for Chinese Research Materials
1527 New Hampshire Ave. NW
Washington, DC 20036
(202) 387-7172

Center for U.S.-China Arts Exchange
423 W. 118th St., Suite 1E
New York, NY 10027
(212) 280-4648

China Institute in America, Inc.
125 E. 65th St.
New York, NY 10021
(212) 744-8181

Chinese Culture Foundation of San Francisco
750 Kearny St.
San Francisco, CA 94108
(415) 986-1822

Chinese-English Translation
Assistance Group
P.O. Box 400
Kensington, MD 20795
(301) 946-7007

Committee on Scholarly Communication with the PRC
National Academy of Sciences
2101 Constitution Ave.
Washington, DC 20410
(202) 334-2718

The Foundation for Books to China
601 California St.
San Francisco, CA 94108
(415) 765-0664

Institute of International Education
809 United Nations Plaza
New York, NY 10017
(212) 883-8200

Joint Committee on Chinese Studies of
the Social Research Council and the
American Council of Learned Societies
Social Science Research Council
605 Third Ave.
New York, NY 10158
(212) 661-0280

National Committee on US-China
Relations
71 W. 23rd St. 19th Fl.
New York, NY 10010-4102
Phone: (212) 922-1385

Northwest Regional China Council
506 SE Mill St.
PO Box 751
Portland, OR 97207
(503) 725-4567
e-mail: nwchina@class.orednet.org

U.S.-China Business Council
1818 N St. NW
Washington, DC 20036
(202) 439-6340

Washington State China Relations Council
Fourth and Vine Building
2601 Fourth Ave., Suite 330
Seattle, WA 98121
(206) 441-4419

*A list of China-related booksellers, trans-
lation services, university centers, outreach
programs, US government agencies, and
PRC institutions in the US is available
from the National Committee on US-China
Relations.*

List of Educational Information Centers in China

The PRC government has established a series of key "learning information centers," to
which the US, British and other governments have donated materials. These can be useful
in-country resource sources. This list is reprinted with permission from the US Information Service, Press and Cultural Section.

BEIJING

**Advisory Center of Foreign Education
Information**
Beijing Languages Institute
Xueyuan Lu #15
Beijing, PRC

Beijing National Library
Wenjin Jie #7
Beijing, PRC

GUANGDONG

**Study Abroad Training Department
Guangzhou Foreign Languages
Institute**
Beijiao Huangpodong
Guangzhou, Guangdong Province PRC

**Study Abroad Information Service
Bureau of Higher Education of
Guangdong Province**
Xihu Lu
Guangzhou, Guangdong Province PRC

Guangzhou Municipal Library
Zhongshan Si Lu #42
Guangzhou, Guangdong Province PRC

Guangdong American Study Information Center
Ground Floor, 46-1 Dezbeng South Road
Guangzhou, Guangdong Province PRC

HEILONGJIANG

Heilongjiang Provincial Library
Fendou Lu
Harbin, Heilongjiang PRC

HUBEI

Hubei Provincial Library
Wuluo Lu #45
Wuchang, Hubei Province PRC

JILIN

Jilin Provincial Library
Changchun, Jilin Province PRC

LIAONING

Study Abroad Training Department
Dalian Foreign Languages Institute
Zhongshanqu Nanshan Lu Jiefangjie #111
Dalian, Liaoning Province PRC

Liaoning Provincial Library
Shenyang Lu Erduan Wenxingli #5
Shenyang, Liaoning Province PRC

SHAANXI

Study Abroad Training Department
Xi'an Foreign Languages Institute
Wujiafen
Xi'an, Shaanxi Province PRC

SHANGHAI

Study Abroad Training Department
Shanghai International Studies University
Xi Tiyuhui Lu
Shanghai, PRC

Shanghai Municipal Library
Nanjing Xilu #325
Shanghai, PRC

SICHUAN

Study Abroad Training Department
Sichuna Foreign Languages Institute
Shapingba
Chongqing, Sichuan Province PRC

Study Abroad Training Department
Chengdu University of Science & Technology
Xingnanmenwai Moziqiao
Chengdu, Sichuan Province PRC

Sichuan Provincia Library
Dongfeng Lu #222
Chengdu, Sichuan Province PRC

Study Abroad Information Centers in Taiwan

The following centers are set up to provide information and counseling services to students who wish to study abroad.

Information Center of International Education
Bureau of International Cultural & Educational Relations
Ministry of Education
100 Aikuo E. Road
Taipei, Taiwan, R. O. C.

Taipei Municipal Library
125 Chienkuo S. Rd, Sec. 2
Taipei, Taiwan, R. O. C.

Kaohsiung Municipal Library
220 Shichuan 1st Road
Kaohsiung, Taiwan, R. O. C.

Taichung Provincial Library
291-3 Chingwu Road
Taichung, Taiwan, R. O. C.

Hualien Hsien Culture Center
6 Wenfu Road
Hualien, Taiwan, R. O. C.

APPENDIX D

Key Universities

Anhui Polytechnical University, Anhui

Anhui University, Anhui

Beijing Aerospace University, Beijing Special Zone

Beijing Institute of Post and Telecommunications, Beijing Special Zone

Beijing Transportation University, Beijing Special Zone

Beijing University of Technology, Beijing Special Zone

Beijing University, Beijing Special Zone

Central Academy of Fine Arts, Beijing Special Zone

Central Conservatory of Music, Beijing Special Zone

Central Minorities Institute, Beijing Special Zone

Chengdu Institute of Radio Engineering, Sichuan

Chengdu University of Science and Technology, Chengdu

China University of Science and Technology, Anhui

China University of Geological Science, Hubei

Chinese People's University (Renda), Beijing

Chongqing Institute of Architectural Engineering, Sichuan

Chongqing University, Sichuan

Daqing Petroleum Institute, Heilongjiang

East China Normal University, Shanghai Special Zone

Fudan University, Shanghai Special Zone

Fuzhou University, Fujian

Guangdong Institute of Technology, Guangdong

Guangxi University, Guangxi

Guizhou University, Guizhou

Harbin Institute of Ship and Boat Engineering, Heilongjiang

Harbin Institute of Science and Technology, Heilongjiang

Henan University, Henan

Hunan University of Science and Technology, Hunan

Hunan University, Hunan

Jiangxi University, Jiangxi

Jilin University, Jilin

Jilin University of Science and Technology, Jilin

Lanzhou University, Gansu

Liaoning University, Liaoning

Nanjing Institute of Meteorology, Jiangsu

Nanjing University, Jiangsu

Nankai University, Tianjin Special Zone

Ningxia University, Ningxia

Northeast Institute of Technology, Liaoning

Northwest University, Shaanxi

Quinghua University, Beijing Special Zone

Shandong University, Shandong

Shanghai Foreign Languages Institute, Shanghai Special Zone

Shanghai Institute of Foreign Trade, Shanghai Special Zone

Shanghai Number One College of Medicine, Shanghai Special Zone

Shanghai Polytechnical University, Shanghai Special Zone

Shanghai Transportation University, Shanghai Special Zone

Shanxi Agricultural University, Shanxi

Shenyang University, Liaoning

Shenzhen University, Guangdong

Sichuan University, Sichuan

South China Agricultural University, Guangdong

South China Institute of Technology, Guangdong

Southwest Institute of Politics and Law, Sichuan

Southwest University, of Transportation, Sichuan

Taiyuan University of Technology, Shanxi

Tianjin University, Tianjin Special Zone

Tibet University, Tibet

Tongji University, Shanghai Special Zone

University of Inner Mongolia, Inner Mongolia

Wuhan University, Hubei

Xi'an Transportation University, Shaanxi

Xiamen University, Fujian

Yunnan University, Yunnan

Zhejiang University, Zhejiang

Zhejiang University of Agriculture, Zhejiang

Zhengzhou University, Henan

Zhongshan University, Guangdong

Index

For updating on Schools
(and New Listings) in China,
visit our Web Site:

www.chinabooks.com

For the best books, tapes and
other materials from and about
China, see our regular catalogs,
visit our retail store, or see our
home page.

China Books & Periodicals, Inc.
2929 Twenty-fourth Street
San Francisco, CA 94110

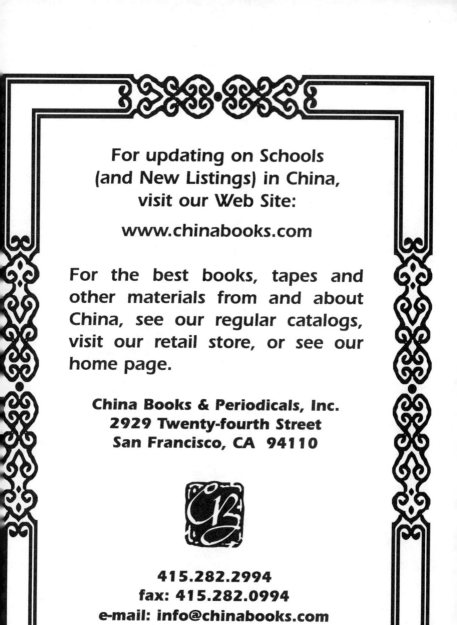

415.282.2994
fax: 415.282.0994
e-mail: info@chinabooks.com

Notes

Notes